Kāma
in the Land of Kāmakalā

Kāma
in the Land of Kāmakalā
Uḍḍiyana-Pīṭha and Erotic Art

Jitamitra Prasad Singh Deo

DK PRINTWORLD
Publishers of Indian Traditions

Cataloging in Publication Data — DK
[Courtesy: D.K. Agencies (P) Ltd. <docinfo@dkagencies.com>]

Singh Deo, Jitamitra Prasad, 1946–
Kāma in the land of kāmakalā / Jitamitra Prasad Singh Deo.
p. cm.
Includes bibliographical references and index.
ISBN 13: 9788124606803

1. Erotic art — India — Orissa. 2. Tantrism— India — Orissa. 3. Yoginīs — Cult — India — Orissa. 4. Orissa (India) — Religion. 5. Orissa (India) — Antiquities. I. Title.

DDC 704.94280954133 22

ISBN 13: 978-81-246-0680-3
First published in India in 2013

Printed and published by:
D.K. Printworld (P) Ltd.
Regd. Office : "*Vedaśrī*", F-395, Sudarshan Park
(Metro Station: Ramesh Nagar)
New Delhi - 110 015
Phones: (011) 2545 3975; 2546 6019; *Fax* : (011) 2546 5926
e-mail: indology@dkprintworld.com
Web: www.dkprintworld.com

Dedicated to

Lord Kāmadeva

Preface

THE Vedic *ṛṣis* and tāntric sages of India turned every aspect of human culture including art, architecture, sculpture, drama, music, medicine, astronomy and language into a tool of spiritual awakening and realization. India, i.e. Bhāratavarṣa, is the land of Vedic culture which is the heritage of mankind. The Mahānadī River Valley region had given its spiritual yogic contributions and developed its own spiritual qualities, bestowed by nature and developed as the land of Kāmakalā, Uḍḍiyāna-Pīṭha (site) and erotic art, where the expression of *kāma* (desire) was exploited during the early and medieval periods of Indian history to its full brim. This background prompted me to write this book, *Kāma in the Land of Kāmakalā.*

Scholars of international repute say, "Ancient India, we feel, has much to teach us" (*ISOTCOC*, p. xx). Therefore, it is an appropriate time for detailed regional studies. Persuasion, intuition and archaeological findings are the key elements in this book. Tantra is a vast subject. It includes all aspects of human life including spirituality, *yoga*, sex and metaphysics. This book is written with an archaeological and historical perspective of the findings in the Mahānadī River Valley of central-eastern India, comprising the states of Chhattisgarh and Orissa.

The author had been doing field surveys, findings, reporting, writing research papers and focusing since 1968. The archaeological findings of the author are preserved at the Khariar Branch Museum, which was specially opened for this purpose by the Government of Orissa in 1976 and also at his personal Palace Museum, at Khariar. After the formation of the new district of Nuāpāḍā in Orissa on 1 April 1993, the Khariar Branch Museum has now been shifted to the district headquarter at Nuāpāḍā.

The comparative observations and study with intuitive insights show that the experiences of yogic teachings find expressions in antiquities, temples and sculptural arts. It also shows us the experiences of the yogic masters of the bygone days.

Every corner of India had its own regional culture, which developed in accordance with the great tradition of India, i.e. Vedic culture. In *Ṛgveda* (I.89.1), it is mentioned:

> आ नो भद्रः क्रतवो यन्तु विश्वतः ॥
> *ā no bhadraḥ kratavo yantu viśvataḥ* ॥

Let noble thoughts come to us from every side.

This book focuses on the development of yogic and tāntric expressions in arts. The twenty-first century is going to be the century of *yoga*. Therefore, it is worth quoting from Swami Vivekananda's speech in Kumbhakoṇam, on "The Mission of the Vedānta" (Lectures from Colombo to Almora, *Complete Works*, vol. 3, *passim*):

> Teach yourselves, teach everyone his (or her) real nature. Call upon the sleeping soul and see how it awakes. Power will come, glory will come, goodness will come, purity will come and everything that is excellent will come when this sleeping soul is roused to self-conscious activity.

Vedic scholar David Frawley, whose Hindu name is Vamadeva Shastri, questions "why are Hindu deities portrayed in erotic forms?" and answers:

> Hindu deities and temple sculptures often appear erotic or voluptuous, so that Western missionaries thought these images were only a glorification of sexuality even though they were a part of a tradition that has always valued asceticism.
>
> God is the ultimate bliss and delight. Union with God is the Supreme Love, in which the male and female sides of our nature, the masculine and feminine aspects of consciousness must be united. To show this Hindu artists have traditionally employed graphic images. Such images are symbolic like that of Rādhā and Kṛṣṇa, who represent the soul and its love of God. To the Hindu mind, all of our passions should be directed to the Divine. For this reason it has not hesitated to portray them as a part of spiritual symbolism. But to confuse these with a glorification of sexuality is to completely misinterpret them. — *Hinduism the Eternal Tradition* (Sanatana Dharma), p. 207.

I am fully indebted to my wife Rajshree Devi, Rani of Khariar, for her relentless support and persuasion to my research work, shouldering a lot of family responsibilities. Thanks are also due to D.K. Printworld for publishing this book.

26 January 2013

Raja Dr. Jitamitra Prasad Singh Deo,
PhD, D.Litt.
Khariar

Contents

Abbreviations

ASCITATTOYAK	*A Systematic Course in the Ancient Tāntric Techniques of Yoga and Kriya*, Swami Satyananda Saraswati 2nd edn., 1989.
EI	*Epigraphia Indica.*
HOTTR	*History of the Tāntric Religion*, N.N. Bhattacharyya, 2nd edn., 1987.
HYP	*Haṭha Yoga Pradīpikā*, Swami Mukti bodhananda Saraswati, 2nd edn., 1993.
IHQ	*Indian Historical Quarterly.*
ISOTCOC	*In Search of the Cradle of Civilization*, G. Feurersten, S. Kak and D. Frawley, 1999.
JBORS	*Journal of the Bihar and Orissa Research Society.*
OHRJ	*The Orissa Historical Research Journal.*
SMTGG	*Śiva Mahadeva: The Great God* — An Exposition of the Symbolism of Śiva, Vasudeva S. Agrawala, 2nd edn., 1984.
THACOTIP	*The History and Culture of the Indian People,* R.C. Majumdar (gen. ed.).
TCOJ	*The Cult of Jagannāth*, K.C. Mishra, 1971.
TCOJATRTOO	The Cult of Jagannāth and the Regional Tradition of Orissa, A. Echman, H. Kulke and G.C. Tripathi, Manohar, New Delhi.
THOMV	*Tāntric Hedonism of Mahānadi Valley (Uḍḍiyāna-Piṭha)*, J.P. Singh Deo, 2004.

Key to Transliteration

VOWELS

अ *a*	आ *ā*	इ *i*	ई *ī*	उ *u*	ऊ *ū*	ऋ *ṛ*	ॠ *ṝ*[1]
(Roman)	(palm)	(it)	(police)	(put)	(rule)	(rig)	
ऌ *ḷ*	ॡ *ḹ*[1]	ए *e*	ऐ *ai*	ओ *o*	औ *au*		
(able)		(there)	(aisle)	(no)	(loud)		

CONSONANTS

Guttural	क *ka* (skate)	ख *kha*[2] (blockhead)	ग *ga* (gate)	घ *gha*[2] (ghost)	ङ *ṅa* (sing)
Palatal	च *ca* (chunk)	छ *cha*[2] (catch him)	ज *ja* (john)	झ *jha*[2] (hedgehog)	ञ *ña* (bunch)
Cerebral	ट *ṭa* (start)	ठ *ṭha*[2] (anthill)	ड *ḍa* (dart)	ढ *ḍha*[2] (godhead)	ण *ṇa* (under)
Dental	त *ta* (path)	थ *tha*[2] (thunder)	द *da* (that)	ध *dha*[2] (this)	न *na* (numb)
Labial	प *pa* (spin)	फ *pha*[2] (philosophy)	ब *ba* (bin)	भ *bha*[2] (abhor)	म *ma* (much)
Semi-vowels	य *ya* (young)	र *ra* (drama)	ल *la*[3] (luck)	व *va*[4] (vile)	
Sibilants	श *śa*[5] (shove)	ष *ṣa*[5] (bushel)	स *sa* (so)	ह *ha* (hum)	
Others	क्ष *kṣa*	त्र *tra*	ज्ञ *jña*		
(*kṣatriya*)	(*triśūla*)	(*jñānī*)			

अं (ं) *ṁ anusvāra* is a nasal off-glide that immediately follows the pronunciation of a vowel as in *saṁskṛti.*

अः *visarga* = *ḥ* consists in abrupt release of breath after a vowel as in *prātaḥ.*

ऽ *Avagraha* shows non-pronunciation, that is, deletion of "a" after "e" or "o" as in *ime 'vasthitāḥ*. In Vedic Sanskrit, it can also show word division.

HINDI LETTERS (extras)

ँ = *m̐* (*candrabindu*)	ं = ṅ (*anusvāra*)	ड़ = *ṛa*	ढ़ = *ṛha*

1 Longer form of the preceding vowel.

2 Aspirated forms of the preceding consonants. The compound words given as examples should be pronounced without a syllabic break at the underlined places. "tha" and "pha" should not be pronounced as fricatives.

3 retroflexed and written as "L *la*" in certain phonetic contexts.

4 Pronounced like "w," without aspiration.

5 "śa" is palatal; "ṣa" cerebral or retroflex.

List of Plates, Figures and Charts

Cover Page: Yawning position, fit for Yoga of Sexual Transformation, Sun Temple Koṇārka, Orissa, thirteenth century CE.

Plates

Pl. 10 Exposed stone sockets. Find-spot: Kharligarh site, Bolaṅgīr district. Preserved at the Manikyapur Museum, Bhawanipatna, Orissa.

Pl. 11 Buddha represented at the centre, like the stone sockets findings. Presentation of Rāhula, cross-bar from Amarāvatī railing, the Archaeological Museum, Amarāvatī, Andhra Pradesh.

Pl. 12 Stone with right angle triangle *yantra*, with three spots (dots), at the three corners. It is *yantra* of creation. Find-spot: Patdaraha region of southern part of Sunabeda plateau, Nuāpāḍā district. Discovered by Rani Rajshree Devi of Khariar on 19 February 2004. Preserved in the Palace Museum of Khariar.

Pl. 13 Dakṣiṇa Kālī as found in a northern niche of the Kedāreśvara Mahādeva temple at Ichhapur village, Kālāhāṇḍī district, Orissa. Modern construction within eighteenth-ninteenth centuries CE.

Pl. 14 *Paṭṭa-citra* painting of Dakṣiṇa Kālī. *Courtesy*: Kishor Chandra Acharya and Dasarathi Acharya of Ichhapur village, Kālāhāṇḍi district. Painting of seventeenth century CE.

Pl. 15 Six-headed and twelve-handed Kārttikeya. Find-spot: Bhubaneswar temple on Tirbandha tank embankment of Khariar town, Nuāpāḍā district, Orissa, twelfth century CE.

Pl. 16 Six-headed and two-handed Kārttikeya as *pārśva-devatā* in a niche of a Śiva temple, within the premises of the Rāmeśvara temple at Sonepur, Sonepur district, Orissa. *Courtesy*: Jogendra Barik. Medieval period.

Pl. 17 Six-headed and two-handed Kārttikeya as *pārśva-devatā* in a niche of a side Śiva temple, within the premises of the Sureśvarī temple at Sonepur, Sonepur district, Orissa. *Courtesy*: Jogendra Barik. Medieval period.

Pl. 18 Six-headed and twelve-handed Kārttikeya as *pārśva-devatā* of the Brajeśvara Śiva temple at Dharamsāgar village, Nuāpāḍā district, Orissa, nineteenth century CE.

Pl. 19 Eight-handed, nude dancing Gaṇeśa. Find-spot: Hari-Śaṅkara site, Bolaṅgīr district, Orissa. Originally it was collected from Rānīpur-Jharial site. Early medieval period.

Pl. 20 Lower portion of eight-handed, nude dancing Gaṇeśa. Find-spot: Hari-Śaṅkara site, Bolaṅgīr district, Orissa. Early medieval period.

Pl. 21 Six-handed Gaṇeśa of yellow colour, worshipped in a side temple, within

Figures

Charts

Explanation of the two folded charts (Purchased by the author from the market of Bada Danda of Puri, in 1973. Such erotic art objects are available for purchase in abundance in the markets of Puri.): Since the composition of *Gīta Govinda* by Jayadeva, the saint-poet of Orissa (modern Odisha province) during twelfth century CE, the amorous themes associated with Lord Kṛṣṇa have become popular in sculptural arts based on "Vāstuśāstra", paintings and palm-leaf etching of Orissa. These are meant to create an amorous delight and devote the sensual mind to *prema-bhakti* (Divine Love) or devotion. In the words of Akhileswar Jha (*Sexual Designs in Indian Culture*, New Delhi: Vikas Publishing House, 1979, p. 163), "If sexual pleasure is the highest pleasure life can give, then to give up this pleasure is, logically, the greatest enunciation; but sexual pleasure remains, positively or negatively, the determinant of both ways."

Introduction

VEDAS are the sources of all religious thoughts, conducts and art of human living. The central theme of the Veda is: "Here, there is none greater, none smaller. All have gathered together here for advancing common welfare of all" (*Ṛgveda*, 5.60.5). Adwaita P. Ganguly[1] states that Vedānta philosophy, on the other hand, looks for cosmic laws, known as *ṛta*s in the *Ṛgveda*, to which we all human beings are conditioned. The cosmic order or law is the only concept of *dharma*, which does not mean faith or tenet of a religion only. *Dharma* means duty, a good act, meritorious deed, fortune, luck, virtue, piety, welfare, justice, righteousness, natural condition, disposition, characteristic quality, conduct, practice approved by the scriptures, law, usage, custom, just consideration, good company, chastity of a woman, etc.[2] *Ṛta* relates all aspects of socio-cultural, religious and art of human living. To this doctrine of reality, the Mahānadī River Valley area of India had its own development of *yoga*, which dealt with *kāma* (desire), during antediluvian culture. It was not much developed technologically, but, spiritually, it was not advanced and pure.

One of the major rivers of the Peninsular India is the Mahānadī which starts from the hilly areas of Sihawa, in the south-east of old Raipur district, now in the Kanker district of the Chhattisgarh state. It flows through the Orissa state to meet the Bay of Bengal at Paradeep. It forms the main water source and, in rainy season, the stream varies in breadth from 2 to 3 km. Its bed is rich in precious stones. This river is also known as "Citrotpalā", which is a name given to a portion of the Mahānadī River between two holy places Śrī Rājīvlocan-Kṣetra (i.e. modern Rājim in Chhattisgarh) and Subarṇapura (i.e. Sonepur) in Orissa. This river is mentioned as Citrotpalā in the *Mahābhārata*, *Mārkaṇḍeya Purāṇa*, *Brahmāṇḍa Purāṇa*, *Kūrma*

---

1. Adwaita P. Ganguly, *Vedanta Philosophy for the Unity of Mankind*, New Delhi: Vikas Publishing House, 1995, p. 69; Madhu Khanna (ed.), *Ṛta: The Cosmic Order*, New Delhi: D.K. Printworld, 2004, *passim*.
2. Gopal Chandra Praharaj (comp.), *Pūrṇṇa Chandra Orḍiā Bhāsha Kosha*, vol. IV, Cuttack, 1934, pp. 3974-76.

Purāṇa, *Vāmana Purāṇa* and *Padma Purāṇa*. There is a description of the Mahānadī in *Skanda Purāṇa* also. A reference to it is found in Ptolemy's work (second century CE.)

With this background, the yogic interpretation of the antiquities of the Mahānadī River Valley is dealt, and the present study shows that this area was the land of Kāmakalā, Uḍḍiyāna-Pīṭha and erotic art, where the expression of *kāma* (desire) is achieved and exploited to its full brim. Therefore in *Mahānirvāṇa Tantram*,[3] it is mentioned:

> The rivers Gaṅgā and Mahāṇadī, the residence of the spiritual guide, and the celebrated shrines, these are the *tīrtha*s or the holy places of pilgrimage in the *Kali-yuga*.

Even the primal alias Ādi Śakti of the Mahānadī River Valley, which is the land of Kāmakalā, Uḍḍiyāna-Pāṭha and erotic art, is found in Nuāpāḍā district of modern Orissa, situated at the central right Mahānadī Valley.

The origin of Śakti worship is shrouded in mystery. J.N. Banerjea[4] considers that the ring stones, the female figurines along with the circular discs and the nude figurines of the historical period collectively establish the long continued existence of the worship of the female principal in aniconic and iconic forms. Ring stones are found in plenty at Nuāpāḍā district and the whole Mahānadī Valley in general. Broken stone piece of a circular disc is found from the Bikrampur site in Nuāpāḍā district and preserved in the private museum of the author at Khariar.

To know about the earliest primal Śakti conception, attention should be drawn to the period of geological formation. It is a truism that the course of human history in a region is in a considerable measure shaped by its physical and geographical features, which, in turn, in the ultimate, are determined by the geological history the region has passed through in the dim vista of time.[5]

When the geological early crust was under formation, in many places the mother earth had formed the shape of female vulva, the external organ. In the words of A. Wall,[6] the external feminine sexual parts, the vulva, is called *yoni* in India; it is still

3 Manmatha Nath Dutt, *Mahānirvāṇa Tantram* (prose translation), Varanasi: Chowkhamba Sanskrit Series Office, 2nd edn., 1979, p. 135.

4 J.N. Banerjea, *Purāṇic and Tāntric Religion*, Calcutta, 1966, p. 111.

5 D.N. Wadia, "The Geological Background of Indian History", *THACOTIP*, vol. I, *The Vedic Age*, 1965, p. 80.

6 O.A. Wall, *Sex and Sex Worship in the World*, Delhi: Inter-India Publication, 1979, p. 464.

very widely worshipped in Asiatic religions and the worshippers of feminine attributes are called *yonicitas*. In further references to the vulva, we will speak of it as the *yoni*.

> *Yoni* in Sanskrit means vulva, uterus or origin; it is the female power in nature. The Supreme Being, wishing to begin creation, divided himself into two parts, Brahman and Nature (Puruṣa and Prakṛti), all females, but the female is regarded as the real force in nature and most deserving of worship.

One such naturally formed female vulva or *yoni* of Mother Earth is found under a bamboo thicket at Pātālagaṅgā, a site near Boden of Nuāpāḍā district, Orissa, and worshipped as *dvārsāni*. It should be regarded as the earliest Śakti-Pīṭha (site) of the entire Mahānadī River Valley. There are other such earthern-formed female vulva or *yoni* sites at other places in India and across the entire earth.

Tantra gives prominence to the female energy of Śakti. Śakti (Kālī) of the Śākta cult is the mother or the Supreme Being. Śiva of the Śiva cult is the father or the Supreme Being. The Tantras attempt to blend these two concepts,the motherhood and the fatherhood of God. Tantra gives importance to the eternal mother, for God's love for the creation is like a mother's love, deep and pure. So, the earliest tāntric site of the Mahānadī Valley is the Yoni Gātra (as named in Yoni Tantra text),[7] worshipped as Dvārsāni deity, in the Nuāpāḍā district. The earliest Pāśupati antiquity of India is found in Kālāhāṇḍī district of Orissa, situated on the central right Mahānadī River Valley.

While dealing about religion of the Indus Valley Civilization, A.D. Pusalker[8] states that among the male gods the most remarkable is a three-faced deity wearing a horned headgear, seated cross-legged on a throne, with *penis erectus* and surrounded by elephant, tiger, buffalo and rhinoceros, with deer appearing under the seat. It wears a number of bangles and has a pectoral round neck, and an inscription of seven letters appears at the top. This representation has at least three concepts which are usually associated with Śiva that he is: (i) Trīmukha (three-faced), (ii) Pāśupati (lord of animals), and (iii) Yogīśvara or Mahāyogī. The first two aspects are apparent from the seal itself. The deity is sitting cross-legged in *padmāsana* posture with eyes turned towards the tip of the nose which evidences

---

[7] J.A. Schoterman, *The Yoni Tantra*, New Delhi: Manohar, 1980, p. 23; J.P. Singh Deo, "Primal (Ādi) Śakti of Orissa Province Is Found in Nuapada District", *OHRJ*, vol. XLVII, no. 3, pp. 38-39.

[8] A.D. Pusalker, "The Indus Valley Civilization", *THACOTIP*, vol. I, *The Vedic Age*, 1965, p. 190.

the Yogīśvara aspect of the deity. It has been suggested by some scholars that this Śiva cult was borrowed by the Indo-Aryans from the Indus culture but as there is a reference to Śiva in the *Ṛgveda* itself (II.1.6; II.33.9.), Śiva may not be a later intruder in the Hindu pantheon.

About the *penis erectus* of the male God of the Indus Valley Civilization, the latest study[9] suggests that what has often been interpreted as an erect phallus could be the part of the belt.

So far as the dating of the seals of the Pāśupati figures is concerned, they may be dated between 3000–4000 BCE. Pusalker[10] says that the archaeological discoveries at Haṛappā, Moheṅjo-Dāṛo and other localities in the Indus Valley have pushed back this limit, at a single stretch, to 3000 BCE, if not to a still remote period and India can now lay claim to the honour of being a pioneer of civilization with Sumer, Akkad, Babylon, Egypt and Assyria.

Since the first archaeological excavations at Indus Valley in CE 1922, much progress has been made on the history and culture of India and scholars of international repute are "in search of the cradle of civilization".[11] Geoffery Bobby[12] rightly remarked, "Indus Valley Civilization is the Cinderella of the ancient world."

Many intensive studies on different aspects of Indological topics are now going on at the international level. One of the distinguished Vedic scholars of the West, is David Frawley.[13] He had done an authoritative study of *The Ṛgveda and the History of India* and suggests:

> There were two main Vedic cultures in ancient India. The first was a Northern Kingdom centred on the Sarasvatī-Dṛṣadvatī River region dominated by the Purus and the Ikṣvākus that produced the existent Veda texts that we have. The second was a Southern Culture along the coast of the Arabian Sea and into the Vindhya mountains, dominated by the Turvaṣas and Yadus and extending into groups yet further south. These northern and southern groups vied for supremacy and influenced each other in various ways as the Vedas and Purāṇas indicate. The northern or Bhārata

[9] *ISOTCOC*, Delhi, 1999, p. 72.

[10] A.D. Pusalker, op. cit., 1965, p. 172.

[11] *ISOTCOC*, Delhi, 1999, *passim*.

[12] Ibid.; G. Bobby, *Looking for Dilmum*, New York: New American Library, 1974, p. 161.

[13] D. Frawley, *The Ṛgveda and the History of India*, New Delhi, Aditya Prakashan, 2001 (flap inner cover).

culture ultimately prevailed, making India the land of Bharata or Bhāratavarṣa and its main ancient literary record the Vedas, though militarily the Yadus remained strong throughout history. The Southern Culture was the older of the two, with the Vedic people coming originally from the south, not the north-west. This was the basis of the maritime symbolism at the core of the Vedic thought, which reflects an ancient heritage.

In addition there was a third or north-west Vedic culture in Punjab and Afghanistan, that of the Anus and Druhyus, which was at first part of the Northern Kingdom but gradually developed its own identity. It was partly assimilated by the Bharatas that became the dominant northern people. Another portion of it extended north and west outside of the Indian subcontinent. Its influence was secondary to that of the Northern and Southern Kingdoms and much of it passed out of the Indic sphere of culture. However, it was the basis of most of the Indo-European and Iranian people and cultures that we find in Europe, Central Asia and the Middle East.

Therefore, we must look at the south and east connections to understand not only Indic civilization and Hinduism, but also to understand the Vedas themselves. The Western connections to the Europeans and Iranians were more an outflow, while the southern connections were more original and enduring. Western scholars, dominated by a European mindset, only traced Indo-European Culture from Europe and the Middle East to India as its eastern border. They failed to see that the boundary was only in their minds.

With this background,[14] let us examine the development of the early upland dwellers of the Mahānadī Valley. This area is no more *terra incognito* to the historical world.

The Stone Age Culture and Megalithic Culture of the whole valley are under study and its explorations are still continuing. The Mahānadī River Valley is situated at the South-eastern part of India, which received cultural and spiritual waves, both from the north and the south. Therefore cultural, religious and spiritual synthesis developed, but the early upland dwellers of the whole Mahānadī Valley had developed their own antediluvian culture. Though technologically the antediluvian culture was not much developed, but spiritually it was much refined, pure and advanced. This is known from the archaeological findings.

The last ruler of the Kālāhāṇḍī State, late Mahārājā Pratāp Kesarī Deo[15], had established the Archaeology Department in his state with late Kedarnath Mahapatra

[14] *THOMV*, New Delhi, 2004, pp. 59-60.

[15] P.K. Deo, *Memories of Bygone Era*, New Delhi: Minerva Press, 2000, pp. 63-64.

as archaeologist and late Padmasri Dr. S.N. Rajguru as epigraphist. The two scholars had done the discovery of the Rock Art of Guḍahāṇḍī jointly, which was first reported in *Journal of Kalinga Historical Research Society*, vol. II, p. 243. H.K. Mahatab[16] refers to this and had mentioned that Guṛahāṇḍī, a place in the district of Kālāhāṇḍī, is famous for some pictographic paintings pertaining to remote Palaeolithic Age. The pictures are at the entrance of some caves in the Guṛahāṇḍī hill.

From Gazetteer[17] it is known that at Guṛahāṇḍī the façades of the natural caves are decorated with drawings mostly of geometrical designs — squares, rectangles, circles and the like figures. These drawings are fast fading away. The most interesting of these pre-historic drawings is a hunting scene which depicts a primitive man throwing a stone missile at a running bison. The missile strikes the game before the agile right hand of the hunter comes to its normal position and the wounded animal casts a pathetic glance at the primitive man turning its head towards him. The face of the man is beaming with joy and his curly hairs become wavy revealing the thrill at the success in the game. The rock shelters in the Guḍahāṇḍī hill have been precisely depicted in the hunting scene indicating that those natural rock shelters were of the habitat of that pre-historic hunter. The Guḍahāṇḍī paintings are, in fact, a great achievement of the primitive artists. The paintings at Guḍahāṇḍī may be placed about fifteenth millennium BCE but those at Yogīmaṭha are somewhat of later period and may be assigned to about tenth millennium BCE.

Sadasiba Pradhan[18] is of the opinion that in the district of Kālāhāṇḍī there is one rock art site under the Guṛahāṇḍī. The site was reported by Rajguru in 1950. The rock art at Guḍahāṇḍī is situated at a distance of about 20 km from Koksara in Kālāhāṇḍī district. Here the shelter located on the left bank of a seasonal nullah preserves 24 specimens of fast disappearing paintings executed in red, blue and black. They include a human figure in red and a variety of geometric patterns of squares and rectangles either empty or filled in with straight and/or diagonal lines or with dots on the borders, circles, wheels with spokes, apsidal patterns, oval shapes with dots executed either in monochrome of red or in polychrome of red, blue and black. In the absence of any thematic depictions, the paintings remain, by and large, enigmatic to any viewer.

---

16 H.K. Mahatab, *History of Orissa*, vol. I, Cuttack: Prajatantra Press, 1959, p. 267.

17 D.C. Kuanr (state ed.), Orissa District Gazetteers, *Kalahandi*, N. Senapati (chief ed.), Cuttack, 1980, pp. 35-36.

18 S. Pradhan, *Rock Art in Orissa*, New Delhi: Aryan Books International, 2001, pp. 30-31.

The enigmatic human figure in red, as found in Guṛahāṇḍī rock art is of interest because, as the author[19] had already stated, in the Peninsular India, the earliest trace of *yoga* is found in the pre-historic rock-shelter painting of Guḍahāṇḍī. The painting of human-like figure has a head which symbolizes a lotus. In *kuṇḍalinī-yoga*, the highest *cakra* of human being is described as a thousand-petalled lotus, i.e. *sahasrāra*. So, it can be claimed that *sahasrāra cakra* is a gift of the central right Mahānadī River Valley to the mankind. In reality *cakra*s are within the realm of the psyche. Consciousness manifests at different levels, in accordance with the *cakra* that is predominantly active. *Sahasrāra* is beyond the beyond (*parātparam*) and it is right here. *Sahasrāra* is the culmination of the progressive ascension through different *cakra*s. It is the crown of expanded awareness. The power of the *cakra*s does not reside within itself, but in *sahasrāra*. The *cakra*s are only switches and all the potential lies in *sahasrāra*.[20]

A minute observation of the human figure with lotus-like head, signifying *sahasrāra cakra* of *kuṇḍalinī śakti*, of the line painting of Guḍahāṇḍī rock art shows that this human figure is standing on an animal. Therefore, it may be stated that this human figure of the pre-historic rock art of Guḍahāṇḍī symbolizes Pāśupati in enigmatic manner and may be accepted as the earliest Pāśupati and *sahasrāra kuṇḍalinī cakra* antiquities of India, because it is much older than the Pāśupati seals, discovered in the Indus Valley Civilization.

As stated by Frawley, there was cultural, yogic and spiritual contact of south peninsular India with the Indus Valley alias Sarasvatī Valley people. Therefore, it may be stated that the Central Mahānadī Valley, now included in modern Orissa state of India, had played a pivotal role in the development of yogic spiritual Pāśupati and *sahasrāra kuṇḍalinī cakra* heritages of India.

According to Vasudeva S. Agrawala,[21] Pāśupati Śiva was much elaborated by the Śaiva teachers of the Pāśupata School of which the founder-teacher was Lakulīśa. He was born at Kāyāvarohaṇa and from there started a serious campaign against false beliefs and preached the religion of *bhakti* to Śiva and his worship in the form of *liṅga*. He was a stern disciplinarian demanding complete detachment (*brahmacarya*) and insisted upon the life of a *parivrājaka* or wandering mendicant

19 J.P. Singh Deo, *THOMV*, New Delhi, 2004, pp. 22-23.

20 Ibid.; Swami Satyananda Paramahansa Sarasvati, *Kuṇḍalinī Tantra*, Munger: Bihar School of Yoga, 1992, p. 201.

21 Vasudeva S. Agrawala, *Śiva Mahādeva the Great God*, Varanasi: Prithivi Prakashan, 2nd edn., 1984, pp. 46-47.

who should carry the message of the divinity of Rudra-Śiva from door to door. In the course of a few centuries the Pāśupata School of Śaivism became predominant throughout north India and all great *tīrthas* like Ujjain, Varanasi, Puṣkara, Mathurā, Prayāga and Thāneśvara became its centres. The purity and drive of these teachers of Pāśupata Śaivism made an eloquent appeal to the people and exercised far-reaching influence on the religious history of India. During the Gupta times it was a faith as powerful and widespread as the religious movement of the great Bhāgavatas who made friends with them and we find the evidence of the same in several Purāṇas which were cast in the moulds of both Pāśupata Śaivism and the Bhāgavata Vaiṣṇavism.

> The principal tenets of the Pāśupata school of Purāṇic Śaivism were the following: *Liṅga* worship, installation of *Śiva-liṅgas*, glorifying Śiva as the Supreme Divine reality, wholesale adoption of the Sāṁkhya metaphysics with the addition of Śiva as the 25th entity (*pañcaviṁśaka sāṁkhya*), *gurucaryā* or the conception of a long succession of teachers from Rudra-Śiva to the last disciple descended from him, *pañcabrahma* doctrine of five-faced Śiva with pentadic scheme of creation as the five heads, Aṣṭamūrti Śiva, Bhasma-dhāraṇa or besmearing the body with ashes, celibacy, mendicancy or self-denying life of poverty, *akiñcanatva* or self-naughting of an extreme type which implied a participation in the affairs of the world but with perfect detachment, study of the Āgamas and the Vedas, intense practice of *yoga* and *prāṇāyāma* and a mastery of *dhyāna*, temple building and worship of the image with visible ceremonies and an enthusiastic approach to all problems of metaphysics, philosophy, religion, art and culture.

The entire Mahānadī River Valley was the land of Kāmakalā, Uḍḍiyāna-Pīṭha and erotic art. The archaeological findings prove that Sunabeda plateau of Nuāpāḍā district and its vicinity was the nucleus of the spiritual culture of the Mahānadī Valley.[22] As this topic is connected with tāntric background, it is worth knowing about "Tantra Śāstra and Veda", as defined by Sir John Woodroffe:[23]

> It is said that in *Satya*, Veda was undivided. In *Dvāpara*, Kṛṣṇadvaipāyana separated it in four parts. In *Satya*, *vaidika upāsanā* was *pradhāna*, that is, prevailed; *sādhakas* worshipping Indra for wealth, children and the like, though *niṣkāma ṛṣis* adored the *sarvaśaktimān* (Devisūkta in *Advaita-Siddhipūrṇa*).

[22] *THOMV*, 2004, p. 71.

[23] Sir J. Woodroffe, *Śakti and Śākta* (Essays and Addresses), Madras: Ganesh and Co., 8th edn., 1975, pp. 56-57.

> In *Tretā*, worship according to Smṛti prevailed. It was then, that Vasiṣṭha is said to have done *sādhanā* of *brahma-vidyā* according to *cīnācāra krama*. Though in the *Dvāpara* there were both Smṛti and Purāṇa, rites were generally performed according to the Purāṇas. There were also then, as always, worshippers of *pūrṇaśakti mahāvidyā*. At the end of *Dvāpara* and beginning of the *Kali* age the Tantraśāstra was taught to men. Then the ten *saṁskāras*, *śrāddha* and *antyeṣṭi-kriyā* were, as they are now, performed according to the *vaidika dharma*: *āśramacara* according to Dāyabhāga and other Smṛti texts; *vratas* according to Purāṇa; *diśā* and *upāsanā* of *Brahman* with Śakti and various kinds of *yoga sādhanā*, according to the Āgama which is divided into three parts; *tantra* (*sattvaguṇa*), *yāmala* (*rajoguṇa*) and *ḍāmara* (*tamoguṇa*). There were 64 Tantras for each of the three divisions — Aśvakrāntā, Rathakrāntā and Viṣṇukrāntā.

Viṣṇukrāntā is the region extending from the Vindhyas up to Chattla, Aśvakrāntā is the region extending from the Vindhyas to Mahācīna and Nepal, and Rathakrāntā is the region from the Vindhyas to the great ocean including Kāmboja and Java.[24] Because of this division, the Mahānadī River Valley is included in the Rathakrāntā division of the Tantra world.

The Rathakrāntā division of the Tantra world had influenced the development of temple architecture in Orissa. "The Phallus and the Chariot: The fusion of motifs and symbols in Indian temple art", has been pointed out by David Miller[25] and he states about the mythological symbol and the architectural style of the chariot temple or shrine from Kaliṅga-Orissa.

A stronger case, that the temples of Bhubaneswar are symbolically chariots, is made by Panigrahi:[26]

> Most likely the Śikhara temple took its shape from the wooden *ratha* or *pagoḍā* which is used in the car festivals annually held at Purī and Bhubaneswar in the months of July and March respectively. Although the date of the origin of the festival cannot be fixed accurately, it is doubtless that it goes back to early antiquity. . . . Curiously enough the term *ratha* is also still associated with one of the principal features of an Orissan Rekha

---

24 D.N. Bose and H. Haldar, *Tantras: Their Philosophy and Occult Secrets*, Delhi: Eastern Book Linkers, 1992, p. 20; J.P. Singh Deo, *Tāntric Art of Orissa*, Delhi: Kalpaz Publication, 2001, p. 15.

25 David Miller, "The Phallus and the Chariot: The Fusion of Motif and Symbols in India Temple Art", *OHRJ*, vol. XLI, nos. 1 to 4, pp. 25-38.

26 K.C. Panigrahi, *Archaeological Remains at Bhubaneswar*, Calcutta: Orient Longmans, 1961, p. 57.

or Śikhara temple, namely the *pāgas* or pilasters, according to the number of which the different varieties of the same type are known as *tri-ratha, pañcaratha, sapta-ratha* and *nava-ratha* temples. The association of a Śikhara temple with a *ratha* is further attested to by the great Koṇārka temple which was actually built as a wheeled car.

According to Swami Satyananda Saraswati:[27]

> In fact, it is a tāntric belief that old texts on Tantra will fade away and new ones will always be written to replace them. The essence of the texts will be the same but the expression and relationship to prevalent social conditions will be different. Tantra has changed and been developed throughout the ages. It has not remained attached to a fixed dogma. It is still growing and adapting itself in the present era and will continue to mould itself to man's need in the future.

Thus, an attempt has been made through intuitive observations of antiquities, temples and sculptures to expose Kāma in the land of Kāmakalā.

The book is divided into seventeen chapters. Detailed studies are done with the support of antiquities discovered so far. Much remains to be excavated at the archaeological sites of different varieties in the Mahānadī Valley. But from the existing discoveries done so far, a detailed study on the *Kāma in the Land of Kāmakalā: Uḍḍiyāna-Pīṭha and Erotic Art* has been done.

---

[27] *ASCITATTOYAK*, 1989, pp. 323-24.

1

The Land of Kāmakalā and Uḍḍiyāna-Pīṭha

Kāmakalā and Uḍḍiyāna-Pīṭha are tāntric-yogic terms. Therefore one should have a yogic intuitive mind to understand the use of these expressions. Study on these two expressions has been done, with supporting archaeological evidences.

Kāmakalā

The author has been doing field surveys, findings and research at personal level since 1968. Author's wife Rani Rajshree Devi drew the attention to the Yoni Gātra, found under a bamboo thicket, at Pātālagaṅgā, near the southern slope of the Sunabeda plateau, in the Boden Block area of Nuāpāḍā district in Orissa. The Yoni Gātra is worshipped as "Dvārasāni", by the tribals of that region. So far eleven *yonis* have been traced in Nuāpāḍā district.

They are:

1. Naturally formed *yoni* (Yoni Gātra) near Pātālagaṅgā site of Nuāpāḍā district.
2. One naturally formed stone *yoni* in Dhangrital village, which is now preserved in author's private museum at Khariar.
3. Three *yoni* formations on the rock belt, on the left bank of the Indra stream, at a distance of 2 km from Chuipain village, at the foothills of the eastern slope of the Sunabeda plateau. This information was first reported by Syamlal Purohit.
4. One stone *yoni* at Soseng village area, on top of the Sunabeda plateau. Because of human vandalism, its middle portion has been damaged. It is now preserved in author's private museum.
5. One chiselled stone *yoni* was discovered while digging the foundation of the spill way of the then proposed Jonk Irrigation Dam, in Māraguḍā Valley. It is kept in author's private museum.

6. Padma Dandasena discovered three *yonis* in Muṇḍapāḍā village, situated on left bank of the Udanti River in Nuāpāḍā district. Out of these *yonis*, one is of special interest, as it was found from the Udanti River and is worshipped as household deity, in the house of Brusabhānu Naik of Muṇḍapāḍā. It is a circular stone, measuring 6½ cm in circumference. There is a triangle and, at its centre, one spot (*bindu*) is found, signifying *bhairavī-yantra*. Goddess Bhairavī is the fifth Goddess of Daśamahāvidyā. In general, a triangle pointed down is a *yoni-yantra*.
7. In 2004, one huge stone *yoni* was discovered within Bireskela and Kerapadar villages of the Boden Block area.

Lot of triangles with spot (*bindu*) at the centre are painted in the rock arts of Orissa, as reported by Sadasiba Pradhan.[1] Hence, it is to be supposed that Bhairavī worship had become very popular in the entire central Mahānadī Valley during the antediluvian and early historical periods.

This benign manifestation of Bhairavī Śakti, according to tāntric text *Śākta Pramoda*,[2] is considered as the giver or bestower of knowledge. So, it is regarded that the early original knowledge of spirituality and *yoga*, sprang up and evolved from the Sunabeda plateau and its vicinity of Khariar ex-estate region, i.e. the present Nuāpāḍā district, situated on the central right Mahānadī Valley.

Yoni is worshipped as Dvārasāni at Sindhekela village of Bolaṅgīr district. One *yoni* is found on the rock surface at Veda Vyāsa site of Sundargarh district. So, it can be comprehended that *yoni* worship was popular in the entire central Mahānadī River Valley, now comprising western part of Orissa.

One broken stone *liṅga* in the actual human *liṅga* shape was collected from the compound of the High School at Bargaon village, situated at a distance of 10 km to the west of Khariar town and preserved in author's private museum.[3] It measures 5 cm in width and 7 cm in length and has similarity with *liṅga* found in Haṛappā.[4]

---

[1] S. Pradhan, *Rock Art in Orissa*, New Delhi: Aryan Books International, 2001, *passim*.

[2] *Śākta Pramoda*, Bombay: Sri Venkatesvara Press, 1951, *passim*.

[3] J.P. Singh Deo, *Tāntric Hedonism of Mahānadī Valley* (*Uḍḍiyāna Pīṭha*), New Delhi: D.K. Printworld, 2004, p. 26.

[4] Ibid.; Pl. 14.

The earliest conceptions of Śakti and Śiva in union have been discovered at the Mahānadī Valley in the form of stone sockets.[5] These are in circular shape with a socket on the lower part and has components in the upper part which fits into the lower socket. Its shape owes its origin to the rock art of Yogīmaṭh Ḍonger (hill) of the neolithic period. Such a stone socket was collected by the author from the Mohangiri site and is preserved at the Manikyapur Museum of Bhawanipatna. It can be interpreted as the union of Śiva and Śakti, which represents the *yoga* of sexual transformation. Later it developed as *vajrolī* and *sahajolī* in the tāntric *haṭha-yoga* practice.

Vajrolī-mudrā: "Thunderbolt attitude" in which the muscles of male sexual organ and lower urinary tract are contracted, redirecting sexual energy upwards. Practice of *haṭha-yoga and tantra.*

Sahajolī-mudrā: practice of *vajrolī* by a woman, wherein contract her lower urinary muscles contract.

Such a socket set was jointly collected by Baba Mishra and Pradeep Mohanty from the Kharligarh site of Bolaṅgīr district. It is exhibited at the Manikyapur Museum of Bhawanipatna. Such an object had also been found from layer III (early historic phase), from Veerapuram in Andhra Pradesh, where it is interpreted as a votive *liṅga*.[6] The shape of such stone sockets had been utilized for the shape of Lord Buddha in the Amarāvatī crossbar railing, showing the presentation of Rāhula.[7] Later this shape got evolved as the image of Lord Jagannātha at Purī[8] and the composite tāntric figure of Mahākāla and Mahākālī at Tala, in Bilāspur district of Chhattisgarh, depicting all *haṭha*-yogic features, throughout the body, relating to the *yoga* of sexual transformation.[9]

Here, it is worth mentioning the finding of a rare stone. The Rānī of Khariar, Rajshree Devi and Yubaraj Deb Prasad Singh Deo came across a rare stone in Patdaraha region, which forms the southern part of the Sunabeda plateau in Nuāpāḍā district,

---

5 J.P. Singh Deo, *Tāntric Hedonism of Mahānadī Valley* (*Uḍḍiyāna Pīṭha*), New Delhi: D.K. Printworld (P) Ltd., 2004, pp. 31-32.

6 T.V.G. Sastri, K.N. Bai, and J.V.P. Rao, *Veerapuram*, Hyderabad: Bhavani Printers, 1984, *passim*.

7 E.R. Stone, *The Buddhist Art of Nagarjuna Konda*, Delhi: Motilal Banarsidas, 1994, Illustration No. 32.

8 J.P. Singh Deo, *Origin of Jagannātha Deity*, New Delhi: Gyan Publishing House, 2nd edn., 2003, Appendix II, pp. 193-99.

9 J.P. Singh Deo, "Composite Tāntric Yogic Figure of Mahākāla and Mahākālī", *Riddle of Indian Iconography* (*Zetetic on Rare Icon from Tala*), Delhi: Sharada Publishing House, 2000, pp. 127-34.

which is believed to have enough tāntric significance, on 19 February 2004.[10] This stone measures 12 cm in length and 9 cm in width, and in a triangular shape. It is a right-angled triangle with three *bindus* (dots) at three corners.

Trikoṇa represents *icchā, jñāna* and *kriyā śaktis*. In the *Śāradātilaka* (I.78), it is recorded that from *saguṇa* Śiva rise Śakti, *nāda* and *bindu*. This *bindu* is threefold: (a) *bindu* (Śiva), (b) *bīja* (Śakti), and (c) *nāda* (Śiva-Śakti).

On "Phonic Emanation", Dirk Jan Hoens[11] states:

> Śakti-Śiva is characterized by both Amṛtānanda and Rāghavabhaṭṭa in the mentioned passages of the *Yoginī-Hṛdaya-Tantra* and the *Śāradātilaka*, by white and red colours suggestive of semen and menstrual flux, the two factors of reproduction in Hindu (including tāntric) embryology. The triad Śiva-Śakti-Nāda obtained the name Kāmakalā, the divine particle (manifesting itself as) desire, personified as Tripurasundarī (*Jñānārṇavatantra* 10.8). In this context, Śiva and Śakti are called Kāmeśvara and Kāmeśvarī. The Kāmakalā symbolizes the creative union of the primeval parental pair, a pulsating cosmic atom with two nuclei graphically represented by a white and red dot which automatically produce a third point of gravity. This situation is often represented graphically as a triangle. This can be done in two ways, with the point upwards or downwards. The second variety which expresses the initial cosmic dynamism would look like this:

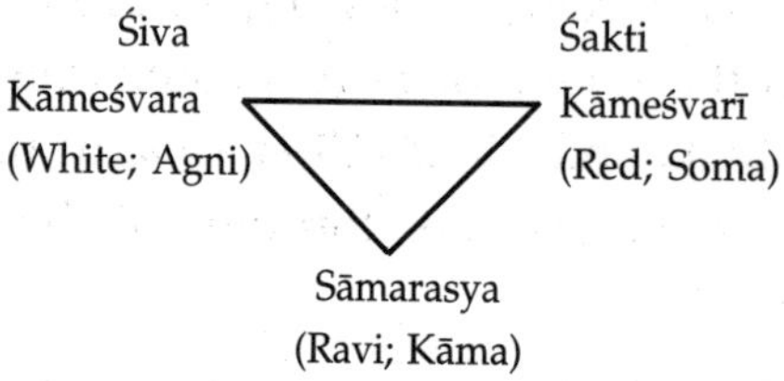

The above discussed discovery of a rare stone with triangle *yantra* from Patdaraha area of Sunabeda plateau proves that the simple triangle *yantra*, as shown by Dirk Jan Hoens is wrong. It should be a right-angled triangle *yantra*. Because, at Bauḍ, three tāntric Śiva temples in right-angled triangle placement are found, which is of advanced tāntric formulae.[12] They are Kapileśvara temple, Bhubaneswar temple and Paścima Somanātha temple, dated to ninth century CE. The placement of these three temples are is as follows:

[10] *The New Indian Express*, English daily, Bhubaneswar, 26 February 2004, p. 4.

[11] Dirk Jan Hoens, "Tantra and Other Constituents of Tāntric Practice", *Handbuch Der Orientalistik*, II, Abt., IV. Band, 2. Abschn; *Hindu Tantrism*, Leiden/Koln: E.J. Brill, 1979, p. 95.

[12] J.P. Singh Deo, op. cit., 2004, pp. 211-24.

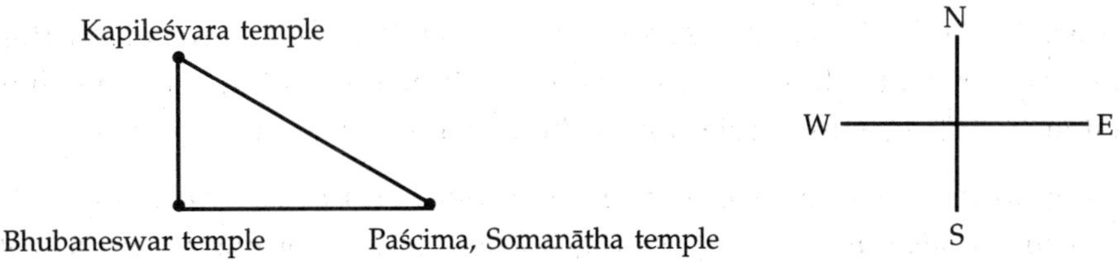

The triangle *yantra* requires explanation thus:

(1) Ordinary triangle, pointed down is *yoni-yantra.*

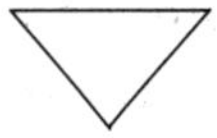

(2) Ordinary triangle, pointed up is *liṅga yantra.*

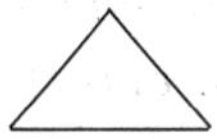

(3) Ordinary triangle pointed down, with a spot (*bindu*) at the centre is *bhairavī-yantra.*

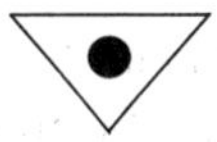

(4) Right-angled triangle is the *yantra* of creation, i.e. (i) Śiva Kāmeśvara, (ii) Śakti Kāmeśvarī, and (iii) *sāmarasya,* (union of Śiva-Śakti).

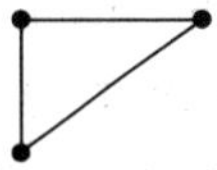

On Kāmakalā, Sir John Woodroffe[13] observes:

> *Parabindu* or *Īśvara tattva* assumes in creation a threefold aspect of the three *bindus* — *bindu* (*kārya*), *nāda* and *bīja*. These three points constitute symbolically a triangle which is known as the Kāmakalā. *Kāma* is of course not here used in the gross sense of desire, sexual or otherwise, but of *icchā*, the divine creative will towards the life of form, which is here explicated from *bindu*, the aspect previously assumed by Śakti through *nāda* (*bindutāmabhyeti*). The undivided supreme *cit-śakti* (*akhaṇḍa-paracicchakti*) becoming desirous of appearing as all the *tattvas* (*samasta-tattva-bhāvena vivarttecchāsa-manvilā*) assumes the *bindu* aspect (*bindubhāvam paryeti*) characterized by a predominance of activity (*kriyā-prādhānya-lakṣaṇā*). Here it may be observed that *icchā* or will is a form of *kriyā* (action), in the sense that it is the preliminary to action and sets the self in motion. Śakti passes from potency through will to action, which through *para-bindu* manifests. *Bindu-bhāva* is that state (*Īśvara tattva*) in

---

[13] Sir John Woodroffe, *The Garland of Letters* (*Studies in the Mantra-Sastra*), Madras: Ganesh and Co., 6th edn., 1974, pp. 175-76.

which it is fully equipped to work and does so. Its threefold aspect as it works are *bindu śivātmaka, bīja śāktyātmaka* and *nāda. Nāda* is *samavāya* that is relationship or connection (*sambandha*) as exciter (*kṣobhaka*), and that which is excited (*kṣobhya*), which relation is the cause of creation (*sṛṣṭihetu*).

According to the *Yoginī-Hṛdaya-Tantra*, the order is (a) *icchā, vāmā, paśyantī;* (b) *jñāna, jyeṣṭhā, madhyamā;* (c) *kriyā, raudrī, vaikharī*. . . . According to the *Kāmakalā Vilāsa, Yogini-Hṛdaya-Tantra* and the *Saubhāgyaśuddhodaya*, the order would appear to be (a) *icchā rajas vāma brahma-paśyanti-śabda;* (b) *jñāna sattva jyeṣṭhā viṣṇu madhyamā-śabda;* (c) *kriyā tamas raudrī rudra vaikharī-śabda.*[14]

For present practical purposes it is sufficient to know that the three *bindus* are Śiva, Śakti, Śiva-Śakti; *prakāśa, vimarśa, prakāśa-vimarśa;* white, red and mixed; *bindu, nāda, bīja;* supreme, subtle, gross; the three *devīs*; the three *devas*, and the three *śaktis* of will, knowledge and action. The supreme at this point thus becomes a trinity of energy.

The *Śabda-Brahman* in its threefold aspect and energies is represented in the Tantras by this triangular Kāmakalā which is the abode of Śakti (*abalālaya*). . . . In the *Āgamakalpadruma* it is said that the *bindu* is *haṁ* (one point) and *visargaḥ* (two points) is *saḥ* or *śakti*. The *Yāmala* thus speaks of this abode: "I now speak of Kāmakalā" and proceeding says "She is the eternal one who is the three *bindus*, the three *śaktis* and the three forms (Trimūrti)." The *Maheśvarī-Saṁhitā* says, "Sun, moon and fire are the three *bindus* and Brahmā, Viṣṇu, Rudra the three lines." The *Lalitā-Sahasranāma* calls the Devī Kāmakalārūpa. Bhāskararāya in his commentary thereon (V.73) says that *kāma* or creative will (*icchā*) is both Śiva and Devī and *kalā* is their manifestation. Hence it is called Kāmakalā. This is explained in the *Tripurasiddhānta:* "O Pārvatī, *kalā* is the manifestation of Kāmeśvara and Kāmeśvarī." Hence she is known as Kāmakalā. Or, she is the manifestation (*kalā*) of desire (*kāma*), that is, of *icchā-śakti*. The *devī* is the great Tripurasundarī.[15]

Man physically and practically is a limited manifestation of this threefold Śakti which resides within himself and is the object of worship. Such worship leads to identification, and so the *Śrītattvārṇava* says, "Those glorious men who worship that body in *sāmarasya* are freed from the waves of poison in the untraversable sea of the universe (*saṁsāra*)." *Sāmarasya,* I may here observe, is a term which is ordinarily applied to the bliss of sexual union (*strīpuṁyogāt*

---

[14] Sir John Woodroffe, *The Garland of Letters* (*Studies in the Mantra-Sastra*), Ganesh and Company, 6th edn., 1974, pp. 177-78.

[15] Ibid., pp. 179-80.

> *yat saukhyam tat sāmarasyam*). For the benefit however of those who are always reading gross meanings into parts of the *śāstra* alien to them it is necessary to explain that *sāmarasya* is both gross (*sthūla*) and subtle (*sūkṣma*). Here the latter is meant. An erotic symbol is employed to denote the merger of the *jīva* and supreme consciousness is ecstasy (*samādhi*).[16]

From *Bhagavad-Gītā*[17] it is known:

> Know that both *puruṣa* and *prakṛti* are beginningless; and know also that all modifications and qualities (*guṇas*) are born of *prakṛti*.

Prakṛti, i.e. nature, is feminine in gender. *Bṛhadyonitantra* describes the *yoni* in this context. In the three corners of the *yoni* are Brahmā, Viṣṇu and Maheśvara (*sṛṣṭi*, *sthiti* and *saṁhāra*).[18]

Sarbeswar Satpathy[19] also states, "Creation is the outcome of divine desire or *kāma* or will (*icchā*)." Therefore, divine is *kāmamayī* or *icchāmayī* in its ultimate consciousness which is symbolized in the *mahāvidyā mantra* as a representation of the divine is *śābdika* or word-form. She is *mantrātmika* or *mantramayī*, *mantra* being *śabda* and *akṣara*. The divine Kāma and the Vāk were united and produced this world.[20] This union became actual as the manifested universe and at its dissolution Śakti as universe re-entered *Brahman* and remained one with *cit* as *cidrūpiṇī* and before that she pervades, as immanent spirit, both mind and matter or *śabda* and *artha*, which are its temporal forms as *mantras* of *akṣara* or imperishable *Brahman*.[21] Because by that *vāk* and that *ātmā* He created all things whatever, the Vedas, metres, sacrifices and all creatures.[22] The *Taittirīya Brāhmaṇa*[23]

---

[16] Sir John Woodroffe, *The Garland of Letters* (*Studies in the Mantra-Sastra*), p. 182.

[17] Sri Sri Paramhansa Yogananda, *God Talks with Arjuna: the Bhagavad Gita*, Kolkata: Yogoda Satsanga Society of India, 2nd impression, 2002, p. 889.

[18] J.A. Schoterman (ed.), *The Yoni Tantra*, New Delhi: Manohar, 1980, pp. 23-24.

[19] Sarbeswar Satpathy, *Śakti Iconography in Tāntric Mahāvidyas*, Calcutta: Punthi Pustak, 1991, pp. 96-97.

[20] Ibid.; (*Pañcaviṁśa Brāhmaṇa*, XX.14.2). W. Caland (ed.), *Pañcaviṁsa Brāhmaṇa*, Calcutta, 1931.

[21] Ibid.; *Śāradātilaka*, I.14 (Varṇātmanā-vīrbhavati), *Śāradātilaka*, with Padārthādarśa Commentary of Rāghavabhaṭṭa, Pandit M.M. Mukunda Jha Sastry (ed.), Varanasi: Chowkhamba Sanskrit Sansthana, 3rd edn., vs 2039.

[22] Sarbeswar Satpathy, Roer (ed.), *Bṛhadāraṇyaka Upaniṣad*, pp. 50-53 (*sā tayā vācā tena ātmanā idaṁ sarvaṁ asrjata . . .*).

[23] Ibid.; (*Taittirīya Brāhmaṇa*, II.8.8.5.) *Taittirīya Brāhmaṇa*, Poona: Anandarshrama Sanskrit Series 37, 3 vols., 1898.

and *Śatapatha Brāhmaṇa*[24] also contain the same idea.

Three parallel lines painted three times in the rock art of Yogīmaṭh Ḍoṅger are dated to the Neolithic period,[25] discovered by the author[26] on 21 December 1970. Another important finding is circular stone in two parts, 25 cm in diameter, with a socket. It makes an overall shape of English numerical 8, thereby showing the union of male and female principles which developed *yoga* of sexual transformation. This shape of stone sockets owes its origin to the rock art of Yogīmaṭh Ḍoṅger. The author has collected such a stone-socket set from the Mohangiri site of Kālāhāṇḍī district. Baba Mishra and Pradeep Mohanty have also collected such a stone set from the Kharligarh site of Bolaṇgīr district. Both these sets are now preserved at the Manikyapur Museum of Bhawanipatna. One half of such a stone socket has been found at the Pātālagaṅgā site, while there is information that two such stone sockets have been found within the ruins of the Śakti temple, on the left bank of the Udanti River, in Bargaon village of Nuāpāḍā district. Such an object has also been found from layer III (early historic phase) at Veerapuram,[27] in Andhra Pradesh, where it is interpreted as a votive *liṅga*. But, in fact, it is not a votive *liṅga*, rather a symbol of union of male and female principles, which developed the *haṭha-yoga* practice of sexual transformation.[28] It can be interpreted as the earliest symbol of Godhead, the Supreme Being, which is both *puruṣa* and *prakṛti* or Śiva-Śakti according to Tantra. Kāmakalā means the art of desire. So, the divine Kāmakalā is symbolized in the shape of two circular components. As these archaeological findings are made in the central Mahānadī River Valley, it can be claimed that the whole Mahānadī Valley is the land of Kāmakalā and as the nucleus of spiritual culture at Nuāpāḍā district.[29]

Uḍḍiyāna-Pīṭha

Kāmakalā-Vilāsa is an ancient and authoritative work on *Śrīvidyā*, composed by Puṇyānandanātha, as *yogī* of Nātha cult, which was founded by Matsyendranāth,

---

24 Sarbeswar Satpathy, *Śakti Iconography in Tāntric Mahāvidyas*, pp. 96-97 (*Śatapatha Brāhmaṇa*, VI.1.1.8.), *Śatapatha Brāhmaṇa* with Sāyaṇa's Commentary, A. Weber (ed.), 2nd edn., Varanasi, 1963.

25 J.P. Singh Deo, "Pre-historic Cave Painting of Jogimath Donger", *OHRJ*, vol. XXII, no. 2, pp. 21-22.

26 J.P. Singh Deo, *Cultural Profile of South Kosala*, New Delhi: Gyan Publishing House, 1987, p. 20.

27 Veerapuram, op. cit., Hyderabad, 1984, *passim*.

28 J.P. Singh Deo, op. cit., 2004, pp. 64-65.

29 Ibid., p. 71.

whose period is uncertain, but is believed to be after Mahāvīra and Buddha in the early Christian era. According to Nātha cult, one should purify the body and its elements through *haṭha-yoga* practice and then should take to the practice of meditation.[30]

According to R.P. Mishra,[31] younger Luipā or Matsyendranāth was the Nātha *siddha* and was born in Cāndradvīpa, Cāndavālī-Dhāmra region of Bālāsore (now Bhadrak district) in the coastal Orissa. This fact finds assertion in the words of H.K. Mahatab,[32] when he states:

> Evidences of Nātha *dharma* in Orissa can be traced since the last quarter of the eighth century. A statue of Matsyendranāth in the form of Padmapāṇi Avalokiteśvara at forest of Rājnagar under Deravisi Block of Kendrapāṛā sub-division is still worshipped by the Nāthas of the surrounding villages. The inscription on both sides of the statue is in Kuṭila-*lipi* or proto-Uḍra-*lipi*. The present Oriyā script had not evolved by then and the period of that script is accepted to be in between sixth and eleventh centuries. The prototype of the same statue is seen at Kendrapāṛā bus stand with the same inscription, and another at Trilochanpur village under Mahājājpur Grām panchayat near Bahūgrām is also worshipped by the Nāthas of the surrounding villages. This proves that towards the last quarter of ninth century, Matsyendranāth and Gorakhanāth were worshipped in Orissa as the incarnations of Viṣṇu and Śiva respectively. The most ancient specimens of Oriyā prose and poetry are ascribed to be the work of Gorakhanāth and other Nātha *siddhas*.

Matsyendranāth was very popular throughout the Mahānadī Valley. Therefore one ferry *ghāṭ* alias bathing *ghāṭ* of the river, within Sonepur township, is named as Matsyendranāth Ghāṭ,[33] and in the hinterland of Amarkaṇṭak, there is one Matsyendranāth temple, constructed during Kaḷacuri period, twelfth-thirteenth century CE.[34]

In the words of Woodroffe:[35]

[30] Swami Muktibodhananda Saraswati (Commentary), *Haṭha-Yoga-Pradīpikā*, Munger: Bihar School of Yoga, 2nd edn., 1993, p. 3.

[31] R.P. Mishra, *Sahajayāna (A Study of Tāntric Buddhism)*, Calcutta: Punthi Pustak, 1991, p. 165.

[32] H.K. Mahatab, "Culture of Orissa", *OHRJ*, vol. XXX, nos. 2-4 and 4, p. 10.

[33] J.P. Singh Deo, *Some Tāntric Esotericism of Orissa*, Calcutta: R.N. Bhattacharya, 2003, p. 290.

[34] Minoti Chakravarty, *Religious Life in the Kalachuri Empire*, Calcutta: Punthi Pustak, 1999, Illustration No. 42.

[35] Sir John Woodroffe (tr.), *Tantrarāja Tantra and Kamakalā-Vilāsa*, Madras: Ganesh and Co., 1971, preface, p. 133.

> The *Kāmakalā-Vilāsa* is an important work in *Śrīvidyā* by Puṇyānanda, an adherent of the Hāḍimata, who is also the commentator on the *Yoginī-Hṛdaya*, a section called Uttaracatuḥśati of the great Vāmakeśvara Tantra. The same Catuḥśati as also the Pūrvacatuḥśati have commentaries by Bhāskararāya. The *Kāmakalā-Vilāsa* which means the spreading or emanation or evolution of the Kāmakalā that is the supreme triangle formed of the *bindu* and *visarga*, of *prakāśa* and *vimarśa*, of Śiva and Śakti, of the "I" (*ahaṁ*) and "This" (*idam*) or universe is, in the supreme sense, the Śiva-*svarūpa* and Śakti-*svarūpa*. To put it quite shortly *Kāmakalā-Vilāsa* is the evolution of the one in its twin aspect as changeless consciousness (*cit* or *saṁvit*) and changing power (*cit-śakti* and *māyā-śakti*) into the multiple universe. This evolution is represented by the greatest of *yantras*, the *śrī-yantra*.

According to Pranab Bandyopadhyay,[36] *śrī-yantra* is a diagrammatic embodiment of the creative sexual activity of the universe.

It is worth quoting verse 51 of *Kāmakalā-Vilāsa*,[37] which goes:

> *āsinaḥ śrīpīṭhe kṛtayugakāle guruḥ śivo vidyāṁ* ।
> *tasyai dadau svaśaktyai kāmeśvaryai vimarśarūpiṇyai* ॥ 51 ॥

> Śiva the *guru* who abides in the Uḍḍiyāna-Pīṭha did in the *Kṛta-yuga* impart the *vidyā* to Her, His own Śakti the *vimarśa-rūpiṇī* Kāmeśvarī. By "Śiva" is meant the *paramātmā* who is the author of all (*sarva-pravartaka*). *Guru* is he who instructs in *jñāna* (*jñānopadeṣṭā*). So it has been said that "the *Guru* is means of success" (*gurur upāyaḥ*);[38]

Commentary — In this verse he further discusses what has been stated in the preceding verse.

The word *gu* signifies darkness and the word *ru* signifies that which dispels it, *guru* is so-called because he dispels darkness.

Who abides in the Uḍḍiyāna-Pīṭha (*āsinaḥ śrīpīṭhe*). By this is meant that the abode of Śiva is the Uḍḍiyāna-Pīṭha within the innermost triangle.

In the *Kṛta-yuga* (*kṛta-yuga-kāle*). By this we are to understand that it was in the beginning of *Kṛta* or *Satya* age that Śiva imparted the knowledge of the *vidyā*. By *vidyā* is meant the *vidyā* which is fully established in all Upaniṣads and thereby a man can realize his oneness with the *ātmā* (*ātmaikya-pradāyinī*).

---

[36] Pranab Bandyopadhyay, *The Goddess of Yantra*, Calcutta: Punthi Pustak, 1987, p. 48.

[37] Sir John Woodroffe, op. cit., 1971, p. 234.

[38] *Kulārṇava Tantra*, XVII.7.

Did impart (*dadau*). Fully instructed (*upādideśa*). Her, His own Śakti (*tasyāi svaśaktyai*). The force of the pronoun "Her" is to press on the reader's attention the fact that it is She who gives boundless happiness to all creatures (*sarva-bhūtānāṁ, niravadhi-kānanda-dāyinī*). His own Śakti (*svaśakti*). By this we are to understand that it is She who enables the Lord to manifest His own being (*svasva-rūpa-satta-saṁpradātri*). So it has been said:

Even the supreme if disunited from Śakti is unable to do anything. O Parameśāni! He is capable (of action) if he is united with Śakti.

Vimarśarūpiṇī. She is so-called because She is the supreme Śakti which is (lit. is the resting place of) the Supreme manifesting Bliss (*anuttarānanda-viśrānti-sthāna-bhūta-śakti-para-rūpiṇī*). So it has been said (*saṁketa-paddhati*). The letter *A* is the first of all and *prakāśa* and the Supreme Śiva and the letter *Ha* is the last which is *kalā* and is called *vimarśa*.

Kāmeśvarī, She is so-called because She at all times and every way grants all objects of desire (*sarvābhiṣṭa-pradāyinī*) and is one with one's own *ātmā* (*svātma-bhūtā*).

This proves that the spot (*bindu*) of the central triangle of *śrī-yantra* is Uḍḍiyāna-Pīṭha, which is the abode of Śiva.

Sri-yantra[39] is the most auspicious and result-giving *yantra*. *Sri-yantra* is the source of attaining all worldly desires and living above want. It bestows popularity with public men and giver of wealth and prosperity. This *yantra* consists of five triangles with their apexes pointed downward, known as *yoni yantras* alias *śakti yantras* and four triangles with their apexes pointing upward, known as *liṅga yantras* alias *śiva yantras*. The centre is marked with a spot (*bindu*), which is Uḍḍiyāna-Pīṭha, as discussed.

The innermost triangle of *śrī-yantra* with apex pointed down is *bhairavī-yantra*,[40] with a spot (*bindu*) at its centre. So, it can be claimed that the central spot (*bindu*) of *bhairavī-yantra* is also Uḍḍiyāna-Pīṭha, where Lord Śiva resides.

As discussed, *bhairavī-yantra* which is the innermost triangle of *śrī-yantra* is found and worshipped as household deity at Muṇḍapāḍā village. The inner plan of the Rājarānī temple at Bhubaneswar is said to be based on *śrīcakra* alias *śrī-*

---

[39] L.R. Chawdhri, *Practicals of Yantras*, New Delhi: Sagar Publications, 1984, p. 19.

[40] David Frawley, *Tāntric Yoga and the Wisdom Goddesses*, Delhi: Motilal Banarsidass, 1996, p. 103.

yantra.[41] The entire Mahānadī Valley is connected with *śrī-yantra*. Therefore, this was the land of Kāmakalā, and *śrī-yantra* was popularized by the Nātha *siddhas*.

As mentioned, triangle pointed down is *yoni-yantra*. Hence it is considered that the central point of the clitoris of every living female is Uḍḍiyāna-Pīṭha, where Lord Śiva resides. Because of the blessings of Lord Śiva, the female reaches orgasm, becomes pregnant and delivers off-springs. Therefore, it is usually observed that females belonging to Hindu religion, do *Śiva-pūjā* (worship) on Monday, which is an auspicious Lord Śiva's day in Hindu calendar.

In the discussed thoughts, three Uḍḍiyāna-Pīṭhas (sites) have been located at the centre of *śrī-yantra*, at the centre of *bhairavī-yantra* and at the central point of the clitoris of every living woman.

Uḍḍiyāna bandha is a Haṭha-yogic practice. According to *Haṭha-Yoga-Pradīpīkā*[42] ch. 3, verses 55-60:

> *Uḍḍiyāna bandha* is so-called by the *yogī*s because through its practice the *prāṇa* (is concentrated at one point and) rises through *suṣumnā*.
>
> — Verse 55
>
> The *bandha* described is called the rising or flying *bandha*, because through its practice, the great bird (Śakti) flies upward with ease.
>
> — Verse 56
>
> Pulling the abdomen back in and making the navel rise is *uḍḍiyāna bandha*. It is the lion which conquers the elephant, death. — Verse 57
>
> *Uḍḍiyāna* is easy when practised as told by the *guru*. Even an old person can become young when it is done regularly.
>
> — Verse 58
>
> The region above and below the navel should be drawn backward with effort. There is no doubt that after six months of practice, death is conquered. — Verse 59
>
> Of all the *bandhas*, *uḍḍiyāna* is the best. Once it is mastered, *mukti* or liberation occurs spontaneously. — Verse 60

Discoveries of circular sockets, showing the union of male and female principles, dated to early historical period in the central right Mahānadī Valley, have already

[41] Bettina Bäumer and Rajendra Prasad Das (eds.), *Śilparatnakośa*, Delhi: Motilal Banarsidass, figs. 53-56, pp. 148 and 151-52.

[42] Swami Muktibodhanana Saraswati, op. cit., 1993, pp. 299-304.

been done. In sculptural art, the earliest eight-handed Naṭarāja with *ūrdhva-liṅga* (*penis erectus*) of India is found at the Archaeological Sculpture Museum of Sirpur,[43] Raipur, Chhattisgarh. Another oldest image of eight-handed Naṭarāja with *ūrdhva-liṅga* (*penis erectus*)[44] was discovered by Nabin Kumar Sahu at the Āsanapaṭ site of Keoñjhar district, Orissa, dated to sixth century CE with an inscription. It is now preserved at the Orissa State Museum, Bhubaneswar.

Ūrdhva-liṅga (*penis erectus*) of Lord Śiva signifies the upflow of semen, i.e. the practice of *yoga* of sexual transformation, which can be practised through Haṭha-yogic, *vajrolī-mudrā, khecarī-mudrā* and *uḍḍiyāna bandha*, which should be learnt from a *haṭha-yoga* master (*guru*).

The archaeological findings discussed above proves that the entire Mahānadī Valley region, which comprises Chhattisgarh and Orissa states of India, was the land of Kāmakalā and Uḍḍiyāna-Pīṭha, during early and medieval periods of the Indian. In the Peninsular India, the earliest trace of *yoga* is found in the pre-historic rock art painting at Guṛahāṇḍī of Kālāhāṇḍī district.[45] This painting of human-like figure has a head, which symbolizes a lotus. In *kuṇḍalinī-yoga*, the highest *cakra* of human being is described as a thousand-petalled lotus, i.e. *sahasrāra*. So, it can be said that *sahasrāra cakra* is the gift of the Mahānadī River Valley to mankind.[46]

---

43 C. Sivaramamurti, *Nataraja in Art: Thought and Literature*, New Delhi: Publication Division, Govt. of India, National Museum, 2nd edn., 1994, pp. 159-60.

44 Ibid., pp. 164-65.

45 *The Journal of Kalinga Historical Research Society*, vol. II, p. 243.

46 J.P. Singh Deo, op. cit., 2004, p. 22.

2

The Land of Kāmakalā and Yoginī Cult

As we have already seen, the Mahānadī Valley is the land of Kāmakalā. Pranab Bandyopadhyay[1] says that *śrī-yantra* is a diagrammatic embodiment of the creative sexual activity of the universe. From various discoveries it is known that the earliest trace of antiquities of Śiva and Śakti in union was in the central right Mahānadī Valley, which had developed the *yoga* of sexual transformation. According to *Haṭha-Yoga-Pradīpikā*,[2] an authoritative text on *haṭha-yoga*, "If a woman practises *vajrolī* and saves her *rajas* and the man's *bindu* by thorough contraction, she is a *yoginī*." After the discovery of this *haṭha-yoga*, it had spread throughout Bhāratavarṣa and finds mentions in mythology.

According to Vanamali:[3]

> Dakṣa had sixty daughters of whom Svadhā was given in marriage to forefathers. She had three daughters of whom Menā was the eldest, Dhanyā, second and Kalāvatī, third. Once the three sisters went to the abode of Viṣṇu in order to have *darśana* of the Lord. A great concourse of sages and *yogī*s was there. It so happened that the four boy sages known as Sanaka, Sananda, Sanandana and Sanatkumāra also arrived to pay obeisance to the Lord. Seeing them, the entire assembly of sages rose up in respect. Submerged in their own thoughts, the three sisters did not rise. Seeing this lack of respect, Sanaka and the others, though steeped in bliss always, became angry in order to fulfil the inscrutable purpose of the Lord. They cursed the sisters that they would be born as human beings on the earth. On hearing this, the sisters became very sad and fell at their feet and begged for forgiveness.

---

1 Pranab Bandyopadhyay, *The Goddess of Tantra*, Calcutta: Punthi Pustak, 1987, p. 48.

2 Swami Muktibodhananda Saraswati (commentary), *Haṭha-Yoga-Pradīpikā*, Munger: Bihar School of Yoga, 2nd edn., 1993, p. 362.

3 Vanamali, *Sri Śiva Līlā*, New Delhi: Aryan Books International, 2002, pp. 53-54.

> Sanaka then said, "The curse of a sage is always for the benefit of the world, so you should not worry. Menā will become the wife of Himavān who is actually a part of Lord Viṣṇu. The Goddess Śakti will be born as Menā's daughter and will be known as Pārvatī. She will become the wife of Lord Śiva. The second, Dhanyā will become a great *yoginī* and will be the wife of the great saint-king of Videha known as Janaka. Lakṣmī herself will be born as her daughter and will be called Sītā. She will become the wife of Viṣṇu in his incarnation as Rāma. The third sister, Kalāvatī shall be born in a vaiśya family of cowherds and will be married to Vṛṣabhāna. Rādhā will be born as her daughter. This Rādhā who will be a resident of Gokula will be the beloved of Kṛṣṇa." The sisters were very happy when they heard this and thanked the sages for their curse, which are actually a blessing, not only to them but also to the whole world.

There is a myth of Karṇa Caurā in Bihar state also.

The Myth of Karṇa Caurā[4]

Munger has always been a spiritual place belonging to the *yogīs*, *ṛṣis* and *munis*. It was a great cultural centre where the chanting of *mantra* and the scriptures took place. Munger is said to have been the kingdom of King Karṇa. At that time it was known as Aṅgadeśa and also included Bhāgalpur. There were different persons by the name Karṇa; which Karṇa actually ruled is not certain. However, it is likely to be Karṇa of the *Mahābhārata*, the son of Kuntī.

Karṇa was a great devotee of *devī* and a devout tāntric. It is said that Karṇa would go to the Caṇḍī Sthāna temple in the early morning via an underground tunnel from *Gaṅgā-darśana*, and perform a horrific sacrifice of his physical body in which he cut himself into pieces and offered these to the 64 *yoginīs*. When he had thrown his whole body into a boiling vat of *ghee*, Caṇḍī would appear and resurrect his body, offering him a boon of 50 kg gold. He would take this gold back to his palace and distribute it to all the beggars and needy people from the now famous platform, Karṇa Caurā. Thus Karṇa became known as Dānavīra or the charitable one.

The story goes that the king of India at that time, called Vikrama (though his identity is not sure, he may be the famous Vikramāditya who ruled from Ujjain),

---

4 *Yoga-Ganga Darshan Issue*, vol. XXI, no. 12, Munger: Bihar School of Yoga, December 1983, pp. 11-12.

wanted to find out how Karṇa was obtaining his gold. So he followed him one morning and watched the whole sacrifice.

Next morning, Vikrama went ahead of Karṇa and performed the same sacrifice. Caṇḍī, being pleased with his offering, appeared to him and offered him the boon. Vikrama asked for the precious stone (*śilā*), the philosopher's stone, which enabled one to have the 50 kg of gold without this torturous sacrifice plus that day's 50 kg of gold. Caṇḍī accepted and gave him what he desired. This meant that whoever performed the sacrifice thereafter could not be saved, nor could they receive any gold. As usual Karṇa came to do his worship that morning. Caṇḍī knowing the present state of affairs turned the boiling vat of ghee upside down so Karṇa could not perform the sacrifice and thereby saved his life. What remains today of the Caṇḍī temple is the inverted cauldron.

These myths show that *yoginīs* and their cult had already become popular in the proto-history period. It is worth discussing how this erotic and esoteric secret or disguised cult became popular and got methodical in the historical period.

Ram Prasad Mishra[5] identifies the birth-place of the great Siddha Matsyendranāth as Candradvipa. As discussed in Chapter 1 Yogī Matsyendranāth was the founder of Nātha cult in the eighth century CE. He believed[6] that before taking to the practices of meditation, one must purify the body and its elements, which is the theme of *haṭha-yoga.* Due to the popularity of the *yoginī* cult gained over the period, he systematized and expounded it in his famous work *Kaulayānanirṇaya*, which later became the authoritative text of the cult.[7]

Kāmakalā-Vilāsa, composed by Puṇyānanda Nātha is an authoritative book of the Nātha cult. Woodroffe[8] mentions that the *Kāmakalā-Vilāsa* is an important work in *śrīvidyā* by Puṇyānanda, an adherent of the Hāḍi *mata*, who is also the commentator on the *Yoginī-Hṛdaya*, a section called Uttara Catuḥśatī of the great *Vāmakeśvara Tantra*. The same *catuḥśatī* as also the Pūrva Catuḥśatī have commentaries by Bhāskararāya. The *Kāmakalā-Vilāsa* which means the spreading or emanation or evolution of the Kāmakalā that is the supreme triangle formed of the *bindu* and *visarga*, of *prakāśa* and *vimarśa*, of Śiva and Śakti, of the I (*aham*) and This (*idam*) or universe is, in the supreme sense, the Śiva-*svarūpa* and Śakti-*svarūpa*. To put it quite

---

5 R.P. Mishra, *Sahajayana: A Study of Tantric Buddhism*, Calcutta: Punthi Pustak, 1991, p. 165.

6 *Haṭha-Yoga-Pradīpikā*, Munger, 1993, p. 3.

7 H.C. Das, *Tantricism: A Study of Yogini Cult*, New Delhi: Sterling Publishers, 1981, p. 3.

8 Sir John Woodroffe, "Preface", *Kāmakalā-Vilāsa*, Madras: Ganesh and Co., 1971, p. 133.

shortly *Kāmakalā-Vilāsa* is the evolution of the one in its twin aspects as changeless consciousness (*cit* or *saṁvit*) and changing power (*cit-śakti* and *māyā-śakti*) into the multiple universe. This evolution is represented by the greatest of *yantras* — the *śrī-yantra* figured on the cover and in a separate plate showing in colours its several *cakras* extending from the point or *bindu* (called *sarvānandamaya*), the Supreme Śiva-Śakti in the centre, to the outermost section of the *cakras* the Bhūpura which is called Trailokyamohana.

The verses 40-44 of *Kāmakalā-Vilāsa*, are of importance, because they deal with the location of *yoginīs* in *śrī-yantra*. They are quoted with the translation and commentary of Woodroffe:[9]

vasukoṇanivāsinyo yāstāḥ saṁdhyāruṇā vaśinyādyāḥ ।
puryaṣṭakamevedaṁ cakratanoḥ saṁvidātmano devyāḥ ॥ 40 ॥

Those that abide in the *cakra* of eight triangles are *vaśinī* and the others who are red like the evening Sun. This (*cakra* of eight triangles) is the eightfold (subtle) body of the *devī*, which is the self thereof in the supreme experience (*saṁvid*).

Commentary: From here onwards he describes the form and nature (*svarūpa-bhāvanā*) of the surrounding *devatās* (*āvaraṇa-devāḥ*), "Those that abide in the *cakra* of eight triangles" (*vasukoṇa-nivāsinyaḥ*). The *cakra* of eight triangles is the *cakra* called *sarva-rogahara* (all disease-destroyer). The eight *śaktis vaśinī* and others abide in this *cakra*. They are powerful to grant the bliss arising from the experience of complete "I-ness" (*pūrṇāhaṁbhāva-dāna-samarthāḥ*). It is because they are able to give the experience of complete "I-ness" that this *cakra* is *rogahara*. For it has been said:

The sense of imperfection is disease and the source of misery (*apūrṇaṁ-manyatāṁ vyādhiḥ kārpaṇyaika-nidānabhūḥ*). These *śaktis*[1] shine like the evening sun and are therefore described as red like the evening sun (*saṁdhyāruṇāḥ*). The *devī* is the supreme experience (*saṁvidātmā*) by which is meant that Her own form (*svarūpa*) is knowledge-in-itself. *Śruti* (in reference to the *Brahman*) speaks of being (*satyam*), knowledge (*jñānam*) and eternity (*anantam*).

Āgama says that the "Devī Tripura is *sva-saṁvid*." By *devī* is meant that she in her desire "to be many" is playfully moving about and active (*viharaṇa-svabhāvā*).

The *cakra* of eight triangles is the eightfold (subtle) body of the *devī* (*cakratanoḥ*

[9] Sir John Woodroffe, *Kāmakalā-Vilāsa*, pp. 219-24.

puryaṣṭakaṁ) in the form of the *śrī-cakra* (*cakrātmikā*). By *cakra* is meant the *śrī-cakra*. The subtle body (*puryaṣṭaka* = eightfold body) is so-called because of the eight triangles which compose it. They are as the *Svacchanda Tantra* says: *citi, citta, caitanya, cetana, indriya-karma, jīva, kalā* and *śarīra*.[2]

Notes: 1. These *śaktis* are called Rahasya Yoginīs (see *Nityaṣoḍaśika*, VIII.161) because they are subtle. **2.** Different stages of *cit-śakti*. Bhāskararāya in his commentary on *Nityaṣoḍaśika*, VIII.160-164 enumerates what constitute the eighfold *sthūla* body of the Devī. They are (1) *karmendriyas*, (2) *jñānendriyas*, (3) *manas*, etc., (4) *prāṇas*, (5) the elements *viyat*, etc., (6) *kāma*, (7) *karma*, and (8) *tamas*.

tadbāhyapaṅktikoṇeṣu yoginyaḥ sarvasiddhidāḥ pūrvāḥ ।
devīdhikarmendriyaviṣayamayā viśadaveśa-bhūṣāḍhyāḥ ॥ 42 ॥

The *yoginī*s in the series of angles outside this (last) are those the first of whom is *sarva-siddhi-pradā*. They are the objects of the *jñānendriya*s and *karmendriya*s of the *devī* and are adorned with white raiment and ornament.

Commentary: In the series of triangles outside this (last) (*tad-bāhya-paṅkti-koṇeṣu*). By "this" is meant *sarva-rakṣākara-cakra*, outside which is the *cakra* called *sarvārtha-sādhaka* (accomplisher of all aims).

In the series of angles (*paṅkti-koṇeṣu*). By this we are to understand that the angles of the triangles of which the *sarvārtha-sādhaka-cakra* is composed are in proximity to the triangles of the *sarva-rakṣākara-cakra*. The *yoginī*s in this *cakra* (*sarvārtha-sādhaka*) are called *kula-kaula*s[1] and they are the ten *śakti*s *sarvasiddhipradā* and others.

They are the objects of the *jñānendriya*s and *karmendriya*s of the *devī* (*devī-dhi-karmendriya-viṣaya-mayāḥ*). These ten *śakti*s are the objects of sense perception such as sound is of hearing and the like. They are clad in white raiment and their adornment is also white (*viśada-veśa-bhūṣāḍhyāḥ*). The sense of this is that these *śakti*s are inseparate from or identical with (*abhedarūpāḥ*) the *mantra*, the *devatā* and the *sādhaka*'s[2] self are white, clad in white raiment and grant *siddhi*.

Notes: 1. Cf. *Nityaṣoḍaśika*, VIII.151-55. **2.** That is, they help the *sādhaka* to realize his identity with the *mantra* and the *devatā*.

bhuvanāracakrabhavanāḥ devīmanukaraṇa vivaraṇa sphuraṇāḥ ।
saṁdhyā savarṇa vāsanāḥ saṁcintyāḥ saṁpradāyayoginyāḥ ॥ 43 ॥

Those (*śakti*s) who have their places in the *cakra* of fourteen triangles are the unfolding movements of the fourteen instruments (of mind and senses) of the *devī*. They are clad in garments (red) like the evening sun and are the *sampradāya-yoginī*s and they should be meditated upon as above.

Commentary: This *cakra* of fourteen[1] triangles is called *sarva-saubhāgyadāyaka* (giver of all prosperity). The fourteen instruments (*manu-karaṇa*) of the *devī* are five of *jñāna* (*pañca-jñānendriyāṇi*), the five or *karma* (*pañca-karmendriyāṇi*) and *manas, buddhi, ahaṁkāra, citta*. Unfolding movements (*vivaraṇa-sphuraṇaḥ*). The movements (*sphuraṇaḥ*) of senses are in the *cakra* of fourteen triangles (*bhuvanāra-cakra*) as the *śakti*s therein. The *devī* herself is in this *cakra* as the fourteen *devatā*s who are her fourteen instruments. The *śakti*s or *devatā*s are *sarvasaṁkṣobhiṇī* and others. They are called *sampradāya-yoginī*s because they are forms of the Ādi-Śakti (*ādi-śakti-mayatvena*). They should be meditated upon as unmanifest (*avyakta*).

Note: 1. The word Manu is used for 14 and *bhuvana* is used for the same number. There are 14 *manas* and 14 *bhuvanas*.

avyaktamahadahaṁkṛtitanmātra svikṛtāṅganākārāḥ ।
dviradacchadana saroje jayanti gupatatarayoginī saṁjñaḥ ॥ 44 ॥

Avyakta, mahat, ahaṁkṛti and the (five) *tanmātra*s having assumed womanly forms abide resplendent in the lotus of eight petals. They are known as the *guptatara yoginī*s.

Commentry: By *avyakta* (unmanifest) is meant the *avyakta-tattva*, i.e. *prakṛti*, by *mahat* or *ahaṁkāra-tattva*. The *tanmātras* are the five *tanmātras* of *pṛthivī* and others. These make eight. These eight have in the *cakra* assumed womanly forms (*svikṛtaṅganākārāḥ*). They are forms of the *devī* (*devyātmikā*).

They are called *guptatara yoginī*s because they are within (*antaraṅga-bhūta*[1]) the *mūla-devī*. These eight *śakti*s who are Anaṅga-Kusumā and others abide in the *cakra* of eight petals which is called *sarva saṁkṣobhaṇa*. Abide resplendent (Jayanti) i.e. they are there excelling all (*sarvotkarṣeṇa vartante*).

Note: 1. *Antaraṅga* = lit. comprehended; inseparable.

The following verse, about a *yoginī*, is found in *Haṭha-Yoga-Pradīpikā:*[10]

पुंसो विदुं समाकुध्य सम्यगभ्यासपाटवात् ।
यदि नारी रजो रक्षेद्वज्रोल्या सापियोगिनी ॥ 99 ॥

puṁso viduṁ samākudhya samyagabhyāsapāṭavāt ।
yadi nārī rajo rakṣedvajrolyā sāpiyoginī ॥ 99 ॥ — ch. 3, verse 99

A lady who practises *vajrolī* alias *sahajolī*, i.e. *yoga* of sexual transformation, is known as *yoginī* in practical purpose.

[10] *Haṭha-Yoga-Pradīpikā*, Munger, 1993, p. 362.

With this Haṭha-yogic action, *siddhi* (perfection, enhanced prāṇic and psychic capacity, *paranormal* or supernormal accomplishment, control of mind and *prāṇa*), a *yoginī* was regarded divine and *yoginī* cult developed. Lists of *yoginīs* are found in *Kālīkā Purāṇa, Skanda Purāṇa, Bṛhada-Nandikeśvara Purānnakto Durgāpūjā Paddhati, Cauṅsaṭha Yoginī Nāmāvalī, Caṇḍī Purāṇa* or *Caṇḍī Yuddha* by Sāralādāsa, Durgā-Pūja (A palm-leaf manuscript of the Orissa State Museum) and *Bṛhannīla Tantra*.[11]

H.C. Das[12] regarded the hypaetheral Sixty-four Yoginī temple at Hirapur, as the earliest one. So far nine *yoginī* temples are found at Bherāghāṭ and Khajurāho in Madhya Pradesh, Rāṇīpur-Jharial in Orissa, Coimbatore district of Tamil Nadu, Shahdol in Madhya Pradesh, Mitauli, Dudahi and Lokhari in Uttar Pradesh and Hirapur in Orissa. It is an irony that without any detailed observation, study, outlook and conviction, H.C. Das[13] considers the Sixty-four Yoginī temple at Hirapur to be the first or the earliest. *Yoginī-Tantra,*[14] a work of eleventh century CE, mentions that first *yoginī pīṭha* (site) is located where Someśvara-Liṅga is worshipped. The Someśvara temple exists at Rāṇīpur-Jharial site.[15] Therefore, Ram Prasad Mishra[16] very correctly remarks:

> It is thus reasonable to believe that Rāṇīpur-Jharial was the ancient Someśvara-*liṅga* Ādipīṭha depicted in *Yoginī-Tantra*. The term *ādi-pīṭha* or primal centre in this *Yoginī-Tantra* must signify the first and foremost place for the tāntric veneration of the *yoginīs*. It is thus reasonable to identify Rāṇīpur-Jharial as the first and foremost tāntric venue of *yoginī*-adoration and as a *tīrtha* it was Ādi-Yoginī Tīrtha or the primary holy place of the tāntric *sādhanās* of the *yoginīs*. It appears that the regions of Khariar and their contiguous regions were known as Kaunripatana under the influence of this *yoginī-pīṭha* because of the popularity of the tāntric practices in these areas, even as late as the time of poet Caitanya Dās of Baḍamūla. This saint-poet of *Viṣṇugarbha Purāṇa* and *Nirguṇa Māhātmya*, flourished in eighteenth century

[11] H.C. Das, *Tantricism: A Study of Yogini Cult*, New Delhi: Sterling Publishers, 1981, pp. 34-41.

[12] Ibid., pp. 12 and 20.

[13] Ibid., pp. 3-4.

[14] K.L. Mishra (ed.), *Yoginī Tantra*, Uttara Khaṇḍa: Prathama Paṭala, Lakshmi Venkatevar Press, Saṁvat 2013 and Śakābda 1878, pp. 241-42, verses 15-19.

[15] Dipakranjan Das, *Temples of Orissa (The Study of a Sub-style)*, Delhi: Agam Kala Prakashan, 1982, pp. 26-29.

[16] Ram Prasad Mishra, "Primal Yogini Pitha, Rāṇīpur-Jharial and Its Influence on the Culture of Western Orissa", *Souvenir*, Bolaṅgir: Bolaṅgir Loka Utsabha, 2001, p. 108.

CE till the rule of Mahārāja Pratāprudra Singh Deo of Khariar, whose ruling period was within CE 1793 to 1818.

The circular and the hypaethral *yoginī* temple in Rāṇīpur-Jharial is perched upon a rocky floor. The exterior circumference of its wall is measured 169' and 3" in length, while its inner circumference in length is measured 145' and 11". Its wall bends inward at a height of 8' and 5". An entrance facing towards the east with steps outside and inside is found with this hypaethral and circular shrine. The entrance shows a measurement of 5' and 9" in altitude and 5' and 3" in width. A small *maṇḍapa* or pavilion roofed with a slab is perched upon the rocky floor at the centre of this *yoginī* temple. The ceiling rests on four pillars erected in four corners of the pavilion. The measurements of this pavilion are 7' in length and 7' and 1" in breadth. This pavilion exhibits on its surface, image of Naṭarāja Śiva with three faces, eight hands and the erectile penis. The image holds by his two hands a serpent and by the other six hands a rosary, a skull, a trident, a pot, a *ḍamaru* (small drum) and an indistinct object. The images of Gaṇeśa, Nandī and eight-handed Pārvatī are also found there. The image of the eight-handed Pārvatī is seen there in her Siddheśvarī or Siddhayogeśvarī Cāmuṇḍā form. As Siddha Yogeśvarī Cāmuṇḍā, she is also called Kālī in tāntric literature. Several tāntric texts delineate Siddha Yogeśvarī Cāmuṇḍā/Kālī as the presiding goddess among the *yoginī*s. All the *yoginī* images in this hypaethral *yoginī* temple are displayed in dancing poses. Naṭarāja as a nomenclature of Śiva denotes his dancing or dance-loving form. In this form or appearance Śiva according to the tāntric mythology performs seven types of dance which are called *tāṇḍava*s. Seven *tāṇḍava*s are known as (1) Kālī Tāṇḍava, (2) Ānanda Tāṇḍava, (3) Sandhyā Tāṇḍava, (4) Gaurī Tāṇḍava, (5) Saṁhāra Tāṇḍava, (6) Tripura Tāṇḍava, and (7) Unmatta Umā Tāṇḍava. In Kālī or Kālikā Tāṇḍava, Naṭarāja Śiva while dancing with Siddha Yogeśvarī Cāmuṇḍā or Kālī in the midst of dancing *yoginī*s enjoys sexual ecstasy or *kāmānanda* in consonance with tāntric mythology. As all the *yoginī*-images of this place are found in dancing poses, Naṭarāja-image with eight hands is seen in *sukhāsana* with *ūrdhva-liṅga* (*penis erectus*) or comfortable sitting with erectile penis and Siddha Yogeśvarī Cāmuṇḍa/Kālī is beheld with eight hands in her sculptural representation, it is undoubtedly a sculptural scene of Kālī Tāṇḍava.

The hypaethral *yoginī* temple of Rāṇīpur-Jharial exhibits on the inner side of its circular wall 64 niches which have been constructed in close and continuous order like the minute marks of a round clock. Each of the niches is measured 1' and 6" in breadth and 3' and 2" in height. It seems that each of the niches had an image of *yoginī* when the hypaethral *yoginī* temple was

> built primarily. Presently 48 niches contain images and the rest are found vacant probably because of the ravages of time and lack of sincere preservation.

K.C. Panigrahi[17] dates the Sixty-four Yoginī temple of Rāṇīpur-Jharial site within ninth-tenth century CE and while dealing on the Cauṅsaṭha Yoginī temple of Hirapur states that it seems that the Somavaṁśī rulers, when they lived in Orissa, built this shrine or helped to build it in the model of the Rāṇīpur-Jharial shrine which lay in their original seat of power. The Hirapur images are the marvellous pieces of art and are comparable to those of the Brahmeśvara and the Liṅgarāja and were evidently the creation of that period. The Brahmeśvara temple and Liṅgarāja temple were built during the eleventh century CE by the Somavaṁśī kings of Orissa.[18] So the construction period of the Yoginī temple at Hirapur may be assigned to the eleventh century CE and not to the early ninth century as forcefully enthralled by Das.[19]

While placing or discussing his opinion Das[20] states, "As regards the date of Sixty-four Yoginī temple at Hirapur, it is evidently the work of Bhauma period." K.N. Mahapatra[21] assigns it to the eighth or early part of the ninth century CE when Brāhmanical tāntric religion made headway in Orissa and several tāntric temples came into existence in the region.

> The work of Hirapur Yoginī temple cannot possibly be placed in the eighth century CE for, the workmanship and ornamentation of the sculptures here far excel the achievement of the eighth century. The temples of Vaitāl, Mohinī, Uttareśvara and Śiśireśvara at Bhubaneswar which are the works of the eighth century CE appear from artistic and iconographic points of view to be inferior to the *yoginī* figures at Hirapur. The suggestion of Mahapatra that the temple belongs to early part of ninth century CE is more plausible. Most probably the temple was built by Hira Mahadevi, Queen of Sāntika II and the present village of Hirapur was named after her.

This discussion and view of Das seem to be speculative and cannot be accepted. The study of Panigrahi looks, more correct and *Yoginī-Tantra* text has strengthened

---

17 K.C. Panigrahi, *History of Orissa*, Cuttack: Kitab Mahal, 1981, pp. 444 and 454.

18 K.C. Panigrahi, *Archaeological Remains at Bhubaneswar*, New Delhi: Orient Longman, 1961, pp. 41-47, 62 and 101.

19 H.C. Das, *Tantricism: A Study of Yogini Cult*, New Delhi: Sterling Publishers, 1981, p. 12.

20 Ibid.

21 Ibid., *OHRJ*, vol. II, no. 2, p. 40.

or confirmed that the first *yoginī* temple was at Rāṇīpur-Jharial site where Someśvara-*liṅga* is worshipped.

Gone are the days of contemplation, theorizing, conjecture, guess-work and hypothesis. At present, we delve upon practical findings of antiquities and their studies. Therefore, it is sensible to summarize that the spiritual culture of the Mahānadī Valley was developed in the Sunabeda plateau of Nuāpāḍā district of the (central right Mahānadī Valley) and its vicinity.[22]

[22] J.P. Singh Deo, *Tāntric Hedonism of Mahānadī Valley (Uḍḍiyāna-Pīṭha)*, New Delhi: D.K. Printworld, 2004, pp. 70-71.

3

Yoginīs of the Puruṣottama Jagannātha Temple

WHILE dealing on "Yoga of Sexual Transformation in Jagannātha Cult", the author,[1] had mentioned that there are *yoginī* images in the Jagannātha temple at Purī. The *yoginī*s are regarded as guardian deities and there is ritual worship also. It is interesting to know about these *yoginī*s. B.C. Pradhan[2] also deals on Śāktism in Jagannātha Cult and mentions:

> The Śākta environment of the temple is further indicated by the fact that the shrine is said to be protected by *aṣṭaśakti*s (eight *śakti*s), namely Sarvamaṅgalā, Bhuvaneśvarī, Indrāṇī, Kūṭamcaṇḍī, Cāmuṇḍā, Dūrgā, Vimalā and Lakṣmī. What is very striking to note is that the *bhoga* (food offered) to Jagannātha as *naivedya* is honoured as *mahāprasāda* only, when the same is offered to the Śākta Goddess Vimalā.

There are temples of Vimalā, Bhuvaneśvarī and Lakṣmī inside the campus of the great temple of Puruṣottama Jagannātha at Purī.

While dealing about the temple and the icon, K.C. Mishra[3] states:

> Now the inner *prākāra* (wall), the *kūrma veḍhā*, starts. . . . At the eastern and southern side we find Satyanārāyaṇa, Vaṭagopāla, Sarvamaṅgalā, Bālamukunda, Vaṭabihārī Jagannātha, Śveta Gaṇeśa, Satyabhāmā and Kalpavaṭa (tree).

Mishra[4] states further that the icons of Goddesses Vimalā, Bhuvaneśvarī and Lakṣmī are worshipped in their respective temples inside the campus of Jagannātha temple:

---

1 *THOMV*, p. 141.

2 B.C. Pradhan, "Śāktism", *Cultural Heritage of Orissa* (vol. II, pt. I), B.C. Ray (ed.), Bhuvaneswar: Centre for Advanced Studies in History and Culture, 1996, p. 123.

3 *TCOJ*, p. 105.

4 Ibid., pp. 112-13.

There are many figures of deities in the temple premises; we shall only give the iconographic features of some of the important ones. Let us take up the figure of the Goddess Vimalā first. This image is made of stone. It is in the standing posture and is four-armed. The upper right hand holds *akṣamālā* (rosary) and lower right is shown in the *varada* pose. The upper left hand holds a beautiful mermaid (*matsyakanyā*). The lower left holds a *pāna-pātra* (drinking vessel). Vimalā is three-eyed, and is wearing *kirīṭa* (crown) and other ornaments. There are two female attendants, naked and fierce-looking, on either side.

The next important Goddess is the four-armed Bhuvaneśvarī, seated on a white lotus in *padmāsana* pose. She holds *aṅkuśa* in the upper-right hand, the lower right being shown in *varada* pose. She holds a *nāgapāśa* in the upper left, the lower one being in *abhaya-mudrā*. She is also three-eyed and has the crescent moon in her crest.

The four-armed Goddess Lakṣmī is seated on a white lotus in the *padmāsana* posture, holding lotuses in her two upper hands, the lower hands being in the *varada* and *abhaya* poses. A few other images of Lakṣmī are shown holding *śaṅkha* and *cakra* in their upper hands. These types of images are found elsewhere.

It is interesting to find that the names of Goddesses Sarvamaṅgalā, Bhuvaneśvarī, Indrāṇī, Kūṭamcaṇḍī, Cāmuṇḍā, Durgā, Vimalā and Lakṣmī, worshipped inside the Jagannātha temple at Purī are found in the lists of *yoginī*s of religious scriptures or texts. The names of Indrāṇī, Durgā, Cāmuṇḍā and Caṇḍī as *yoginī*s[5] are found in the list of *yoginī*s, according to *Kālikā Purāṇa*. The name of Lakṣmī[6] as *yoginī* is found in the list of *yoginī*s, according to *Bṛhad Nandikeśvara Purāṇokto Durgāpūjā Paddhati*.

The name of Bhuvaneśvarī as a *yoginī*[7] is found in the list of *yoginī*s according to *Cauṅsaṭha Yoginī Nāmāvalī*. The name of Sarvamaṅgalā as a *yoginī* is found in the list according to *Durgāpūjā* (a palm-leaf manuscript).[8] Das[9] has laboured to find out the *yoginī*s of different groups, from different scriptures and has included Vimalā as a *yoginī*.

---

5 H.C. Das, *Tāntricism: A Study of the Yoginī Cult*, New Delhi: Sterling Publishers, 1981, p. 34.

6 Ibid., p. 35.

7 Ibid., p. 36.

8 Ibid., p. 38.

9 Ibid., p. 41.

According to tāntric text, *Haṭha-Yoga-Pradīpikā*,[10] a *yoginī* is one who practises *vajrolī*:

> पुंसो विंदुं समाकुंच्य सम्यगभ्यासपाटवात् ।
> यदि नारी रजो रक्षेद्वज्रोल्या सापि योगिनी ॥
>
> *puṁso viduṁ samākudhya samyagabhyāsapāṭvāt* ।
> *yadi nārī rajo rakṣedvajrolyā sāpi yoginī* ॥
>
> — verse 99, chapter 3

If a woman practises *vajrolī* and saves her *rajas* and man's *bindu* by thorough contraction, she is a *yoginī*.

Vajrolī is a Haṭha-yogic-mudrā. It means "thunderbolt attitude" in which the muscles of the male sexual organ and lower urinary tract are contracted, redirecting sexual energy upwards. A practice of *haṭha-yoga* and *tantra*,[11] *sahajolī-mudrā* is a practice of *vajrolī* by a woman, involving contraction of the lower urinary muscles.[12] To sum up it can be said that women practising *yoga* of sexual transformation are *yoginī*s.

A painting of the eighteenth century CE, showing *yoginī*s oracle in the cremation ground, is found exhibited at Bharat Kala Bhavan, Benares. The painting depicts a crowned king praying by touching the feet of a *yoginī*.[13] This proves that real *yoginī*s received obedience and respect from the people in general in ancient days.

The existence of Goddesses inside the boundary of Jagannātha temple at Purī, who are included in the lists of *yoginī*s, proves that *yoga* of sexual transformation existed in Jagannātha cult.

There exists a small Budar Caṇḍī temple, inside the Jagannātha temple compound, near the *navagraha*. As She is a form of Caṇḍī, she may be included as a *yoginī*, inside the temple campus.

A mystic tale of Goddess Budar Caṇḍī may be narrated. The author's wife Rani Rajshree Devi of Khariar is the second daughter of late Thatraj Raj Raj Deb of Purī. From her, the author has come to know that her father as the Thatraj and superintendent for some period, used to roam inside the campus of Jagannātha

---

10 *HYP*, 1993, p. 362.

11 Ibid., p. 564.

12 Ibid., p. 558.

13 Nik Douglas, *Tantra Yoga*, New Delhi: Munshiram Manoharlal, 1971, *passim*.

temple during night and in many nights, he had witnessed a dog coming from somewhere, entering the small temple of Budar Caṇḍī. Because of this, he believed that Budar Caṇḍī takes the form of a dog and guards the premises of the temple of Jagannātha at night. So, it can be said that the *yoginīs* inside the campus of this great temple act as guardian deities. Further, it is known that the image of Budar Caṇḍī is an inhaling or breathing reality.

Further, while discussing about the obscene or erotic sculptures on the Jagannātha temple, Mishra[14] writes:

> There is a story in the *Bhāgavata Purāṇa*[15] according to which Indra was guilty of the sin of *brahma-hatyā*. He divided his sin into four parts and gave it to four units (1) the earth, (2) the water, (3) tree, and (4) women. As regards the part which fell to the share of women, it was granted by Indra that they would always cherish the passion of love, though their monthly sickness would symbolize the part of the *brahma-hatyā* sin shared by them. Under Indra's injunction nobody should take away or disturb the love affairs of women when they are in union with men. This is also supported by *Pāraskaraguhyasūtra Garbhādhāna-prakaraṇa*. Even the *vajra* of Indra will never strike the structure such as a temple, where the *mithunas* have been carved. This Paurāṇic story may explain in a way the presence of these human couples engaged in different sex acts indicative of their mutual love and passion. On the basis of this story, the carving of such scenes on temple walls can be regarded as prophylactic in nature. These *mithunas* assumed so much importance that in the tāntric world they were worshipped. They are called *yoginīs*. The *Tantrarāja Tantra* and *Kaulāvali Tantra*[16] say that offering should be made to the fifty *mithunas*. It is strange that on the *anaṅgatrayodaśī* day the *mithuna* images on the temple of Jagannātha are actually worshipped. The first *mithuna* that is worshipped is *anaṅgāturā* carved on the outer northern wall of the Jagamohana.

The great tradition of the cult of Puruṣottama Jagannātha has absorbed the little tradition of *yoginī* cult into its fold. S.K. Ramachandra Rao[17] observes that there are *yantras* for minor or attendant deities (like Hanumān, Garuḍa, Vīrabharda,

---

14 *TCOJ*, 1971, p. 116.

15 *Bhāgavata Purāṇa*, Chapters VI and VII, pp. 2-40. "Pāraṣkaraguhyasūtra Garbhādhāna Prakaraṇa, Taittirīya Bhāṣya: *Bhabatinam Kāmabodhantā Pātakiṣyat*."

16 *Kaulāvali Tantra*, Ch. XXI, *ślokas* 88-96.

17 S.K. Ramachandra Rao, *Yantras*, Delhi: Sri Satguru Publications, 1988, p. 14.

Gaṇeśa, Sāstā, Bhairava, Khaḍga and Yoginī). Saint-poet Balaram Das[18] in his composition *Bata Avakāsa* mentions that Lord Jagannātha is attended by sixty-four Yoginīs, Kātyāyanīs, Saptamātr̥kās, Vimalā and Virajā.

[18] *Journal of the Bihar and Orissa Research Society*, vol. II, p. 419.

4

Yoginīs and the Cosmic Creative Forces

Positions of *yoginīs* in *śrī-yantra* are found in verses 40 and 42-44 of *Kāmakalā-Vilāsa*, an important text of the Nātha cult, which considers *haṭha-yoga* as the preliminary practice for Tantra, *rāja-yoga, kuṇḍalinī-yoga* and *kriyā-yoga*. Satyananda Paramahamsa[1] states:

> When the *ṛṣis* discovered the science of *haṭha-yoga*, they did not have *yoga* therapy in mind. Although *yoga* has proved to be very effective in the treatment of many impossible and incurable diseases, the therapeutic effect of *yoga* is only a by-product and incidental.
>
> The main objective of *haṭha-yoga* is to create an absolute balance of the interacting activities and processes of the physical body, mind and energy. When this balance is created, the impulses generated give a call of awakening to the central force (*suṣumnā nāḍī*) which is responsible for the evolution of human consciousness. If *haṭha-yoga* is not used for this purpose, its true objective is lost.

The interplay of the inner energy:

> In order to make the subject clear, it was termed as *haṭha*, i.e. *ha* and *ṭha yoga*, a combination of two *bīja mantras*. It has been explained in *haṭha-yoga* that *ṭha* represents *prāṇa*, the vital life force, and *ha* represents mind, the mental energy. So *haṭha-yoga* means the union of the prāṇic and mental forces. When union between the praṇic and mental forces takes place, a great event occurs in man. This is the awakening of higher consciousness.
>
> *Prāṇa śakti*, the life force, and *manas śakti*, the mental force, are the two fundamental creators. Every object in the universe, right from the smallest atoms to the largest stars, is composed of these two *śakti*s or energies. When

[1] Satyananda Paramahamsa, "Swamiji Speaks on Hatha Yoga", *HYP*, 1993, pp. 6-7.

they interact with each other, when the interplay of these two *śakti*s takes place, then creation begins to unfold.

When the two *śakti*s are separated from each other, or they are dissolved back in their source, then the creation is dissolved. That is the great *pralaya*, i.e. the total annihilation of matter. In the field of physics also they speak along the same lines.

All matter in this creation is alive. This is the first point. It is also conscious. This is the second point. Therefore, everything has potential consciousness and everything is alive. In *yoga*, life and consciousness are known as *prakṛti* and *puruṣa*, in *tantra* they are known as Śakti and Śiva. In *haṭha-yoga* they are called *iḍā* and *piṅgalā*; in Taoism, *yin* and *yang*, and in physics, matter and energy. They have their own names in different times, in different philosophies. This physical body as it is seen, is the gross perception. If you look at this body with psychic eyes, or with specialized and sophisticated electronic eyes, perhaps you would understand that it has its own subtle counterpart also.

What is happening internally whenever you start to think? If you have never thought about it, please start thinking from now. What is thought? What happens within us when a thought is emerging and a thought is diminishing and when one is superseded by another, or when thoughts intercept each other? This is called the interplay of *śakti*.

In *Haṭha-Yoga-Pradīpikā*,[2] the following verse is found:

योगिनी वक्रसंमान्यः सृष्टिसंहारकारक ।
न क्षुधा न तृषा निद्रा नैवालस्यं प्रजायते ॥ ५५ ॥

yoginī vakrasaṁmānyaḥ sṛṣṭisaṁhārakāraka ।
na kṣudhā na tṛṣā nidrā naivālasyaṁ prajāyate ॥ ५५ ॥

— verse 55, ch. 2

He is adored by the circle of *yoginī*s and becomes the controller of creation and dissolution, being without hunger, thirst, sleep and laziness.

Swami Muktibodhananda Saraswati explains that according to this *śloka*, the perfectionist of *sītkāri* is adored or worshipped by the *cakra* or circle of *yoginī*s, but what exactly is the *cakra* or *yoginī*? *Cakra* usually refers to a particular circle which is a source of energy. *Yoginī* is a female *yogī*, the embodiment of *śakti*, the cosmic creative force. In *tantra* there is an order of sixty-four *yoginī*s who represent the sixty-four *tantra*s and sixty-four perfections of *yoga*.

[2] Satyananda Paramahamsa, "Swamiji Speaks on Hatha Yoga", *HYP*, 1993, pp. 221-22.

The aspects and evolution of cosmic *śakti* from its source are represented by the *śrī-yantra* or *cakra*. *Sri-yantra* is the formula of creation, manifestation and dissolution of the macro and micro cosmos. It is constituted by a number of interlacing triangles which are known as *yoginīs*. They represent the cosmic *śakti* and manifestation of human existence. *Sri-yantra* also represents each individual.

The *cakra* of *yoginīs* symbolizes every function of the gross subtler bodies, the functions of mind and integration with the soul. Our entire existence is controlled or operated by various forms of *śakti* or a specific *yoginī* or *devī*. Each individual person is a manifestation of the *cakra* of *yoginīs*.

fig. 1: *Sri-yantra*

Thus it is said that through the practice of *sītkāri* the whole body comes under the control of the practitioner. In fact, perfection of any of the *prāṇāyāmas* leads to control of the body mechanisms, stabilization of the mental tendencies and deeper awareness of the mind/body complex.

Sītkāri particularly works on the heat/cold aspect of the body. Control of any two opposite forces in the body/mind leads to control of the other aspects of the physical, mental, emotional and psychic make-up.

> Swatmarama specifically mentions that *sītkāri* eliminates indolence and the need and desire to eat, drink and sleep.

Swatmarama is the author of the *Haṭha-Yoga-Pradīpikā* text and *sītkāri* is a Haṭha-yogic term, whose full term is *sītkāri prāṇāyāma*[3] meaning "hissing breath", which is done by inhaling through the clenched teeth; exerts a cooling effect upon the whole body.

With these backgrounds, it can be claimed that the land of Kāmakalā and Uḍḍiyāna-Pīṭha, which developed the *yoginī* cult, had also helped in the process or evolution of *śrī-yantra*. Therefore, the innermost triangle of *śrī-yantra*, which is *bhairavī-yantra*, is found as an antique stone by Padma Dandasena and worshipped as a household deity in Brusabhanu Naik's and Narsingh Naik's joint family house in Muṇḍapala village, on the left bank of the Udanti River, within Sinapali Block area of Nuāpāḍā district. The full-fledged *śrī-yantra* is found as the inner plan alias plan of *garbha-gṛha* of the Rājarānī temple of Bhubaneswar or this temple has ground plan with *śrī cakra* superimposed.[4]

Here one has to recall the mention of Mahānadī Valley as the land of Kāmakalā in the tāntric text *Kāmakalā-Vilāsa*, composed by Nāṭha Yogī Puṇyānanda Nātha.[5]

Pranab Bandyopadhyay observes:[6]

> In *śrī-yantra*, which is the most important of all tāntric *yantras*, each of the outer triangles is occupied by the *devatās* which represent the sub-divided energy-self of the Goddess.
>
> Some of the lesser *yantras* are obviously segments out of the *śrī-yantra*. This all-embracing great *yantra* is the very image of the process of creation, metaphysically sexual. To a tāntric creation is a continuous process. So the form the desire (*kāma*) assumes is that of his female identity by making the world for him to enjoy as bliss, consciousness and ultimately the being.
>
> The motive force underlying the whole process of Tantra is a transcendental desire with sexual undertone. Desire creates its object, as cosmic desire created the world. When desire is multiplied, it creates objects. It becomes

---

[3] Satyananda Paramahamsa, "Swamiji Speaks on Hatha Yoga", *HYP*, 1993, p. 560.

[4] Bettina Bäumer, Rajendra Prasad Das (eds.), *Śilparatnakośa* (*A Glossary of Orissa Temple Architecture*), Delhi: Motilal Banarsidas, 1994, figs. 53-56.

[5] Sir John Woodroffe (tr. and Commentator), *Kāmakalā-Vilāsa*, Madras: Ganesh and Co., 1971, *passim*.

[6] Pranab Bandyopadhyay, *The Goddess of Tantra*, Calcuta: Punthi Pustak, 1987, pp. 49-50.

> a special inner radiance known only to the tāntric, when withdrawn and focused on the veil of ultimate reality.
>
> Certain diagrams show the cosmos in a side-elevation like a calyx of a flower or a world-tree which a tāntric sees as an image of the Goddess-function, an alternative icon of her joyful play.
>
> In *Tantrarāja Tantra,* the use of the flat cosmic diagram in meditation has been mentioned. It places the great Goddess at the centre.
>
> The tāntric vision comes from the outermost circuit which envelopes all other aspects of the diagram. The gigantic wheel of time set into the complex motion by the creative desire of the Goddess, has its twelve shining spokes summarizing the months, and in it are incorporated the motion of the planetary cycles.
>
> Nothing exists in space without existing in time. Creation is time. The Goddess in Her function as *māyā* (measurer) weaves the substance of events in time and space.

This gigantic wheel of time, set into the complex motion, by the creative desire of the Goddess finds full expression in the twenty-four wheels of the Sun temple of Koṇārka,[7] which is the finest efflorescene of the artistic genius of Orissa state, made in the form of a chariot.

---

[7] Rustam J. Mehta, *Koṇārka — The Sun Temple of Love,* Bombay: D.B. Taraporevala Sons and Co., 1969, pp. 1-46;

Arjun Joshi, *New Light on the Cultural Heritage of Orissa,* Cuttack: Baneeshree, 1979, pp. 157-63.

5

Rare Sculptural Arts

SCULPTURAL arts are not the free imaginations of sculptors. They have been guided by deep yogic masterminds (*sthāpakas*). Two such sculptures are Nandī, the great bull with *yoni* symbols on its body and six-headed Kārttikeya.

Nandī, the Great Bull with *Yoni* Symbols on Its Body

In the Nāsadiya-Sūkta (hymn of creation) of the *Ṛgveda* (10.129), it is stated that *kāma* was the first to be created and it was the seed of the creator's mind from which sprouted the entire cosmic creation. Love is the predominant impulse in the heart of all creatures and therefore its regulation, control and purity are of the highest significance for the integration of one's personality. Śiva as *yogī* must therefore be realized within the heart of each individual who aspires to conquer death, darkness of matter and limitation in all its basic forms, and who wishes to ascend to the higher world of light, divine powers and immortality. It is after the mastery of *kāma* that Śiva attains the perfection of *yoga* and *samādhi,* and becomes entitled to join his female energy Kuṇḍalinī or Śakti or Pārvatī and attain the form of Ardhanārīśvara.[1]

Kāmadeva as the power of sex has been considered to be the greatest disturber of *yoga*. It was therefore essential for Śiva to sublimate the instinct of love before he could be able to effect his *samādhi*. This is the meaning of the burning of Kāma known as *madana-dahana*. This great legend has been related at length in the *Kumārasambhava* of Kālidās. The conception of Śiva in his Kāmāntaka form or conquering the God of Love is the greatest exploit of the Great God and confers on him the highest rank amongst the divine beings.[2]

As Lord Śiva has mastery on *kāma*, it is only he, who is entitled, has right or claim to make the great bull his vehicle and sit on its back.

---

[1] *SMTGG* 1984, pp. 13-14.

[2] Ibid., p. 13.

In the words of Vasudeva S. Agrawala:[3]

Nandī as the great bull is said to be the vehicle of Śiva. Śiva loves to ride on his bull who has become a member of his Lord's family. Śiva became propitiated with Nandī and made him the leader of all his hosts.

What is the symbolism of Nandī the bull? The bull is known as *vṛṣabha* or *vṛṣa*. He is the great sprinkler of the seed. He represents the fecundating energy of Kāma or the God of Love. As we have seen in a preceding chapter Śiva the Lord of *yoga* conquered the God of Love, thus naturally he became the Lord or rider of the bull, Nandīśvara. Kāmadeva is the greatest sprinkler of the seed in all beings. He represents the instinct of sex and procreation by which all creatures fulfil the cycle of life; the creative process is inherent in all beings.

This we may designate as the mastery of the sprinkling of the seed by the bull. *Prāṇa* is that great bull in the individual centre; Sūrya is also the bull who is dispersing his energy through the radiation of his thousand rays; he is the great God as bull (*mahādeva vṛṣabha*). He is fastened in three places, namely the head, the breast and the feet, i.e. he is the master of the *trayī vidyā*, the threefold power of *Ṛg*, *Yajus* and *Sāma* — in which the *Ṛg* is the expanding diameter. *Yajus* is the pulsating centre and *Sāma* is the delimiting circumference; this is mentioned in the *Ṛgveda* as the threefold fastening of the bull (*tridhā baddho vṛṣabhaḥ* — *ṚV*, 4.58.3). The fastening has reference to the bull being brought under a regulated system or order of the triadic pattern symbolized also by Śiva's trident.

This bull is ceaselessly roaring; the roaring is a manifestation of his great energy produced from *ākāśa*, or the most subtle material element. The roaring of the bull is a sign of his robust vitality and of the perfect assimilation and integration of all the five elements on the level of matter. The bull roars when he is impelled by his grandiloquent energy; this roaring is the symbol of the God of Love, Kāmadeva, which is an irrepressible instinct that manifests itself through the mind. The sound of its roar is ceaseless and overrides or drowns all other voices.

That is the *vṛṣa* aspect when the springs of sexual energy flow downwards. But the other aspect is that of the upward flow of sex power when that ascends to the brain and saturates the highest centres of the mind and thus contributes to the *samādhi* of Śiva. The bull is thus both a sprinkler and preserver of the energy that is with Śiva.

---

[3] *SMTGG* 1984, pp. 14-15.

One Nandī bull with three *yoni* marks chiselled on both sides of the body was found in the forest around the vicinity of Nangalbod village of Nuāpāḍā district, Orissa. It is now installed in front of the Hara-Pārvatī temple, situated to the east of Khariar. This proves that *yoga* of sexual transformation was discovered in this area during antediluvian culture. Though technologically the antediluvian culture was not much developed, spiritually, the yogic methods were much refined, pure and advanced, as known from the archaeological findings. Therefore, the finding of a Nandī bull with six *yoni* marks on its body, in this hinterland of Orissa, is not a paradox. It is in reality and authenticity that *yoga* of sexual transformation, from sex to super-consciousness or from sex to salvation was discovered in the central right Mahānadī Valley, which influenced the entire central Mahānadī Valley from Sundargaṛh district in the north to Korapūṭ district in the south.

Six-headed Kārttikeya

The concept of Skanda Kārttikeya is found in Vedic literature — *Rāmāyaṇa, Mahābhārata* and Purāṇas.[4]

The mythological story of Śiva and Prajāpati Dakṣa and establishment of 52 *śakti-pīṭhas* (sites) in India are well mentioned in *Tantracūḍāmaṇi*. The Dakṣa's *yajña* (sacrifice) finds mention in *Vāyu Purāṇa* also. According to Agrawala,[5] the limbs of the body of Satī dropped down severally by which 108 centres of Śakti worship (*śakti-pīṭhas*) were formed which are said to continue up to this day. The moral of this story is the broad-based apotheosis of the motherland conceived in the form of energized centres for tāntric and yogic *sādhanā* or for practising special meditation and spiritual discipline.

The story goes on to say that Śiva[6] after his roaming with the body of Satī had his consternation somewhat overcome and in order to attain peace he began to perform meditation or *samādhi*. He sat down in the forest of *devadāru* trees in the Himalayas and went into *samādhi*. It was an intensive exploration of the powers of his own mind and through unbroken meditation he desired to integrate them once again. His *samādhi* continued for thousands of years and the fate of gods against the *asuras* remained undecided. So they counselled and planned to break

---

[4] Asim Kumar Chatterjee, *Cult of Skanda-Kārttikeya in Ancient India*, Calcutta: Punthi Pustak, 1970, pp. 1-28; Kanchan Sinha, *Kārttikeya in Indian Art and Literature*, Delhi: Sundeep Prakashan, 1979, pp. 1-40.

[5] *SMTGG*, 1984, pp. 10-11.

[6] Ibid., p. 17.

his *samādhi* by the intervention of the God of Love, Kāmadeva. He resorted to the place and created an atmosphere of disturbing the meditation of Śiva. Just then Pārvatī as the female energy filled with the pride of physical beauty and outer charm wanted to wean away Śiva's mind like the magnetic needle doing to the iron. Śiva then thought within himself:

> A *yogī* who has got control over the power of the *cakra*s of the body and the mind, cannot fall a prey to the temptations of the senses and the God of Love, how can physical beauty attract him to the world of sense pleasure?

Thus thinking, he opened his third eye of wisdom in search of some extraneous centre of disturbance. He saw the God of Love, Kāmadeva, aiming his shaft against Śiva in *samādhi*. The great God opened his eye of wisdom and consumed Kāmadeva to ashes, that is, burned his physical body so that all objective existence of Kāma was annihilated. The God of Love became merely an idea that springs in mind and can be conquered by the illumination of the mental powers.

> When the youthful Pārvatī, the embodiment of beauty and charm, witnessed this phenomenon and the irrestible power of Śiva's mind, she became frustrated. She realized that physical beauty was not the way to win Śiva and, therefore, she herself took to the path of *yoga* and *samādhi*, or *tapas*. She continued to live there on the Himalayas performing severe austerities and denying all physical pleasures. She tried to discover the laws of *samādhi* or the highest mental concentration. At last, Śiva became pleased and came to her *āśrama*. She received him with decorum and affection and both became pleased with each other covenanting to marry with the approval of Pārvatī's parents. This was done in accordance with the detailed ceremonies proper to the sacrament of marriage.
>
> In the years following, Śiva and Pārvatī lived in union in their heritage on Kailāsa. To them a son was born named Skanda or Kumāra who became the leader of the divine forces or husband of Devasenā. Being nursed in the six centres of *suṣumnā* which is symbolized as Agni, he is conceived of as the six-headed son of fire whose symbolism has been explained in an earlier chapter. Skanda is conceived of as the fiery God more lustrous and resplendent than even the Sun-God Āditya. He is the very symbol of the prāṇic element within each individual body whose *śakti* like Indra's thunderbolt vindicates against all āsuric forces especially Tārakāsura or the demoniacal darkness of the mind. He is known as *senānī*, the leader of the divine powers of *devas*.

> It may also be noted that his vehicles are both a cock and a peacock. The cock is the symbol of fire or prāṇic energy whose sound is expressed as three accents, namely short, long and circumflex; that is the threefold nature of Agni or Vāk that is inherent in all beings. The sound is the honey-tongued speech which is the sign of life as expressed in matter. Later on the cock was replaced by the peacock. Since the latter is a bird that is inimical to vipers or serpents where the pea-fowl is present the serpents are rendered ineffective. The serpent represents poison, that is the sign of death. The birth of Kumāra or Skanda is the signal that the death-conquering aspect of prāṇic energy has come into full play and will not permit a loophole for the *asura*s to invade the realm of life. On the one hand there are vipers coiled on the body of Śiva; and on the other hand his son Skanda comes to have the peacock as his vehicle and both of them are considered to be reconciled in the family of the great God Śiva, Mahādeva.

The *Viṣṇudharmottara* describes a six-faced figure under the name of Kumāra with clear-cut features as endowed with six-faces.[7] The *Samarāṅganasūtradhāra*[8] describes the images of Kārttikeya elaborately. This work mentions that Kārttikeya is to be represented like the morning sun, clothed in red garments and having a fiery red colour. His form is required to be beautiful, and though youthful, should be tending towards childhood. He is required to have a garland of *muktā-maṇi*. He can have either six heads or only one head. He is to be shown with his *śakti* (spear), the very embodiment of his prowess. The number of his arms, however, varies according to the place. In a town he is to be adorned with twelve arms, in the *kheṭaka* with six arms and in a village with two arms only. In the twelve-armed variety, his five right hands are to carry *śakti* (his most characteristic weapon), arrow, sword, *musuṇṭhī* and *mudgar* (hammer) and the sixth one to be shown spreading; in the five left hands are to be shown bow, flag or victory, bell (*ghaṇṭā*), *kheṭaka* and cock and the sixth one to be displayed in *saṁvardhana* pose.

In *Matsya Purāṇa*,[9] it is mentioned that in a rustic town, his image is required to have twelve arms, in a *karbaṭa* four arms, while in a forest or a village only two

---

[7] *Viṣṇudharmottara Purāṇa*, Bombay: Venkatesvara Press, 1912. Translation of Book III, *Treatise on Indian Painting and Image Making*, by Stella Kramrisch, 2nd edn., Calcutta University Press, 1928, ch. 77, vv. 3-5.

[8] D.N. Shukla, *Hindu Canons of Iconography and Painting*, Gorakhpur, 1958, pp. 296-97.

[9] *Matsya Purāṇa*, tr. Rama Pratapa Tripathi, Delhi: Hindi Sahitya Sammelan, Prayag, Saṁ 2003, also Jamna Das Akhtar (ed.), Delhi, 1972, ch. 260.47.

arms. The twelve-armed Kārttikeya should hold a spear, a noose, a sword, an arrow and a trident in five of the right hands, while the remaining sixth right hand should be left blank, being displayed in the attitude of offering some gift and holding out the idea of "no-fear". He is also required to exhibit arrow, flag, fist, pointed ring finger and *kheṭaka* by the five left hands, the sixth hand being shown carrying a cock.[10]

One of the earliest six-headed and twelve-armed figure of Kārttikeya, chiselled on a lintel is found at Pawāyā in the former Gwalior state, now in Madhya Pradesh.[11]

Asim Kumar Chatterjee[12] deals with the Kārttikeya images of Orissa state:

> Probably the oldest image of Kārttikeya from Orissa was that discovered from Dhudhuā.[13] The image is weather-beaten and primitive. The God sits astride a peacock and not cock as supposed by Vāsu. The right hand holds a spear (*śakti*) but the attribute of the left hand cannot be recognized. The image is in a bad state of preservation and is not graceful.
>
> The temples of the sacred city of Bhubaneswar contain some interesting images of the war-god.[14] One such image is to be found in the temple of Paraśurāmeśvara situated at a distance of less than a furlong from the sacred Kedārakuṇḍa. The God sits on a throne, carved with a peacock, killing a serpent. The image is placed in the central niche of the temple. Another very elegant sculpture is found in the Megheśvara temple (late twelfth century CE). A number of beautiful images of Skanda are found in the Bhubaneswar temple complex. On the western niche of the *vimāna* of the temple can be seen the figure of Kārttikeya, standing on a pedestal of lotus. The part of the pedestal below the lotus, referred to, presents a nice front carved with artistic floral devices. This highly ornamented figure has all the characteristics of the medieval Orissan sculpture. The peacock, with broken head, is represented with all its glory. The side deities hold garlands and are represented with equal skill. Two four-headed images of Kārttikeya can be noticed in the temple of Vṛṣabha. The figures hold *khaḍga* (sacrificial

---

10 *Matsya Purāṇa*, ch. 260.46.

11 *Proceedings of the Indian History Congress*, X Session, pp. 137 ff; Annual Administrative Report of Archaeological Department, Gwalior State, 1924-25, p. 10.

12 Asim Kumar Chatterjee, op. cit., pp. 122-24.

13 N.N. Vasu, *Archaeological Survey of Mayurbhanj*, vol. I, fig. 6.

14 M.M. Ganguli, *Orissa and Her Remains: Ancient and Medieval* (*District Puri*), London: W. Thacker and Co., 1912, *passim*.

scimitar), *kamaṇḍalu* (bowl), *triśūla* and *ḍamaru*. The figures are seated on the peacock. Another image of a twelve-armed, six-headed Kārttikeya can be seen on one of the walls of the temple of Vimalā, situated in the compound of Bhubaneswar temple. The image has following attributes — *dhanuṣa, śara, gadā, śaṅkha, triśūla, pināka, abhaya, varada, padma, pāśa, cakra* and *aṅkuśa*. A number of beautiful images of Kārttikeya are also to be noticed on the walls of the Mārkaṇḍeśvara temple at Purī.

A tenth-century standing Kārttikeya from Purī is preserved in the Asutosh Museum, Calcutta. The image is two-armed, but the hands are broken. It is a highly graceful sculpture with all the fine characteristics of the Orissan art. Another Kārttikeya image from Bhubaneswar is preserved in the Indian Museum, Calcutta.[15] This is a typical specimen of the latest phase of the later medieval Orissan art.

Kanchan Sinha[16] also mentions about six-headed and twelve-armed Kārttikeya in India. They are the following:

1. A highly interesting image of Kārttikeya belonging to the medieval period has been found in the Avantīśvara temple, situated on the right bank of the river Vitastā, about 29 km above Srinagar. It is a six-headed but six-armed image of the God,[17] dated ninth century CE.
2. The Nagpur Museum also possesses an interesting six-headed and twelve-armed image of Kārttikeya, bearing various attributes and wild cock in them. The God, however, does not sit on the back of his mount, the peacock, the figure of which is to be seen by his side.[18] The attributes held by the deity in the hands are generally those which have been mentioned in the *Matsya Purāṇa*. This image is also a product of the medieval period.
3. At Ranoda, in the former Gwalior state, was also found a unique six-headed and twelve-armed image of Kārttikeya. This is entirely unconventional and has nothing to do with any of the known images of the deity.[19]
4. There is a highly artistic twelve-armed image of Kārttikeya in the shrine of Khermai, modern village of Tewar, the ancient Tripurī, the capital of the

[15] *Memoirs of the Archaeological Survey of India*, no. 44, Pl. VIII, fig. 6.

[16] Kanchan Sinha, op. cit., pp. 128-29, 135-36 and 140-42.

[17] Ibid.; *Archaeological Survey of India* (*Annual Report*), 1913-14, p. 53.

[18] Ibid.; *Descriptive List of Exhibits at the Nagpur Museum*, p. 16, Pls. V and 6.

[19] Ibid.; G.H. Khare, *Mūrtti Vijñāna* (Marāṭhī), Poona, 1939, fig. 61.

Haihayas (alias Kaḷacuris).[20] According to R.D. Banerji, the temple was probably built during the reign of Karṇadeva or in the time of anyone of his immediate successors. The deity has been shown standing on the ground and his peacock is to be seen behind him. It is three-headed (other two heads being not shown) figure of God, with all the twelve arms broken. A female attendant, presumably his consort with a garland is shown on his either side. They too have been beautifully represented. There are also four other male attendants, the figures of all of them also being damaged. Stylistically, the image is entirely different from the other images of the God.

5. Kārttikeya also makes his appearance on the great *toraṇa* of Gurgi, now re-erected in front of the Mahārāja's Palace at Rewa.[21] According to Banerji, this *toraṇa* originally formed a part of the great Śiva temple which was constructed by Yuvarāja I. Although the deity has been endowed with six heads, strangely enough, he has been provided only with ten arms, standing under a tree with a fringe of mangoes. The peacock stands to the left of the deity. A number of his hands are broken. However, he holds a *kamaṇḍalu* in one of his hands, and a shield in the other. Two of his right hands hold a bird (cock?) and a lotus stalk.

6. The central niche of the north side of the temple of Baijanāth, near Garur in the Almoṛā district (the ancient Kārttikeyapur), contains an image or Kārttikeya.[22] The God, shown as seated on the peacock, is represented six-faced (Ṣaḍānana), but only with four hands. The image belongs to the late medieval period (early thirteenth century CE).

7. Kārttikeya has very rarely been represented as dancing. In this connection, mention may be made of an early medieval stone relief, assignable to the eighth-ninth centuries CE, now studded into a well at Choṭī-Khaṭāu in the Nagaur district of Rajasthan. It represents a six-headed and six-armed Kārttikeya dancing and feeding the peacock.

8. The Śiva temple at at Paṭṭīśvaram has a beautifully carved six-faced and twelve-armed figure of Subrahmaṇya.[23] Depicted as Ṣaṇmukha, the front

[20] Kanchan Sinha, op. cit., *Memoirs of the Archaeological Survey of India*, 23, p. 92, Pl. XXX.b.

[21] Ibid., p. 72.

[22] Ibid.; *Archaeological Survey of India* (*Annual Report*), *1905-06*, p. 21, fig. 4.

[23] Ibid.; T.A.G. Rao, *Elements of Hindu Iconography*, vol. II, Madras, 1916, Pls. CXXCVI and 3.

right and left hands of the God are held in the *abhaya* and the *varada* poses, respectively, while remaining ones carry *śakti, ṭaṇka, cakra, khaḍga* and *mūsala* (or *pāśa*?), and *vajra, dhanuṣa, bāṇa, kheṭaka* and *śaṅkha*. Behind Subrahmaṇya is his vehicle, the peacock, facing the left.

9. There is an almost similar image of Ṣaṇmukha Subrahmaṇya from Nellur in bronze.[24] In addition to the attributes held in the twelve arms, it however, also shows a *śakṭyāyudha* made separately and kept leaning on the back arms of the God. The lotus seat upon which the image of the God stands is hexagonal, made specially so in other to agree with the six faces of the deity from whom it serves as a pedestal.

10. A stone image of Ṣaṇmukha Subrahmaṇya is preserved in the Worcester Art Museum.[25] Like the previous images representing the Ṣaṇmukha aspect of Subrahmaṇya, this image has also twelve arms. This is a typically south Indian image. The most remarkable feature of the image is the representation of the three back heads on the reverse side of the relief. The plumage of the peacock has very softly been graded, offering finely graded features of the image.

11. A granite stone image of Subrahmaṇya was discovered from Rajahmundry, which was the capital of the eastern Cāḷukyas.[26] It also represents the Ṣaṇmukha aspect of Subrahmaṇya and fortunately all its twelve arms are intact with the attributes *abhaya, triśūla, gadā, kukkuṭa, lāṅgali, vajra, dhanuṣa*, battle-axe, *pāśa, padma, ghaṇṭā* and *varada*. The deity is crowned and his face is lit up with a benign smile. An inscription of the Śaka year 994 (i.e. CE 1072) was also discovered from the same site. As such the image may reasonably be assigned to the second half of the eleventh century CE.

12. There is a highly attractive image of the six-faced and twelve-armed image of Subrahmaṇya in the interior of the temple at Perur. Ṣaṇmukha Subrahmaṇya has been shown seated in the *ardhaparyaṅka* attitude on the back of his mount, the peacock Paravāṇi facing the right[27].

---

[24] Kanchan Sinha, op. cit., pp. 128-29, 135-36 and 140-42, p. 447, Pl. CXXVIII.

[25] Ibid.; *Rūpam*, no. 1, 1926, p. 36.

[26] Ibid.; *Proceeding and Transactions of the 7th All India Oriental Conference*, Baroda, 1938, pp. 773-74.

[27] Ibid.; Veronica Jons, *Indian Mythology*, London, 1968, fig. on p. 85.

13. At Halebiḍ as well, Ṣaṇmukha Subrahmaṇya has been shown seated on the back of his mount, the peacock, in *ardhaparyaṅka* attitude. The bird is, however, facing the left.[28]

With this much information on six-headed Kārttikeya, across India, let us deal the findings of six-headed Kārttikeya images in western Orissa specifically. They are dealt district-wise.

NUĀPĀḌĀ DISTRICT

1. One Śiva temple exists on the embankment of the Tribandha Tank of Khariar town. This temple has triple *āmalaka*s and snakehood-like projections on its body, like the Kaḷacuri temples of Chhattisgarh region.[29] Therefore, this temple has been identified as a temple of Kaḷacuri style, dating within the twelfth-thirteenth centuries CE. One six-headed and twelve-armed Kārttikeya is found on the pillared *maṇḍapa* of this temple.

2. Raja Brajaraj Singh Deo was the fourteenth Chauhan Raja of Khariar. His ruling period was within CE 1889–1907. He had built a Śiva temple at Dharamsāgar. His father Raja Padman Singh had excavated a huge tank at Tannote village, named after him as "Padman Sāgar", covering 12 acres and one huge tank named "Dharam Sāgar", covering 15 acres 30 decimal.[30] After ascending the throne of Khariar on 10 June 1889, Raja Brajaraj Singh Deo had taken up many development works and one of them was the construction of a Śiva temple at Dharamsāgar. One of the *pārśva-devatā*s of the temple is a six-headed Kārttikeya.

KĀLĀHĀṆḌĪ DISTRICT

1. In the Nīlakaṇṭheśvara temple at Dadpur, one six-headed Kārttikeya image is found. About this six-headed Kārttikeya image, Baba Mishra and Pradeep Mohanty[31] are of the opinion:

---

[28] Kanchan Sinha, op. cit., pp. 128-29, 135-36 and 140-42, R.S. Gupte, *Iconography of the Hindus, Buddhists and Jains*, Bombay, 1972, fig. 81.

[29] S.N. Kesharwani, "The Sītā Mātā Temple at Deorbijā", *Prachya Pratibha*, vol. V, no. 2, July 1977, Delhi: Agam Kala Prakashan, pp. 39-41, Pl. 2.

[30] J.P. Singh Deo, "Socio-Culture History of Orissa: A Case Study of Khariar Estate", *Glimpses of Orissa*, Calcutta: Punthi Pustak, 1986, p. 65.

[31] Baba Mishra and Pradeep Mohanty, "Archaeological Heritage of Dadpur Region, District Kalahandi, Orissa", *Journal of Bengal Art*, vol. 4, 1999, pp. 352-53.

Six-headed Kārttikeya of Dadpur seems to be another *pārśva-devatā* of the former shrine. Kārttikeya image according to *Śilpa-Prakāśa* should be placed on the back wall of the temple (Vidya Dehejia, *Early Stone Temples of Orissa*, 1979, p. 68). *Viṣṇudharmottara*, while dealing with the image-making process shows that Kumāra should be rendered with six faces and adorned by the feather of a peacock, having a peacock for his *vāhana*. He should wear a red cloth, while his right hand should hold cock and ball, the *vaijayantī* flag and spear should be in left hand. (Kramrisch, ed. 1993: 93)

Kārttikeya image of Dadpur, however measures 24 x 17 cm and is carved out of a soft red stone. The God has six heads and four hands and grips the beak of his mount peacock in lower right hand. While weapon in upper left hand is illegible, the lower left hand is shown in *varada-mudrā*. His mount peacock is shown in a profile of standing posture. The architect has modelled this sculpture in its youthful vigour. The said Kārttikeya icon has no parrallel in Orissan art. Multiheaded Kārttikeya iconography traversed from central India to Orissa. (Donaldson, 1987: 1061)

2. One six-headed Kārttikeya was found at Junagarh. It is reported[32] that the standing six-headed image of Kārttikeya was brought from the hill fort of Junagarh by the superintendent of Orissa State Museum, C.B. Patel. This image is of the time of Kaḷacuri. The peacock as an essential element in the iconography of Kārttikeya prominently appears in the back of the image. It is a four-handed image made of red sandstone. It measures 19 × 13 × 5". The upper right hand holds trident and the palm of the left lower hand is placed on the beak of the peacock. The lower left hand holds an indistinct object. The upper right hand is partially damaged. The figure is ornamented with heavy anklets in the half damaged foot. A big garland (*rudrākṣamālā*) encirled round the neck of the deity, which touches the belly of the image.

SONEPUR DISTRICT

1. One six-headed and two-handed Kārttikeya is found as *pārśva-devatā*, in a niche of a side Śiva temple, within the premises of the Sureśvarī temple at Sonepur.
2. A six-headed and two-handed Kārttikeya is seen as *pārśva-devatā*, in a niche of a side Śiva temple, within the premises of the Rāmeśvara temple at Sonepur.

These two six-headed Kārttikeyas found in Sonepur are made of red stones.

Knowledge is imitative, derivative, repetitive, educative and intuitive in nature.

[32] C.B. Patel, "Rare New Collections of Orissa State Museum", *OHRJ*, vol. XLVI, no. 3, p. 93.

Intuitive knowledge can be acquired through *yoga*. There are ten kinds of *yoga* — *jñāna-yoga, rāja-yoga, bhakti-yoga, karma-yoga, haṭha-yoga, kuṇḍalinī-yoga, tantra-yoga, japa-yoga, laya-yoga* and *yoga* of sexual transformation.[33]

About transforming the primal energy, Swami Satyananda Saraswati[34] states:

> When no sexual desires of any kind manifest in an aspirant anymore, and when there is no more personal attraction, that means *kuṇḍalinī* has passed beyond *svādhiṣṭhāna cakra*. However, when dealing with the subject of sex, your understanding must be very thorough. Although you may not be having any sexual awareness at the moment, that doesn't mean your desires have been exterminated. They might be in a suppressed state. There is an automatic process of suppression in the human constitution, and that is inherent in our own mental being.
>
> Hindu *ṛṣis* have stated that sexual awareness and desires can manifest at any stage of evolution. They are very acute and clearly expressed when one is in *svādhiṣṭhāna* and having continual fantasies, but sexual awareness never really dies because it is fuelled by the primal energy which is present all throughout. Sex is only an expression of that, and therefore it can manifest at any stage, and one should never think that he has transcended it. It is even present when one is in the highest state of consciousness. The only difference is that in *svādhiṣṭhāna* it is in a very disturbed state, whereas in the higher centres of evolution it is in a seed form. After all, what is *bhakti* or devotion; what is union? They are the sublimated pure form of sexual energy.
>
> Energy at different levels is known by different names. At the highest level it is called spiritual experience. On the emotional level it is known as love. On the physical level it is known as sex, and at the lowest level it is known as *avidyā* or ignorance. So therefore, when you talk about sex, you must understand that it is only a particular formation of energy. Just as curd, butter and cheese are different formations of the one thing — milk, energy has different manifestations. Matter is the grossest manifestation of energy; in the ultimate state, matter is energy. Therefore, energy and matter are intraconvertible. A thought is an object and an object is a thought. This body is consciousness and consciousness has become this body. In the same way that you understand this, you have to reanalyse and redefine sexual awareness.

---

33 J.P. Singh Deo, *Tāntric Art of Orissa*, Delhi: Kalpaz Publications, 2001, p. 29.

34 Swami Satyananda Saraswati, *Kundalini Tantra*, Munger: Bihar School of Yoga, 2nd edn., 1992, pp. 161-62.

> The *ṛṣi*s say that the same energy which flows through passion, when channellized, manifests as devotion. Channellize this same energy again and it manifests as spiritual experience. That is why spiritual aspirants love God in various manifestations. Some picture him as a father, a mother, a child, a friend, husband or lover. In this way, they can sublimate the form of their emotional energy and even transform the primal energy into a divine experience.

About the six heads of Kārttikeya, Agrawala[35] gives an authentic yogic explanation:

> According to the yogic texts, Śiva is the deity of the mind and has his seat in the higher brain. From there he controls all the nerves centres and the entire mechanical, vital and psychical activities and functionings within the body. As the great God he has to be present everywhere and direct the subtle vibrations of the entire constitutional system. His son is only a transformation of his nature and power and in the form of Skanda who controls the activity of the six *cakra*s and who is conceived of as the leader of the divine forces or activities released by the power of the *cakra*s, nerve centres in the spinal cord. Five such centres exist in the spinal column, one above the other, and the sixth is the brain itself. *Yoga* teachers relate them to the five elements of matter as follows:
>
> 1. *Mūlādhāra cakra*: The coccygeal region named after coccyx, the lowest most sector of the spinal column in which the four vertebrae are joined together. It is related to earth, the grossest element. This centre controls the elimination of faecal matter. Here resides the power known to the *yoginī*s as *kuṇḍalinī* or the coiled serpent-mother which releases all physical energy when it is awakened by the conscious effort of the *yogin*.
>
> 2. *Svādhiṣṭhāna cakra*: The sacral region. This region consists of five vertebrae which are joined together as the bone called sacrum. These are much better developed as individual entities. The functions relating to the organs of generation are controlled by the nervous ganglia of this *cakra*. It is said to correspond to the element of water which takes the form of *retas* or the fecundating seed in the human body which is the most subtle and condensed form of *soma* (*īśvaraḥ sarvabhūtānām hṛddeśerjuna tiṣṭhati* — *Gītā* 18.61). In mythical language these are various gods and goddesses that have taken their stations in the human body and continue to perform their functions or do their duties while the full session of life lasts.

[35] *SMTGG*, 1984, pp. 5-7.

3. *Maṇipūra cakra*: This is the lumbar region. It consists of five vertebrae and its centre is in the navel which controls the digestive system. The element of fire presides over this *cakra*. It should be noted that there is no flame or burning fuel in the nerves that are here but the fiery energy takes the form of so many gastric juices and acidic secretions which digest the food and process it for extracting life-building saps and secretions. It is in fact the foundation of the entire life-force and therefore, Skanda is conceived as the son of Fire. Although the seed which gave him birth was thrown into waters or the mother-principle, it is an interconnected sort of thing by which the life-principle within the body is produced and maintained at its highest efficiency and in an inscrutable way.

4. *Anāhata cakra*: This is the dorsal region. It is a long sector of twelve vertebrae having its location in the place near the heart with air as its element. This is responsible for the circulation of the blood pumped by the contraction and expansion (diastole and systola). It is the rushing of the air through the arteries and veins that makes the blood go forward from the heart and come back to it and oxygenating the life stream or blood to burn its impurities. The Vedic thinkers speak of *gad vāyu* as the manifest form of *Brahman* or concretize the divine aspect as *prāṇa* entering the lungs and performing the miracle of keeping life within the body.

5. *Viśuddhi cakra*: This is the cervical region. It is made up of seven vertebrae and its centre is the throat. Its element is *ākāśa* or space which produces sound.

These are the five elements associated with the five nerve centres in the spinal column and the spinal canal (*suṣumnā*).

6. *Ājñā cakra*: This is the name of the higher brain or mind which is the place of intelligence and consciousness. It corresponds to the so-called third eye of the *yoginīs* and also the thousand-petalled lotus which is the seat of Śiva and his consort Pārvatī or his female energy. The spinal canal enters the brain in a bend and through a large hole known as *magnum foramen*; therefore the spinal cord itself is known as the curved one (*kuṭila*) and the big hole as the curved door (*krauñca dvāra*). When Śiva and Pārvatī are together in the highest centre of the mind their union produces the miraculous baby known as Kumāra or Skanda. The five centres in the spinal column related to the five elements of gross matter and the sixth one in the brain representing the psychical energy are conceived of as the six mothers and also as the six faces of the young hero named Skanda. It is, in fact, the yogic terminology for the new youthful energy of *prāṇa* over which the *yogin* has perfect control. He

becomes the leader of the divine army or all the divine powers that function in the body. Psychologically he is the hero of all the conscious and subconscious powers and becomes the conqueror of the hosts of *asura*s whose leader is Tārakāsura. The meaning of Tāraka is transparent; Tāraka means a star; that star is the moon which is the symbol of the mind. It is stated in the *R̥gveda* that the moon represents the mind of the creator (*candramā manaso jātaḥ*, 10.90.13).

Sometimes the number of *cakra*s is taken to be eight by reckoning three *chakra*s in the brain, namely lower, middle and higher brain, or cerebellum, medulla oblongata and cerebrum respectively. In the *Atharvaveda*, the body is said to have eight *cakra*s (*aṣṭacakrā navadvāra devānām pūrayodhyā*, i.e. the body is the city of gods named Ayodhyā having eight *cakra*s and nine doors). It seems that in the ancient-most yogic doctrine the number of *cakras* was counted as eight and the three parts of the brain were distinguished one from the other in a clear manner. However, it was permissible to look upon all the centres of the mind as a unit and then count them as one making a total of six *cakra*s which were conceived as the six mothers of Skanda–Kārttikeya who was, therefore, named as the son of six mothers. These were symbolized as the constellation Pleiades which consists of six twinkling stars. The babe himself was thought to have six heads or six faces with which he sucked the milk of his six mothers. The plain meaning is that the new fiery energy which is generated by the union of Śiva and Pārvatī or Śiva and Śakti, in a new sublimated form, is all-conquering which brings under its control all the psychical and vital functions of the body. The one pre-eminent quality or characteristic feature of Skanda is his leadership over the hosts of all Gods who combine to prepare for him a grand chariot in which he moves; and he carries his irresistible spear (*śakti*) whence he is known as Śaktidhara which gives him complete mastery over all the *asura*s. He is, therefore, spoken of as Viraka, the conquering hero who is the Lord of all the ugly deformed and grotesque hosts known as *gaṇa*s. There are two kinds of prāṇic powers: One set is manifested in sacrifice (*yajña*) leading the life of order and harmony; the other comprises of all kinds of aberrations and out of the plumb-line or the vertical axis of the life-force. The latter are the *asura*s, the genii of darkness and evil. These are the gnomes, the ghouls and the goblins of all mythologies. They are also known as the *bhūta*s.

The victorious hero is Skanda who is but another form of Śiva for all practical purposes in the mythology of Śiva. He is the pre-eminent *deva*, the son of Fire and more brilliant than Āditya or Sūrya. Skanda is the resplendent energy of Śiva who has been nursed from one *cakra* to another in a rising order until in the sixth *cakra* his full splendour becomes manifest. It is said that a *yogin* who has attained to *samādhi* in the sixth *cakra* of the mind is never assailed by the darkness of the five elements of matter. In him the *deva*s have eternal victory over the *bhūtas*. The highest centre of the mind is the region of ethereal light in which the vibrations of matter are eliminated.

The mind is said to represent the two aspects of light and darkness. It waxes and wanes in the two halves of the month, but, in fact, is receiving constantly the reflection of the light of the sun which is always there. The mind region always under the influence of light is the higher mind or intelligence. It is the divine mind called *vijñāna*, but the other aspect of mind is that which turns away from the reflection of the Sun or higher intelligence and falls a prey to darkness; this is the lower mind which is represented as an *asura* named Vṛtra in the Vedas and Tāraka in the Purāṇas. Although the body has its normal and autonomous functions dependent on *prāṇa*, the real power belongs to the mind which controls all the conscious, subconscious and unconscious realms of personality. In *yoga*, the mind is everything which is withdrawn from all external sensuous affections and becoming introvert is made the instrument of meditation in order to realize the universal intimations. It then becomes merged in the universal centre known as *hṛd* in Indian definitions of *yoga*. The *hṛd* is the centre or point of the transcendent divine reality.

While speaking of Śiva as *deva* one has to take into account the Indian conception of Śiva Mahādeva; one has to take into account the great myth of Skanda known as Kumāra in the Brāhmaṇas and Purāṇas or the miraculous baby (*citra śiśu*) of the *Ṛgveda*. Just as Śiva rides in his mountain chariot for a victory over the *asura*s, so does Kumāra; the one holds the trident, the other the spear. The implication of the fiery energy of both is a complete triumph over the *asura*s or powers of darkness, untruth and death.

The quoted discussion shows the six heads of Kārttikeya to represent the main six *cakra*s of *kuṇḍalinī śakti*. According to Swami Satyananda Saraswati,[36] *kuṇḍalinī* does not belong to the physical body, though it has to be searched for there, nor is

---

36 Buddhananda Chela, *Moola Bandha the Master Key*, Munger: Bihar School of Yoga, 2nd edn., 1984, *passim*.

the mental body or even in the astral body. It is in the unconscious causal body, in that particular state of awareness where the concept of time, space and object is completely lost. The seat of the unconscious in man is in the perineum, known in yogic terminology as *mūlādhāra*. It is a gland, a muscle, it is a body in which all the unconscious powers and initiatives of man are hidden.

With this background, it is worth to know about the conditions and spiritual consciousness, when *kuṇḍalinī* rises, from the pen of Sudhir Ranjan Sengupta,[37] who is indebted to Swami Vairabananda Jyotibhusan Deb, popularly known as Mahatma Seeta Nath, who left his mortal coils in 1925, and to Shreemat Purnananda Paramahamsa, who was born in 1834 and after fulfilment of his divine mission in life, he left his mundane body on 30 April 1928 by entering into *nirvikalpa samādhi*, seated in the posture of *padmāsana*.

> *Samādhi* or self-absorption *Samādhi* starts with the absorption of self in the duality of structure in consciousness and ends in the absorption of self in identification with secondless unique self of the Supreme Self. Self-absorption with duality of structure in consciousness is called *savikalpa samādhi*. Self-absorption without any sense of duality is called *nirvikalpa samādhi*. *Savikalpa samādhi* is of four types and *nirvikalpa samādhi* is of two types, one having three sub-divisions.
>
> These are briefly described below:
>
> SAVIKALPA SAMĀDHI
>
> 1. *Savitarka samādhi*: Self-absorption in the duality of structure in consciousness with latent sense of controversy in the consciousness is called *savitarka samādhi*.
> 2. *Savicāra samādhi*: Self-absorption in the duality of structure in consciousness with a latent sense of discretion in the consciousness is called *savicāra samādhi*.
> 3. *Sānanda samādhi*: Self-absorption in the duality of structure in consciousness with an all-absorbing bliss is called *sānanda samādhi*.
> 4. *Sasmita samādhi*: Self-absorption in the duality of structure on consciousness with a latent sense of self-existence is called *sasmita samādhi*.
>
> NIRVIKALPA SAMĀDHI
>
> 1. *Bhāva pratyaya videha samādhi*: Consists in self-absorption without the least trace of duality in consciousness with complete self-identification with nature of God, without

---

[37] Sudhir Ranjan Sengupta, *Mother Cult*, Calcutta: Firma K.L.M., 1977, pp. 106-07.

the light of consciousness. *Bhāva pratyaya videha samādhi* has three sub-divisions, viz. *prakṛti pratyaya, aham pratyaya* and *mahat pratyaya*, i.e. self-consciousness lost in nature, self-consciousness lost in egotism and self-consciousness lost in *bodhisattva*.

2. *Pūrṇa pratyaya samādhi*: Self-absorption in the secondless unique conscious Absolute Self of the Supreme Self without the least trace of duality is called *pūrṇa pratyaya samādhi*. The *pūrṇa pratyaya nirvikalpa samādhi* is possible when the five waves of mind cease to function and the *sādhaka* transcends the basic evolution. *Pūrṇa samādhi* attained as a result of the realization of the identity of self with the absolute self of God, without the least trace of duality in the self-revealed consciousness, liberates an individual soul from the ills of the world and world series, as he knows no other existence except the Supreme Being. The sages say that of these eight varieties of *samādhi, pūrṇa pratyaya samādhi* alone can liberate an individual soul.

It is worth quoting *Īśāvāsya Upaniṣad* and *Viśvasāra Tantra* thus:

Īśāvāsya Upaniṣad[38] says:

That is full, this full.
From full, the full is taken,
the full has come.
If you take out the full from the full,
the full alone remains.

Viśvasāra Tantra[39] says:

What is here is elsewhere;
What is not here is nowhere.

Two more six-headed (Ṣaṇmukha) Kārttikeya found in Orissa may be mentioned. They are: (i) the six-faced (Ṣaṇmukha) Kārttikeya found in the Vimalā temple, at Purī and (ii) the six-headed Kārttikeya specimen in the Guṭeśvara temple of Algum.

---

[38] Swami Satyananda Saraswati, *A Systematic Course in the Ancient Tāntric Techniques of Yoga and Kriyā*, Munger: Bihar School of Yoga, 2nd edn., 1989, p. 330.

[39] Ibid., p. 337.

6

Bhairava Cult and Gāṇapatya Tantra in Orissa

THE evolution of the Bhairava cult and Gāṇapatya Tantra in Orissa are of interest and their narrations have been done in two parts.

Bhairava Cult

From the *Bhagavad-Gītā*[1] it is known that:

> प्रकृतिं पुरुषं चैव विद्धयनादी उभावपि।
> विकारांश्च गुणांश्चैव विद्धि प्रकृतिसम्भवान् ॥
>
> *prakṛtiṁ puruṣaṁ caiva viddhyanādī ubhāvapi* ।
> *vikārāṁśca guṇāṁścaiva viddhi prakṛtisambhavān* ॥ 13.19 ॥
>
> Know that both *puruṣa* and *prakṛti* are beginningless; and know also that all modifications and qualities (*guṇas*) are born of *prakṛti*.

This is the conception of Śiva-Śakti.

It is usually regarded that the earliest Śiva Pāśupati antiquity is found in the seals of Moheṅjo-Dāṛo, dating 2000–3000 BCE. According to Vasudeva Sharan Agrawala,[2] it is seated Pāśupati in *padmāsana* or Śiva as the lord of animals. This is the ancient-most representation of Śiva as an anthropomorphic image with a trident-shaped headgear. Probably the figure shows Śiva as Tryambaka with three faces, one frontal and two lateral. Another noteworthy feature is Śiva as Ūrdhvaretas, i.e. the *membrum virile* in an erect form which is the characteristic mark of numerous images of Śiva in the Pāśupata sect of the great teacher Lakulīśa. Between the legs of Śiva is seated the figure of an antelope which was also associated

---

[1] Sri Sri Paramahansa Yogananda, *God Talks with Arjuna: the Bhagvad-Gita*, vol. II, Kolkata: Yogoda Satsanga Society of India, 2nd impression, 2002, p. 889.

[2] Vasudeva S. Agarwala, *SMTGG*, 1984, p. 60 and Pl. I.

with the Mṛgavyādha or Śiva as great hunter. The God is wearing a triangular necklace with five strings on the chest and his arms are covered with profuse bangles (*khādayaḥ*) from shoulder to wrist showing him to be the father of the Maruts. The God is surrounded by four animals — rhinoceros and bison on proper right, and elephant and tiger on proper left. Above the head is an epigraph in the pictographic script of the Indus Valley. The animals partake of the conception of *catuṣpada-paṅkti*, i.e. a row of quadrupeds treated as a sacred symbol on many ancient monuments. These are all wild beasts showing the element of strength of the primeval forest. These animals are also represented moving in a file on a prismatic seal of the Indus Valley (Archaeological Survey of India, *Annual Report, 1924-25*, Pl. xxiii) and also on a clay seal from Tell Asmar (*Annual Bib. of Indian Archaeology for 1932*, vol. VII, Pl. Ib).

> The date of this Pāśupati sealing is *c.* 2000 BCE a fact rooted in the archaeology of the Indus Civilization where the people were worshippers of Pāśupati (Śiva) whose legacy was transmitted to the historical period of Śaivism. Pāśupati Śiva is mentioned several times in the *Yajurveda*, cf. the hundredfold invocation (*Śatarudriya*).
>
> Because of the cross-legged seat, Ūrdhvaretas, three-horned headdress, the antelope below the seat and the four big animals, the identification of the God as Pāśupati Rudra is beyond all doubts.

About this finding in the Indus Valley Civilization, A.D. Pusalker[3] states:

> Among the male gods the most remarkable is a three-faced deity wearing a horned headdress, seated cross-legged on a throne, with penis erectus, and surrounded by elephant, tiger, buffalo and rhinoceros, with deer appearing under the seat. It wears a number of bangles and has a pectoral round the neck, and an inscription of seven letters appears at the top. This representation has at least three concepts which are usually associated with Śiva, viz. that he is (i) Trimukha (three-faced), (ii) Pāśupati (lord of animals), and (iii) Yogīśvara or Mahāyogī. The first two aspects in a *padmāsana* posture with eyes turned towards the tip of the nose which evidences the Yogīśvara aspect of the deity. It has been suggested by some scholars that this Śiva cult was borrowed by the Indo-Aryans from the Indus culture but as there is a reference to Śiva in the *Ṛgveda* itself,[4] Śiva may not be a later intruder in the Hindu pantheon.

---

3 A.D. Pusalker, "The Indus Valley Civilization", *THACOTIP*, vol. I, *The Vedic Age*, 1965, pp. 190-91.

4 Ibid.; *Ṛgveda*, II.1.6; 33-39; X.92.9; Mookerji, *Proceedings of the All-India Oriental Conference*, VIII, p. 452.

> Two more seals of Śiva have been found in the course of further excavations. The deity is always nude save for a cincture round the waist, and has a horned headdress. In one seal the deity is three-faced and seated on a low dais, while the second has one face in profile; both have a sprig of flowers or leaves rising from the head between the horns. This sprig suggests that the deity so ornamented is a vegetation or fertility god — another link with Śiva, who personifies the reproductive powers of nature. A horned archer dressed in a costume of leaves displays the divine hunter aspect of Śiva.
>
> It thus appears that Śiva was one of the principal deities of the people along with the Mother Goddess. His worship was, however, not merely iconic, but also phallic, as would appear from the presence of a large number of conical and cylindrical stones. These conical and cylindrical stones probably symbolize fertility and are connected with the cult of Śiva as *liṅgas*. Many scholars find a contemptuous reference in the *R̥gveda* to phallus worship and regard it as a veiled allusion to the religious customs of the pre-Aryan people of the Indus valley, but it has been suggested by others that the passage in question simply alludes to sensuous or lustful persons.[5]

The seal findings of Śiva alias Pāśupati in the Indus Valley Civilization are not the earliest such findings in India. The latest findings of the author[6] proves that in penisular India the earliest trace of *yoga* is found in the pre-historic rock-shelter painting at Guḍahāṇḍī. This painting of human-like figure has a head which symbolizes a lotus. In *kuṇḍalinī-yoga*, the highest *cakra* of human being is described as a thousand-petalled lotus, i.e. *sahasrāra* (*fig.* 2). So, it can be claimed that the *sahasrāra cakra* is a gift of the Mahānadī River Valley. It seems that *kuṇḍalinī śakti* was first experienced by the early upland dwellers because among the pre-historic arts of Guḍahāṇḍī, line painting of Pāśupati is found with a head, symbolized by a flower, which seems to mean the *sahasrāra cakra*. It is believed to belong to about fifteenth millennium BCE.[7] Therefore, the earliest trace of Pāśupati Śiva is found in the rock art of Guḍahāṇḍī.

The author discovered on 21 December 1970 the rock art of Yogīmaṭh Ḍoṅger (*fig.* 3). It has three triple parallel lines and indicates creation. It is assigned to

---

[5] A.D. Pusalker, "The Indus Valley Civilization", *THACOTIP*, vol. I, *The Vedic Age*, 1965, pp. 190-91; A.D. Pusalker, *Prācyavāṇī*, I, pp. 29-31.

[6] *THOMV*, 2004, pp. 22 and 64.

[7] D.C. Kuanr (state ed.), *Orissa District Gazetteers, Kalahandi,* N. Senapati (ed.), Cuttack, 1980, p. 36.

fig. 2: Pre-historic rock art at Guḍahāṇḍī, Kālāhāṇḍī district, Orissa, fifteenth millennium BCE

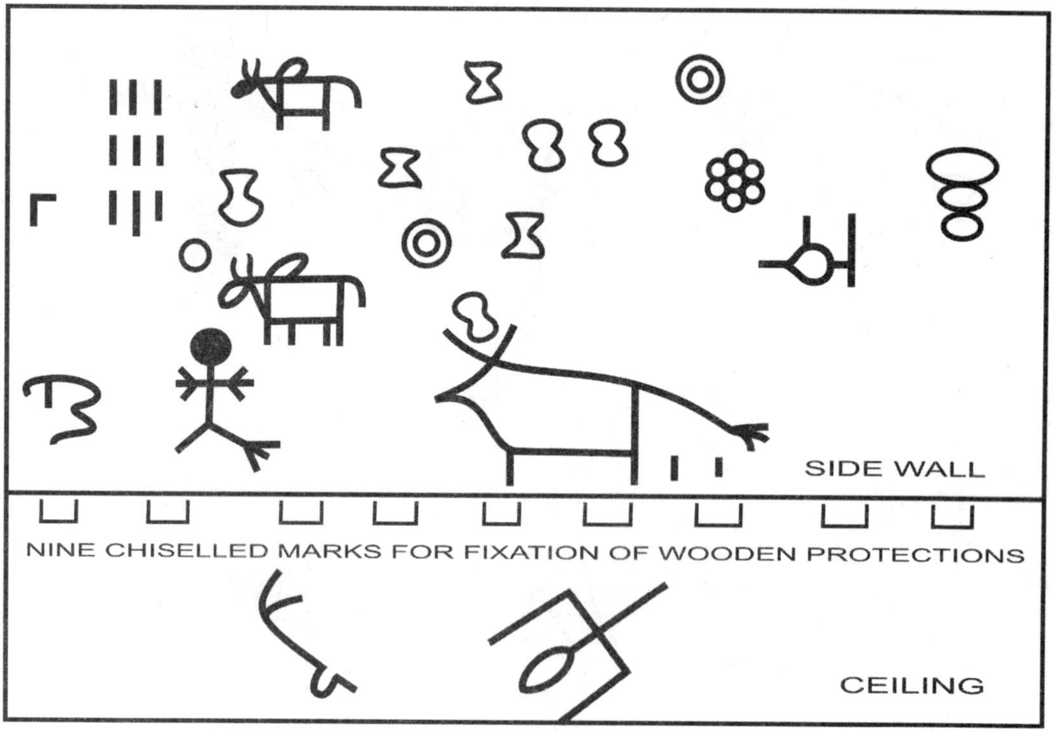

fig. 3: Pre-historic rock art at Yogīmaṭha Ḍoṅger, Nuapāḍā district, Orissa, tenth millennium BCE

about tenth millennium BCE.[8] These prove that the early yogic conception of India was first developed in the central right Mahānadī River Valley and it gradually shifted to the Indus–Sarasvatī Valley.

These findings strengthen the view of David Frawley:[9]

> when he states that there were two main Vedic cultures in ancient India. The first was a northern kingdom centred on the Sarasvatī-Dṛṣadvatī River region dominated by the Purus and the Ikṣvākus that produced the existent Veda texts that we have. The second was a southern culture along the coast of the Arabian Sea and into the Vindhya mountains, dominated by the Turvaṣas and Yadus and extending into groups yet further south. These northern and southern groups vied for supremacy and influenced each other in various ways as the Vedas and Purāṇas indicate. The northern or Bhārata culture ultimately prevailed, making India the land of Bhārata or Bhāratavarṣa and its main ancient literary record the Vedas, though militarily the Yadus remained strong throughout history. The southern culture was the older of the two, with the Vedic people coming originally from the south, not the north-west. This was the basis of the maritime symbolism at the core of Vedic thought, which reflects an ancient heritage.

In addition, there was a third or north-west Vedic culture in Punjab and Afghanistan, that of the Anus and Druhyus, which was at first part of the northern kingdom but gradually developed its own identity. It was partly assimilated by the Bharatas that became the dominant northern people. Another portion of it extended north and west outside of the Indian subcontinent. Its influence was secondary to that of the northern and southern kingdoms and much of it passed out of the Indic sphere of culture. However, it was the basis of most of the Indo-European and Iranian peoples and cultures that we find in Europe, Central Asia and the Middle East.

Therefore, we must look at the south and east connections to understand not only Indic civilization and Hinduism, but also to understand the Vedas themselves. The western connections to the Europeans and Iranians were more an outflow, while the southern connections were more original and enduring. Western scholars, dominated by a European mindset, only traced Indo-European Culture from Europe

[8] D.C. Kuanr (state ed.), *Orissa District Gazetteers, Kalahandi,* N. Senapati (ed.), Cuttack, 1980, p. 36.

[9] David Frawley, *The Ṛgveda and the History of India,* New Delhi: Aditya Prakashan, 2001, inner flaps.

and the Middle East to India as its eastern border. They failed to see that the boundary was only in their minds.

Recent archaeological findings of the Indus alias Sarasvatī Valley Civilization have evidences of Vedic features. Therefore Bhagwan Singh[10] deals with them as "The Vedic Haṛappans". With this cultural civilization, the central Mahānadī Valley had contact and it is proved by the finding of a broken stone *liṅga* at Baṛagāon village in Nuāpāḍā district, which has similarity with a stone *liṅga* finding of Haṛappā.[11] This broken *liṅga* finding may be regarded as the earliest *liṅga* finding in the entire Mahānadī River Valley. One steatite figure of a priest, wearing a robe falling from the left shoulder was discovered in the compound of the house of late Jagabandhu Das in Khariar. Similar steatite figure of a priestess is found at the Indus alias Sarasvatī Valley Civilization site at Gumlā in Pakistan.[12] These prove that the cult of Śiva alias Pāśupati first developed in Kālāhāṇḍī and Nuāpāḍā regions of Orissa.

Historically, Bhairava worship began from Vedic Ajaikapāda Bhairava. In *Śiva Purāṇa*, Bhairava is regarded as prūrarūpa of Śaṅkara. Bhairava is the protector of creation and is terrific.

While dealing about "Śiva and Dakṣa", Agrawala[13] states:

> In one *mantra*, Aditi is defined as being identical with heaven and earth or the spatial extension; with past and future, or temporal extension; with father, mother and son or the biological manifestation; with all the gods or divine powers whether on earth or in heaven (*viśvedevāḥ*); or with the five tribes (*pañcajana*s), that is, all the classes of human beings on the sociological level. Aditi is the mother of all the worlds. This grand conception refers to the universal form of Aditi or Motherhood and therefore she is conceived of as the great Mother Goddess, as the presiding *śakti* of the universal *yajña*. But as the Great Mother she has a number of youthful daughters and a son named Dakṣa the principle of dexterity which becomes manifest in each individual *yajña*. Dakṣa is the energy of the Great Mother as her son and the universal Aditi and the individual Dakṣa must be reconciled to each other so that the process of sacrifice remains whole and the rhythm of

---

[10] Bhagwan Singh, *The Vedic Harappans*, New Delhi: Aditya Prakashan, 1995, *passim*.

[11] *THOMV* 2004, Pls. 14 and 15.

[12] J.P. Singh Deo, *Some Tāntric Esotericism of Orissa*, Kolkata: R.N. Bhattacharya, 2003, pp. 39-42.

[13] *SMTGG*, 1984, pp. 10-11.

energy does not become short-circuited. Dakṣa in this scheme represents the individual ego or centre of consciousness, *ahaṁkāra*. He thinks that his sacrifice can continue without the universal energy of Aditi descending in his centre. His daughter was Satī an incarnation of Aditi or transformation of the Universal Śakti for the performance of the individual sacrifice. When he organizes a session of his *yajña* he sends an invitation to all his daughters and all gods except Satī who was the eldest daughter and a goddess married to Śiva. Satī learned that her father was performing a sacrifice and so she asked her husband Śiva to accompany her to Dakṣa's home. Śiva said that he had not been invited and could not go adding that Satī also did not have the proper invitation. But Satī insisted on going and she came alone to the *yajña* of Dakṣa. There she was not well received and she also saw that each god was given the share of offering in the *yajña* excepting the God of gods, Śiva Mahādeva. She so resented this slight to her husband that she dropped down dead at the altar of the sacrifice. This implied a breakdown to the sacrifice of Dakṣa. When Śiva learned of this he assumed a terrible form as Bhairava-Vīrabhadra and came to the spot where Satī's body had fallen. He made short work of Dakṣa's sacrifice where everything was thrown into commotion and disorder. The implication is that no *yajña* in the individual centre can become complete without the descent of the Universal Energy into it as Satī and Śiva. The story says that Dakṣa lost his head and with him the sacrifice also became headless. The head is the symbol of mind and life or the two universal aspects of energy (*manas-prāṇa*). God Śiva was approached and propitiated and it is said that the detached head of Dakṣa was restored by joining a goat's head to his body. The goat in Sanskrit is called *aja* or the unborn universal to which Dakṣa was brought into union again. As to Śiva himself he picked up the body of Satī and throwing it on his shoulder went about the whole land where the limbs of the body of Satī dropped down severally by which 108 centres of *śakti* worship (*śakti-pīṭhas*) were formed which are said to continue up to this day. The moral of this story is the broad-based apotheosis of the motherland conceived in the form of energized centres for tāntric and yogic *sādhanā* or for practising special meditation and spiritual discipline.

During his wanderings, Śiva became Bhairava the terrible aspect of Rudra, and roamed over the earth with a begging bowl in hand crying for food from the goddess Annapūrṇā which is another name of Mother Earth, the eternal source of food and sustenance. Without the energy of the great goddess even the earth does not produce food and therefore the various limbs of the great mother goddess Satī or Aditi got mingled with the earth, which thus became the mother of abundance and fertility.

> The power of Śiva as auspicious god becomes efficient against the substratum of the motherly energy: Thus the seeds grow the energy of the earth and the infinite power of generation that is in the Mother Earth.

It is worth to know about the origin of ten wisdom goddesses or concept of *daśamahāvidyā*, because in tāntric text, the ten goddesses are conceived as Bhairavī and their consorts are Bhairavas.

According to Frawley,[14] the first clear reference to the ten wisdom goddesses occurs in the *Śiva Purāṇa* (v. 50).

> According to this story a demon named Durgama, took control of the four Vedas, by a boon of the creator, Lord Brahmā, and through them gained power over the entire universe. This caused a tremendous drought on earth for many years in which all creatures suffered greatly. Hence the gods called upon the Goddess to save the world. The Goddess, who always responds to the wishes of her devotees, first eliminated the drought and filled all the waters of the earth. Then the gods asked an additional boon to destroy the great demon and reclaim the Vedas. In her battle with the demon, the Goddess brought ten great forms out of her body — the *daśamahāvidyā* and then took the forms of innumerable goddesses. She defeated the demon and returned the Vedas to the gods. As the conqueror of Durgama, the Goddess was named Durgā.
>
> The ten wisdom goddesses are originally associated with the myth of restoring the Vedic teaching, which through the process of time had fallen under the forces of decay and corruption. From the Vedas to the Tantras is an unbroken line of mantric and meditation teachings centred in the Goddess, who herself is the divine word the Vedas and who periodically renovates the teaching in order to sustain it in this world bound by time and death.

The goddesses of *daśamahāvidyā* are Kālī, Tārā, Tripurā, Bhuvaneśvarī, Bhairavī, Chinnamastā, Dhūmāvatī, Bagalāmukhī, Mātaṅgī and Kamalātmikā.

The finding of two split-head or headless icons, on the back of the block office of Junagarh in Kālāhāṇḍī district is of interest. Baba Mishra[15] describes the iconography of these split-head icons thus:

---

[14] David Frawley, *Tāntric Yoga and the Wisdom Goddesses*, Delhi: Motilal Banarsidass, 1996, p. 62.

[15] Baba Mishra, "Split-Head Icons in the Temple Art of Kalahandi", Kala Jharan, *Kalahandi Utsav, 2002*, Souvenir, District Council of Culture, Bhawanipatna, English section, pp. 33-34.

1. The icon is two armed and measures 26 x 35 cm. It is a male figure and it holds its own chopped off head by a tuft of hair in the left hand, and a dragger is shown in the right hand. The figure is nude and has sturdy body and muscular limbs. The sculpture figure has a slender waist and broad-boned chest. The icon is carved in "*samabhaṅga* posture", on the semi-circular pedestal of granite stone. A dog is fashioned on the left ridge of the pedestal. The overall shape of the figure is round and the surface is polished. The striking aspect of the figure is that it is headless. The modelling of the figure was abruptly completed when the fashioning of chest and limbs were finished. The upper part of the shoulder is not only devoid of throat and head but at the same time, it looks polished which was deliberate.
2. It measures 30 × 20 cm. The icon is two-armed and is fashioned in "*samabhaṅga* posture" on a slab of granite stone, but the arms are obliterated. It is considerably damaged than its counterpart icon no. 1. It is also nude and severed head carried in the left hand is missing. Also, the dog carved on the pedestal is worn out. A separate rectangular pedestal is designed on a slab of granite stone to position the icon in *samabhaṅga* posture. The said image is also headless. The modelling abruptly stops with the completion of chest and limbs. As usual the shoulder remains finished and polished.

Remarkable identification of these two split-head icons has been done by Baba Mishra[16] and, while ascertaining the identity, he remarks that the Śaiva-Śākta tāntric tradition and its sacred literature reveal the headless divine male principle as a counter-part of headless female energy. In the hoary antiquities of Śaiva-Śākta creed, the idea embodied that male principle is the best support of energy, whose quality is feminine. It led eventually to the fruition of the concept of Śiva and Śakti.

> Śiva and Śakti are two aspects of the same truth, the static and dynamic, the negative and the positive, the abstract and the concrete and the male and the female. According to the second concept neither of it is real without the other as Śakti cannot be conceived of without Śiva, so also Śiva becomes *śava* (dead) without Śakti. The third view makes of Śakti, the highest truth and Śiva is conceived of as the best support of Śakti. Śiva is therefore invariably found to be entangled with his Śakti or vice versa.

---

[16] Baba Mishra, "Split-Head Icons in the Temple Art of Kalahandi", Kala Jharan, *Kalahandi Utsav, 2002*, Souvenir, District Council of Culture, Bhawanipatna, English section, pp. 34-35.

Tāntric texts further elaborate this concept in *daśamahāvidyā* or ten goddesses, who were emanated from the primordial Mother Goddess, Durgā Pārvatī alias Satī. In the tāntric text, these ten goddesses have also been conceived as Bhairavī. *Todala Tantra* thus postulates nine Bhairavas as the consorts of these nine Bhairavīs of *mahāvidyā*. Devī Dhūmāvatī being widow, no Bhairava is assigned to her. Devī Chinnamastā of *mahāvidyā* thus has her Bhairava known as Kabandha or Kabandha-Bhairava, who was deemed to be the best support of Devī Chinnamastā. As such, the God Kabandha-Bhairava appropriates the cardinal physical traits of Chinnamastā and Bhairava aspect in his person.

Consequently, in the delineation of Kabandha-Bhairava, some cardinal aspects like headlessness, nudity and two arms with attributes are discerned. But at the same time to demonstrate the Bhairava aspect, the deity is shown along with the dog on the pedestal. The headless icons of Junagarh can thus be successfully identified as Kabandha-Bhairava, a composite figure of Chinnamastā and Bhairava.

Kālāhāṇḍī region of modern Orissa breathes with strong Śaiva-Śākta tradition. A number of dilapidated stone and brick temples belonging to Śaiva-Śākta creed are found throughout the district. Different aspects of Lord Śiva and Bhairava as well as Mother Goddess were carved during the medieval period for installation in those temples. These icons are found scattered in this district after the demolition of those shrines.

The worship of the goddesses of *daśamahāvidyā* seems to have pervaded in the ninth-tenth centuries CE. The worship of Goddess Chinnamastā of *daśamahāvidyā* was adjusted later on with the creed of Maṇikeśvarī or vice versa in Kālāhāṇḍī.

During the tenth-eleventh centuries CE a shrine of Śākta Goddess was built at Junagarh near the present block office. Today the temple site is full of debris after its demolition. But amidst the heap of debris, cultish images like Caṇḍī, Trimūrti, Bhairava, Gaṇeśa and the above-discussed Kabandha-Bhairava, etc. are found.

It can be conjectered that the modelling and installation of Kabandha-Bhairava in the temple art of the land was inspired by Śaiva-Śākta tāntric tradition.

The finding of Kabandha-Bhairava in the hinterland central right Mahānadī Valley is noteworthy, because according to *Todala Tantra*, the goddesses of *daśamahāvidyā* had their consorts as Bhairavas.

The centres of Bhairava worship in Kālāhāṇḍī district are Medinipur,

Gudralipadar, Icchapur, Uditnarayanpur and the main centre is Lañjigaṛh, where a Bhairava temple exists. One four-handed Bhairava image with a dog at the bottom is found within Kāleśvara Mahādeva temple at Churiāgaṛh of Kālāhāṇḍī district. It measures 17" in height and 9½" in width. It is of Kaḷacuri period within the twelfth-thirteenth centuries CE.[17] Two Bhairavas are found in Māṇikgaṛh fort area, within the Māraguḍa Valley of Nuāpāḍā district.

It is known from tāntric texts that Kāla-Bhairava is a synonym of Amardaka.[18] Amardaka *tīrtha* is identified with modern Amarda of Mayūrbhañj district, where tāntric Śaiva Siddhānta School was popular.

It seems Bhairava worship became popular in Orissan Śaivism from eighth century CE. It is known from inscriptions that Bhañjas who ruled over Khiñjalimaṇḍala were devout worshippers of Bhairava. *Tad bhairavam haravapuḥ bhavataḥ prapātu* is the common prayer in the preamble of the charters of Bhañjas of Khiñjalimaṇḍala.

The Bhañjas of Khijjiṅgakoṭṭa were also worshippers of Bhairava. One Ajaikapāda Bhairava is found at Museum of Baripāḍā and one Bhairava is found at Museum of Khichiṅg.

Two Bhairavas are found in Vaitāl (Vetāl) temple of Bhubaneswar. In *Svarṇādri Mahodaya*, Chapter XXVII, this temple is called Kāpālinī.

Bhairavas are associated with *yoginī* cult. According to Āgamic texts there are sixty-four Bhairavas divided into eight groups and they are the counterparts of the sixty-four *yoginī*s. At Hirapur the images of Ajaikapāda Bhairava, Svacchanda Bhairava and Caṇḍa Bhairava, on the niches of *yoginī* temple are very fine images. In this Sixty-four Yoginī's temple at Hirapur, on the *caṇḍī maṇḍapa*, late Kedārnath Mahapatra[19] had noticed an image of Ajaikapāda Bhairava with four arms and one leg standing on a full-blown lotus. This Bhairava was wearing a garland of skulls, a tiara over his head and bracelets and armlets. It had a *khaḍga* in his upper right hand, a shield in upper left hand and the backbone of a fish in the lower left hand. The lower right hand was broken. Now this image is missing.

Bhairava images are found at Jajpur, Ajaikapāda Bhairava in Siṁhanātha temple in Baramba ex-state area, Junagarh and Biswanathpur and adjoining

[17] J.P. Singh Deo, *Some Tāntric Esotericism of Orissa*, Kolkata: R.N. Bhattacharya, 2003, pp. 50-51.

[18] J.P. Singh Deo, *Tāntric Art of Orissa*, Delhi: Kalpaz Publications, 2001, pp. 120-21.

[19] Kedarnath Mahapatra, "A Note on the Hypaethral Temple of Sixty-four Yoginis at Hirapur", *OHRJ*, vol. II, no. 2, pp. 23-44.

Ṭopīgāon villages of Kālāhāṇḍī district and many other places of Orissa and Chhattisgarh. One Bhairava image taken from Biswanathpur is installed in a temple of Lañjigaṛh, which is known as Bhairava Temple. Another Bhairava image taken from Biswanathpur ruins is now worshipped as Daṇḍa-Bhairava, at Ambadola. Hari-Hara with *ūrdhva-liṅga* (*penis erectus*) at Saṅkuśgaṛh is worshipped as Bhairava locally. Two *tantra* goddesses and one dancing Bhairava are found at Menda. Prabhat Mukherjee[20] had informed that an image of Bhairava was worshipped along with Jagannātha for a long time at Purī. From documents of the East India Company, it is known that in nineteenth century CE an image was removed from the throne of Lord Jagannātha at Purī, by the priests of the temple, when the throne was under repair. The priests refused to re-install the image after the repair of the throne. It is further reported that the priests destroyed the image into pieces which was thrown into the sea.

L.K. Panda[21] deals about the evolution of Bhairava cult, during the age of the Bhañjas and talks about Bhairavas found in the Mayūrbhañj, Keoñjhar and Bālāsore districts. One Ajaikapāda alias Ekpāda monolithic image is found in Bhairava Ḍuṅgrī in Ghodar village of Bolaṅgīr district.[22]

With the development of the *yoginī* cult in the central right Mahānadī Valley, Bhairava cult also expanded, because each of the 64 *yoginīs* was furnished with a male consort Bhairava. In the words of H.C. Das,[23] it finds expression:

> In connection with the *yoginīs*, the cult of Śiva which is widespread in different parts of India and finds mention profusely in mythology particularly in *Śiva Purāṇa*, *Liṅga Purāṇa*, etc. appears to be significant. The cult of Śiva has two aspects, benevolent (*saumya*) and malevolent (*ugra*). Among various types of the terrific or *ugra* forms of Śiva mention may be made of his Bhairavas, Aghora, Vīrabhadra and Virupākhya forms. According to Āgamic texts there are sixty-four Bhairavas,[24] divided into eight groups and they are the counterparts of the sixty-four *yoginīs*.

---

[20] P. Mukherjee, "The Missing Bhairava Image of the Jagannātha Temple", *Orissa Review*, July 1970, vol. XXXVI, no. 12, pp. 23-44.

[21] L.K. Panda, *Śaivism in Orissa*, Delhi: Sundeep Prakashan, 1985, pp. 68-77.

[22] Ram Prasad Mishra, *Fragments of Indian Culture*, Kolkata: Punthi Pustak, 1995, Pls. 34 and 35.

[23] H.C. Das, *Tāntricism: A Study of the Yogini Cult*, New Delhi: Sterling Publishers, 1981, pp. 27-29.

[24] Ibid.; N.N. Bhattacharya, *History of the Śākta Religion*, New Delhi: Munshiram Manoharlal, 1974, *passim*.

A story of *Vāmana Purāṇa* highlights the origin of the mystic Bhairavas. In ancient times there was a fierce battle between Mahādeva and Andhakāsura. Andhaka hit the head of Mahādeva with his mace. As a result blood oozed out from the wound and flowed down to four sides. From the stream of blood that gushed out of the head of Mahādeva the Bhairavas were created. From the blood stream flowing to the east was born Bhairava known as Vidurājra decked with beautiful ornaments and looking like a blazing fire. From the flow to the south was born Rāmarāja Bhairava, deep black in colour associated with *pretas*, from that of flow to west, Nāgarāja decorated with leaves and *atasi kusuma* in colour and from that of the north was born Bhairava known as Svacchandarāja, black in colour holding *triśūla* (trident) and lastly from the total flow of the blood came out a Bhairava known as Lambitarāja.[25] Eight names of Bhairavas, who are worshipped on the occasion of autumnal Devī worship are Mahā-Bhairava, Saṁhāra-Bhairava, Asitāṅga-Bhairava, Ruru-Bhairava, Kāla-Bhairava, Krodha-Bhairava, Kapāla-Bhairava and Rudra-Bhairava. According to *Tantrasāra*, Asitāṅga, Ruru, Caṇḍa, Krodha, Unmatta, Kapāli, Bhīsaṇa and Saṁhāra are the eight Bhairavas. We also find the mention of Bhairavas along with Mahāvidyās.[26]

The eight Bhairavas such as Asitāṅga, Ruru, Caṇḍa, Krodha, Unmatta, Kapāla, Bhīṣana, Saṁhāra, multiplied in course of time into sixty-four are given in the tabular form.[27]

Vidya Dehejia[28] also mentions sixty-four Bhairavas in her studious work, *Yogini Cult and Temple: A Tāntric Tradition.*

According to K.C. Mishra[29] the cult for Jagannātha is formulated as a result of the remarkable synthesis between tāntric Buddhism, Nāthism, Vaiṣṇavism and Śāktism.

25 H.C. Das, *Tāntricism: A Study of the Yogini Cult*, New Delhi: Sterling Publishers, 1981, pp. 27-29; *Viśva Koṣa* (Beṅgālī), vol. 13, p. 548.

26 Ibid., pp. 548-49.

27 Ibid.; R.S. Gupte, *Iconography of the Hindus, Buddhists and Jains*, Bombay: Taraporevala, 1974, p. 76.

28 Vidya Dehejia, *Yogini Cult and Temples: A Tāntric Tradition*, New Delhi: National Museum Publication, 1986, p. 222. (64 Bhairavas, see Manuscript in Madras devoted to their *pūjā* (worship), as stated by Gopinath Kaviraj in his work *Tāntrika Sāhitya*, Delhi, 1972, pp. 19-23; 64 *mantras* in P.C. Bagchi, *Kaulajñānanirṇaya*, and some minor texts of the School of Matsyendranāth, Paṭala VIII, Calcutta, 1943.)

29 K.C. Mishra, *The Cult of Jagannātha*, Kolkata: Firma K.L. Mukhopadhyay, 1971, p. 158.

In the tradition of Sāralā Dāsa's *Mahābhārata*, Mishra[30] states that Sāralā Dāsa appears to ascribe the origin of the worship of Jagannātha to that of Mādhava or Nīlamādhava, also named Śabarināraāyaṇa by the Śabara community of the bygone days. The God Nīlamādhava reassured Jarā (Vasu — Śabaras father) that he would incarnate himself as Buddha in Nīlagiri. In this manner Jagannātha deity is associated with Nīlamādhava and Nīlagiri.

According to R.G. Bhandarkar,[31] Ānanda-Bhairava or Mahā-Bhairava, which is the name given to Śiva, is the soul of, or is composed of, the nine collections of things of which the world is made up, such as time and its various forms (*kāla-vyūha*), existing things like the blue substance (*kula-vyūha*), names (*nāma-vyūha*), perception (*jñāna-vyūha*), the five faculties, viz. consciousness, heart, will, intelligence and mind (*citta-vyūha*). Mahā-Bhairava is the soul of the goddess; therefore she also is the soul of, or composed of, the nine collections. Both, therefore, constitute one entity. When there is *sāmarasya*, or community of joy or intense love between them, creation follows. The female element, or Mahābhairavī, however, is predominant in the process of creation and the male element, or Mahā-Bhairava, in the work of destruction.[32]

Lord Puruṣottama Jagannātha of Purī is regarded as Bhairava by the Śaiva and tāntric worshippers. *Bhairavī-yantra* is chiselled on Ratna Siṁhāsana of Purī temple and Lord Puruṣottama Jagannātha is placed on *bhairavī-yantra*. According to Niranjan Satapathy,[33] the cult of Jagannātha incorporated in itself all faiths and all religions that flourished in Orissa by the end of the Gaṅga rule. The *mantra*[34] which is uttered at the time of the worship of Jagannātha at Purī sums up the findings of this work. It declares that Jagannātha is the same as the Supreme God of the Vaiṣṇavas, Śaivas, Śāktas, Jains and Bauddhas. He admits all interpretations with a broad smile. As a unique symbol of religious synthesis he sits there majestically in his temple and confers his blessings on all people, irrespective of caste, colour and creed.

---

[30] K.C. Mishra, *The Cult of Jagannātha*, Kolkata: Firma K.L. Mukhopadhyay, 1971, p. 79.

[31] R.G. Bhandarkar, *Vaiṣṇavism, Śaivism and Minor Religious Systems*, Varanasi: Indological Book House, 1965, p. 145.

[32] Ibid., *Saundaryalaharī*, verse 34.

[33] N. Satapathy, *Religious Life in Orissa: A Study of the Interrelation of Cults*, Kolkata: R.N. Bhattacharya, 2000, pp. 181-82.

[34] Ibid., p. 184.

D.C. Bhattacharyya[35] had quoted the *mantra*, which is uttered at the time of the worship of Jagannātha at Purī:

> *yoginām haṁsatattvam hariharanāmitaṁ śrīpatiḥ vaiṣṇavānāṃ* । *śaivānāṁ bhairavākhyāṁ pāśupatiparaman śāktatattve ca sevitaṃ* । *bauddhānāṁ buddha sākṣāi rūpabhayādiharo jainasiddhāntamūrtiḥ* ॥

Gāṇapatya Tantra

About Gāṇapatya sect, Swami Satyananda Saraswati[36] says that the followers of this sect venerate the chubby elephant deity known as Gaṇapati or Gaṇeśa. He is the son of Śiva and Pārvatī (Śakti) and represents the understanding that comes through the mind. In other words, it is through consciousness and its manifestation (Śiva–Śakti) that one gains mental understanding.

> Gaṇeśa is an aspect of the absolute and is widely worshipped throughout India in almost all Hindu rites and ceremonies. The worshippers invoke Lord Gaṇeśa before commencing any important undertaking, for nothing can be achieved without mental understanding. This applies to everyday duties as well as enlightenment. Gaṇeśa is the controller of all accomplishments. Without the grace of understanding, nothing can be achieved. It is for this reason that he is such an important deity, and why a specific sect has arisen around him. Without mental understanding how can anything be initiated or successfully carried out?
>
> Followers of this sect are more prevalent in western India. Huge processions are entirely devoted to the veneration of Gaṇeśa. However, this sect has really ceased to be a distinct tāntric group as such and has been absorbed into the mainstream of Hinduism.
>
> Gaṇeśa is traditionally regarded to be the scribe of many of the important scriptures of India, including the Tantras. That is, when Śiva, Śakti, Kṛṣṇa or any other deities, together with *ṛṣis*, seers, etc. discoursed, Gaṇeśa wrote everything down. He represents the higher understanding that must accompany all scriptures before they can be written, and before they can be utilized by the reader. In fact, Gaṇeśa is invoked at the beginning of many of the tāntric texts; the very first words are: *śrī gaṇeśāya namaḥ*, which means salutations to the blessed Gaṇeśa. This is done to encourage correct understanding by both the writer and the reader. There is also a well-known

[35] N. Satapathy, D.C. Bhattacharya, *Iconology of Composite Images*, New Delhi 1980, p. 65.

[36] *ASCITATTOYAK*, 1989, p. 328.

tāntric text called the *Gaṇeśa Tantra*.

This system of Tantra is simple, direct and yet sublime and it can lead to

Name of the Bhairavas	Objects in Hand	Colour
1. ASITĀṄGA 1. Asitāṅga 2. Viśālākṣa 3. Mārtaṇḍa 4. Modakapriya 5. Svachchaṇa 6. Vighnasaṁtuṣṭa 7. Khecara, and 8. Sacarācara	Trident, sword, drum and noose	Golden
2. RURU 1. Ruru 2. Kroḍa-daṁṣṭra 3. Jaṭādhara 4. Viśvarūpa 5. Virūpākṣa 6. Nānārūpadhara 7. Mahākāya, and 8. Vajrahasta	Rosary, goad, lute (*vīṇā*) and book	White
3. CAṆḌA 1. Caṇḍa 2. Pralayāntaka 3. Bhūmikampa 4. Nīlakaṇṭha 5. Viṣṇu 6. Kulapālaka 7. Muṇḍapāla, and 8. Kāmapāla	Fire (*agni*), spear, mace and *kunta*	Blue
4. KRODHA 1. Krodha 2. Piṅgalākṣaṇa 3. Adhararūpa 4. Dharāpāla 5. Kuṭila 6. Mantranāyaka 7. Rudra, and 8. Pitāmaha	Sword, shield, long sword and battle axe	smoke coloured

Name of the Bhairavas	Objects in Hand	Colour
5. UNMATTA 1. Unmatta 2. Vaṭuka-nāyaka 3. Śaṅkara 4. Bhūta-Vetāla 5. Varada 6. Pārvatīvāsu 7. Trinetra, and 8. Tripurāntaka	*Kuṇḍa* or *kunta*, shield, *parigha* (a kind of club) and *bhiṇḍipāla*	White
6. KAPĀLA 1. Kapāla 2. Śaśibhūṣaṇa 3. Hasticarmā-baradhara 4. Yogīśa 5. Brahmarākṣasa 6. Sarvajña 7. Sarvadeveśa, and 8. Sarvabhūtahṛdisthita	*Kuṇḍa* or *kunta*, shield, *parigha* and a *bhiṇḍipāla*	Golden yellow
7. BHĪṢAṆA 1. Bhīṣaṇa 2. Bhayahara 3. Sarvajña 4. Kālāgni 5. Mahāraudra 6. Dakṣiṇa 7. Mukharā, and 8. Asthira	*Kuṇḍa* or *kunta*, shield, *parigha* and a *bhiṇḍipāla*	Red
8. SAṀHĀRA 1. Saṁhāra 2. Atiriktāṅga 3. Kālāgni 4. Priyaṇkara 5. Ghoranāda 6. Viśālākṣa 7. Yogīśa, and 8. Dakṣasaṁsthita	*Kuṇḍa* or *kunta*, shield, *parigha* and a *bhiṇḍipāla*	Colour like lightning

> spiritual heights. It is by invoking and focusing one's powers on mental understanding (personified by Gaṇeśa) that one can actually bring about a high level of understanding in oneself. All that is required is the overwhelming need to know a need that springs from the very depths of one's heart. This is the same as worshipping Gaṇeśa, provided one understands the significance of Gaṇeśa. From this understanding will come many other things, including illumination and bliss.

It may be asked, why the elephant's head was chosen as the symbol of Gaṇapati. The answer is that the elephant's head was made the symbol of the inflated ego or the conscious "I", the first principle which emanated from the unmanifest Prajāpati, for the simple reason that the elephant is of the most huge size amongst all creatures. That is the nature of *ahaṁkāra* (ego), also, since it is the modification of *mahat*, or what in the *Gītā* has been named as Mahad-Brahmā (*Gītā*, 14, 3-4).[37]

In the words of N.N. Bhattacharyya:[38]

> As Gaṇādhipati Gaṇeśa was more akin to Rudra, as we have seen, and this probably explains why in later tradition he was regarded as the son of Rudra, Śiva and Pārvatī. In the *Atharvaśiras Upaniṣad*, Rudra has been equated with Vināyaka and Vināyaka is the other name of Gaṇeśa. The *Amarakoṣa* gives many names of Gaṇeśa:
>
> *vināyaka-vighnarāja-dvaimātura-gaṇādhipāḥ,*
> *apyekadanta-heramba-lambodara-gajānanāḥ.*
>
> In the *Mahābhārata* Gaṇeśvaras and Vināyakas are described as the lords of the world. If properly propitiated they remove all obstacles. In the *Mānava Gṛhyasūtra* four Vināyakas have been mentioned — Sālakaṭaṅkaṭa, Kūṣmāṇḍarājaputra, Uṣmita and Devayajana. In the Purāṇas, such as the *Śiva, Liṅga, Varāha, Skanda, Brahmavaivartta,* etc. we have various conflicting anecdotes regarding the birth of Gaṇeśa. Iconological texts mention twenty-four forms of Gaṇeśa: Vināyaka, Gaṇādhīśa, Vighneśa, Pramathādhipa, Gaṇeśa, Bījagaṇapati, Heramba, Vakratuṇḍa, Bālagaṇapati, Bhakta-vighneśa, Śaktigaṇeśa, Dhvajagaṇādhipa, Piṅgalagaṇapati, Ucchiṣṭagaṇapati, Lakṣmī-Gaṇeśa, Mahāgaṇeśa, Bhuvaneśa, Gaṇapati, Nṛtyagaṇapati, Ūrdhvagaṇeśa, Prasannagaṇeśa, Unmattavināyaka and Haridrāgaṇeśa.

---

[37] *SMTGG*, 1984, p. 54.

[38] *HOTTR*, 1987, pp. 270-72.

In Ānandagiri's *Śaṅkaradigvijaya*, and also in its *Diṇḍimākhya* commentary, six branches of the Gāṇapatyas or followers of the creed of Gaṇeśa (*gāṇapatyamiti khyātaṃ ṣaḍbhirbhadaiḥ samanvitaṃ*) are known as Mahāgaṇapati, Haridrāgaṇapati, Ucchiṣṭagaṇapati, Navanītagaṇapati, Svarṇagaṇapati and Santānagaṇapati. According to the worshippers of Mahāgaṇapati, Gajānana, also known as Ekadanta Gaṇapati, who is in eternal union with his Śākti, is the creator of the world and the ultimate reality. According to the worshippers of Haridrā Gaṇapati, Gaṇapati is the original cause of this phenomenal world and the other Gods like Brahmā are his parts; they used to depict the head of Gaṇeśa on their hands.

The worshippers of Ucchiṣṭagaṇapati were undeniably followers of Tantrism. They visualized Gaṇeśa with four arms, three eyes, lasso (*pāśa*), goad (*aṅkuśa*), club (*gadā*) and in *abhaya-mudrā*. His trunk is shown as drinking intoxicating liquor. Seated on a *mahāpīṭha* he is engaged in kissing and embracing his Śakti who sits on his left lap:

caturbhujaṁ trinayanaṁ pāśāṅkuśa gadābhayaṁ ।
tuṇḍāgra tibramadhukaṁ gaṇanāthamahaṁ bhaje ॥

mahāpīṭha niṣannaṁ taṁ vāmāṅga parisaṁsthitaṁ ।
devīmāliṅgya cumbantaṁ spṛśaṁaṣṭuṇḍena vaibhagam ॥

The Ucchiṣṭagāṇapatyas did not differentiate between merit and demerit. They did not find any fault in indiscriminate sexual intercourse among men and women. They did not obey caste distinctions nor observe various *saṁskāra*s like marriage, etc. They drank wine. Their sect mark was a red circle on the forehead.

With this background, it is worth to study the development of *Gāṇapatya* worship and *Gāṇapatya Tantra* in Orissa. The early Gaṇapati images are found in the temples of Orissa. According to Arjun Joshi,[39] in Orissa, particularly at Bhubaneswar, still there are Gaṇapati images of earlier periods. In the Orissa State Museum there are four panels containing the images of Gaṇeśa. Out of these four, the one, having a mouse vehicle has been dated by scholars to the Gupta period. The other three figures were brought from the neighbourhood of the Śatrughneśvara group of temples and hence may be dated to seventh century CE. It is interesting to note that these museum specimens have similar features with the sculptures preserved

[39] Arjun Joshi, *New Light on the Cultural Heritage of Orissa*, Cuttack: Baneeshree, 1980, pp. 52-53.

in the niches of the Paraśurāmeśvara temple (seventh century CE), the Uttareśvara temple (seventh century CE), the Mohinī temple (eighth century CE) and the Śiśireśvara temple (eighth century CE) within the compound of the Vaitāl (Kapālinī) temple. The Gaṇeśa sculptures preserved in the museum have similar features with the Gaṇeśa image carved in the centre of a door lintel preserved in the museum. K.N. Mahapatra, told me that the door lintel was acquired from the neighbourhood of the Śatrughneśvara group of temples and it belongs to one of the temples of that group. There is a similar door lintel with Gaṇeśa figure in the southern door of Jagamohana of the Paraśurāmeśvara temple. Thus all these figures of Gaṇeśa belong to the temples of ancient period. The three images of the Śatrughneśvara group of temples preserved in the museum are artistically earlier than the Gaṇeśa sculptures in the niches of the temples of Paraśurāmeśvara, Uttareśvara, Mohinī and Śiśireśvara. For example, the Śatrughneśvara group of images have no halo, but the Paraśurāmeśvara and the Śiśireśvara images have halos. In both the images of the Paraśurāmeśvara temple — beaded boarded halo of the image in the niche of *vimāna* and simple halo of the image in the door lintel of Jagamohana — halo is clearly carved out. This proves that the temples of Śatrughneśvara are earlier than the Paraśurāmeśvara and other temples. The temples of this group may hence be regarded as the earliest temples of Orissa.

During Somavaṁśī period separate shrines for Gaṇeśa were erected. The Siddha Gaṇeśa temple was built by the side of the river Dayā, at the foothills of Dhauli, Gaṇeśa shrine in the premises of the Bhava Kuṇḍaleśvara temples of village Tankapāṇi in the Bhārgavī Valley, Gaṇeśa temples at Agrahāṭ near Chauḍwār, Teraboi in the Dayā Valley, in Prācī Valley, at Jaipur and many other places. This was probably the formative period of the cult of Gaṇeśa which later grew into an important cult with the establishment of the Mahā-Vināyaka-Kṣetra at Kapilasa.[40]

Arjun Joshi[41] further states that generally the Gaṇeśa images found in India have two eyes. There are some Āgamas which prescribe three eyes for him in certain particular aspects. It is interesting to note that all the four images in the museum have three eyes, the third eye being at the middle of the forehead. But there are other Āgamas which prescribe either two or three eyes.

The Gaṇapati image may have two, four, eight, even sixteen hands. But in majority cases they have four hands. The images in Orissa, particularly those

---

[40] J.P. Singh Deo, *Tāntric Art of Orissa*, Delhi: Kalpaz Publications, 2001, p. 117.

[41] Arjun Joshi, op. cit., 1980, p. 55.

described in this article, have four hands. Several Āgamas also prescribe four hands. The dancing Gaṇeśa image preserved in the Khiching Museum and another image at Purī have eight hands.

Gaṇapati images of the later period such as the one installed in the southern niche of the celebrated Liṅgarāja temple and the images preserved in the Khiching Museum are represented as standing or dancing in *tribhaṅga* pose. One eight-handed *nṛtya* (dancing) Gaṇeśa in *tribhaṅga* pose is found as *pārśva-devatā* of Trilochanpur temple at Sathalapuri village in Jagatsinghpur district.

Gaṇeśa alias Gaṇapati images are found throughout the country like Śiva-Śakti ruins. Let us know the important images of Gaṇeśa, which have tāntric influence in Orissa. The most ancient image of Gaṇeśa with tāntric influence was found at Rāṇīpur-Jharial site, whose ruins are assigned to the sixth-twelfth centuries CE. About this tāntric image of Gaṇeśa, Sasanka Sekhar Panda[42] remarks:

> Unique of its kind, the figure of an eight-handed Nṛtta Gaṇapati (dancing Gaṇeśa) of the height of around 4' has been shifted from Rāṇīpur-Jharial by some Chauhan ruler of Patnagarh long ago and since then housed in the Hariśaṅkara temple. This image is exquisitely carved and heavily ornamented. The lord is in a *tribhaṅga* dancing pose, on a full-blown lotus or *padmāsana*. His left leg is slightly bent but firmly placed on the *padmāsana*, while the right leg is also bent but the heel is up. He is seen wearing a *sarpa* as *yajñopavīta*. He is seen to be wearing *hāra*, *keyūra* and *kaṅkaṇa*. Two crouching *yakṣa*s are carved beside both feet of the lord and flying *gandharva* as well as *gandharvī* on both sides overhead. Out of eight hands, two left hands are broken. In both his raised upper hands, he is seen holding a *sarpa* (snake), and in his lower third and fourth right hands an *akṣamālā* and a broken *danta* (tusk), his second right hand is on his chest with palm in a dancing *mudrā*. In his third left hand, Gaṇeśa is seen holding a *laḍḍū-pātra*. On the pedestal of this figure are carved figures of three devotees playing kettle-drum, cymbals and other musical instruments. A profile figure of his *vāhana* mouse is carved on the pedestal eating something held by a devotee. It is a very fine piece of sculpture, perfect in modelling as well as execution and pleasing in effect. Such Gaṇeśa figure in dancing pose is said to be a tāntric manifestation.

[42] S.S. Panda, "Some Archaeological Remains of Bolangir District", *OHRJ* vol. XXXX, nos. 1-4, p. 61.

This Nṛtta (dancing) Gaṇeśa is nude. Its scrotum is visible, over which a small snake is chiselled. The snake on the scrotum is the symbol of *kuṇḍalinī śakti* and resembles the upflow of semen, i.e. the practice of *yoga* of sexual transformation. Its *liṅga* (penis) is not visible and this symbolizes that the Gaṇapati is practising *vajrolī* and through this *haṭha-yoga* the muscles of the penis, i.e. the external male sexual organ, have been sucked up, like the head and legs of a tortoise — a *haṭha-yoga* practice of sexual transformation. Finally the *uḍḍiyāna bandha* (abdominal extraction lock: drawing in of the abdomen and stomach towards the backbone after exhaling) is done.[43]

Sasanka Sekhar Panda[44] brings to limelight another such image of Nṛtta Gaṇeśa, inside the *garbha-gṛha* of a Śiva temple in Godhaneśvara village, situated on the left bank of the Mahānadī, in Bīrmahārājpur sub-division of the Sonepur district:

> Inside the *garbha-gṛha*, the image of an eight-handed Nṛtta Gaṇapati is kept leaning against the northern wall. In both his raised upper hands he is seen holding a snake over his head. In his second upper left hand there is a *laḍḍū-pātra*, from which, he is seen picking *laḍḍu* by touching it with his proboscis. His third left hand is in *abhaya-mudrā*, while the fourth (lowest) hand is broken. His lowest right hand is on the chest-portion, in the *gajahasta* posture. In his third right hand he is seen holding a small bow, but object in his second right hand is not clear. He is seen wearing a conical-shaped *mukuṭa* on his head. His *vāhana* mouse is standing on the pedestal in profile, near his right leg. This image is of the height of around 2' and breadth of 2' also. In the back side of this image, a long inscription in six lines is carved. This inscription is having the proto-Oriyā characters of the late Gaṅga period and palaeographically can be taken to be of the thirteenth century CE.

Such an eight-handed Nṛtta (nude) Gaṇeśa is found chiselled on the wall of right side of the door of the Vimalā temple, inside the compound of Puruṣottama Jagannātha temple, Purī. Inside the compound, one Gaṇeśa temple facing south is found in front of the Vimalā temple. The main deity of this Gaṇeśa is in the shape of eight-handed Nṛtta Gaṇeśa as found at Hariśaṅkara site and Godhaneśvara village, as already described. The upper two hands hold a snake, which symbolizes the conquest or rise of *kuṇḍalinī śakti*. This proves that the concept of Gāṇapatya

---

[43] J.P. Singh Deo, *Some Tāntric Esotericism of Orissa*, Kolkata: R.N. Bhattacharya, 2003, pp. 279-80.

[44] S.S. Panda, "Some Arhaeological Remains of Bolangir District", *OHRJ*, vol. XXXX, nos. 1-4, p. 78.

Tantra was evolved in the central Mahānadī River Valley and migrated to coastal Orissa, to be finally merged in the great tradition of the Puruṣottama Jagannātha cult, which is all embracing.

These eight-handed *nṛtta* images of Gaṇeśa are replicas of images of eight-handed Naṭarāja of Sirpur, dated fifth century CE and Āsanpaṭ, dated sixth century CE,[45] from which developed the separate cult of *Gāṇapatya Tantra*.

One six-handed Gaṇeśa, worshipped in a side temple, within the premises of the Rāmeśvara temple at Sonepur is found.[46] This concerned tāntric Ganeśa is yellow in colour. With the influence of Tantra, Gaṇeśa under the name of Gaṇapati, thus became an important deity towards the tenth century CE when the Gāṇapatya sect alias cult set up the cult of Śakti-Gaṇapatis called: Ucchiṣṭa-Gaṇapati, four-armed, red in colour; Mahā-Gaṇapati, ten-armed red; Ūrdhva-Gaṇapati, six-armed, yellow; Piṅgala-Gaṇapati, six-armed; Lakṣmī-Gaṇapati, four or eight-armed, white; while the Śakti is yellow and carries a lotus.[47] The concerned Tāntric Gaṇesa of Sonepur is Ūrdhva-Gaṇpati; six armed and yellow coloured.

It is only Lord Śiva, who is Liṅgarāja with his *ūrdhva-liṅga* (*penis erectus*).[48] The Gāṇapatyas were *liṅga* worshippers and the Gaṇapati liṅga was considered second only to the Svayambhū, which was enshrined in the innermost sanctuary of a temple and never gazed upon by its worshippers. The Gaṇapati liṅga, being less sacred, was shown to the members of the Gāṇapatya sect. It was in form somewhat in the shape of a citron, a cucumber or a wood apple and its worship was believed to have been set up by the *gaṇa*s at a very early date.[49]

A.K. Bhattacharya[50] is of the opinion that:

> The Gāṇapatya sect, or more precisely the Ucchiṣṭa Gāṇapatya sect, grew in conjunction with the *yoginī* sect that originated in *c.* eleventh century CE. A variety of Gaṇeśa or Gaṇapati accompanied by consort (Śakti) is known

---

45 C. Sivaramamurti, *Nataraja in Art, Thought and Literature*, New Delhi: Publication Division, Govt. of India, 2nd edn., 1994, pp. 159-60 and 164-65.

46 J.P. Singh Deo, *Some Tāntric Esotericism of Orissa*, Kolkata: R.N. Bhattacharya, 2003, p. 295.

47 Alice Getty, *Gaṇeśa: A Monograph on the Elephant-faced God*, New Delhi: Munshiram Manoharlal, 1992, p. 20.

48 J.P. Singh Deo, op. cit., 2003, p. 296.

49 Alice Getty, op. cit., 1992, p. 21.

50 A.K. Bhattacharya, "A Study on the Iconography of Five Ucchista-Ganapati Figures", *OHRJ*, vol. XLII, nos. 1-4, pp. 72-73.

> as Ucchiṣṭa-Gaṇapati. It is thus a kind of Śakti-Gaṇeśa or Śakti-Gaṇapati. The distinctive feature of this variety is constituted by the fact that the Śakti or the female consort is invariably shown nude and she is either seated on the left lap of Gaṇeśa or standing beside him at left. Though this kind of representation is by itself vulgar, there is a further tinge of sexuality in them and this sexual vulgarity is what is indicated by the appellation by which these figures are known, namely, Ucchiṣṭa-Gaṇapati. The derivation of the term *ucchiṣṭa* has to be taken as *ut* (opposed to) and *śiṣṭa* ("civil" or "polite" or "chaste"), thus *ucchiṣṭa* is what is "not civil or chaste", i.e. vulgar. The sexuality of these "Ucchiṣṭa-Gaṇapati" type of figures is, however, expressed in many ways. The feature of Gaṇapati touching the pudendum mulie of Devī (Śakti) and the latter holding the genital organ of the Lord, is described in two verses in the *Sāradā Tilaka Tantram*,[51] where, in both cases, Gaṇapati is four-armed and both the varieties come under *Śakti-Gaṇādhipa*.

A.K. Bhattacharya gives details of: (1) Ucchiṣṭa-Gaṇapati of stone material found in the Nāgeśvarswāmī temple of Kumbhakoṇam, dated tenth century CE, (2) Ucchiṣṭa-Gaṇapati of stone material at Barsur, in Madhya Pradesh, dated tenth-eleventh centuries CE, (3) Ucchiṣṭa-Gaṇapati made of stones, at Nañjangūḍu in Karnataka, dated twelfth-thirteenth centuries CE, (4)Ucchiṣṭa-Gaṇapati painting of Jammu-Kashmir school, eighteenth century CE of National Museum, New Delhi, and (5) Ucchiṣṭa-Gaṇapati of ivory material, Orissa, late ninteenth century CE of National Museum, New Delhi. In ivory figure from Orissa[52] datable in the late ninteenth century CE now preserved in the National Museum, New Delhi, Gaṇapati is shown four-armed with his upper right hand holding the broken tooth of his own, and the lower, an *akṣa-mālā* (rosary of beads), the upper left has a serpent, while the lower left caresses the Śakti at her left shoulder. With traces of scanty lower garment, Gaṇapati is richly ornamented with *ratna-mukuṭa, valaya, hāra*, jewelled *kaṭi-bandha*, and anklets. He wears an *upavīta* going over his bulging belly. With all this Gaṇapati is shown to touch the private parts of Śakti by his proboscis, thus helping to designate the composition as Ucchiṣṭa-Gaṇapati. The Śakti is two-armed, richly bedecked with ornaments and beautifully sculpted. She holds a lotus in her right hand and places the left on her thigh.

In addition to these Ucchiṣṭa-Gaṇapati figures, there is another Ucchiṣṭa-Gaṇapati

---

[51] A.K. Bhattacharya, "A Study on the Iconography of Five Ucchista-Ganapati Figures", *OHRJ*, vol. XLII, nos. 1-4, *Śāradā-Tilaka-Tantram*.

[52] Ibid., pp. 75-76.

inside the compound of the temple of Puruṣottama Jagannātha at Purī. It is known as Kāñcī Gaṇeśa alias Bhaṇḍa Gaṇeśa locally. A separate temple is built for this Kāñcī Gaṇeśa, to the back of the main Puruṣottama Jagannātha temple. This Kāñcī alias Bhaṇḍa Gaṇeśa temple, mostly remains closed and is opened only for a short ritual worship daily.

The reigning period of Gajapati Puruṣottamadeva of Sūryavaṁśī is assigned between CE 1467-97 and K.C. Panigrahi[53] asserts that there is still an image of Gaṇeśa in the compound of the Jagannātha temple which is taken to have been brought by Puruṣottama from Kāñcī. So it is positive to mention that *Gāṇapatya Tantra* existed in Orissa state.

From Purāṇas it is known that Gaṇeśa had married Siddhi and Buddhi. Mamta Das[54] mentions about these marriages of Gaṇeśa:

> In the *Gaṇeśa Purāṇa*,[55] we come across the description of Gaṇeśa's marriage. The narration of the story differs from the one in *Śiva Purāṇa*. When Mayūreśa became fifteen years old, Śiva and Pārvatī thought of his marriage. Once when Nārada visited Śiva, the divine couple requested him to find out a suitable bride for their son, Mayūreśa. Nārada told them that Brahmadeva had two marriageable daughters, Siddhi and Buddhi. Śiva-Pārvatī approved the proposal and arranged for the wedding. The marriage procession proceeded towards Brahmā's residence. On the way they confronted many demons, the notable among them was Sindhu. Mayūreśa killed the demons and married Siddhi and Buddhi. Here however we do not come across any mention about Gaṇeśa's brother Kārttikeya.

The same Purāṇa[56] at another place gives a queer account of how Gaṇeśa accepted Siddhi and Buddhi as his wives. It narrates that once Brahmā worshipped Gaṇeśa. At the time of offering *dakṣiṇā*, two beautiful daughters of Brahmā came. They had graceful appearance and were decked with jewelled ornaments and had put on divine clothes. They also worshipped Gaṇeśa with flowers and sang the *sahasranāma* in praise of him. Being pleased with their worship, Gaṇeśa accepted them as his wives and taking them with him he disappeared:

---

53 K.C. Panigrahi, *History of Orissa*, Cuttack, Kitab Mahal, 1981, pp. 208 and 217.

54 Mamta Das, *Origin and Development of Ganeśa in the Purāṇas*, Berhampur, Orissa: Upagupta Publications, 1996, pp. 111-14.

55 Ibid.; *Gaṇeśa Purāṇa*, II, 108.

56 Ibid.; *Gaṇeśa Purāṇa*, I, 15, 34-39.

ततः प्रसन्नो भगवान् विध्नकर्त्ता गजाननः।
सिद्धिबुद्धि गृहीत्वा तु अन्तर्धानमगद् विभु॥

tataḥ prasanno bhagavān vighnakarttā gajananaḥ ।
siddhibuddhī gṛhītvā tu antardhānamagad vibhu ॥
— *Gaṇeśa Purāṇa*, I.15.39

Another passage of the same Purāṇa mentions Gaṇeśa with Siddhi and Buddhi. Pleased with sage Gṛtsamada's penance, Gaṇeśa appeared before him riding on a lion and accompanied by his two wives:

सिद्धिबुद्धियुतः श्रीमान् कोटिसूर्याधिकद्युतिः।
अनिर्वाच्यस्वरूपोऽपि लीलयाऽसीत् पुरो मुनेः॥

sidhibuddhiyutaḥ śrīmān koṭisūryādhikadyutiḥ ।
anirvācyasvarūpo 'pi lilayā 'sīt puro muneḥ ॥
— *Gaṇeśa Purāṇa*, I.37.13

The *Nārada Purāṇa* describes Siddhi sitting close to Gaṇeśa holding a lotus in her hand and meditating on Gaṇeśa:

पाशाकुंशांभयवरान् दधानं कंजलस्तथा।
पत्न्याश्लिषृं रक्ततनुंत्रिनेत्रं गणपं भजेत्॥

pāśāṁkuśābhayavarān dadhānaṁ kañjalastathā ।
patnyāśliṣṛṁ raktatanuṁtrinetraṁ gaṇapaṁ bhajet ॥
— *Nārada Purāṇa*, III.66.139

The *Gaṇeśa Purāṇa* describes Siddhi and Buddhi as the wives of Gaṇeśa. He is described as the God who bestows Siddhi and Buddhi, i.e. "success" and "knowledge" on men:

भक्तानां वरदं सिद्धिबुद्धिभ्यां सेवितं सदा।
सिद्धिबुद्धिप्रदं नृणां धर्मार्थकाममोक्षदम्॥
ब्रह्मारुद्रहरीन्द्राद्यैः सस्तुतं परमर्षिभिः।

bhaktānāṁ varadaṁ siddhibuddhibhyāṁ sevitaṁ sadā ।
siddhibuddhipradaṁ nṛṇāṁ dharmārthakāmamokṣadam ॥
brahmārudraharīndrādhaiḥ sastutaṁ paramarṣibhiḥ ।
— *Gaṇeśa Purāṇa*, I.49.23-24

Purāṇic Passages Mentioning Siddhi and Buddhi as Wives of Gaṇeśa

Several passages from different Purāṇas describe Siddhi and Buddhi as the wives of

Gaṇeśa. A few references are quoted below:

The *Mudgala Purāṇa* mentions Gaṇeśa as the husband of Siddhi and Buddhi:

सिद्धिबुद्धिपतिं चैव सिद्धिबुद्धिप्रदायकम्।
siddhibuddhipatiṁ caiva siddhibuddhipradāyakam ।
— *Mudgala Purāṇa*, I.38.42

नानासिद्धिप्रदं चैव हृदि बुद्धिप्रकाशकम्॥
nanāsiddhipradaṁ caiva hṛdi buddhiprakāśakam ॥
— *Mudgala Purāṇa*, I.49.28

According to the same Purāṇa, Vināyaka married Siddhi and Buddhi, the two beautiful daughters of the Sage Dharmadatta of Kāśī:

ततो मुनिः सुभावेनापूजयेत्तं विनायकम्।
कन्ये प्रददौ तस्मै सिद्धिबुद्धी सुलक्षणे॥

tato muniḥ subhāvenāpūjayettaṁ vināyakam ।
kanye pradadau tasmai siddhibuddhī sulakṣaṇe ॥
— *Mudgala Purāṇa*, II.57.3

Another passage of the same Purāṇa describes Brahmā giving his daughters Siddhi and Buddhi in marriage to Gaṇeśa:

तत्र ब्रह्मा प्रहर्षेन सस्मार तनये स्वके।
सिद्धिबुद्धि समायते रूपलावण्यसंयुते॥

tatra brahmā praharṣena sasmāra tanaye svake ।
siddhibuddhi samāyate rūpalāvaṇyasaṁyute ॥
— *Mudgala Purāṇa*, VI.41.28

मालां गले गणेशस्य ततश्चिक्षिपतुर्विधिः।
तस्मै समर्पयामास सिद्धिं बुद्धिं विधानतः॥

mālāṁ gale gaṇeśasya tataścikṣipaturvidhiḥ ।
tasmai samarpayāmāsa siddhiṁ buddhiṁ vidhānataḥ ॥
— *Mudgala Purāṇa*, VI.41.35

Ṛddhi and Buddhi as Wives of Gaṇeśa

The *Matsya Purāṇa*, while giving instructions as to the iconography of Gaṇeśa, mentions Ṛddhi instead of Siddhi as one of the wives of Gaṇeśa. However, Buddhi is also described along with Ṛddhi in the text:

युक्तं तु ऋद्धिबुद्धिभ्यामधस्तान्मूषिकान्वितम्।

yuktaṁ tu ṛddhibuddhibhyāmadhastānmūṣikānvitam ।

— *Matsya Purāṇa*, ch. 259.55

Puṣṭi as Wife of Gaṇeśa

The *Brahmavaivartta Purāṇa* mentions Puṣṭi as the wife of Gaṇeśa. Similar reference also occurs in the *Devī Bhāgavata*:

पुष्टिं ददौ विवाहेन गणेशाय महामुने ॥

puṣṭiṁ dadau vivāhena gaṇeśāya mahāmune ॥

— *Brahmavaivartta Purāṇa*, III.18.20b.

यथा शची महेन्द्रे च यथा पुष्टिभगणेश्वरे ।

yathā śacī mahendre ca yathā puṣṭi-gaṇeśvare ।

— *Devī Bhāgavata*, IX.18.18a

The *Mudgala Purāṇa* states Puṣṭi, daughter of Lakṣmī born by penance, was given in marriage to Gaṇeśa:

ततो लक्ष्मीसुता पुष्टिस्तपसा च वभूव ह ।
तां ददौ स गणेशाय विष्णुः परमहर्षितः ॥

tato lakṣmīsutā puṣṭistapasā ca vabhuva ha ।
tāṁ dadau sa gaṇeśāya viṣṇuḥ paramaharṣitaḥ ॥

— *Mudgala Purāṇa*, II.63.38

Śani praises Gaṇeśa as the lord of Puṣṭi:

नमस्ते गणनाथाय पुष्टिकान्ताय ते नमः ।

namaste gaṇanāthāya puṣṭikāntāya te namaḥ ।

— *Mudgala Purāṇa*, II.63.14a

Sons of Gaṇeśa

The *Mudgala Purāṇa*[57] mentions Lakṣa and Lābha as sons of Gaṇeśa from Siddhi and Buddhi, respectively. Lakṣa and Lābha are allotted the responsibility of protecting the devotees of Gaṇeśa and bestowing them desired fruits:

सिद्धिपुत्र (लक्ष) महाभाग मद्भक्तान् रक्ष यत्नतः ।
बुद्धिपुत्रः स्वयं लाभः फलदाता भविष्यति ॥

siddhiputra (lakṣa) mahābhāga madbhaktān rakṣa yatnataḥ ।
buddhiputraṁ svayaṁ lābhaḥ phaladātā bhaviṣyati ॥

— *Mudgala Purāṇa*, II.72.36b, 37a

57 *Mudgala Purāṇa*, II.72.36b, 37a. Cf, VI.13-32.

स्वानन्दनगरं यस्य सिद्धिर्बुद्धिः प्रिये परे ।
लक्षलाभौ सुतौ प्राक्तौ वाहनं मूषिकः परः ॥

svānandanagaraṁ yasya siddhirbuddhiḥ priye pare ।
lakṣalābhau sutau prāktau vāhanaṁ mūṣikaḥ paraḥ ॥

— *Mudgala Purāṇa*, VI.13.32

Conclusion

Dr. Syamakantaji Dwivedi[58] puts forward a philosophical interpretation of Gaṇeśa's marriage with Siddhi, Buddhi and Puṣṭi (Ṛddhi) and says that in the field of spiritual *sādhanā*, the *sādhaka*, after the attainment of *Śivatva* acquires the power of destroying all obstacles. Then all the Puṣṭis (Ṛddhis) and Siddhis (prosperities and successes) come under his control. In other words, as long as the *sādhaka* does not control the world of names and forms and its power of illusion, he cannot be the master of all prosperity, success and knowledge (Puṣṭi (Ṛddhi), Siddhi, Buddhi) and the father of Lakṣa and Lābha.

The idea of the marriage of Gaṇeśa seems late as comparatively older Purāṇas like the *Padma, Matsya, Liṅga* and *Skanda* etc. which depict the life of Gaṇeśa are silent about his married life. Gaṇeśa is shown as an idependent deity detached from his parents' mythology. Orthodox gods like Brahmā and Viṣṇu feel proud of themselves to honour him by giving their daughters in marriage to him. It speaks of a developed sect of Gaṇeśa which gives integrity to his personality by showing him as a family man like other deities of the Hindu pantheon.

The Ucchiṣṭa-Gaṇapati, known as Kāñcī Gaṇeśa alias Bhaṇḍa Gaṇeśa, inside the campus of Puruṣottama Jagannātha temple at Purī, is in *lāṭa-mudrā,* like Umā-Maheśvara and Lakṣmī-Nārāyaṇa images, which are concerned with *haṭha-yoga* of tāntric sex, which is used for pleasure, procreation and *samādhi* purposes.

Swami Vimalānanda and his disciple Robert E. Svoboda,[59] describe the *lāṭa-mudrā*:

> When a man and a woman come together for *lāṭa-mudrā* the woman must sit on the man's left thigh and hold his penis with her right hand. He must cup her left breast with his left hand. Like a creeper she drapes herself

[58] Shyamkantaji Dvivedī, *Sri Gaṇeśa kī Utpatti, Svarūpa aur Sampradāya* (Hindi), Kalyāṇa Varṣa 48, Aṅka 1, p. 129.

[59] Robert E. Svoboda, *Aghora*, New Delhi: Rupa & Co., 1993, pp. 271-72.

around him, clinging tightly like a delicate vine; and he permits himself to be clung to, offering her support.

There are three types of *lāṭa-mudrā*: mundane, spiritual and one which is beyond both the mundane and the spiritual. The mundane gives maximun sexual excitement, the spiritual is for *sādhanā* and "beyond" is too advanced to be dealt with here. In all types the female counts *japa* with her left hand, the male with his right. The *mantra*s are specific for each type. He forgets who he is and she forgets who she is. He thinks, "I am Lord Śiva in the form of Bhairava (the fearful lord), and this is my Śakti, my Bhairavī." She thinks, "This is my Lord Śiva, and I am his grand consort, His Bhairavī (the fearful goddess)."

If the couple is doing it for mundane purposes they must concentrate on exciting each other. Without realizing it she will begin to breathe through her left nostril and will direct that Śakti to him. His right nostril will be working and that Śakti of his will be directed to her. Hypersecretion of all the glands will result, and at the moment of greatest excitation cessation of breathing occurs for a moment. Then the male mounts and discharges his semen convulsively. Because of hypersecretion he will now eject three teaspoonsful of semen as opposed to his normal one teaspoonful. Because the vagina and cervix have become utterly loose and dilated the sperm will go directly to the mouth of the cervix. The result is a child, if this is done at the right time of the month. This is the *brahmacarya* appropriate to the ordinary householder, because by such sex, satiation occurs for a month or more and *ojas* is not wasted by frequent orgasms.

The spiritual *lāṭa-mudrā* is quite different. The Śiva must control his Śakti very carefully to ensure that she does not become sexually excited. The couple should be able to sit together for at least three hours without the least excitation, no twitching or oozing. The girl must understand that she will not get an ordinary orgasm this way. If she waits patiently, she will eventually get a super orgasm: which will make her forget sex for ever. If this *mudrā* is done properly she will go into *bhāva samādhi*. Her emotions will crescendo until her mind becomes totally one-pointed, directed toward Śiva, and she will partly forget her worldly existence for a while. Even *mahābhāva samādhi*, which I call emotional highlight, is possible — total immersion in Śiva but with retained awareness of the bliss. Wonderful!

Haṭha-yoga became popular throughout the country after Mahāyogī

Matsyendranāth reintroduced the proper system and founded the Nātha cult.[60] With the practice of *haṭha-yoga*, the process of spiritual alchemy developed, for it fuses the individual consciousness with the supreme consciousness. It transmutes the mortal into the immortal. Man finds his real nature. It is by looking inside that one discovers the secrets of the universe and the supreme secret.[61] David Gordon White[62] has recently studied "the alchemical body", which centres within the Indian context, of the medieval *siddhas*, which opens the way to a new and more comprehensive understanding of medieval Indian mysticism, within the broader context of South Asian Hinduism, Buddhism, Jainism and Islam. Because of these backgrounds, the tāntric Gāṇapatya cult developed in the medieval period.

Mention may be made of Gaṇapatis found in "Dr. N.K. Sahu Museum", of the Sambalpur University. According to P.K. Nayak,[63] the University Museum contains as many as nine Gaṇapati images both of metal and stone. Out of these nine, seven are made of stone and the rest two of bronze. The Gaṇapatis are: (i) Haridra Gaṇapati, (ii) Vīra Gaṇeśa, (iii) Gaṇeśa in *ardha-paryaṅka* pose, (iv) Unmatta-Ucchiṣṭa-Gaṇapati, (v) Śakti-Gaṇapati, (vi) Bāla-Gaṇapati, (vii) Prasanna-Gaṇapati, (viii) Dhvaja-Gaṇapati, and (ix) Gaṇapati image of poorly cast specimen, which looks crude and meant for catering to the need of the rural worshippers.

About Gaṇeśa in sculptural traditions of Orissa, K.S. Behera[64] is of the opinion that the extant reliefs and single sculptures of Gaṇeśa give us an idea of the iconography and the typical Orissan mode of representation. Gaṇeśa usually appears as a *pārśva-devatā* in a Śiva temple and his depiction without mouse seems to be an earlier convention. The Gaṇeśa images of Orissa generally fall under four categories, Sthānaka, Āsīna, Nṛtta and Devī-Sahita. Several seated and standing forms of Gaṇeśa are known from Bhubaneswar which teems with numerous Śiva temples. Beautiful representations of the seated form are available at Paraśurāmeśvara, Śiśireśvara and other temples. One of the finest standing types of Gaṇeśa is seen in the southern niche of the Liṅgarāja temple. Several *nṛtta mūrtis* (dancing forms) of Gaṇeśa are known from Khichiṅg, Campanāth, Bhubaneswar,

---

60 *HYP*, 1993, pp. 2-3.

61 *ASCITATTOYAK*, 1989, p. 338.

62 David Gordon White, *The Alchemical Body*, New Delhi: Munshiram Manoharlal, 2004, *passim*.

63 P.K. Nayak, "The Ganapati Icons", *New Aspects of History of Orissa*, vol. II, Dept. of History, Sambalpur University, Burla, 1978, pp. 31-35.

64 K.S. Behera, "Traditions in Sculpture", *Art Tradition of Orissa*, Bhubaneswar: Orissa Sahitya Akademi, 1983, pp. 48-49.

Parahat, Algum and other places. Gaṇeśa is shown along with the Devī in a specimen from Jagannātha temple compound. Images of five-headed Gaṇeśa, one in the British Museum and another fixed on the wall of Siddha Mahāvīra temple, illustrate altogether unique iconographic types. Pañcamukha Gaṇeśa is found as mural painting in the Jagamohana of Lakṣmī temple, inside the Puruṣottama Jagannātha temple compound at Purī. According to H.D. Bhattacharyya,[65] even a five-faced Gaṇeśa, in imitation of his five-faced (*pañcānana*) father, has been unearthed both in Orissa and in the ruins of Rāmpāl (Dacca).

Gaṇeśa image assigned to seventh century CE in the Someśvara temple, Jajpur,[66] deserves a special mention, because the image is a rare Śakti-Gaṇapati. Gaṇeśa is depicted, raising his Śakti by his trunk.

---

[65] H.D. Bhattacharyya, "Gaṇeśa", *THACOTIP*, vol. IV, *The Age of Imperial Kanauj*, 1964, p. 345.

[66] Nrusinha Charan Behuria (chief ed.), *Orissa State Gazetteer, Orissa state*, vol. II, Cuttack, 1991, p. 445.

7

Mattamayūra Śaivism in Mahānadī Valley

MATTAMAYŪRA was a sect or cult of Śaivism, which had much impact on the socio-religious life of Indians during the medieval period, because the *siddha* Śaiva *ācārya*s of this sect had established their spiritual yogic centres, from the Himalayan belt in North India to the Kanda region in South India.

The earliest reference to the name "Mattamayūra", is found in the Sabhā-Parva of *Mahābhārata* (II.32.4-5) as the *Mattamayūra* kṣatriya tribes of Rohitaka region adjoining Delhi, who fought against the Pāṇḍavas, for autonomy of their lands. Because of this reference N.K. Sahu[1] and S.C. Behera[2] are of the opinion that Mattamayūra Śaivācāryas were spread from the Rohitaka region. R.P. Mishra[3] defines this and mentions that he had an opportunity of having a discussion with late Sri Dinabandhu Badpanda, a prolific astrologer of the village Pankeldadar near Binka. Sri Badpanda while voicing an analysis on the nature and definition of *kāla* in astrology had expressed a few points on Śaivism, antiquity of the *liṅga* of the Kapileśvara temple of Charada near Binka and on Mattamayūra Śaivism from an old palm-leaf manuscript called *Kapileśa-Māhātmya.* All his points recited in Sanskrit verses naturally allured me to obtain the manuscript. But in spite of several approaches at his door, all attempts ended in fiasco. The verses, cited by Sri Badpanda during his discussion were as follows:

vr̥ndārakairūpāsitaṁ mattamayūraḥ saṁjñitaṁ
dr̥śyate sthāṇuliṅgoyaṁ kadamba sumabāsitam ।
kurutūrthe kurukṣetre koṣavane manorame
asmintīrthe bhavam dhātvā naraḥ mucyate kilviṣai ॥

---

[1] N.K. Sahu, *Oḍiā Jātira Itihāsa* (Oriya), Part I, Bhubaneswar: Orissa State Bureau of Text Book Preparation and Production, 1974, p. 343.

[2] S.C. Behera, *Rise and Fall of the Sailodbhavas,* Calcutta: Punthi Pustak, 1982, p. 173.

[3] R.P. Mishra, "Mattamayūra Śaivism in Orissa", *Culture and Collections,* Calcutta: Punthi Pustak, 1996, pp. 109-10.

If at all, these verses are believed to have been impregnated with truth then it will be a fact that the Mattamayūra Śaivism originated in the Koṣatraya forest of Kurutīrtha near Kurukṣetra with the enshrinement of a *liṅga* called Mattamayūra. The Nāthas, who generally believe the Śaivāgamas based on Siddhānta doctrine as their sacred religious texts, assign the nomenclature Siddhamata or "Siddhānta" to their centripetal religious doctrines.[4] They also delineate the beautiful Koṣatraya forest near Kurukṣetra as the seat of their primal Lord Śiva, called Ādinātha.

The genealogy of the Śaiva Ācāryas of the Mattamayūra clan prepared by V.V. Miradhi[5] is shown on page 97. According to R.P. Mishra,[6] many of the Śaiva ascetics enlisted in the Mattamayūra Śaivācārya tradition appeared to have been associated with the Śaivite cultures of Orissa. Kadambaguhādhivāsin Mattamayūra Śaivācārya means a Mattamayūra Śaiva ascetic who had his abode in a cave called Kadambaguhā. Kadambaguhā is identified as Kadwaha in Madhya Pradesh by some of the scholars while few other scholars identify it with Kadambagiri of the Rīṭāpur copper plates of Bhavattavarman.[7] But as in Sanskrit language *guhā* means a cave and the ascetics of ancient India used to live in the caves of mountains, this Kadambaguhā may resonably be identified with the cave of a mountain. Either the locality Kadwaha or the village Kadambagiri cannot be identified with Kadambaguhā. Śaṅkhamaṭhikādhipati means master of Śaṅkhamaṭhika. This *maṭhika* or *maṭha* may reasonably be identified with the famous Śaṅkhākāra Maṭha of the Āsanapaṭ stone inscription of the King Śatrubhañja of Nāga ruling dynasty.[8] This Śaṇkhākāra Maṭha was located in Ahicchatraka[9] which is identified with the modern Ramnagar of Bareilly district of Uttar Pradesh. As from the palaeographical standpoint, the Āsanapaṭ stone inscriptions were placed in the fourth century CE and as in this lithic record Śatrubhañja figures as a donor of abundant charity, it is conclusive that this *maṭha* had already been established in its glory and grandeur by the fourth century CE. As there are records of prayers of the Naṭarāja countenance of Lord Śiva,[10] in the Candrehe stone inscriptions of Prabodhaśiva, the Ranod stone

[4] R.P. Mishra, "Mattamayūra Śaivism in Orissa", *Culture and Collections*, Calcutta: Punthi Pustak, 1996, Pūrṇanāthjī, *Gorakṣha Siddhānta Saṁgraha* (Hindi), p. 151.

[5] *IHQ*, vol. XXVI, no. 1, pp. 1-10; *OHRJ*, vol. III, no. 2, p. 69.

[6] R.P. Mishra, op. cit., pp. 111-19.

[7] Ibid.; *OHRJ*, vol. III, no. 2, p. 69; N.K. Sahu, op. cit., pp. 341-42.

[8] Ibid.; S.N. Rajguru, *Oḍishā-ra-Itihāsa*, pt. I (Oriyā), Cuttack: Grantha Mandir, 1985, p. 278; *OHRJ*, vol. XIII, no. 2, pp. 1-18 (Āsanapaṭ Stone Inscription edited).

[9] Ibid. (both).

[10] Ibid.; *EI*, vol. XXI, p. 149, vol. I, pp. 354-55 and vol. I, p. 254.

Chart 1: The Genealogy of the Śaiva Ācāryas of the Mattamayūra Clan

Kadambaguhādhivāsin
(The inhabitant of Kadambaguhā)
↓
Śaṅkhamaṭhikādhipati
(The Lord of Śaṅkhamaṭhikā)
↓
Terambipāla
(The protector of Terambi)
↓
Āmardakatīrthanātha
(The Lord of Amardakatīrtha alias Rudraśiva)
↓
Purandara alias Mattamayūranātha

- Kavacaśiva
  ↓ Sadāśiva
  ↓ Hydayeśa
  ↓ Vyomaśiva (Gaganaśiva I)
  ↓ Pataṅga Śambhu
- Dharmaśambhu
  ↓ Sadāśiva
  ↓ Purandra alias Madhumateya
  ↓ Cūḍāśiva
  - Hṛdayaśiva
    ↓ Aghoraśiva
  - Prabhāvaśiva
    ↓ Praśāntaśiva
    - Īśānaśiva
      ↓ Gaganaśiva II
    - Prabodhaśiva (CE 972)

inscriptions of Yaśovarman and the Bilhari stone inscription of Cedi kings, it is invariably believed that this form of Śiva had accumulating popularity among the adherents of Mattamayūra Śaivism.

In the Mattamayūra Śaiva centre, Rāṇīpur-Jharial, a Naṭarāja image is found seated in the centre of the Yoginī-Pīṭha of this place. In the upper portion of the Āsanapaṭ stone inscriptions, an image of Naṭarāja Śiva is found inscribed conspicuously. Mantric adoration of Lord Śiva is a prominent feature of Mattamayūra Śaivism. For this, the Śaivācāryas of this Śaivite school were not only reciting the Śaiva *mantras* but were also composing *mantras* with a meditative perception.[11] Verse XXIII of the Ranod stone inscriptions records the testimony about the composition of *mantra* by the ascetics and preceptors of this school.[12] In the Āsanapaṭ stone inscriptions, Śatrubhañja is endowed with the epithets, *mahārudrasya caturbhī yugānta cala kīrtti* and *lakṣamantradhāraṇaikadakṣaḥ.*[13] In significance of his epithet *lakṣamantradhāraṇaikadakṣaḥ,* Śatrubhañja may be described to have been initiated into several *mantras*. All these facts traceable from the Āsanapaṭ stone inscriptions have much in common with the features of Mattamayūra Śaivism and on these affinities Śatrubhañja, the donor of these inscriptions, may reasonably be accepted as a devotee of Mattamayūra Śaivism. Possibly from the time of Śatrubhañja, the king of Vindhyāṭavi Kingdom in the fourth century CE, Mattamayūra Śaivism began to exercise its influence on the culture of Orissa. Kadambaguhā was most probably a cave in the mountainous region of north India in a reliable nearness with *Ahicchatraka*.

> The exact time of the efflorescene of the Mattamayūra Śaiva ascetics delineated in the above Mattamayūra Śaivācārya tradition is yet a controversial issue in the pages of history. Scholars profess diametrically opposite views with regard to their time of efflorescene. Although no source materials became available to upraise the iron curtain of mutual anthithesis among the scholars it appears reasonable to believe that the Śaiva ascetics Kadambaguhādhivāsin and Śaṅkhamaṭhikādhipati remained efflorescent in the intervening period from CE 340 to 425. Most possibly Śatrubhañja travelled to Śaṅkhākāra Maṭha of Ahicchatraka towards the closing years of fourth century CE when Kadambaguhādhivāsin had already experienced the separation of his body and soul and his disciple Śaṅkhamaṭhikādhipati

[11] R.P. Mishra, op. cit., *EI*, vol. I, pp. 351-56.

[12] *EI*, vol. I, verse 23 of Ranod Stone Inscription.

[13] Ibid.; S.N. Rajguru, op. cit., p. 278. Pariśiṣṭa (kha).

had risen to prominence. The author is inclined to place the time of Kadambaguhādhivāsin from CE 300 to 350 and that of his disciple from CE 340 to 425. The image of a Śaiva saint inscribed at the right hand side of the image of Naṭarāja Śiva on the Āsanapaṭ stone inscription may be identified with Śaṅkhamaṭhikādhipati. The Śaivācārya Terambipāla succeeded Śaṅkhamaṭhikādhipati and may be suggested as an ascetic of fifth century CE. This Terambipāla who had his *maṭha* or monastery in Terahi of Madhya Pradesh was prominent for preaching this Śaivism in the Central Province of India. He most probably lived from CE 400 to 480. Rudraśambhu of Mattamayūra Śaivācārya tradition was popularly known as Amardakātīrthanātha. The place Amardaka Tīrtha is acquainted with Amod in Madhya Pradesh by some scholars, but this identification does not appear reasonable. Amardaka Tīrtha is described in the Senakapaṭ stone inscription of Mahāśivagupta Bālārjuna,[14] in the Saurashtra Haddala copper plate in Śaka era CE 836 or 914[15] and in the Rajorgaṛh stone inscription[16] of Rajasthan in Vikrama Saṁvata CE 1016 or 959. This Amardaka may be identified with Amarda in Mayūrbhañj district of Orissa. In this Amarda, the Gaganeśvara Śiva temple was found in a good condition until the Muslim rule in Orissa. The Someśvara temple constructed by Gaganaśiva II in Rāṇīpur-Jharial displays an inscription on the upper portion of the doorway of the chamber where the Someśvara-*liṅga* is found enshrined. In this inscription Śiva is prayed as *gaganaikastavyaṁ prabhuḥ*.[17] As the word *gagana* denoting sky occurs commonly in Gaganaśiva, Gaganeśvara and in the above-noted inscriptions and as in Mattamayūra Śaiva theology Lord Śiva is conceived as illimitable and omnipresent as the all-pervading sky, the Gaganeśvara Śiva worship in Amarda may be conceived of as a product of Mattamayūra Śaiva influence. Most possibly the Śiva temple of Gaganeśvara in Amarda was built with the effort of Āmardakātīrthanātha Rudra-Śambhū in the closing part of fifth century CE. Rudra-Śambhū may be believed to have been alive in between CE 450 and 500. The Śaiva ascetic Mattamayūranātha Purandara was the disciple of this Rudra-Śambhu. It may be believed that Purandara assumed the honorific title Mattamayūranātha, at the time of his initiation to this Śaivism in Amarda by his preceptor Rudra-Śambhu. He may be believed to be the founder of Rāṇīpadra penance-grove in Rāṇīpur-Jharial in the first-half of sixth century CE.[18] In his presiding supervision the

---

14 R.P. Mishra, op. cit.; *EI*, vol. XXXI, pp. 31-36.

15 Ibid.; *Indian Antiquary*, vol. XII, pp. 190 ff.

16 Ibid.; *EI*, vol. III, pp. 266 ff.

17 Ibid.; *EI*, vol. XXIV, p. 239.

18 Ibid.; *EI*, vol. I, pp. 351-56. Ranod Stone Inscription, verse 15.

Siddheśvara temple in Rāṇīpadra might have been built with the enshrinement of *liṅga* named Siddheśvara Śiva in adherence to the practice of *siddhānta* theories. Siddheśvara of Someśvara temple inscription of Rāṇīpur-Jharial is identified by Puṇḍit Kedarnath Mahapatra as Lord Buddha by mistake.[19] On his erroneous identification Mahapatra has been inclined to acquaint the image of a contemplative ascetic at the door wall of the *garbha-gṛha* or the sanctum as the image of Lord Buddha.[20] As this image is found seated in a meditative pose, as there is a sign of semi-circular moon over the head of this image and the image is found embellished with a sacred thread or *yajñopavīta* on its body, it is undoubtedly an image of a Śaiva-ascetic within the fold of orthodox Brāhmanism or Vedicism and can in no way be an image of Lord Buddha. As the gesture shown by this image indicates a praying pose towards Lord Someśvara, it is also not the image of Siddheśvara Śiva as narrated in Someśvara temple inscription. It is undoubtedly the image of a Śaiva *saṁnyāsī* and most probably that of Īśāna-Śambhu, the preceptor of the architect of this temple. It is possible that Siddheśvara Śiva described in later Someśvara temple inscription was worshipped in this place in a different temple at the centre of this place the remains of which are seen at present at the centre of the huge rockbed of this place. These remains present a dumb witness to the worship of Siddheśvara Śiva in a temple constructed by Mattamayūranātha Purandara who most probably travelled from this place to Avantī and initiated the king of Avantī into Mattamayūra Śaivism.[21] He may be believed to have been prominent in the first half of sixth century CE. From this time onward the adoration of Siddeśvara appears to have acquired popularity in this place and centring around his veneration, the tāntric cult of Siddha Yogeśvarī Cāmuṇḍā in seventh century CE and *siddhi*-conferring *yoginī*s evolved in the later part of eigth or opening part of ninth century CE. In a corner of this huge rockbed the image of Cāmuṇḍā is found inscribed on a large stone on one side and on the opposite side of this large stone the inscribed images of Saptamātṛkās, Gaṇeśa and Vīrabhadra are observed clearly. As this Cāmuṇḍā is found seated on a corpse holding in her hand a pot of wine and munching a piece of bone besides other traditional features, as Vīrabhadra is marked with a corpse as his vehicle and as in the Yoginī-Pīṭha of this place the *yoginī*s display poses of exhilarated dancing around the image of Naṭarāja Śiva it is believed that the Vāmācārin tāntric cult was also efflorescent in

19 *OHRJ*, vol. III, no. 2, p. 71.

20 Ibid.

21 Ibid.; S.C. Behera, op. cit., 1982, p. 172, fn. 60.

this place assigning centripetal importance to Lord Siddheśvara. This tāntric trend most probably developed in ninth century CE although the worship of Siddheśvara was established from sixth century CE. Mattamayūra Śaiva ascetics Kavacaśiva, Sadāśiva and Hṛdayaśiva may be confided to have been prominent in this school of Śaivism in the later half of sixth century CE. Śadāśiva is believed to have performed his penance in Rāṇīpadra or Rāṇīpur-Jharial.[22] Vyomaśiva of the above-noted Śaivācārya tradition was the disciple of Hṛdayaśiva. He is believed to have ascended to the acme of popularity in the first half of seventh century CE in the penance-grove of Rāṇīpadra. His time of consecration to popularity is fixed erroneously by Paṇḍit Kedarnath Mahapatra in the periphery of ninth century CE.[23] Paṇḍit Guṇaratna and Rājaśekhara suggest the composition of *Vyomavatī* or *Vyomamatī* commentary by this Vyomaśiva on the *Praśastapādabhāṣya* of Vaiśeṣika philosophy.[24] The time of the rise of Guṇaratna and Rājaśekhara are generally assigned in tenth century CE although a scholar has unreasonably suggested this time as fourteenth century CE.[25] As the time of Guṇaratna and Rājaśekhara does not precede tenth century CE it is logical to assign the duration of the composition of *Vyomavatī* and that of the rise of its author before tenth century CE. But priority to tenth century CE does not particularize ninth century CE. It may mean any century before tenth century CE. Paṇḍit Mahapatra, to comprise the time of *Vyomavatī* as also of its author misinterprets the word *śaṅkara*, in verse 37 of Ranod stone inscriptions of King Yaśovarmā in the significance of Śaṅkarācārya. But as this verse is recorded as *sarvajñaḥ spuṭa meṣa kopi bhagavān anya kṣitau śaṅkaraḥ*,[26] and as the word *śaṅkara* in this verse is not accompanied either with the prefix or suffix *ācārya*, it is a gross mistake to accept this word as a synonym of Śaṅkarācārya of ninth century CE in the absence of distinctive particularization. As this verse suggests, Śaivācārya Vyomaśiva had attained the status of omni intelligent Lord Śiva because of his yogic perfection. Hence in this verse he is compared with Lord Śiva, and not with Śaṅkarācārya of ninth century CE and on this reasonable ground it may be asserted that neither can he be

22 *OHRJ*, *EI*, vol. I, pp. 351-56. Ranod Stone Inscription, verse 17.

23 *OHRJ*, vol. III, no. 2, September 1954, p. 68.

24 *IHQ*, vol. X, 1974, p. 165.

25 Ibid.; S.N. Dasgupta, *A History of Indian Philosophy*, vol. V, pp. 8 and 15; *Kāvyamīmāṁsā* (G.O.S. Baroda), no. 1, p. XXXI.

26 Ibid.; *EI*, vol. I, pp. 351-56, verse 37 of Ranod Stone Inscription quoted by Pt. K.N. Mahapatra in *OHRJ*, vol. III, no. 2, September 1954, p. 68.

called the second Śaṅkarācārya nor can he be placed in ninth century CE. Further in the *Śāṅkarabhāṣya, Śaiva Siddhānta* is blamed as anti-Upaniṣadic in nature.[27] As Mattamayūra Śaivism is a school of Śaiva Siddhāntas, it must have been blamed by Śaṅkarācārya as anti-Upaniṣadic and anti-Vedic. On the Vaiśeṣika philosophy, Praśastapāda wrote his commentary in fifth century CE.[28] According to Ranod stone inscription of Yaśovarman,[29] Vyomaśiva elucidated the real definition of matter having composed *Vyomavatī* commentary on *Praśastapādabhāṣya*. As with the rise of sun the darkness disappears and the entire world becomes visible with light, the *Vyomavatī* commentary according to this inscription removed ignorance and revealed the real definition and nature of matter. Śaṅkarācārya refuted the atomism of Vaiśeṣika philosophy.[30] Vyomaśiva, a protagonist of Vaiśeṣika philosophy and also its theory of atomism, an exponent in giving the reasonable definition of matter and an advocate of Siddhānta theory must not have been compared with Śaṅkarācārya even at a much later date of the exposition of the Ranod inscription. A patron of Vaiśeṣika philosophy, he must not have been compared with Ācārya Śaṅkara, an antagonist of that philosophy even at a later date by the Mattamayūra Śaivas. As Vyomaśiva was the preceptor of Pataṅgaśambhu who may be identified with Pataṅgaśiva of Dharmaliṅgeśvara copper plates of the Eastern Gaṅga King Devendravarman, it seems logical to believe that Vyomaśiva flourished in first half of seventh century CE and during this period he composed *Vyomavatī* and several *mantras* in the penance-grove of Rāṇīpadra.[31] With the effort of this eminent recluse, the Mattamayūra Śaivism attained popularity in many parts of Orissa and Madhya Pradesh. S.C. Behera considers the God Śiva invoked and prayed to by the Śailodbhava king at the opening of their several charters as Mattamayūra Śiva because in consistence with his suggestion, it is observed that Lord Śiva narrated in Buguḍa copper plates of King Mādhavavarman differs from the Pāśupata Śiva described in *Ṣaḍdarśanasamuccaya,* of Ācārya Haribhadra in appearance, attire and ornaments.[32] The features of Śiva delineated in this Buguḍa copper plates maintan a resemblance with those of Śiva prayed to in Khaṇḍipada Nuāpalli

---

27 *IHQ,* S.N. Dasgupta, *A History of Indian Philosophy,* vol. V, p. 70.

28 Ibid.; A.L. Basham, *The Wonder that Was India,* London: Sidgwick and Jackson, 1969, p. 326.

29 Ibid.; *EI,* vol. I, pp. 351-56. Ranod Stone Inscription, verse 23.

30 Ibid.; A.L. Basham, op. cit., p. 499.

31 Ibid.; *EI,* vol. I, pp. 351-56, Ranod Stone Inscriptions, verses 23 and 32.

32. Ibid.; S.C. Behera, *Rise and Fall of the Sailodbhavas,* op. cit., 1982, pp. 169-75.

copper plate[33] of Caramparāja Ayaśobhīta I who flourished in seventh century CE and this Śaivism enjoyed royal patronage of the Śailodbhavas most probably owing to the influence of Amardaka and preaching of the prolific Śaivite scholar Vyomaśiva.

Pataṅgaśambhu in the Mattamayūra Śaivācārya tradition figures as disciple of Vyomaśiva. According to Dharmaliṅgeśvara copper plates of Devendravarman, the Eastern Gaṅga king of Kaliṅga, he is described as a scholar of Veda, Vedāṅga, Itihāsa, Purāṇas and Nyāya and a genius of Siddhānta theories of his school.[34] He, according to this charter, initiated King Devendravarman into his Śaivism and accepted the village Haḍuvaka in Puṣpagiri Pāñcālī Viṣaya as a charity in view of his initiation from this king.[35] From the land grant that he received, he donated half of the area of lands for the worship of Yogeśvara-Śiva and the residue to his disciples and thus maintained the lofty ideal of Indian asceticism in a conspicuous sincerity.[36] His disciples as it is known from this charter lived happily in Kaliṅga accepting these gifts with the pleasure of their preceptor[37] and became helpful in promoting the cause of Mattamayūra Śaivism. This Pataṅgaśiva is identified with Pataṅgaśambhu of Mattamayūra Śaivācārya tradition. Dharmaliṅgeśvara copper plates were issued in Gaṅga era 184 which may correspond to the Christian year CE 682.[38] Pataṅgaśambhu or Pataṅgaśiva also played an active role in spreading this Śaivism in Koṅgodamaṇḍala. Mahāśivagupta Bālārjuna the Pāṇḍuvaṁśī alias Sōmavaṁśī King of South Kosala was also a devoted patron of this Śaivism. He began his rule in South Kosala in the last phase of eighth century CE.[39] In the 57th year of his reign he issued his Lodhia copper plates.[40] According to this copper plate inscription, Ācārya Śūlapāṇi came to South Kosala from Pañcayajña penance grove of Dvaitavana near Delhi and Kurukṣetra region and accepted land grant for the worship of Īśāneśvara Śiva enshrined in a temple of Khadirapadraka. The villages Vaidyapadraka and Khadirapadraka narrated in this copper plate may be identified with Vanjipadar and

[33] *IHQ*, pp. 70-71: *EI*, vol. XXVI, pp. 62-65.

[34] Ibid.

[35] Ibid.

[36] Ibid.

[37] Ibid.

[38] *EI*, vol. XXVI, pp. 62-64 and *Inscriptions of Orissa*, vol. II, pp. 69-71.

[39] *Inscriptions of Orissa*, vol. IV, 1966, p. 354.

[40] Ibid.; *EI*, vol. XXVII, pp. 319-25.

> Khairpadar near Rāṇīpadra or Rāṇīpur–Jharial. Śūlapāṇi also seems to have played a significant role in spreading Mattamayūra Śaivism in South Kosala. The Senakapaṭ inscriptions of Mahāśivagupta Bālārjuna while recording a graphic description of the dancing of Naṭarāja Śiva also suggest the advent of Sadāśivācārya from Amardaka to South Kosala.[41] As Amardaka played a vital role for disseminating Mattamayūra Śaiva culture this Sadāśaiva is also believed as a Mattamayūra sage age. From the standpoint of historical chronology this Sadāśiva seems different from the Śaiva saint of consemblent nomenclature in Mattamayūra Śaivācārya tradition. The role of this Śaiva ascetic is also worth accountable for the growth of this Śaivism in South Kosala.

This narration of R.P. Mishra gives a comprehensible view of the impact or role of Mattamayūra Śaivism in the Mahānadī River Valley during early medieval period. But the author does not agree with the view of R.P. Mishra that *siddhi*-conferring *yoginī*s evolved in the later part of eighth or opening part of the ninth century CE. As discussed in earlier chapters the *yoginī*s had already evolved during proto and ancient Indian historical periods.

The *ācārya*s of the Mattamayūra Śaiva sect preached their doctrine in the entire Mahānadī River Valley. Many tāntric Śaiva temples were built during the reign of Pāṇḍuvaṁśī king Mahāśivagupta Bālārjuna, which came to be known as the "Kosalī style of Rekha temple architecture", in the upper Mahānadī Valley.[42]

Because of the development of Kosalī style of Rekha temple architect in South Kosala, i.e. the upper Mahānadī River region, the author[43] had expressed the view, after comparative study, that the Kosalī style of temple architecture was developed in South Kosala during the early Somavaṁśī rule and influenced the neighbouring territories. Thus, it influenced the Mukteśvara temple of Bhubaneswar, the temple within the Nurpur fort and the thousand pillar temple of Warangal.[44] It seems, the Kosalī style of temple architecture had influenced the Lakṣmaṇa temple at Sirpur and the Indralath temple at Rāṇīpur-Jharial, to some extent, as these temples also consist of the sanctum proper and *maṇḍapa* in front, with an antechamber (*antarāla*)

---

[41] *Inscriptions of Orissa, EI,* vol. XXXI, pp. 31-36, verses 1 and 17.

[42] J.P. Singh Deo, *Cultural Profile of South Kosala,* Delhi: Gyan Publishing House, 1987, pp. 152-58 and 329-32; J.P. Singh Deo, *Tāntric Art of Orissa,* Delhi: Kalpaz Publications, 2001, pp. 86 and 175-79; *THOMV,* pp. 185-10.

[43] J.P. Singh Deo, "Kosalī Style of Temple Architecture", *OHRJ,* vols. XXIV, XXV and XXVI, pp. 175-76.

[44] Ibid.; *Caravan,* June (First), 1977, no. 60, p. 52.

connecting the two. The *kumbha*-shaped mouldings of Kosalī style of temples connecting the *maṇḍapa* and the *antarāla* of these two temples are practically the same. The pillared *maṇḍapa* of the Indralath temple has fallen since long. Its scattered stone pillars are now used as seats by the Orissa State Archaeology. Some influence is also noticeable between the Kosalī style of temples and the temples of *pañcaratha* plan, when the sharp edges of the early Kosalī style rounded up in later years. The Nīlakaṇṭheśvara temple of Dadpur, Kālāhāṇḍī, is a stone structure and seems to be a late medieval structure, with the influence of Kosalī style of temple architecture in its plan. Here, it will be interesting to note the view of K.S. Behera, on the Brāhmanical temples of Orissa, under the Somavaṁśīs. While giving the account, Behera[45] mentions that the Somavaṁśīs, who succeeded the Bhauma-Karas, came from South Kosala, but they did not introduce any unfamiliar line of development in art and architecture. The pillared *maṇḍapa* of the Kosaleśvara temple at Baidyanātha district Bolaṅgīr (now Sonepur), with lateral trancepts and large sculptures in the interior, suggests that when the Somavaṁśīs were ruling in the upper Mahānadī Valley, there was some central Indian influence on the temple architecture but as they proceeded towards the coastal region, they strengthened the traditional temple style. Here, it is to be noted that there was influence on the plan of Kosalī style of temple architecture.

> As mentioned above, the number of intersecting squares developed particularly in the Cāḷukyan monuments of the eleventh-twelfth centuries CE in Gujarat. Even in the Hoysaḷa temples of Mysore the star-shaped plan becomes the usual fashion.[46] The maturity of structure influenced each other to such an extent that Cāḷukya–Hoysaḷa school of architecture gradually developed in eleventh, twelfth and thirteenth centuries CE. This shows the plan of intersecting two squares of Kosalī style of early phase to have prevalence over these styles of architecture later.

While dealing with "Progress of the Śaiva Siddhānta System: Śaivism in South Kosala", L.K. Panda[47] narrates erroneously:

> Purandara's disciple, Dharmaśambhu, is not mentioned in any of the available Somavaṁśī inscriptions. But Dharmaśambhu's disciple Sadāśiva[48]

45 J.P. Singh Deo, "Kosalī Style of Temple Architecture", *Orissa Review — Monument Special*, January 1976, p. 60.

46 Ibid.; *THACOTIP*, vol. V, *The Struggle for Empire*, 2nd edn., 1966, p. 24.

47 L.K. Panda, *Śaivism in Orissa*, Delhi: Sundeep Prakashan, 1985, pp. 89-90.

48 Ibid.; see line 14 of *Inscriptions of Orissa*, vol. IV, p. 49.

> seems to be identical with Sadāśivācārya of the Senakpaṭ inscription. It is likely that Sadāśivācārya was very young when he proceeded to Śripura, the capital of South Kosala, along with his great-grand teacher Rudraśiva Ācārya of Amardaka fame. Sadāśiva's disciple, Purandara was the founder of the School of Madhumatteya.[49] In this line there flourished the great Śaivite teacher Prabhavaśiva, same as Sadbhavaśambhu,[50] who established the tradition of Golakī Maṭha. This Śaivite tradition was very much prevalent in the south. A branch of the Golakī Maṭha was established at Bherāghāṭ about 10 miles from Tripurī, the Kaḷacuri capital. In accordance with the ideology of the Golakī Maṭha the tāntric temple of Sixty-four Yoginīs was established in that Śaivite centre. In the line of Prabhavaśiva there flourished the towering Śaiva ascetic called Gaganaśiva II,[51] the disciple of Īśānaśambhu who possibly carried the tradition of Golakī Maṭha from Tripurī to Kosala. Inspired by the ideology of these Sixty-four Yoginīs of Bherāghāṭ, Gaganaśiva II seems to have built a similar shrine of Sixty-four Yoginīs at Rāṇīpur-Jharial by the side of the temple of Someśvara near Titilagaṛh in the Bolaṅgīr district of Orissa. There are only four Yoginī temples in India, the other two being at Khajurāho in Madhya Pradesh and Hirapur near Bhubaneswar. All these four temples appear to have been built within a range of about one century. Gaganaśiva II is known to us from the Someśvara temple inscriptions,[52] located at Rāṇīpur-Jharial. The Śaiva Siddhānta School of the line of Kadambaguhāvāsī which passed through several phases in course of its evolution, resulted in the manifestation of the Tāntric form of Śaivism with Rāṇīpadra identified with Rāṇīpur as the nerve centre of this system.

Panda seems to have no idea of the *yoginī* cult and its founder, therefore comes this wrong view. As studied in earlier chapters, the *yoginīs* had early origin in proto-historic *Mahābhārata* period and their *yoga* is related with the *yoga* of sexual transformation. Hence H.C. Das[53] is very correct when he states that Matsyendranāth, in view of popularity of the *yoginī* cult gained over the period, systematized and expounded it in his famous work *Kaulayānanirṇaya*, which has become the authoritative text of the cult. The great *yogī* Matsyendranāth was the

---

49 L.K. Panda, *IHQ*, vol. XXVI, no. 1, p. 16.

50 Ibid.

51 Ibid.

52 Ibid.; *EI*, vol. XXIV, p. 239.

53 H.C. Das, *Tāntricism: A Study of Yogini Cult*, New Delhi: Sterling Publishers, 1981, p. 3.

founder of Nāthism or the Nātha cult. So, in no way the Mattamayūra Śaivism and their Śaivācārya tradition, which was *siddhānta* doctrine of ancient Śaivāgamas, according to Mādhavācārya,[54] had anything to do with the *yoginī* cult.

Mattamayūra Śaivism has become extinct throughout the Mahānadī River Valley now.

54 V.S. Sharma, *The Sarvadarśana Saṁgraha of Mādhavācārya*, Varanasi: Chokhamba Vidya Bhavan, 1964, pp. 297-390, chs. VI-IX.

8

Kosalī Style of Temple Architecture

THE style of temple architecture had developed in South Kosala, the administrative state of ancient and medieval periods of Indian history, comprising the upper Mahānadī River Valley. The earliest text on the Orissan temple architecture is *Bhuvana-Pradīpa*.[1] While naming thirty-six types of Rekha temples, this text mentions one variety as "Kosalī", and three as Khākharā temple styles. The description of Kosalī Khākharā temple[2] is given here:

(क) कोसोलि भाग ६० रथक ९ शिखर
नास्ति रेख गुण खाखरा खखर ५ ॥
(रथक) ५-५-८-८ मेलाण ३ (?) । १११०-१११०-१= (शेष पृष्ठा)

(ग) ए कासील भाग ६० रथक ६ सिखर नास्ति
रेखगुणाघाठ ३० (६८ पृ:)
कोसलिभाग ६० रथक ९ सिखर नास्ति
रेखगुलखाखर (रथक) ५-५-४-६-६
(मेलाण) २-२१११०-१११०-१=०-(?) (१८२ पृ:)
कोसल भाग ६० रथक ९ सिखर नास्ति
रेखगुण खखर (रथक) ? (मेलाण)
२-१-१११०-११० (१८३ पृ:)
कोसली भा १८ रथक भा ५ सिखर नास्ति
रेखगुणीघाठ ४ (रथक) ३-३-२-३ (मेलाण)
२-१-११० (२०२ पृ:)

(ka) *kosoli bhāga* 60 *rathaka* 9 *śikhara*
nāsti rekhā guṇa khākharā khakhara 5 ॥
(*rathaka*) 5-5-8-8 *melāṇa* 3 (?), 1110-1110-1= (*śaṣa pṛṣṭhā*)

---

[1] N.K Bose, *Canons of Orissan Architecture*, New Delhi: Cosmo Publications, 1982, p. 124.

[2] Ibid., pp. 172-73; Nirmal Kumar Bose, *Orissa Architecture*, Calcutta, 1931, p. 124 and pp. 172-73; J.P. Singh Deo, *Cultural Profile of South Kosala*, Delhi: Gyan Publishing House, 1987, pp. 331-32.

(ga) *e kāsīla bhāga* 60 *rathaka* 6 *sikhara nāsti*
rekhaguṇāghāṭha 30 (68 *pṛ.*)
kosalibhāga 60 *rathaka 9 sikhara nāsti*
rekhagulakhākhara (*rathaka*) 5-5-4-6-6
(*melāṇa*) 2-2110-1110-1=0-(?) (182 *pṛ.*)
kosala bhāga 60 *rathaka* 9 *sikhara nāsti*
rekhaguṇa khakhara (*rathaka*) ? (*melāṇa*)
1-1-1110-110 (183 *pṛ.*)
kosali bhā 18 *rathaka bhā* 5 *sikhara nāsti*
rekhaguṇāghāṭha 4 (*rathaka*) 3-3-2-3 (*melāṇa*)
2-1-110 (202 *pṛ.*)

The Kosalī consists of 60 *bhāgas*, 9 *rathakas*. It has no *śikharas*. The *rathakas* are in the ratio of 5–5–4–6–6, their projections being 6–1–¾–½ *ān*.

Indian, i.e. Bhāratīya, religious Sanskrit literatures and arts have spiritual symbolism, which is not easily understood by lay academic scholars, whose spread is only the educative knowledge. One should have intuitive knowledge to understand them.

One example can be given of the late Jagadguru Śrī Śaṅkarācārya, His Holiness Bhāratī Kṛṣṇa Tīrtha of the Govardhana Maṭha in Purī. He was a scholar of great repute and a revered spiritual leader of millions of Hindus. His Holiness gave an intimation of the less-than-obvious meanings that could be drawn from Sanskrit literature and his unique discovery of the whole science of mathematics in sixteen seemingly unrelated verses in the *Atharvaveda*. The renowned Śaṅkarācārya, found in these *ślokas* of the *Atharvaveda*, the *Gaṇita Sūtras* — which have been dismissed by many Western scholars as "unintelligible nonsense" — unique formulas applicable to mathematics in all its branches from simple arithmetic to calculus and physics and all forms of applied mathematics. (See *Vedic Mathematics*, written by His Holiness Bhāratī Kṛṣṇa Tīrtha, published by Motilal Banarsidass, Varanasi, 1965.) In 1958, His Holiness, head of the Govardhana Maṭha in Purī, and a direct spiritual successor of the Ādi Śaṅkara — toured the United States under the auspices of self-realization fellowship. During his three-month tour, he spoke on Vedic metaphysics and mathematics in major universities across the country. It was a historic event — the first time any Śaṅkarācārya had travelled to the West.[3]

[3] Sri Sri Paramahansa Yogananda, *God Talks with Arjuna: the Bhagavad Gita*, Kolkata: Yogoda Satsanga Society of India, vol. I, 2nd impression, 2002, pp. XXXV, fn. and 280 fn.

Similarly, when we study the Kosalī style of Rekha temple architecture, one has to keep in mind that the plan of this variety of temple architecture has yogic and spiritual symbolism. The study is divided into three parts.

Jugglery of the Opinions, on the Plan of Cheliā Temple in Rāṇīpur-Jharial Complex

On the left side of the road leading to the Sixty-four Yoginī temple of Rāṇīpur-Jharial site in Bolaṅgīr district of Orissa, a mound was found with four stone pillars, within Kansil village area. When A.N. Tiwari was Director of Cultural Affairs Department, he got it excavated through the Orissa State Archaeology Department. Locally this mound is called Cheliā Temple. The stellate plan of two squares placed diagonally and intersecting each other at angles of 45° was exposed, which is a brick structure, over a stone pavement.

While writing on the Kosalī style of temple architecture, the author[4] had mentioned:

> Rāma temple at Sirpur (*c.* CE 595–605), Indal Duel at Kharod (*c.* CE 650-60), Siddheśvara temple at Palari (*c.* CE 675-85) and Sabari temple at Kharod (*c.* CE 700-10) have stellate plans. Another group of temples having the plans of two squares placed diagonally and intersecting each other at angles of 45°, which gives the shape of eight-pointed star are: (1) the Pātāleśvara Śiva temple at Būḍhī Komnā (at present in Nuāpāḍā district), (2) the Chitawari Devī temple at Dhobni near Damakeda village (Raipur district), (3) a temple in ruin at Kansil village area (in Rāṇīpur-Jharial complex Bolaṅgīr district), and (4) a temple ruin at Adhabhara village situated roughly 8 km south of Kharsia (Bilaspur district). *Bhuvanapradīpa*, the earliest or ancient architectural text of Orissa, mentions 36 types of Rekha temples and among these, one specification of "Kosalī" Rekha temple is found. As single temples with different types of stellate plans are found and as four (4) temples with the plans of two squares placed diagonally and intersecting each other at angles of 45° are traced in South Kosala region, it seems, it will be proper for the temples which are more in number, with same plans, to be identified with "Kosalī Style of Rekha Temple". The Pātāleśvara Śiva temple at Būḍhī Komnā, situated in western Orissa, should be taken as Rekha temple of "Kosalī Style", standing in full form dating from seventh-eighth centuries CE.[5]

---

[4] J.P. Singh Deo, op. cit., 1987, p. 330.

[5] J.P. Singh Deo, "Kosalī Style of Temple Architecture", *OHRJ*, vols. XXIV, XXV and XXVI, pp. 169-76.

In the meantime a scholarly work of R.P. Mishra, *Fragments of Indian Culture* was published in 1995.[6] During that period, the author was writing a book *Tāntric Art of Orissa,* and the author[7] in search of "Reality or Truth of the Temple Architecture" had to comment:

In the newly published work *Fragments of Indian Culture,* R.P. Mishra has done an error, while describing the plan of the ruined brick temple at the Rāṇīpur-Jharial complex,[8] whose plan is of two squares placed diagonally and intersecting each other at angles of 45°.

R.P. Mishra states:

> On the left side of the approach road leading to the main temple site of Rāṇīpur-Jharial the ruins of a damaged brick temple is found. This brick temple does not show the present-day *mukhaśālā, antarāla* and *garbha-gṛha.* It shows only the *pīḍha* on which the temple had been built. In the midst of the relics of this temple few large stone pillars basement built of bricks and star-shaped layout are clearly observed. The *garbha-gṛha* being evidently a square shape is measured 6′ and 4" both in length and breadth. The damaged doorway of the temple is 3′ and 5" in breadth and 6′ and 1" in height. A lotus carved on a stone was found here. This is perhaps the part of a ceiling of this temple. Brick used in the erection of this temple is 1′ and 2" in length, 8" in breadth and 3" in height. The people of Rāṇīpur-Jharial call it Cheliā temple. In a tāntric Buddhist manuscript called *Vajratoṣaṇa Tantra,* the tāntric Buddhists or Vajrayānists are instructed to adore the primal Buddha Vajrasattva with tāntric rites in a star-shaped edifice.
>
> As this *tantra* suggests the tāntric Buddhists should enshrine Vajrasattva in association with his consort Vajranārī or Prajñā and other members of *vajra* family on a pedestal shaped as conjoint double lotus. This double lotus pedestal should be erected on a square-shaped pavilion encompassed by a circle of perfect tranquillity. This circular space of tranquillity should be located in a star-shaped edifice. As so-called Cheliā temple is a star-shaped edifice and as in a reliable proximity of this temple an image of Lord Buddha is found, it is reasonable to believe that this Cheliā temple was originally a

---

[6] R.P. Mishra, *Fragments of Indian Culture,* Calcutta: Punthi Pustak, 1995, *passim;* ibid; pp 76-77; J.P. Singh Deo, *Tāntric Art of Orissa,* Delhi: Kalpaz Publications, 2001, pp. 177-79.

[7] J.P. Singh Deo, *Tāntric Art of Orissa,* Delhi: Kalpaz Publications, 2001, pp. 177-79

[8] R.P. Mishra, "Indralat Brick Temple of Rāṇīpur-Jharial and Its Cultural Heritage", *Souvenir, Bolangir Loka Utsaba 2003,* Bolaṅgīr, 2003, pp. 74-75.

fig. 4: Buddhist *yantra*

shrine for worship of the supermost tāntric Buddhist god, Vajrasattva along with his *śakti* and *vajrakula*.

It is interesting to mention that what R.P. Mishra thinks to be six-pointed star-shaped temple is in reality a plan of two squares placed diagonally and intersecting each other at angles of 45°, thereby making an aerial view of eight-pointed star.

When only one wall of this brick temple was existing, in early part of the twentieth century, N.K. Bose of Calcutta University had visited Rāṇīpur-Jharial and had reported (vide: THACOTIP, vol. V, *The Struggle for Empire*, 1966, p. 556).

In recent years American scholar Thomas E. Donaldson[9] had visited Rāṇīpur-Jharial and had recorded the plan and measurements of the ruined brick temple and states: "A similar brick temple composed of intersecting squares producing an eight-pointed stellate ground plan existed at Kansil near Rāṇīpur-Jharial though only the foundation of *deul* and *antarāla* has survived along with the *pīṭha*, the *jagamohana* being completely destroyed. The temple faces east and the intersecting squares measure 14' on each side. The *antarāla* has a large pillar on either side of its door opening but nothing of the frame has survived whereas the jambs of the sanctum door, also of stone, are partly intact but relatively plain. A stone slab, 42" square, is decorated with a Lotus rosette and probably served as a ceiling ornament

[9] Thomas E. Donaldson, *Hindu Temple Art of Orissa*, vol. I, Leiden, The Netherlands: E.J. Brill, 1985, pp. 212-15.

for the *antarāla*. The Sanctum, 7′ square, has a stone pillar set into the brick foundation at each corner. A water spout pierces the north wall. Only the lower two mounding of the *pābhāga* of the exterior have survived, a *khurā* at the base and a *kumbha* above. The outlines of a *kirīṭa* are visible on the *khurā* moulding while three *campaka* leaves hang down from the *kumbha*. There are no surviving sculptures. Stylistically the temple is closely aligned to the Pātāleśvara temple of Būḍhī Komnā and can likewise be dated to the late ninth or early tenth century CE."

These studies contradict with the opinions of R.P. Mishra.

The observation of the author has the support of eminent scholars of international fame like N.K. Bose, S.K. Saraswati and Donaldson. However, R.P. Mishra reacts:

> The ruins of the eight-angled brick stellate traceable in this place was most probably a tāntric Buddhist temple of Vajrasattva in the past. Learned scholar Jitamitra Prasad Singh Deo criticizes the view of this author as wrong although the tāntric Buddhist diagram given by me occurs on the cover page of his book.[10] It appears that the erudite scholar Singh Deo has failed to understand what I have written. While analysing the archaeological remains of this stellate or star-shaped edifice in pages 75-76 of my *Fragments of Indian Culture*, I have written it neither as a six-angled stellate nor as an eight-angled stellate. This stellate is called Cheliā temple by the local people. In reviewing this nomenclature which has been developed by the local people towards its popularity, I have simply written. As a star displays six angular points in its pictorial representation and thus evidently as a star-structural temple, the name was corrupted to Chaliā or Cheliā in course of time. The criticism of Singh Deo is a monument of his folly, not of his intelligence. As it has been discussed above Rāṇīpur-Jharial in the midst of the peaceful co-existence of several religious followers of different religious ideologies professed a sense of harmonious tolerance between different religions. The brick Indralatha temple had probably been instrumental in disseminating the ideals of Hari-Hara unity, amalgam and assimilative tolerance between different Indian religions, Ramaite Vaiṣṇavism and Rāmāyaṇic ideals.

With this much of jugglery, it can be safely stated that the plan of Cheliā temple originally is based on two squares placed diagonally and intersecting each other at

---

[10] J.P. Singh Deo, *Tāntric Art of Orissa*, 2001, pp. 178-79.

angles of 45°.[11] As stated above its plan has similarity with the plan of Pātāleśvara Śiva temple at Būḍhī Komnā and has a water spout piercing the north wall. So, originally Cheliā temple was a Śiva temple, whose plan is based on *Kāmakalā-yantra*, based on the *mantras* of "*Ānandalaharī*, verse 20 and *Saundaryalaharī* verses 20 and 42", of Ādi Śaṅkarācārya and was built in "Kosalī Style of Rekha Temple Design alias Plan". The author invokes the attentions of the interested persons and scholars to visualize the plan of Cheliā temple of Kansil village area of Rāṇīpur-Jharial complex personally and form their opinions, about the authenticity of the author's claim, with comparative study of other temples of the same plan, which is *Kāmakalā yantra*.

D.R. Das[12] of the Calcutta University also states, "The ruined brick temple at Kansil seems to have a parallel in the Pātāleśvara temple at Būḍhī Komnā." This proves that the author is correct and Ram Prasad Mishra is in bewilderment or perplexity.

Cheliā Temple of Kansil Village:
Originally a Śiva Temple

While approaching the main site of Rāṇīpur-Jharial, one visualizes a ruined mound on the left side of the road within Kansil village area. S.K. Saraswati[13] states:

> Another temple of a similar plan may be recognized in a ruined brick monument at Kausuli (i.e. Kansil) near Rāṇīpur-Jharial, old Patna state.[14] Only one wall of this building now remains. But the exterior face leaves no doubt about its plan being obtained on the principle of two intersecting squares, as in the above-mentioned temples of Bauḍh, to which, as carvings indicate, it was probably co-eval in date.

This statement proves that in the early part of twentieth century N.K. Bose had visited Rāṇīpur-Jharial site, while only one wall of the brick temple in Kansil village area was standing and had reported about its plan being obtained on the principle of two intersecting squares. In course of time, because of vagaries of nature, the

---

[11] J.P. Singh Deo, *Some Tāntric Esotericism of Orissa*, Kolkata: R.N. Bhattacharya, 2003, pp. 301-08 and 311.

[12] D.R. Das, *Temples of Rāṇīpur-Jharial*, Calcutta University, 1990, pp. 37 and 48; Ibid., "Stellate Temples of Orissa", *Art and Culture*, no. 1, July 1983, pp. 7 and 9.

[13] S.K. Saraswati, "Architecture", *THACOTIP*, vol. V, *The Struggle for Empire*, 1966, p. 556.

[14] N.K. Bose, Calcutta University, kindly supplied the required information.

temple ruin of Kansil area had formed a mound, with its supporting stone pillars, projecting out. After excavation the stellate plan, on the principal of intersecting two squares placed diagonally and intesecting each other at angles of 45 degrees was found. This plan is based on *yantra*, based in Śaiva Tantra, as mentioned in the *mantras* of *Ānandalaharī*, (v. 20)[15] and *Saundaryalaharī* (vs. 20 and 42)[16] of Ādi Śaṅkarācārya. As these *mantras* are based on Śaiva Tantra, it can safely be said that originally the Chelia temple ruin, in its innate inborn natural quality, was a Śiva temple.

Cheliā temple was a Śiva temple and it can be confirmed, as it has similarity with the temple of the same plan at Pātāleśvara Śiva brick temple at Būḍhī Komnā. Donaldson[17] confirms it, while dealing about the brick temples in the Upper Mahānadī Valley and Būḍhī Komnā, Kausuli (i.e. Kansil) stellate brick temples thus:

> A similar brick temple composed on intersecting squares, producing an eight-pointed stellate ground plan, existed at Kausuli (i.e. Kansil) near Rānīpur–Jharial though only the foundation of the deul and *antarāla* has survived along with the *pīṭha*, the *jagamohana* being completely destroyed. The temple faces east and the intersecting squares measure 14 ft on each side. The *antarāla* has a large pillar on either side of its door opening but nothing of the frame has survived whereas the jambs of the sanctum door, also of stone, are partly intact but relatively plain. A stone slab, 42 inches square, is decorated with a lotus rosette and probably served as a ceiling ornament for the *antarāla*. The sanctum, 7 ft square, has a stone pillar set into the brick foundation at each corner. A water spout pierces the north wall. Only the lower two mouldings of the *pābhāga* of the exterior have survived, a *khura* at the base and a *kumbha* above. The outlines of a *kirīṭa* are visible on the *khura* moulding while three *campaka* leaves hang down from the *kumbha*. There are no surviving sculptures. Stylistically the temple is closely aligned to the Pātāleśvara temple and can likewise be dated to the late ninth or early tenth century.

D.R. Das[18] of the Calcutta University has also studied the Kansil site and states:

---

[15] Devabrata Ghosh (ed.), *Ānandalaharī*, Calcutta: Sanskrit Book Depot, 1986, p. 29.

[16] V.K. Subramanian, *Saundaryalaharī of Śaṅkarācārya*, Delhi: Motilal Banarsidass, 1986, pp. 11-12 and 23. For the *yantras*, vide pp. 66 and 77.

[17] Thomas E. Donaldson, *Hindu Temple Art of Orissa*, vol. I, Leiden, Netherlands: E.J. Brill, 1985, p. 215.

[18] D.R. Das, "Stellate Temples of Orissa", *Art and Culture*, no. 1, July 1983, p. 9.

> Situated not far from Rāṇīpur-Jharial, Kansil is a hamlet of little consequence. Excavating a mound at this village the Department of Orissa State Archaeology has unearthed the ruins of a temple. It was a composite construction in which the frame of the structure was built in stone and the remaining part was completed in bricks. From what has been exposed it appears that the temple had a *baḍa deula* and a *mukhaśālā* with a vestibule connecting the two. The temple was facing east. The plan of the *baḍa deula* is stellate and identical with that of the Pātāleśvara. Probably in elevation also, it did not differ from the example at Būḍhī Komnā. Among its different vertical divisions, only a portion of the *pābhāga* is preserved. In the damaged *pābhāga*, two mouldings, viz. *pāda* (*khura* type) and *kumbha* can be deciphered. Bricks used in constructing this temple measure 17" X 8.8" X 2.75".

In a second report, D.R. Das[19] again confirms:

> The ruined brick temple at Kansil seems to have a parallel in the Pātāleśvara temple at Būḍhī Komnā in the Kālāhāṇḍī district (now Nuāpāḍā district).

Fate of Kosalī Style of Rekha Temples

The earliest text on temple architecture, found in Orissa is *Bhuvana-Pradīpa*, which gives names of thirty-six Rekha temples and three types of Khākharā temples. Among the thirty-six types of Rekha temples, Kosali,[20] is found and among the three types of Khākharā temples Kosali,[21] is found with description, as stated above.

While searching for the Kosalī variety of Rekha temple,[22] the author had stated:

> The stellate plans and the plans of two squares placed diagonally and intersecting each other at angles of 45° probably developed by basing on *Vāstupuruṣamaṇḍala*, at the territory of South Kosala. Tantra aims at attaining salvation with the help of mystic diagrams and *mantras*. Therefore it can definitely be said that the plans of the concerned temples of South Kosala developed with Tantra influence.

The Pātāleśvara Śiva temple at Būḍhī Komnā[23] situated in Nuāpāḍā district of

---

[19] D.R. Das, *Temples of Rāṇīpur-Jharial*, Calcutta University, 1990, p. 48.

[20] N.K. Bose, op. cit., 1982, p. 124.

[21] Ibid., p. 172.

[22] J.P. Singh Deo, op. cit., 1987, pp. 330-31.

[23] J.P. Singh Deo, "Kosalī Style of Temple Architecture", *OHRJ*, vols. XXIV, XXV and XXVI, pp. 169-76.

western Orissa rises precipitously from the ground, which is a brick work and has stone door-jamb, where *navagrahas* with the figure of Gaja-Lakṣmī at the centre is found. This shows synchronization of Śaivism and Vaiṣṇavism. The *kumbha*-shaped moulding, which acts as *antarāla* connecting the temple with the pillared *maṇḍapa* (now delapsed, but has modern construction now), in front is a peculiarity of the Kosalī style of Rekha temple. The plan of two intersecting squares of Kosalī style of Rekha temple, seems to have influenced the growth of *pañcaratha* plan. With the rise of Somavaṁśīs, the *pañcaratha* plan of temples became very famous and this seems to be a great contribution of South Kosala to the development of Kaliṅga style of temple architecture in the coastal belt. Beginning from the Bhauma-Kara period, the cultural knit had begun as *pañcaratha* plans are excavated from the ruins of Ratnagiri and the temple architecture of coastal area became fully matured with the development of *pañcaratha* temples in Orissa.

Further addition to the number of intersecting squares of the plan, gradually developed and can be judged in the Cāḷukyan monuments of the eleventh-twelfth century CE of Gujarat in the west, the Hoysaḷa temples of Mysore in the south, the Candella temples of Khajurāho in the north and the Kaliṅga style of temple architecture in the east. This shows that the Kosalī style of Rekha temple architecture had influenced the development of temple architectures in all directions. This contribution of South Kosala seems to have been possible, because of its centralized-eastern location, in the heart of the country.

The question arises, in what circumstance the Kosali Style of Rekha Temple architecture" developed? It is generally known that the origin of Tantra is lost in mystery, but H.D. Bhattacharyya[24] states that it is only in later literature, from about the fifth or sixth century CE, that Tantra as a special religious or philosophical concept gradually came into use. Similarly, mother earth has naturally taken the form of *yoni* and is worshipped as "Duārsani", near Pātālgaṅgā site of Nuāpāḍā district. It seems to be the earliest Śakti of Orissa.[25] Further, ten *yonis* were discovered in Nuāpāḍā district. Duārsani deity of Sindhekela village in Bolaṅgīr district is also in the form of a *yoni*. Another *yoni* is found at the Veda-Vyāsa site of Sundargaṛh district. Lots of *yonis* in the triangle forms are found in the rock art sites in Orissa.[26]

---

24 H.D. Bhattacharyya, "Tāntric Religion", *THACOTIP*, vol. IV, *The Age of Imperial Kanauj*, 1964, pp. 315-16.

25 J.P. Singh Deo, *Tāntric Art of Orissa*, Delhi: Kalpaz Publications, 2001, p. 45; "Primal alias Ādi Śakti of Orissa Province Is Found in Nuapada District", *OHRJ*, vol. XLVII, no. 3, pp. 38-39.

26 Sadasiba Pradhan, *Rock Art in Orissa*, New Delhi: Aryan Books International, 2001, *passim*.

Sadasiba Pradhan[27] informs that all the rock art sites in Orissa are found in the western districts of (1) Jharsuguḍa, (2) Kālāhāṇḍī, (3) Mayūrbhañj, (4) Nuāpāḍā, (5) Sambalpur, (6) Sundargaṛh, and (7) Sonepur. Bisected triangle or triangle with a dot at the centre resembling vulvas (female genitalia) remains the hallmark of all representations both in painting and engraving. Its repeated occurrence in different contexts of the rock panels gives an impression as if there was a deliberate attempt for symbolic representation of the Venus, the primordial mother responsible for all creations. Fertility has been of supreme concern throughout the history of mankind to ensure prosperity. Concept of fertility can be expressed in many forms: (i) the women herself, (ii) depiction of vulva — symbol of generative power of procreation and nourishment, (iii) depiction of copulation, (iv) female puberty ritual, etc. Fertility practices varied in different areas, but there has been a widespread consistency in the use of symbolic representation of the human vulva. Vulva motif may take many forms while still referring to the same basic concept for continuation of life and maintenance of human fertility.

The discoveries of *yoni*s alias female vulvas discussed above prove that the middle Mahānadī River Valley was the birth-place of *yoni* worship in India. The *yantra* symbolizing *yoni* is a triangle pointed down, which happens to be the *yantra* of Bhairavī, the fifth Goddess of Daśamahāvidyā.[28] According to *Śākta Pramoda*,[29] Bhairavī alias Tripurabhairavī is the benign manifestation of *śakti* and is considered as the giver of knowledge.

Bhairavī is also known as Tripurabhairavī, because her *yantra* has three points or corners and according to the *Bṛhadyonitantra*, in this context in the three corners of the *yoni* are Brahmā, Viṣṇu and Maheśvara (*sṛṣṭi*, *sthiti* and *saṁhāra*); on the right side of the triangle the river Yamunā flows, on the left side the Sarasvatī and on the top the Jāhnavī (the Ganges); in the centre of the triangle the abode of Kāmākhyā is situated, who is identified with *kuṇḍalinī* and *prakṛti* in the form of the menstrual flux (*puṣparūpiṇī*); the *yoni* itself is Kāmarūpa, the Yonipīṭha.[30]

---

27 Sadasiba Pradhan, "Rock Art Heritage in Orissa", *Souvenir (Orissa History Congress: Silver Jubilee Session)*, 2-3 November 2003, History Department, Sambalpur University, 2003, pp. 10-11.

28 David Frawley, *Tāntric Yoga and the Wisdom Goddesses*, Delhi: Motilal Banarsidass, 1996, p. 103.

29 Pushpendra Kumar, *Śakti Cult in Ancient India*, Varanasi: Bharatiya Publishing House, 1974, p. 157; *Śākta Pramoda*, Sri Venkatesvara Press edn., Bombay: 1951, p. 262.

30 J.A. Schoterman, *The Yoni Tantra*, New Delhi: Manohar, 1980, pp. 23-24.

This fact is also confirmed by the *Bhagavad-Gītā*[31] (chapter 13):

1. Know that both *puruṣa* and *prakṛti* are beginningless; and know also that all modifications and qualities (*guṇas*) are born of *prakṛti* (verse 19).
2. In the creation of the effect (the body) and the instrument (the senses), *prakṛti* is spoken of as the cause; in the experience of joy and sorrow, *puruṣa* is said to be the cause (verse 20).
3. *Puruṣa* involved with *prakṛti* experiences the *guṇas* born of nature. Attachment to the three qualities of *prakṛti* causes the soul to take embodiment in good and evil wombs (verse 21).
4. The Supreme Spirit, transcendent and existing in the body is the detached beholder, the consenter, the sustainer, the experiencer, the Great Lord and also the highest self (verse 22).
5. Whatever his mode of life, he who thus realizes *puruṣa* and the threefold nature of *prakṛti* will not again suffer rebirth (verse 23).

It is worth knowing about the eruption of Tāntricism in the South Kosala region, during the historical period. According to S.R. Nema,[32] the reigning period of last Pāṇḍuvaṁśī alias Somavaṁśī king of South Kosala, Mahāśivagupta Bālārjuna was CE 595–655 and he informs, Mahāśivagupta, being a great devotee of Śiva, enjoyed the epithet "Paramamāheśvara" in his charters and also had the Śaivite emblem of the bull on his seal, while the seal of his ancestor (grandfather's brother) Tīvara who was a "Parama Vaiṣṇava", bore the Vaiṣṇava emblem of Garuḍa.[33] He as well as his subordinate chiefs gave patronage to Śaivism. We know from the Senakapaṭ inscription[34] that "Durgārakṣita", son of Devarakṣita, was a bee at the feet, i.e. a servant of Mahāśivagupta Bālārjuna. He being a worshipper of Śambhu constructed a temple of Śiva at the village (modern) Senakapaṭ and made it over to an ascetic, Sadāśivācārya who was probably the spiritual successor of Sadāśivācārya, hailing from the penance grove, entitled Amardaka. In Ladhia plates, as seen above, the donee Śūlapāṇi was a disciple of Pramathācārya who is said to be an inhabitant of Pañcayajña-tapovana in Dvaitavana. Here it is sufficient to say that these Śaivācāryas,

---

[31] Sri Sri Paramahansa Yogananda, *God Talks with Arjuna: The Bhagavad Gita*, Yogoda Satsaṅga Society of India, Kolkata, 2nd impression, 2002, pp. 889-94.

[32] S.R. Nema, *Political History of the Somavamsi Kings of South Kosala and Orissa*, New Delhi: Oriental Publishers & Distributors, 1978, pp. 128 and 135.

[33] *EI*, vol. XXXI, p. 32.

[34] Ibid., pp. 32-33.

probably belonged to a sect of Tāntric-Śaivism who later came to be called Mattamayūra and as such, it may be assumed that Mahāśivagupta may have accepted the doctrine of Pāśupata *dharma*.[35]

The influence of Mattamayūra Śaiva Tantra School seems to have great impact on Mahāśivagupta Bālārjuna and it is appropriate to suppose that during his rule "Kosali Style of Temple Architecture" was developed. As mentioned above, temples with the same plan of two squares placed diagonally and intersecting each other at angles of 45° are found at four sites — (1) Būḍhī Komnā, (2) Dhobnī, (3) Adhabhara (modern Adbhar), and (4) Kansil.

Having analysed the history of the Kosala style, let us peep into the conditions of these temples which exist at four sites of the ancient South Kosala region.

BŪḌHĪ KOMNĀ

The Pātāleśvara Śiva temple at Būḍhī Komnā, situated in Nuāpāḍā district of Orissa, is in perfect original shape and is a brick structure. It is now conserved by the Orissa State Archaeology Department. Its *maṇḍapa* had fallen and in recent period a modern *maṇḍapa* has been built in front of the main temple.

DHOBNĪ

Dhobnī village is situated in Raipur district of Chhattisgarh. The Citavari Devī temple stands there. The lower portion of the temple, till its *jaṅghā* portion is built of stone and the upper portion is built of bricks. The original *maṇḍapa* and the front portion of the temple have collapsed.

The author[36] had accompanied Nrusingha Prasad Tripathi in his visit to Dhobnī village on 22 February 1986, and found the Śiva-liṅga deity painted in red by vandalists, the Śakti of the *liṅga* removed and kept near the back wall of the sanctum and worshipped as Citavari Devī. Originally, it was a Śiva temple.

ADHABHARA

Same thing has happened at Adhabhara also. In "Bilaspur Gazetteer, 1978", it is mentioned that there are two ornamental doorways of an old ruined temple of a Devī, in the Adhabhara village. The ruined temple of Adhabhara was a Śiva temple, which was visited and have been recorded by N.K. Bose of the Calcutta University, during the early part of twentieth century CE and reported in his work, *Indian*

---

[35] S.N. Rajaguru, *Inscriptions of Orissa*, vol. IV, pp. 349-50.

[36] J.P. Singh Deo, *Tāntric Art of Orissa*, 2001 pp. 177 and 179.

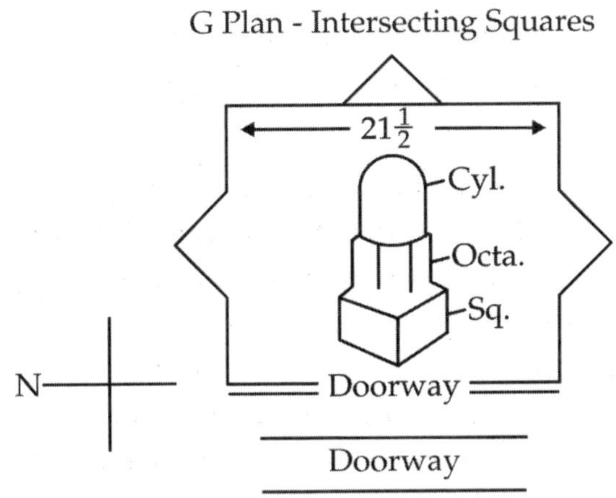

fig. 5: Plan of Kosalī Rekha temple at Adbhara, Bilāspur district, Chhattisgarh

Temple Designs, 1981.[37] From the sketch made by Bose and published, it is known that originally the plan of Adhabhara temple was of two intersecting squares and was a Śiva temple, where a lotus ceiling was found. One eight handed Naṭarāja sculpture was found near the temple ruin.

KANSIL

The study on the Kosalī style of Rekha temple architecture, of Kansil village of Bolaṅgīr district has fallen on intellectual misunderstanding.

This study shows the fate of Kosali style of Rekha temples and how false developments have accumulated on them. All the four Kosalī style of Rekha temples were Śiva temples originally. With flux of time understanding of them have fallen into false, erroneous, haggard and hazardous one-sided scholars. This is the period of confrontation and globalization in search of truth. Any false claim is going to fall like a pack of cards. Vedas are the heritage of human beings. Therefore, *Ṛgveda* (5.60.5) declares, "Here there is none greater, none smaller. All have gathered together here for advancing common welfare of all." The studies of the Vedas show that the Vedas constitute the root of all religions and the social, cultural, political and economic thoughts of mankind. The existential blissful consciousness is the source of all creations. The energy of the Lord or by whatever name one recognizes it, it is truth, beauty and goodness. The Vedas are his breath, man is his expression. The tenets of Vedic Sanātana Dharma with its scientific and yogic rationalism can help human

[37] *Tāntric Art of Orissa*, 2001, p. 175; N.K. Bose, *Indian Temple Designs*, Calcutta: R.N. Bose, 1981, pp. 169-70.

beings in the flowering of their genius to its fullest potential. The fundamental truths of life, as revealed to us by the Vedas, can make our lives healthy, wealthy and wise.

The origin of Kosalī style of Rekha temple style has its origin in Vedic cosmology, because the square grid of the Vāstumaṇḍala reflected Vedic cosmology, which saw the world as square, and in its construction could be related to the actual piling of bricks for the altar. Construction of a square using gnomon and cord is described in the *Śulba-Sūtras* of the Veda.[38] The plan of Kosalī Style of Rekha Temple has two squares placed diagonally and intersecting each other at angles of 45°, which is studied as *Kāmakalā yantra*, which is a mirror of consciousness in art, creativity and bliss. Originally, the Kosalī Style of Rekha Temples were Śiva temples, because Lord Śiva likes to reside in fortresses, which are impregnable, well guarded and provided with every convenience, according to *Śivānandalaharī*, verse 42, of Ādi Śaṅkarācārya.[39]

---

[38] M.W. Meister, "Muṇḍeśvarī: Ambiguity and Certainty in the Analysis of a Temple Plan", *Kaladarsana (American Studies in the Art of India)*, J.G. Williams (ed.), New Delhi: Oxford and I.B.H. Publishing Co., 1981, pp. 79 and 83.

[39] T.M.P. Mahadevan, *The Hymns of Śaṅkara*, Delhi: Motilal Banarsidass, 1986, pp. 81 and 121-22.

ANNEXE

fig. 6: Plan of Cheliā brick temple, situated within Kansil village area, in Rāṇīpur – Jharial Complex, Bolaṅgīr district, Orissa, according to Kosali style of Rekha temple

9

Mysticism of the Tāntric Temples of Bauḍh

BAUḌH town is the headquaters of Bauḍh district, situated in central Orissa, on the right bank of the Mahānadī River. Bauḍh town has several temples. However, some of them deserve special mention such as the Rāmeśvara or Rāmanātha temple, the Candracūḍa (Śiva) temple on the bank of Mahānadī River, the Jagannātha and the Bhairavī temples near the palace of the ex-ruler and the Hanumān temple in the midst of the Mahānadī River. The Hanumān temple, it is reported, was constructed by a religious mendicant about thirty-five years back on public donation and the affairs of the temple are now being managed by the Endowment Department. The temple being in the midst of the river commands a beautiful view, especially during the rainy season, when the Mahānadī River is full with water. The most important, however, are the three Śiva temples, locally known as the Rāmanātha temple. These magnificent temples built of red sandstone are profusely carved and are stated to have been constructed in the mid-ninth century CE. The temples with their rich texture and carved surfaces are strikingly noteworthy. Each of these temples stands by itself on a raised platform and each consists of a cell and an attached portico. The minute recesses and angularities produce a charming effect of light and shade and confer an appearance of greater height from the continued cluster of vertical lines than they really possess.[1]

The Gazetteer[2] mentions:

> A group of three temples of Śiva at Bauḍh called the Rāmeśvara or Rāmanātha temples, dating back to the ninth century CE are reputed for their special features.

---

[1] D.C. Kuanr (state ed.), *Gazetter of India, Orissa, Bauḍh-Khondmals*, N. Senapati (chief ed.), Cuttack, 1983, p. 376.

[2] Ibid., p. 33.

In the words of R.D. Banerjee:

> The decorative motifs and the plastic art of the three temples at Bauḍh are certainly superior to and older than the great Liṅgarāja-Anantavāsudeva group . . . one particular feature of the Bauḍh temples is worth particular attention, their plan is quite different from that of any other temples. . . . In plan these temples are eight-rayed stars and the *argha-paṭṭa* of the *liṅga*s are also similar.[3]

The Rāmeśvara or Rāmanātha temple is a modern construction, which was never completed. Its construction was started by the last ruling chief Rājā Narāyan Dev of the former Bauḍh State. It remained incomplete, because of the Second World War. In its compound, the three tāntric Śiva temples are existing in triangle setting.

About these three tāntric Śiva temples at Bauḍh, K.S. Behera[4] states:

> At Bauḍh town there are three small temples, within the compound of the Rāmeśvara temple, which have great significance from the architectural point of view. Of these temples, one faces west and the other two with the same architectural and sculptural features, face the east. J.D. Beglar,[5] who visited the place in 1874-75 has left a concise account of the temples.

Each of these temples stands by itself on a raised platform and each consists of a cell and its attached portico only. The plan will show the minute recesses and angularities which produce so charming an effect in the variety of light and shade and confer an appearance of greater height from the continued cluster of vertical lines they really possess. With these recesses and angularities the ground plan is in the shape of an eight-rayed star. The plan has been obtained on the principle of intersecting squares, but obviously this unique ground plan was due to tāntric necessity for not only the ground plan of the temple, but also the Śakti of the star-shaped Śiva-liṅga.

On the temples we find *navagraha* slabs, which are common in later temples. These are so profusely ornamented that Beglar remarked that "though small they are gems of art in their own humble way".[6] The clear-cut interlacing of *caitya*-windows on the *śikhara* is arresting and similar designs are seen on the *anurathapāga*

---

[3] R.D. Banerjee, *History of Orissa*, vol. II, pp. 355-56.

[4] K.S. Behera, *Temples of Orissa*, Bhubaneswar: Orissa Sahitya Akademi, 1993, pp. 35-36.

[5] Cunningham, *Archaeological Survey of India*, vol. XIII, pp. 118-19.

[6] Ibid.

of the *deula* of the Mukteśvara temple at Bhubaneswar. These two temples, as K.C. Panigrahi points out, possess many decorative elements in common[7] and therefore may not have been far removed from each other in time. In shape and style of decorative treatment they differ considerably from the temples of the earlier period, but at the same time they do not possess the characteristics of the temples like the Brahmeśvara at Bhubaneswar, which was erected by the mother of the Somavaṁśī king Uddyotakeśarī. Therefore, we may assign them to the early period of the Somavaṁśī rule in Orissa.[8]

Vidya Dehejia[9] had studied the Śiva shrines at Bauḍh and stated:

> Śiva shrines in the compound of the later Rāmeśvara temple in the town of Bauḍh are three shrines, star-shaped in plan with a tiny rectangular portico in front taking the place of the *mukhaśālā*. Each temple houses a *liṅga* placed on a star-shaped Yoni-Pīṭha, and each shrine is raised on a high plinth with steps leading up to it.
>
> The triangular placing of the temples within the courtyard is quite unusual. They definitely do not represent three of the four corner shrines of a one-time *pañcāyatana* temple in which the main shrine has been obliterated. Banerjee's sketch shows quite clearly that the placing is not correct for such a temple and his suggestion that the configuration has significance may be accepted for want of any other explanation. (R.D. Banerji, "Antiquities of Bauḍh State", *JBORS*, vol. 15, 1929, pp. 64-86.)
>
> Though unique in certain aspects, the Bauḍh shrines bear striking resemblances to the temples just considered, and belong quite definitely to the culmination phase. Base mouldings of each shrine are of category III, but more elaborate than those we have considered as there is here one extra-rectangular level above the *ḍamaru-garbha*. The leaf-like strip extends all the way down the four levels ending at the top of the arch decorating the *khurā*, and each level is painstakingly carved with bands of leafy scrolls. The treatment of the wall surfaces too is typical of the culmination phase. However the star-like plan results in the shrine having seven *koṇaka*s, each treated as pilasters decorated with a *kanyā*, scroll and *kīrttimukha* with garlands. The most popular *kanyā* is the *dalamālikā* holding a branch of a tree, and the *koṇaka*s terminate with *abhāra-vāhaka* as is standard in the temples

---

[7] K.C. Panigrahi, *Archaeological Remains at Bhubaneswar*, Calcutta, 1961, pp. 158-59.

[8] Ibid., p. 159.

[9] Vidya Dehejia, *Early Stone Temples of Orissa*, New Delhi: Vikas Publishing House, 1979, pp. 147-49.

we have looked at. The facets between are treated as *anartha*s and display a niche completed as a barrel-vaulted shrine. The pilasters flanking the niches are decorated with the scroll and *kīrttimukha* garland. The star plan results in the absence of any *rāha*s. Beyond the plain recessed *bandhana,* the *koṇaka*s of the *śikhara* are divided into five units of three levels each. The decoration includes that tracery of *caitya* arches which is so striking a feature of all culmination temples.

The tiny entrance portico is flanked by pillars rising out of a *ghaṭa,* with a shaft decorated with the scroll motif and *kīrttimukha* with garlands. Above the portico and cutting across all the facets is a projecting front *rāha* treated as a niche which is today empty. The sides of this projection have large *dalamālikā kanyā*s carved against them. The shrines have *navagraha* lintels over the entrances. Despite the many questions raised by these unusual shrines by their placing and by their significance, one fact is certain — the shrines were built definitely during the culmination phase of the early Orissan temple.

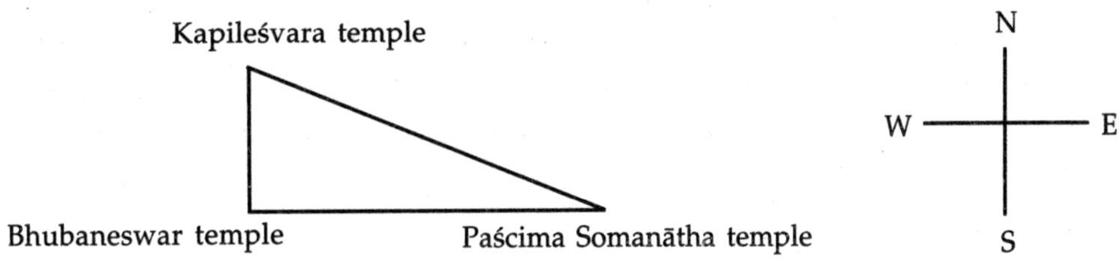

If the three tāntric temples of Bauḍh were built during the culmination phase of early Orissan temple, as stated by Vidya Dahejia, the base of their origin or the nucleus and their development has to be traced out. The author's field surveys and archaeological findings show that the nucleus of human culture in the Mahānadī River Valley had emanated, sprung, flashed and focused from the Sunabeda plateau region of Nuāpāḍā disctrict of Orissa.

As stated in an earlier chapter, the three tāntric Śiva temples of Bauḍh represent Śiva Kāmeśvara, Śakti Kāmeśvarī and Sāmarasya, with advanced tāntric formulae. Their placement has its nucleus from the Sunabeda plateau. So, it can be claimed that the culmination of early Orissan temple had tāntric influence fully, with its mysticism of *Kāmakalā-Vilāsa.*

Kamakalā-Vilāsa[10] is a tāntric text, composed by Puṇyānanda Nātha. It is an authoritative work on Śrīvidyā. Kāma means desire, Kalā means art and Vilāsa

[10] Sir John Woodroffe, "Preface", *Kāmakalā-Vilāsa,* Madras: Ganesh and Co., 1971, p. 133.

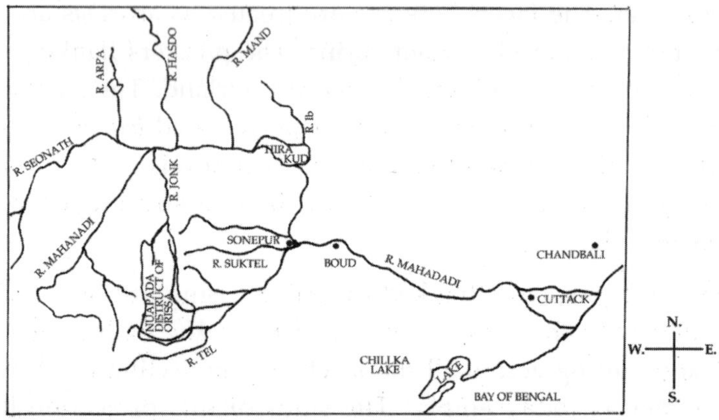

fig. 7: Nucleus of spiritual and material cultures of the Mahānadī River Valley. These cultures were developed at Nuāpāḍā district, Orissa, and gradually spread to different directions.

alias Bilāsa means play, enjoyment of pleasure, amusement, playfulness, joy, merriment, sport, dalliance, amorous exhibitions, manifestation, etc. The highest pleasure is beatitude, which is happiness of the highest kind alias heavenly happiness. So *Kāmakalā-Vilāsa* means the art of desire in beatitude, which is enjoyed by the creator.

Sir John Woodroffe mentions:

> The *Kāmakalā-Vilāsa* is an important work in Śrīvidyā by Puṇyānanda, an adherent of the Hāḍi-mata, who is also the commentator on the *Yoginī-Hṛdaya*, a section called Uttaracatuḥśatī of the great Vāmakeśvara Tantra. The same Catuḥśatī as also the Pūrvacatuḥśatī have commentaries by Bhāskararāya. The *Kāmakalā-Vilāsa* which means the spreading or emanation or evolution of the *kāmakalā* that is the supreme triangle formed by the *bindu* and *visarga*, of *prakāśa* and *vimarśa*, of Śiva and Śakti, of the "I" (*ahaṁ*) and "This" (*idaṁ*) or universe is, in the supreme sense, the Śiva-*svarūpa* and Śakti-*svarūpa*. To put it quite shortly *Kāmakalā-Vilāsa* is the evolution of the one in its twin aspect as changeless consciousness (*cit* or *saṁvit*) and changing power (*cit-śakti* and *māyā-śakti*) into the multiple universe. This evolution is represented by the greatest of *yantra*s, the *Śrī-yantra*.

The whole Mahānadī River Valley is the land of Kāmakalā, because this thought seems to have developed in this area by the Nātha Yogī, Puṇyānanda Nātha.

The founder of Nāthism was Yogī Matsyendranāth. Though there are controversies about his birthplace, R.P. Mishra[11] emphasizes that younger Luipa or Matsyendranāth was the Nātha *siddha* and was born in Candradvīpa, Cāndavāli-Dhāmra region of Bālāsore (now Bhadrak district) in Orissa.

Archaeological support to this opinion of R.P. Mishra is found in the statement of H.K. Mahatab,[12] when he states:

> A statue of Matsyendranāth in the form of Padmapāṇi Avalokiteśvara at forest of Rajnagar under Deravisi block of Kendrapāṛā sub-division is still worshipped by the Nāthas of the surrounding villages. The prototype of the same statue is seen at Kendrapāṛā bus stand with the same inscription, and another at Trilochanpur village under Mahajajpur Gram Pañcāyat near Bahugrām is also worshipped by the Nāthas of the surrounding villages.

Śrīvidyā seems to have developed in the Mahānadī River Valley, because there are archaeological findings supporting this view. *Śrī-yantra*[13] Śrīvidyā, is the diagrammatic embodiment of the creative sexual activity of the universe and is the well-known *yantra*.

The *Śrī-yantra* as shown in *fig*. 1 has a *bindu* (point) at the centre. It consists of four triangles with their apexes pointing upward, known as *Śiva yantra*s and the five triangles with their apexes pointing downward, which are the *Śakti yantras*.

The innermost triangle of *Śrī-yantra* is *bhairavī-yantra*.[14] Bhairavī is a benign manifestation of Śakti and is considered as the giver of knowledge, according to *Śākta Pramoda*[15] text.

An archaeological remain of *bhairavī-yantra* has been found with the help of Padma Daṇḍasena, on a round stone, which is a quartzite stone, ferruginous in colour and measuring 6½ cm in circumference, from the sand of the Udantī River in Nuāpāḍā district and is kept as household deity, in the house of Brusabhanu Naik and Narsingh Naik, in Muṇḍapala village of Nuāpāḍā district, situated on the left bank of the Udantī River.

So, from the archaeological point of view, it can be mentioned that the nucleus

---

[11] R.P. Mishra, *Sahajayāna (A Study of Tāntirc Buddhism)*, Calcutta: Punthi Pustak, 1991, pp. 114 and 165.

[12] H.K. Mahatab, "Culture of Orissa", *OHRJ*, vol. XXX, nos. 2-4, 1984, p. 48.

[13] Pranab Bandyopadhyay, *The Goddess of Tantra*, Calcutta: Punthi Pustak, 1987, p. 48.

[14] David Frawley, *Tāntric Yoga and the Wisdom Goddesses*, Delhi: Motilal Banarsidass, 1996, p. 103.

[15] *Śākta Pramoda*, Sri Venkatesvara Press edn., Bombay, 1951, p. 262. Vide Pushpendra Kumar, *Śākti Cult in Ancient India*, Bharatiya Publishing House, Varanasi, 1974, p. 157.

of *Śrī-yantra* had its origin in Nuāpāḍā district of Orissa and finds its full expression in the inner ground plan with *Śrī-yantra* alias *Śrī-cakra* superimposition of Rājarānī temple, Bhubaneswar.[16]

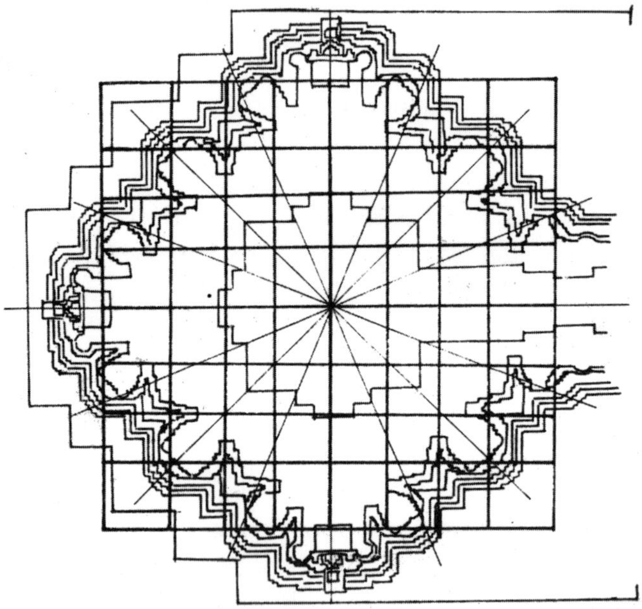

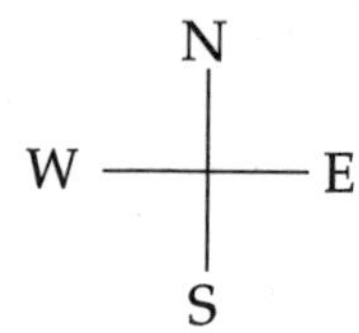

fig. 9

fig. 8

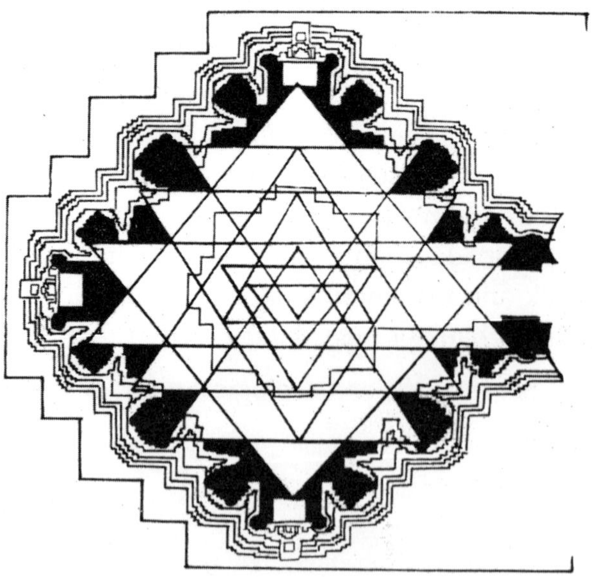

figs. 8-9: Rājarānī temple ground plan with *cakras* and *koṇas*. The plan shows *Śrī-cakra* alias *Śrī-yantra* superimposed. (*Source*: Bettina Bäumer and Rajendra Prasad Das (tr.), *Śilparatnakośa (A Glossary of Orissan Temple Architecture)* by Sthapaka Niranjana Mahapatra), New Delhi: Indira Gandhi National Centre for the Arts and Motilal Banarsidass, 1994, vide figs. 52-56.)

[16] Bettina Bäumer and Rajendra Prasad Das, *Śilparatnakośa* (*A Glossary of Orissan Temple Architecture* by Sthapaka Niranjana Mahapatra), Delhi: Motilal Banarsidass, 1994, figs. 52-56.

With this archaeological background, it can be claimed that the Mahānadī River Valley is the land of Kāmakalā and the Nātha Dharma tāntric text *Kāmakalā-Vilāsa* was fully implemented in this land.

As already stated, the three tāntric temples at Bauḍh are based on the plan of *Kāmakalā yantra*. The result of the culmination of the early temple architecture influenced the fully developed *pañcaratha* temple architecture of coastal Orissa, which earned a name of its own as "Kaliṅga Style of Temple Architecture", as mentioned in an inscription on the capital of a pillar in the *mukhamaṇḍapa* of the Amṛteśvara temple at Holal (Bellary district).[17]

Behera[18] states, "The Somavaṁśīs, who succeeded the Bhauma-Karas, came from South Kosala, but they did not introduce any unfamiliar line of development in art and architecture." This is a wrong statement, because the Somavaṁśīs of South Kosala had matrimonial relationship with the Bhauma-Karas. With the Somavaṁśī's cultural affiliation[19] *pañcaratha* temples developed in coastal Orissa and finally Somavaṁśī rule extended to coastal Orissa, which helped in the development of Mukteśvara temple and fully matured Kaliṅga style of temple architecture in the Liṅgarāja temple, Bhubaneswar. This is the mystic undercurrent or role in the development of temple architecture in the Mahānadī River Valley in general.

---

[17] K.S. Behera, *Temples of Orissa*, Bhubaneswar: Orissa Sahitya Akademi, 1993, p. 2.

[18] Ibid., p. 32.

[19] B.K. Rath, *Cultural History of Orissa*, Delhi: Sundeep Prakashan, 1983, pp. 173-87; Bina Kumari Sarma, *The History of Somavaṁśī Rule in Orissa*, Calcutta: Punthi Pustak, 1983, pp. 78-93.

10

Impact of Nātha Cult on the Mahānadī Valley

NĀTHISM originated from the lower level of society, which was influenced by Ājīvikism, Jainism, Buddhism and Tantrism. Mīnanātha also known as Matsyendranāth was a fisherman, Gorakṣanātha was either a fisherman or a Keetiya or Kaivartta and Hāḍipā alias Jālandharipā, was a *hadi* (or a net-holder according to another tradition) who served as a stable sweeper in the palace of Queen Maināmatī of Pāṭikā.[1]

According to Swami Satyananda Saraswati:[2]

> After about five hundred years or so, the popularity and influence of Buddhism declined and so did these tāntric sects and their practices. Then in the fourth, fifth and sixth centuries CE, after the period of Buddhist decadence in India, some great *yogī*s took this science and set out to purify the tāntric system. Matsyendranāth, Gorakhanāth and a few other *yogī*s in the tradition found that this important science was being ignored by the serious minded people and was being wrongly taught by others. So they separated the *haṭha-yoga* and the *rāja-yoga* practices of Tantra from the rest and they left out the rituals of Tantra altogether, and they did not even mention it.

The Nātha cult developed as an amalgam. Therefore, P.K. Bandyopadhyay[3] is of the opinion that the Nātha cult which has derived much of its character from esoteric Tantrism and the Śaivite tradition is a perfect example of amalgam.

Mahāyogī Mīnanāth alias Matsyendranāth was the founder of the Nātha cult and the *yoginī* cult. His chief disciple, Gorakhanāth, bows down to him, in his composition *Gorakṣa Śataka*.[4] R.P. Mishra[5] is of the opinion that Matsyendranāth was

---

1 J.P. Singh Deo, *Tāntric Art of Orissa*, Delhi: Kalpaz Publications, 2001, pp. 86-87.

2 *HYP*, p. 3.

3 P.K. Bandyopadhyay, *Nātha Cult and Mahānadī* (*A Study of Syncretism*), Delhi: B.R. Publishing Corporation, 1992, p. 5.

4 George Weston Briggs, *Gorakhnāth and the Kānphaṭa Yogīs*, Delhi: Motilal Banarsidass, 1989, p. 284.

5 R.P. Mishra, *Sahajayāna*: *A Study of Tāntric Buddhism*, Calcutta: Punthi Pustak, 1991, p. 165.

a Nātha *siddha* and was born in Candradvīpa, Cāndāvāli-Dhāmra region of Bālāsore (now Bhadrak district) in Orissa.

While dealing on "Sahajayāna and the Religions of Medieval Orissa", R.P. Mishra[6] states:

> According to *Kaulajñāna Nirṇaya*, Matsyendra was called Matsyaghna or a killer of the fish when he killed a big fish in Candradvīpa and rescued the text of sacred wisdom from its belly.[7] According to S.C. Behera, the Mattamayūra School of Śaivism flourished in North Orissa as early as the seventh century CE under the leading role of a preceptor called Rudraśiva[8] who in consonance with the delineations of Bilhari and Ranod inscriptions was the lord of Amardaka *tīrtha*.[9] Amarda with a Gaganeśvara Śiva temple[10] was, most probably, the Amardaka *tīrtha* of these incriptions. It is curious to observe that the disciple of Rudra-Śiva is endowed with no epithet Mattamayūra Nātha although he is known by the name Purandara.[11] As suggested earlier, the Mattamayūra Śaiva teachers came to different parts of India from the neighbourhood of Delhi.[12] Even during the rule of Somavaṁśīs of Orissa, this Śaiva sect was very influential and continued to enjoy royal patronage. In Lodhia plates of Mahāśivagupta, Śrī Śūlapāṇi, the disciple of Pramathācārya figures as the donee of lands donated by this king.[13] Pramathācārya here is described to have hailed from Pañcayajña Tapovana of Dvaitavana.[14] In the Senakapaṭ inscription of the time of Mahāśivagupta Bālārjuna, Amardaka figures as a centre of Śaivism.[15] The Mattamayūra School, believing in Śaiva Siddhānta thus exerted preponderant influence on the Śaivas of western and northern Orissa. This school as it is suggested by a learned scholar, believed in a system of *yoga* which centred around "the method of the restraints of breath, abstraction, meditation, concentration and absorption in thought (*samādhi*) and the positions of the circles in the body beginning with the root circle (*mūlādhāra* or navel)".[16] Entertaining Upaniṣadic influence, in its prayer of Lord Śiva, this school most

---

6 R.P. Mishra, *Sahajayāna: A Study of Tāntric Buddhism*, Calcutta: Punthi Pustak, 1991, pp. 280-82.

7 Ibid.; S.B. Dasgupta, *Obscure Religious Cults*, Calcutta: Firma K.L.M., 1976, p. 384.

8 Ibid.; S.C. Behera, *Rise and Fall of Sailodbhavas*, Calcutta: Punthi Pustak, 1982, p. 173.

9 Ibid., pp. 171-72.

10 Ibid., p. 172 (Amarda in Mayūrbhañj district).

11 Ibid., p. 172.

12 Ibid., p. 173.

13 Ibid.; S.N. Rajaguru, *Inscriptions of Orissa*, vol. IV, p. 87, lines 12-14.

14 Ibid., p. 87, lines 12-13.

15 Ibid., p. 49, verse 16.

16 Ibid.; R.G. Bhandarkar, *Vaiṣṇavism, Śaivism and Minor Religious System*, Varanasi: Indological Book House, 1965, p. 126.

probably followed the *yoga* of Atharvavedic Upaniṣads of the later days; which also influenced the *yoga* system of tāntric Buddhism. It appears that from this School of Śaivism, the cult of Nātha originated in Orissa and as the neighbourhood of Delhi was the primal seat of this school, the Nāthas treated Kurukṣetra as the seat of their primal lord or Ādinātha Śiva.[17] Candradvīpa where Matsyendra rescued the text of the sacred knowledge from the belly of a fish was most probably the Cāndavāli-Dhāmra regions of Orissa, which is even at present a popular citadel of the cult of Śaivism and the Nāthas. The Nātha as a School of Śaivism appears to have accultured much from different religious systems in the primary days of its genesis. It admitted the influence of Upaniṣads, Śāktism, Vaiṣṇavism and tāntric Buddhism although its adherents criticized a number of religious systems. Its Supreme Reality is called Saccidānanda,[18] the Absolute Truth,[19] the Real Truth transcending all dualism and non-dualism[20] and thus carries on the influence of Upaniṣads. Śakti figures as inseparable from Śiva in this cult.[21] The Supreme Reality in this cult is accompanied with Viṣṇu from the right hand side and with Śiva from the left hand side.[22] So Śiva as the Supreme Reality of this cult is quite different from the Śiva of other Śaiva School.[23] He is *Parama-Brahman* and is beyond all thought constructions.[24] The cult of Nātha most probably accultured the doctrine of *sahaja* both from the later Upaniṣadic culture and Sahajayāna. In *Akula Vīra Tantra*, ascribed to Matsyendranāth, *sahaja* is described as a state of supreme equilibrium which transcends all perceptual knowledge with positive and negative attributes. In this state, the *yogī* becomes one with the whole universe and realizes a non-dual existence.[25] In *Nātha Nirvāṇa Vyākhyā*, *sahaja* is defined as the knowledge of oneness of the Supreme Reality and the universe.[26] In *Maṇḍala Brāhmaṇopaniṣad*, Saccidānanda *Brahman* is described as the unsegregated circular light,[27] signifying as the

---

17 R.P. Mishra; Pūraṇanāthji, *Gorakṣa Siddhānta Saṁgraha* (in Hindi), p. 151. "*Saptakrośa pramāṇena ādinātho vased bhuvi, karakṣetre madhyedeśa koṣatraya vane sthitaḥ.*" (*Tantra Mahārṇava* quoted).

18 Ibid.; Babu Rawa Joshi, *Santa Kāvya meṅ Parokṣa Sattā Kā Svarūpa* (Hindi), p. 130, Gwalior: Kailash Pustak Sadan, 1968. (*Siddhasiddhānta Paddhati* quoted): *svajyoti satyameka jayanti tavapadaṁ saccidānanda mūrteḥ.*

19 *Satyameka* here signifies the only one Absolute Truth.

20 Ibid., p. 129. The real truth transcends both dualism and non-dualism; according to this text.

21 Ibid., p. 128.

22 Ibid.; Pūraṇanāthjī, *Gorakṣa Siddhānta Saṁgraha*, p. 2.

23 Ibid.; B.R. Joshi, *Santa Kāvya meṅ Parokṣa Sattā Kā Svarūpa*, p. 150.

24 Ibid.; Pūraṇanāthjī, *Gorakśa Siddhānta Saṁgraha*, p. 34.

25 Ibid.; N.K. Sahu, *Buddhism in Orissa*, Cuttack: Utkal University, 1958, pp. 173-74.

26 Ibid.; Yogi Narahari Nāth Sastri, *Siddha-Siddhānta-Paddhati-Nātha Nirvāṇa Vyākhyā*, quoted in Dolagovinda Sastri, *Nātha Dharma kā Krama Vikāsa* (Oriyā). A Doctoral Thesis of Utkal University, Cuttack, 1971, p. 213.

27 Ibid.; Sri Ram Sharma Acarya, 108 *Upaniṣad* (Brahmavidyā-Khaṇḍa), *Maṇḍalabrahmanopaniṣad*, p. 92.

> one and the absolute manifestative potency of the universe. Since one and the only one potency manifests in the universe, the potency and the universe are undoubtedly one. The realization of this oneness of the supreme cause potency and the universe is the *sahajānanda* of this Upaniṣad. Mind dissolved in *sahajānanda* becomes as peaceful as that of Śambhu, who is beyond all thought-discriminations.[28] *Sahaja* in Sahajayāna also reveals similar impressions as stated above.

Mahipati, a Marathi writer, had written the stories of Indian saints in his book, *Bhaktavijaya*. Mahipati was born in the little village of Taharabad, in the Ahmednagar district, in the year CE 1715 and died in the year CE 1790.[29]

Birth of Matsyendra

About Mahāyogī Matsyendranāth's birth, Mahipati gives the following narration:[30]

> While Śiva was giving her instructions the fair-complexioned one was unconscious. Just at that moment there was a foetus in the womb of a crocodile. It replied from there that it understood the instructions being given. In the midst of the violent waves of the sea this foetus remained hidden in the womb of the crocodile. Hearing the instructions given by Śiva to Pārvatī, it held it in its memory; just as when Kayādhu was in a prison, Nārada came suddenly there and kindly gave her instructions, Prahlād still in the womb heard it, so now as the enemy of Madan (Śiva) was instructing Pārvatī. His words reached into the womb of the crocodile. At that moment, Matsyendranāth was born, a saviour of the world. He was in truth the *avatāra* of Śiva. He was the very mount Meru of those indifferent to earthly things, an ocean of intelligence, descending as an *avatāra* to save the world. Matsyendranāth was supremely wise in all divine knowledge. He was the wish-tree giver of the highest form of final deliverance, the internal witnesser of every life, or the second Viṣṇu himself, the *homa* of the qualities, one in the form of intelligence, a moon becoming a full moon. Although he came with a body, he was separate from it. He was a statue of the Supreme *Brahman*, the essence of the highest form of happiness made manifest to this world. As he came out of his mother's womb he did not forget that he was the Supreme *Brahman*. He was not touched by the violent winds of ignorance. He at once came out of the water. He began to think of himself, "I want to see all the sacred bathing places". From there, Matsyendra wandered about as he wished from town to town, and ate whatever was given to him. Afterwards he was accustomed to go into the jungle and sit by himself alone. Thus, indifferent to all earthly things, twelve years of his life passed away. On one occasion, however, he arrived casually at a certain town.

---

28 *Satyameka* here signifies the only one Absolute Truth, p. 126.

29 E. Abbott and N.R. Godbole (eds.), *Stories of Indian Saints*, Delhi: Motilal Banarsidass, 1999, p. XXII.

30 Ibid., 1999, pp. 359-60.

About the historicity of the Nātha cult in Orissa, H.K. Mahatab[31] states:

> Evidences of Nātha *dharma* in Orissa can be traced since the last quarter of the eighth century. A statue of Matsyendranāth in the form of Padmapāṇi Avalokiteśvara at forest of Rajnagar under Deravisi block of Kendrapāṛā sub-division is still worshipped by the Nāthas of the surrounding villages. The inscription on both sides of the statue is in Kuṭila *lipi* or proto-Uḍra *lipi*. The present Oriyā script was not evolved by then and the period of that script is accepted to be in between sixth and eleventh centuries. The proto-type of the same statue is seen at Kendrapāṛā bus stand with the same inscription, and another at Trilocanpur village under Mahajajapur Grām Pañcāyat near Bahugrāma is also worshipped by the Nāthas of the surrounding villages. This proves that towards the last quarter of ninth century, Matsyendranāth and Gorakhanāth were worshipped in Orissa as the incarnations of Viṣṇu and Śiva respectively. The most ancient specimens of Oriyā prose and poetry are ascribed to be the works of Gorakhanāth and other Nātha *siddhas*.
>
> The theory of *piṇḍa-brahmāṇḍa* (cosmos in microcosm) of Gorakhanāth serves as the backbone of Orissan Vaiṣṇava philosophy of the Pañcasakhā literature as in the case of *nirguṇa santa kāvyas* of Hindī, Punjābī and Gujarātī literatures of the ancient and medieval periods.
>
> Since the dates of Sāralā Dās, the Nāthas of Orissa found to be mentioned as Rudraja and Śiśuvedī brāhmaṇa (*śiśuvedī haive pañcaviṁśā sahasra brāhmaṇa* — Madhya-Parva; *śiśumuna vedena ve lakṣeka dvija* — Sabhā-Parva). They observe most of the Vedic Brāhmanical rites so far as social customs are concerned, with some variations. The sacred thread, according to the Nāthas, is ever pure (*pavitra*) even during the period of uncleanliness due to birth and death. The dead body is buried seated in *yogāsana* in a compound specially preserved in the premises of *maṭhas* or homestead land. The *samādhis* are treated as sacred shrines. Śiśuveda of the Nāthas is regarded as the fifth Veda. A person from any caste or religious sects can accept Nātha *dharma*, but he must use the title of "Nātha" after his name after due initiation. Hundreds of *maṭhas*, *pīṭhas* and *gaddīs* are scattered all over Orissa. Although idolatry is forbidden in Nātha *dharma*, it came to be mixed up first with Buddhism, then with Hinduism. Buddhist and brāhmaṇa idols were accepted by the Nāthas as theirs. It is the Nātha *dharma* which made *yoga* popular in Orissa.
>
> One interesting fact is that Orissa is the state where in ancient times *Atharvaveda* was the prevalent Veda. This was known when research was made on *Paipallāda Sūtra* of *Atharvaveda* which was taken to be lost but manuscripts of which were found in many villages in Orissa. When *Atharvaveda* was downgraded during ascendency of Brāhmanism many changed over to *Yajurveda* but they cannot dispense with some rituals of *Atharvaveda* during ceremonies such as marriage, etc.
>
> That the influence of these religious currents and cross-currents worked in Orissa cannot be gainsaid.

31 H.K. Mahatab, "Culture of Orissa", *OHRJ*, vol. XXX, nos. 2-4, 1984, pp. 10-11.

The development of Nātha cult in the Mahānadī Valley gave much impulse to the development of Oriyā language and literatures. Chittaranjan Das[32] discusses this impact:

> The early Oriyā specimen of the Nātha literature also seems to fall into this category. Nātha cult was itself built upon an exclusive emphasis on *haṭha-yoga* which was prevailing in India as a very old tradition. At a time when the higher strata in society took pleasure in philosophical Buddhism or dabbled in the Brāhmanic injunctions, the lower strata got an outlet in the Nātha doctrine of the perfect body. It could reach all the lay quarters in society which had been forbidden an access to the religions of the elite and appeared as it were as a popular edition to traditional *yoga,* Tantra and Vajrayāna Buddhism of the Indian Great Tradition. Besides those who had run away, there were also many others of the cult in Orissa and they had taken to names in imitation of the great names of the cult, Gorakhanāth and Matsyendranāth. What these *yogīs* composed and sang as their cult literature has definitely served as an intermediary step in helping the then prevailing Apabhraṁśa reach a state of further distinction and in the long run earn a distinguished shape called Oriyā. As in Hindī as well as Beṅgālī, there is some poetry of the cultish variety associated with the name of Gorakhanāth and this has led some scholars at times to believe that the original Gorakṣa was actually from Orissa itself.
>
> The *Kaḷasā Cauṅtīsā* of Bachā Dāsa is a brilliant piece of a specimen in the Oriyā literature of all ages, though it has been ascribed to the pre-Sāralā period. *Cauṅtīsās* are poems where the stanzas begin, one by one, with the letters of the Oriyā alphabet, which number thirty-four. The *kaḷasā* depicts in lucid poetry the marriage of Śiva with Umā, the main emphasis being on the humour with which the poet has depicted the whole episode. Bachā Dāsa describes the would-be wed bridegroom as a disabled old man, decrepit with asthma and Umā's agony at the thought that she has cast her lot with this queer odd thing for a whole life. It may be that in the process of being copied and copied again through the ages, the original text has managed to get a chastened form in which it appears today, but the *kaḷasā* continues to remain an inimitable instance of the fact that so much mirth can be created and made available to the reader by presenting a God as a laughable old stock of a bridegroom that in appearance is no match for the most beautiful bride contemplated on earth. *Kaḷasā* in its own time became without doubt so much adored as a piece of poem that the musical metre in which it was written continued for many centuries after it, to be used by many other poets. In view of the very developed language and style of the *kaḷasā*, Bachā Dāsa, the author is sometimes considered to have belonged to a much later period. But it can be nevertheless claimed that whatever the age, he is by far the best among the many *cauṅtīsā* writers in Oriyā. We are not sure if he has written only one *cauṅtīsā,* or if he has written *cauṅtīsās* only. But unfortunately nothing more has been available of him. All glory to a literature that has so lucid and so profound

---

32 Chittaranjan Das, *A Glimpse into Oriya Literature*, Bhubaneswar: Orissa Sahitya Akademi, 1982, pp. 52-54.

> a poet at its early stages. Though *kaḷasā* presents its author primarily as a *bhakta* who has Lord Śiva as his object of adoration, yet there is no trace in it of the self-mortifying type of *bhakti* in Bachā Dāsa, a *bhakti* that only asks for and complains about what all one wanted to get and has not got yet. The real *bhakti* literature is perhaps one which speaks with a sense of proximity with the object one wants to attain and to adore, a sense that brings you nearer and nearer, so nearer that it gives you that total and integral feeling of healthy-mindedness which takes away from you all the fever and the anguish associated with seeking.

In the *Tantra-Mahārṇava*, quoted in the *Gorakha Siddhānta Saṁgraha*, Gorakhanāth is described as residing in the forest of Jagannātha (Orissa). This proves that Gorakhanāth was connected with the Orissa region.

The Nātha *siddhas* believe that Ādinātha is the first Nātha, the founder of all esoteric sciences. He is very often equated with Śiva and Vajrasattva. The Hara-Gaurī conception of Nāthism is an adaptation of both the Mahāyānic *karuṇā* and *śūnyatā*, and the Vajrayānic *upāya* and *prajñā*. The Śūnyavāda of the Mādhyamika system is also accepted in Nāthism. According to Nāgārjuna, *śūnya* or vacuity is of four kinds — *śūnya, atiśūnya, mahāśūnya* and *śarvaśūnya*. The followers of Nāthism believe in three kinds of *śūnya* — *adiśūnya, madhya-śūnya* and *antaḥ-śūnya*. This *śūnya* is to be realized through *yoga*. The process has been described in a text called *Hāḍimālā*, which says that by the yogic control of breath thirty knots in the spinal cord can be loosened, as a result of which the two vital winds, *prāṇa* and *apāna*, can enter the spinal cord and move upwards as *haṁsa* through the six nerve plexuses — *mūlādhāra, svādhiṣṭhāna, maṇipūra, anāhata, viśuddha* (*vaisandhari*) and *ājñā* (*ādya*) — and on reaching the *sahasrāra* region assume the nature of *śūnya*. There are 72,000 nerves within the body of which sixty-four can be distinctly located and fifteen are utilized for yogic purposes. In the *Yogacintāmaṇi* section of the *Gorakhavijaya*, we have the concept of *navacakra* which is the addition of three extra stages to the tāntric *ṣaṭcakra*. These extra stages are the three forms of *śūnya* — *ādi, madhya* and *antaḥ*. It also deals with *ulṭā-sādhanā* which is a yogic method of making the vital fluid flow upward. This shows that the Nātha *siddhas* practised *vajrolī*.[33]

In nothern, western and southern India centres of Nāthism had spread.[34] Nātha movement, which became the Nātha cult, was an all-India movement inspiring literature in many of the local vernaculars in most parts of India.

---

33 J.P. Singh Deo, *Tāntric Art of Orissa*, Delhi: Kalpaz Publications, 2001, pp. 89-90.

34 George Weston Briggs, *Gorakhnāth and the Kānphaṭa Yogīs*, Delhi: Motilal Banarsidass, 1989, *passim*; Shashibhusan Das Gupta, *Obscure Religious Cults*, Calcutta: Firma K.L.M., 1995, pp. 367-81; P.K. Bandyopadhyay, *Nātha Cult and Mahānād* (*A Study in Syncretism*), Delhi: B.R. Publishing Corporation, 1992, *passim*.

In the entire Mahānadī River Valley, Nātha cult was popular and it is still a living cult in India. One ferry *ghāṭa* alias bathing *ghāṭa* of the Mahānadī River side, within Sonepur township, is named as Matsyendranāth Ghāṭ.[35] One Macchendranātha temple still standing in full form, built during the Kaḷacuri period (twelfth–thirteenth centuries CE) at Amarakaṇṭak.[36] This temple has *antarāla, maṇḍapa* and *garbha-gṛha* and all of which are joined in an axial length. The sanctum is *pañcaratha*. The three parts of this temple form parts of a unified scheme and according to scholars, they represent advancement from the early Nāgara form.[37] With the exception of the *śikhara* and the back-rests of branches, it is in a fairly good state of preservation. Certain portions of the *śikhara* bear traces of white wash, which may indicate that it was partly re-built at some later date. Access is obtained to the interior of the *maṇḍapa,* through an opening on the western side or the front of the *maṇḍapa,* where a stone door-frame has been fitted.[38] Unlike other temples, this temple faces the west and the floor of the *garbha-gṛha* is far below that of the *maṇḍapa*.

Tantrarāja Tantra[39] is a text of Nātha *dharma*. It is a haṭha-yogic text where *kūrma sthiti* is mentioned thus:

> He who does *jāpa* without knowing *kūrma sthiti* not only fails to get the fruit thereof but he meets with destruction. Therefore *kūrma* should be first known. *Kūrma* is of four kinds namely firstly *para kūrma*. This which is steady (*sthira*) and extends to 50 *koṭi*s (500,000,000) of *yojana*s (between 8 and 9 miles) supports *pṛthvī*. The others are *deśagata, grāmaga* and *gṛhaga*. That is just as the supreme tortoise supports the whole universe, the others support particular countries, villages and dwellings.

Kūrma sthiti means that higher austerities of yogic asceticism should be kept secret and the yogic masters (*guru*s) should teach the disciples to maintain *kūrma sthiti,* for spiritual progress. Archaeological remains of *kūrma sthiti* is found at the Mohangiri site of Kālāhāṇḍī district. Therefore, the author[40] had mentioned:

---

35 J.P. Singh Deo, *Some Tāntric Esotericism of Orissa*, Kolkata: R.N. Bhattacharya, 2003, p. 290.

36 Minoti Chakravarti, *Religious Life in the Kalachuri Empire*, Calcutta: Punthi Pustak, 1999, p. 114 and Pl. 42.

37 Ibid.; R.K. Sharma, *The Kalachuris and Their Times*, New Delhi: Sundeep Prakashan, 1980, p. 264.

38 Ibid., for details, see R.D. Banerji, *The Haihayas of Triputi and Their Monuments*, Memoirs of Archaelogical Survey of India, no. 23, Calcutta, 1931, pp. 60 f.

39 Sir John Woodroffe (ed.), *Tantra-Rāja-Tantra* (*A Short Analysis*), Madras: Ganesh & Co., 1971, p. 33.

40 *THOMV*, p. 113.

> While collecting antiquities in 1992, to start a multipurpose museum at Bhawanipatna, the author had visited the Mohangiri site. It was apparent from the ruins of the Śiva or the Bhairava Temple at Mohangiri that it faced east and stood on a stone platform. At the north-west portion of the platform or stone basement, four tortoises were chiselled. The name Vyādha-Bhairava, found in the inscriptions proves that the site was important because the tāntric, yogic and esoteric *sādhanā*s were practised here, which are inner, secret, mysterious *sādhanā*s. The most esoteric *sādhanā* is the *yoga* of sexual transformation, or the *haṭha-yoga* practice of the union of male and female principles. The remnant of four chiselled tortoises found on the platform of the Śiva alias Bhairava temple, now named "Dhabaleśvar Śiva temple", at Mohangiri reminds the author about the secret doctrinaire of *kūrma sthiti*, as mentioned in the *Tantrarāja Tantra*, a *haṭha-yoga* manual, meant for daily *sādhanā*s of the Nātha *haṭha-yogī*s. The existence of four tortoises in different sizes chiselled in one line at Mohangiri site, is Kālāhāṇḍī's gift to the esoteric *haṭha-yoga* of Nātha *dharma*.

The epitomic haṭha-yogic, tāntric sculptural masterpiece of India, which is identified as the composite tāntric-yogic figure of Mahākāla and Mahākālī, by the author,[41] stands at Tala site of Bilaspur district of Chhattisgarh state, in the upper Mahānadī Valley. This composite gigantic haṭha-yogic image seems to be the outcome of the combination of all tāntric schools of Aghora Śaivism, Mattamayūra Śaivism[42] and the Nātha cult. Aghora Śaivism and the Nātha cult are still living religious practices of alchemical body, which were the *siddha* traditions of the medieval India.

---

41 J.P. Singh Deo, "Composite Tāntric Yogic Figure of Mahākāla and Mahākālī", *Riddle of Indian Iconography* (*Zetetic on Rare Icon from Tala*), L.S. Nigam (ed.), Delhi: Sharada Publishing House, 2000, pp. 127-34; *THOMV*, 2004, pp. 155-71.

42 V.V. Mirashi, *Corpus Inscriptionum Indicarum*, vol. IV, pt. I, Ootacamund, 1955 (Archaeological Survey of India), pp. clxii-clxiv; L.K. Panda, *Śaivism in Orissa*, Delhi: Sundeep Prakashan, 1985, pp. 78-99; R.P. Mishra, "Mattamayūra Śaivism in Orissa", *Culture and Collections*, R.P. Mishra (ed.), Calcutta: Punthi Pustak, 1996, pp. 101-39.

11

Land of Kāmakalā
Originator of Puruṣottama Jagannātha Cult

THE Mahānadī River Valley was the land of Kāmakalā and Uḍḍiyāna-Pīṭha, during the medieval period of Indian history. It is here in this valley that Puruṣottama Jagannātha deity and the Jagannātha cult got developed, being Purī as its headquarters.

From time immemorial Puruṣottama (the highest self) was worshipped at Purī. While discussing *God Talks with Arjuna*: *The Bhagavad-Gītā*, Sri Sri Paramahamsa Yogananda[1] discusses about Puruṣottama, the uttermost being and gives English translation of the Sanskrit verses (ch. 15):

Eternal Aśvattha: The Tree of Life

श्रीभगवानुवाच
ऊर्ध्वमूलमधः शाखमश्वत्थं प्राहुर्व्ययम् ।
छन्दांसि यस्य पर्णानि यस्तं वेद स वेदवित् ॥ 1 ॥

śrī bhagavānuvāca
ūrdhvamūlamadhaḥ śākhamaśvatthaṁ prāhurvyam ।
chandāṁsi yasya parṇāni yastaṁ veda sa vedavit ॥1 ॥

The Blessed Lord said:

They (the wise) speak of an eternal *aśvattha* tree, with roots above and boughs beneath, whose leaves are Vedic hymns. He who understands this tree of life is a Veda-knower.

अधश्चोर्ध्वं प्रसृतास्तस्य शाखा गुणप्रवृद्धा विषयप्रवालाः ।
अधश्च मूलान्यनुसन्ततानि कर्मानुबन्धीनि मनुष्यलोके ॥ 2 ॥

---

[1] Sri Sri Paramahamsa Yogananda, *God Talks with Arjuna: the Bhagavad-Gītā*, vol. II, Kolkata: Yogoda Satsanga Society of India, 2nd impression, 2002, pp. 927-52.

adhaścordhvaṁ prasr̥tāstasya śākhā guṇapravr̥ddhā
viṣayapravālāḥ ।
adhaśca mūlānyanusantatāni karmānubhandhīni
manuṣyaloke ॥ 2 ॥

Its branches spread and below, nurtured by the *guṇas*; its buds are the sense objects; and downward, into the world of men, extend the rootlings that force man to actions.

न रूपमस्येह तथोपलभ्यते नान्तो न चादिर्न च सम्प्रतिष्ठा।
अश्वत्थमेनं सुविरूढमूलमसङ्गशस्न्नेण दृढेन छित्वा ॥ 3 ॥
ततः पदं तत्परिमार्गितव्यं यस्मिनाता न निवर्तन्ति भूयः।
तमेख चाद्यं पुरूषं प्रपदो यतः प्रवृतिः प्रसृता पुराणो ॥ 4 ॥

na rūpamasyeha tathopalabhyate nānto na cādirna ca sampratiṣṭhā ।
aśvatthamenaṁ suvirūḍhamūlamasaṅgaśasnneṇa dr̥ḍhena chitvā ॥ 3 ॥

tataḥ padaṁ tatparimārgitavyaṁ yasminātā na nivartanti bhūyaḥ ।
tameva cādyaṁ puruṣaṁ prapado yataḥ pravr̥ttiḥ prasr̥tā purāṇo ॥ 4 ॥

The true nature of this tree, its beginning, its end and its modes of continuity — none of these is understood by ordinary men. The wise, having destroyed the firmly rooted *aśvattha* with the powerful axe of non-attachment; thinking, "I take refuge in the primeval Puruṣa from whom alone issued the immemorial processes of creation", seek the supreme goal. Reaching it, they return to phenomenal existence no more.

The Abode of the Unmanifest

निर्मानमोहा जितसङ्गदोषा अध्यात्मनित्या विनिवृत्तकामाः।
द्वन्द्वैर्विमुभाः सुखदुःखसञ्ज्ञैर्गच्छन्त्यमूढाः पदमव्ययं तत् ॥ 5 ॥

nirmānamohā jitasaṅgadoṣā adhyātmanityā vinivr̥ttakāmāḥ ।
dvandvairvimuktāḥ sukhaduḥkhasaṁjñairgacchantyamūḍhāḥ padamavyayaṁ tat ॥ 5 ॥

न तद्भासयते सूर्यो न शशाङ्को न पावकः।
यद्गत्वा न निवर्तन्ते तद्धाम परमः मम ॥ 6 ॥

na tadbhāsayate sūryo na śaśāṅko na pāvakaḥ ।
yadgatvā na nivartante taddhāma paramaṁ mama ॥ 6 ॥

Where no sun or moon or fire shines, that is my Supreme Abode. Having reached there, men are never reborn.

How Spirit Manifests as the Soul

ममैवांशो जिवलोके जीवभूतः सनातनः।
मनःषष्ठानीन्द्रियाणि प्रकृतिस्थानि कर्षति ॥ 7 ॥

mamaivāṁśo jivaloke jīvabhūtaḥ sanātanaḥ ।
manaḥṣaṣṭhānīndriyāṇi prakṛtisthāni karṣati ॥ 7 ॥

An eternal part of myself, manifesting as a living soul in the world of beings, attracts to itself the six senses, including the mind, which rest in *prakṛti*.

शरीरं यदवाप्नोति यच्चाप्युत्क्रामतीश्वरः।
गृहीत्वैतानि संयाति वायुर्गन्धानिवाशयात् ॥ 8 ॥

śarīraṁ yadavāpnoti yaccāpyutkrāmatīśvaraḥ ।
gṛhītvaitāni saṁyāti vāyurgandhānivāśayāt ॥ 8 ॥

When the Lord as the *jīva* acquires a body, He brings with Him the mind and the senses. When He leaves that body, He takes them and goes even as the wind wafts away scents from their dwelling places (in flowers).

श्रोत्रं चक्षुः स्पर्शनं च रसनं घ्राणमेव च।
अधिष्ठाय मनश्चयं विषयानुपसेवते ॥ 9 ॥

śrotraṁ cakṣuḥ sparśanaṁ ca rasanaṁ ghrāṇameva ca ।
adhiṣṭhāya manaścayaṁ viṣayānupasevate ॥ 9 ॥

Presiding over the mind, and the senses of hearing, sight, touch, taste and smell, He enjoys the sensory world.

उत्क्रामन्तं स्थितं वापि भुञ्जानं वा गुणान्वितम्।
विमूढा नानुपश्यन्ति पश्यन्ति ज्ञानचक्षुषः ॥ 10 ॥

utkrāmantaṁ sthitaṁ vāpi bhuñjānaṁ vā guṇānvitaṁ ।
vimūḍhā nānupaśyanti paśyanti jñānacakṣuṣaḥ ॥ 10 ॥

The deluded do not perceive Him staying or departing or experiencing the world of the *guṇas*. Those whose eye of wisdom is open see Him.

यतन्तो योगिनश्चौनं पश्यन्त्यात्मन्यवस्थितम्।
यनन्तोऽप्यकृतात्मानो नैनं पश्यन्त्यचेतसः ॥ 11 ॥

yatanto yoginaścaunaṁ paśyantyātmanyavasthitam ।
yananto 'pyakṛtātmāno nainaṁ paśyantyacetasaḥ ॥ 11 ॥

The *yogīs* striving for liberation see Him existing in themselves; but those who are unpurified and undisciplined are unable to perceive Him even when they struggle to do so.

यदादित्यगतं तेजो जगद्भासयतेऽखिलम् ।
यच्चन्द्रमसि यच्चाग्नौ तत्तेजो विद्धि मामकम् ॥ 12 ॥

yadādityagataṁ tejo jagadbhāsayate 'khilam ।
yaccandramasi yaccāgnau tattejo viddhi māmakam ॥ 12 ॥

The light of the sun that illumines the whole world, the light from the moon, and the light in fire — know this radiance to be mine.

गामाविश्य च भूतानि धारयाम्यहमोजसा ।
पुष्णामि चौषधीः सर्वाः सोमो भूत्वा रसात्मकः ॥ 13 ॥

gāmāviśya ca bhūtāni dhārayāmyahamojasā ।
puṣṇāmi cauṣadhīḥ sarvāḥ somo bhūtvā rasātmakaḥ ॥ 13 ॥

Permeating earth with my effulgence, I support all beings; having become the watery moon, I bring forth all plant forms.

अहं वैश्वानरो भूत्वा प्राणिनां देहमाश्रितः ।
प्राणाणनसमायुभः पचाम्यन्नं चतुर्विधम् ॥ 14 ॥

ahaṁ vaiśvānaro bhūtvā prāṇināṁ dehamāśritaḥ ।
prāṇāṇanasamāyuktaḥ pacāmyannaṁ caturvidham ॥ 14 ॥

Having become Vaiśvānara (fiery power), I exist in the body of living creatures; and, acting through *prāṇa* and *apāna*, I digest food that is eaten in four ways.

सर्वस्य चाहं हृदि सन्निविष्टो मत्तः स्मृतिर्ज्ञानमपोहनं च ।
वेदैश्च सर्वैरहमेव वेद्यो वेदान्तकृद्वेदविदेव चाहम् ॥ 15 ॥

sarvasya cāhaṁ hṛdi sanniviṣṭo mattaḥ smṛtirjñānamapohanaṁ ca ।
vedaiśca sarvairahameva vedyo vedāntakṛdvedavideva cāham ॥ 15 ॥

Also, I am seated in the heart of all beings; and from me come memory and knowledge, as well as their loss. Verily I am that which is to be known through the Vedas; indeed, I am the Veda-knower and the author of the Vedānta.

The Supreme Spirit: Beyond the Perishable and the Imperishable

द्वाविमौ पुरुषौ लोकेश्वरश्चक्षर एव च ।
क्षरः सर्वाणि भूतानि कूटस्थोऽक्षर उच्यते ॥ 16 ॥

dvāvimau puruṣau lokeścaraścakṣara eva ca ।
kṣaraḥ sarvāṇi bhūtāni kūṭastho 'kṣara ucyate ॥ 16 ॥

There are two beings (*puruṣas*) in the cosmos, the destructible and the indestructible. The creatures are the destructible, the *kūṭastha* is the indestructible.

उत्तमः पुरुषस्त्वन्यः परमात्मेत्युदाहृतः।
यो लोकत्रयमाविश्य बिभर्त्यव्यय ईश्वरः॥ 17॥

uttamaḥ puruṣastvanyaḥ paramātmetyudāhṛtaḥ ।
yo lokatrayamāviśya bibhartyavyaya īśvaraḥ ॥ 17 ॥

But there exists another, the highest being, designated the "Supreme Spirit" — the Eternal Lord who, permeating the three worlds, upholds them.

यस्मात्क्षरमतीतोऽहमक्षरादपि चोत्तमः।
अतोऽस्मि लोके वेदे च प्रथितः पुरुषोत्तमः॥ 18॥

yasmātkṣaramatīto 'hamakṣarādapi cottamaḥ ।
ato 'smi loke vede ca prathitaḥ puruṣottamaḥ ॥ 18 ॥

I (the Lord) am beyond the perishable (*prakṛti*) and am also higher than the imperishable (*kūṭastha*). Therefore, in the worlds and in the Veda (the intuitive perception of undeluded souls) I am proclaimed Puruṣottama, the uttermost being.

यो मामेवमसम्मूढो जानाति परुषोत्तमम्।
स सर्वविद्भजति मां सर्वभावेन भारत॥ 19॥

yo māmevamasammūḍho jānāti puruṣottamam ।
sa sarvavidbhajati māṁ sarvabhāvena bhārata ॥ 19 ॥

Whosoever, freed from delusion, knows me thus as the Supreme Spirit, knows all, O descendant of Bhārata (Arjuna). He worships me with his whole being.

इति गुह्यतमं शास्त्रमिदमुक्तं मयानघ।
एतद्बुद्ध्वा बुद्धिमान्स्यात्कृतकृत्यश्च भारत॥ 20॥

iti guhyatamaṁ śāstramidamuktaṁ mayānagha ।
etadbuddhvā buddhimānsyātkṛtakṛtyaśca bhārata ॥ 20 ॥

Herewith, O sinless one (Arjuna), have I taught thee this most profound wisdom. Understanding it, a man becomes a sage, one who has successfully fulfilled all his duties, and yet continues in dutiful actions.

ॐ तत्सदिति श्रीमद्भगवद्गीतासूपनिषत्सु ब्रह्मविद्यायां योगशास्त्रे
श्रीकृष्णार्जुनसंवादे पुरुषोत्तमयोगो नाम पञ्चदशोऽध्याय॥

> *oṁ tatsaditi śrīmadhbhagavadgītāsūpaniṣatsu*
> *brahmavidyāyāṁ yogaśāstre śrīkṛṣṇārjunasaṁvāde*
> *puruṣottamayogo nāma pañcadaśo 'dhyāya* ।
>
> *aum, tat, sat* ।
>
> In the Upaniṣad of the holy *Bhagavad-Gītā* — the discourse of Lord Kṛṣṇa to Arjuna, which is the scripture of *yoga* and the Science of God-realization — this is the fifteenth chapter, called "union with the Supreme Spirit".

While dealing with the antiquity of Jagannātha Purī as a place of pilgrimage, K.N. Mahapatra[2] states:

> We now turn to the *Anargha-Rāghava Nāṭakam*, by Murari Mishra, written half a century since Śaṅkara's visit to Purī. This drama was presented at the time of a festival (*yātrā*) of God Puruṣottama, who was being worshipped on the sea-shore:
>
> नान्द्यन्ते सूत्रधार-अलमतिबिस्तरेण। भो भो लबणोद-वेला-वनाली नमालतुर कन्दलस्य त्रिभुवनमौलि-मण्डन-महानीलमणेः कमला कुच-कलश केलि कस्तूरिका पत्राङ्क भागवत ८ पुरुषोत्तमस्य यात्रायां मुपस्थानीया सभासद॥ ८[3]॥
>
> *nāndyante sūtradhāra-alamatibistareṇa* । *bho bho labaṇoda-velā-vanālī namālatura kandalasya tribhuvanamauli-maṇḍana-mahānīlamaṇeḥ kamalā kuca-kalaśa keli kastūrikā patrāṅka bhāgavata* 8 *puruṣottamasya yātrāyāṁ mupasthāniyā sabhāsada* ॥ 8 ॥
>
> This world famous God Puruṣottama, the consort of Kamalā, worshipped on the sea-shore, in whose *yātrā*, this great drama was presented before an audience of learned people, can be no other than Jagannātha in Purī, who must have been well known throughout India, by the time of Murari, who is assigned to the ninth century CE.[4] Murari, who wrote his drama *Anargha-Rāghava*, in imitation of *Mahavīracarita*, of Bhavabhūti, got it performed, at the time of *yātrā* (perhaps car festival) of God Puruṣottama in Purī, who must have been the family-deity of his Royal patron, whose name is not given.

K.N. Mahapatra has confused the names "Puruṣottama" and "Jagannātha", to be the same. By that time "Puruṣottama Jagannātha", deity had not yet evolved, developed,

---

[2] K.N. Mahapatra, "Antiquity of Jagannātha: Purī as a Place of Pilgrimage", *OHRJ*, vol. III, no. 1, June 1954, pp. 9-10.

[3] Ibid.; *Anargha-Rāghava Nāṭakam*, Act I, p. 8, published by Nirnaya Sagara Press.

[4] Ibid.; Dasgupta and De, *History of Sanskrit Literature*, vol. I, *Classical Period*, p. 449.

and installed as the presiding deity of Puruṣottama Kṣetra Purī. It is a great misnomer of K.N. Mahapatra's understanding, therefore a misunderstanding.

The information on Puruṣottama and his consort Kamalā in *Anargha-Rāghava Nāṭakam* of Murari Misra, dated to the ninth century CE is of importance. The name Kamalā is used both for Goddesses Pārvatī and Lakṣmī. So, it seems that during that period the image of Puruṣottama was Umā-Maheśvara or Lakṣmī-Nārāyaṇa. This shape represents *lāṭa-mudrā*, a *haṭha-yoga* practice, which is the premier *mudrā* before the sexual act for pleasure or for *yoga* of sexual transformation. Interaction between man and woman, Tantra-wise are for three purposes — pleasure, procreation and *samādhi*.[5] In yogic conception, when man and woman come together, they should first perform haṭha-yogic *lāṭa-mudrā* and after its practice, they can use their sexual energy for pleasure, procreation and *samādhi*. So, it is worth knowing details about *lāṭa-mudrā*.

About *lāṭa-mudrā*, B. Bhattacharya[6] says:

> This is the ultimate secret of *lāṭa-sādhanā*, the female entwines the body of the male like a creeper, as do the snakes. The erotic in the human body creeps through the body and becomes love and understanding. That is Śaṅkara's burning of Kāma with the third eye. You know the legend. That is the end of *sādhanā*. Let the serpent lie tame as a friend clinging to the body.
>
> Didn't you seek the secrets of the *lāṭa-sādhanā*? The male–female *āsanas* clinging over long hours are parts of this *sādhanā*. The (*cadavar*) *śava āsana* too is another type of *lāṭa-sādhanā*. Did you not want to know?
>
> Watch them, the two, the male and the female, "O" they lie quite on you as two earthworms, like two hands joined in prayer, yet how powerful they are. Death in life, life in death.

This discussion proves that Purī was originally Puruṣottama-Kṣetra (site) and Puruṣottama was worshipped at Purī from time immemorial in *lāṭa-mudrā* haṭha-yogic pose (*mudrā*).

The present presiding deity of Purī is Puruṣottama Jagannātha. Therefore the evolution of "Jagannātha" name has to be studied and how it became synthesized

---

5 J.P. Singh Deo, *Tāntric Art of Orissa*, Delhi: Kalpaz Publications, 2001, p. 31.

6 B. Bhattacharya, *The World of Tantrā*, New Delhi: Munshiram Manoharlal Publishers, 1992, pp. 447-48.

as Puruṣottama Jagannātha is to be known.

While dealing on the "Origin and Antiquity of Jagannātha", H.K. Mahatab[7] mentions that Jagannātha has been referred to for the first time in *Jñānasiddhi* of Indrabhūti, written in CE 717. This statement is completely wrong. It is therefore proper to know about the use of the word "Jagannātha".

The Use of the Word "Jagannātha"

From *Vālmīki Rāmāyaṇa*, Uttara Kāṇḍa, 108, 28, it is known that the family deity of Ikṣvāku dynasty was Jagannātha.[8] Regarding the composition period of the *Mahābhārata*, M.A. Mehendale[9] remarks, "The *Mahābhārata* cannot have received its present form earlier than the fourth century BCE and later than the fourth century CE." N.K. Sahu[10] is of the opinion that in Sanskrit literature Jagannātha as a deity is unknown before *Jñānasiddhi*. Jagannātha mentioned in the Śānti Parva of the *Mahābhārata* of Baṅgabāsī edition and even in early publication of Baṅgabāsī edition is an interpolation as this is not found in Poona edition or Kumbakoṇam edition, and even in early publication of Baṅgabāsī edition, Purī (Puruṣottama Purī) is the seat of Puruṣottama and not of Jagannātha. In the tenth century CE a religious revolution synthesized Jagannātha of Sambalpur with Puruṣottama of Purī.

In a manuscript discovered by Nicolas Notovitch,[11] at Himis Buddhist monastery of Ladakh, one comes across the word "Jagannātha". Notovitch[12] informs that the principal scrolls — which were written in India and Nepal, at different epochs, as the events happened — are in Lhasa; several thousands in number. In some great convents are to be found copies, which the Lamas, during their sojourn in Lhasa, have made at various times, and have then given to their cloisters as souvenirs of the period they spent with the Dalai Lama.

This shows that the manuscript of the "The Unknown Life of Jesus Christ",

---

7 H.K. Mahatab, "Culture of Orissa", *OHRJ*, vol. XXX, nos. 2-4, 1984, p. 15.

8 *TCOJ*, 1971, p. 73; Baba Mishra, *Medieval Orissa and Cult of Jagannātha*, New Delhi: Navrang, 1995, p. 49.

9 M.A. Mehendale, "*The Mahābhārata*", *THACOTIP*, vol. II, *The Age of Imperial Unity*, 1968, p. 251.

10 N.K. Sahu, "Padma Sambhava (Appendix III)", *Gazetteer of India, Orissa, Sambalpur*, N. Senapati (chief ed.), Cuttack: 1971, pp. 96-97.

11 N. Notovitch, *The Unknown Life of Jesus Christ*, J.H. Connelly and L. Landsberg (tr.), Calcutta: Nababharat Publishers, 1981, p. 85.

12 Ibid., p. 38.

was written in different periods, and the actual period of composition is not known. This author had already examined this aspect,[13] where it is mentioned:

> From the discovery of a manuscript in the Himis monastery in Ladakh, by noted Russian traveller Nicholas Notovitch and Swami Abhedānanda, an apostle of Sri Ramakrishna Paramahamsa (Bengali Book, *Kashmere-O-Tibbete*), it is known that Jesus Christ had visited Purī, where he was taught to read and to understand the Vedas, to cure physical ills by means of prayers, to teach and to expound the sacred scriptures, to drive out evil desires from man and make him again in the likeness of God. It seems, the site of modern Purī had already become popular, as a religious and spiritual centre with its *vedī*, during that period.

From Nicolas Notovitch's[14] work, it is known that Jesus Christ spent six years in Jagannātha, in Rājagṛha, in Benares and in other holy cities. The common people loved Issa, for he lived in peace with the vaiśyas and the śūdras, to whom he taught the holy scriptures.

It becomes necessary to know the use of the title Jagannātha and how it came into use in Sanskrit literature. H.V. Stietencron[15] states that it appears that the decisive factor in bringing about the correlation of Jagannātha with Viṣṇu was Śāktism and more particularly the enormous popularity of one of its most important texts, the *Devī Māhātmya*. The text which was composed by a gifted poet in the late Gupta or early medieval period and therefore became an integral part of the *Mārkaṇḍeya Purāṇa*, refers in its first chapter to Viṣṇu as Jagannātha. Its influence was considerable, as can be proved by the countless images of the Goddess in her various aspects which are inspired by the descriptions of the *Devī Māhātmya*. And it was mainly due to this text that the combination of the title Jagannātha with Viṣṇu became known throughout India. But in the *Devī Māhātmya*, the reference is to Viṣṇu as primordial deity, sleeping on the cosmic waters. It is not to the particular god enshrined in a temple at Purī or elsewhere, nor to Purī's wooden images, of unique and unmistakable shape which later became constitutive for all Jagannātha temples in India.

---

13 J.P. Singh Deo, *Origin of Jagannātha Deity*, New Delhi: Gyan Publishing House, 1991, pp. 78-79.

14 Nicolas Notovitch, op. cit., p. 85.

15 H.V. Stietencron, "Early Temples of Jagannātha in Orissa: The Formative Phase", *The Cult of Jagannātha and the Regional Tradition of Orissa*, New Delhi: Manohar, 1978, p. 62.

The composition form of *Mārkaṇḍeya Purāṇa* is of late Gupta period, not later than CE 600 according to R.C. Hazra.[16] Further, Stietencron[17] is of the opinion that the title "Jagannātha (Lord of the World)", itself is unspecific. It has been applied to Buddha, to Śiva and to Viṣṇu. Its uncompounded variant *Jagato-nātha* was similarly used for each of those three deities. The same is true for its synonyms "Lokanātha" and "Lokeśvara", which could be used for Śiva, Viṣṇu and a form of the Bodhisattva Avalokiteśvara. Other titles Īśvara (ruler) or Parameśvara (Supreme Ruler) were equally unspecified up to the post-Gupta period and could be applied both to Viṣṇu and Śiva. All these terms simply denote the all-embracing power of protection and lordship vesting in the Supreme God.

In *Padma Purāṇa* (ch. 70, *śloka* 1), Maheśa has been addressed as Jagannātha. In the same Purāṇa (ch. 17, *śloka* 51) Puruṣottama has been called as Jagannātha. Hazra[18] thinks that *Vāmana, Liṅga, Varāha, Padma, Agni, Skanda, Brahma-vaivartta* and *Bhaviṣya* are the results of destructive recasts and *Padma Purāṇa* has late appendages composed after CE 800 and 900. *Padma Purāṇa* cannot be dated earlier. Jagannātha, a form of Viṣṇu is also mentioned in the *Trikāṇḍaśeṣa Abhidhamma* of Puruṣottama Dev, a supplement of the famous *Amarakoṣa*, compiled in the ninth century CE.

Indrabhūti ruled Sambhala, in Uḍḍiyāna during eighth century CE as claimed by N.K. Sahu.[19] Indrabhūti opens his famous work *Jñānasiddhi*, with an invocation to Lord Jagannātha and Jagannātha is mentioned four more times in other verses.

Published under the title *Two Vajrayāna Works*, Gaekward's Oriental Series, the opening verse of ch. I is as follows:

> प्रणिपत्य जगन्नाथं संबजिनवराच्चितं ।
> सर्ब बुद्धमयं सिद्धिं व्यापिनं गगनोपमं ॥
>
> *praṇipatya jagannāthaṁ saṁbajinavarāccitaṁ* ।
> *sarba buddhamayaṁ siddhiṁ vyāpinaṁ gaganopamaṁ* ॥
>
> — *Jñānasiddhi*, ch. I, v. 1

Jagannātha is mentioned in four other verses of this work

---

[16] R.C. Hazra, "The Purāṇas", *The Cultural Heritage of India*, vol. II, Calcutta: The Ramakrishna Mission Institute of Culture, 1969, p. 256.

[17] H.V. Stietencron, "Early Temples of Jagannātha in Orissa: The Formative Phase", op. cit., p. 61.

[18] R.C. Hazra, op. cit., pp. 260-61.

[19] N.K. Sahu, *Buddhism in Orissa*, Cuttack: Utkal University, 1958, *passim*.

सः गुरुः शिष्यसंग्राहो सर्बबुद्धानुकारकः।
इत्युवाच जगन्नाथो नान्ये वै गुरवः स्मृताः॥

saḥ guruḥ śiṣyasaṁgrāho sarbabuddhānukārakaḥ ।
ityuvāca jagannātho nānye vai guravaḥ smṛtāḥ ॥
— *Jñānasiddhi*, ch. I, v. 27

तान् प्रयुक्ता जगन्नाथः वज्रसत्त्वविभावनैः।
भुजवरार्ण समायुक्त मुद्रा मराडल केस्तथा॥

tān prayuktā jagannāthaḥ vajrasattvavibhāvanaiḥ ।
bhujavarārṇa samāyukta mudrā marāḍala kestathā ॥
— *Jñānasiddhi*, ch. I, v. 92

अतएव जगन्नाथा वालानां प्रतिबोधने।
निवणिं दशेयन् त्येव रूपस्यानित्य दर्शकाः॥

ataeva jagannāthā vālānāṁ pratibodhane ।
nivaṇiṁ daśeyan tyeva rūpasyānitya darśakāḥ ॥
— *Jñānasiddhi*, ch. II, v. 28

सर्बज्ञः सर्बदर्शी च सर्वलोकार्य कारकः।
तन्त्र तन्त्र जगन्नाथः दर्शितः करुणात्मभि॥

sarbajñaḥ sarbadarśī ca sarvalokārya kārakaḥ ।
tantra tantra jagannāthaḥ darśitaḥ karuṇātmabhi ॥
— *Jñānasiddhi*, ch. V, v. 8

In a Buddhist literature, *Bodhicaryāvatāra*, Buddha is named as "Jagannātha", which goes thus:

अद्यैव शरणं यामि जगन्नाथा तू महाबलान्।
जगद्रक्षार्थमुद्युक्तान् सर्वत्रासहरान् जिनान्॥

adyaiva śaraṇaṁ yāmi jagannāthā tū mahābalān ।
jagadrakṣārthamudyuktān sarvatrāsaharān jinān ॥
— *Bodhicaryāvatāra* 2.48

The Pāla king of Bengal, Anaṅgavajra and his *guru* (master) Padmavajra a Buddhist tāntric composed *Hevajra Tantra*, in eighth century CE[20] and it is mentioned there that "Jagannātha" and "Kātyāyanī" were worshipped in Oḍradeśa. The author[21] has already discussed this and has clarified that it has already been mentioned

[20] G. Mohapatra, *Śrī Jagannātha Tatwa* (Oriyā), Cuttack: Nalanda, 1989, p. 217; D.C. Sircar, *The Śākta Pīṭhas*, Delhi: Motilal Banarsidass, 1973, p. 12.

[21] J.P. Singh Deo, *Origin of Jagannātha Deity*, p. 29.

that the term Jagannātha was used for Viṣṇu-Śiva and Buddha. Hence, the term Jagannātha used in *Hevajra Tantra*, a Buddhist tāntric text, is addressed to Buddha image and Buddhist worship in Oḍradeśa. The word Jagannātha used in the Buddhist Tantra scriptures and Hindu Tantra, before ninth century CE volumes are used for Lord Buddha and Lord Śiva.

Ramakanta Rout[22] informs that in ninth century CE Siddhasena Dibakar composed *Vardhamān Dwārisika*, a Jaina religious literature and in it, Mahāvīra has been addressed as Jagannātha.

Ādi Śaṅkarācārya addressed Śiva as Jagannātha, in his composition *Śiva Bhujaṅgam*, which goes thus:

जगन्नाथ! मन्नाथ! गौरीसनाथ!
प्रपन्नानुकम्पिन्! विपन्नार्त्तिहारिन् ।
महस्तोममूर्ते! समस्तैकबन्धो ।
नमस्ते नमस्ते पुनस्ते नमोऽस्तु ॥[23]

jagannātha! mannātha! gaurīsanātha!
prapannānukampin! vipannārttihārin ।
mahastomamūrte! samastaikabandho!
namaste namaste punaste namo 'stu ॥

So, it is definite that the name Jagannātha was not yet used or installed as a separate deity and it was used for addressing Viṣṇu, Śiva, Buddha and Mahāvīra, like Lokanātha and Viśvanātha.

Without observing the use of the word Jagannātha in its proper perspective and use, scholars are doing repeated mistakes. There are three instances as example.

In recent years, a scholar Pandit Gouri Kumar Brahma of Orissa is boastful in claiming that he has traced the word "Jagannātha" in the Veda.[24] The learned personage should find out that in which perspective, the word is used. This information was first given by Gaganendra Natha Dash (*Hindus and Tribals — Quest for Co-existence*, Decent Books, New Delhi, 1998, pp. 14-15), when he states that the famous Vedic commentator, Sāyaṇa, while commenting on a *sūkta* in the

---

[22] Ramakanta Rout, "Śrī Jagannātha Dharma-ra-Baichitra-o-Baisistha: Eka Tawitka Anusilan", *Jhankar*, Justice Harihara Mahapatra (ed.), Cuttack: Prajatantra Press, July 1991, p. 348 (Oriyā).

[23] *Sankara The Missionary*, Bombay: Central Chinmaya Mission Trust, 1978, p. 129.

[24] Information gathered from author's second brother Patayet Nilalohita Prasad Singh Deo of Khariar, Member, Orissa Sahitya Academy on 13 December 2004.

R̥gveda, claimed that in the said *sūkta* Puruṣottama Jagannātha on the sea-shore at Purī had been referred to (*R̥gveda*, 10.155.3). Sāyaṇa or any other Vedic commentator did not ever claim that in Vedic *sūkta*s any other Hindu shrine or deity had been referred to, as to them, it was most unlikely. Therefore, Sāyaṇa's discovery of this reference to Puruṣottama Jagannātha of Purī in a *sūkta* of *R̥gveda*, however improbable that might be, is quite significant. It only points out the primary importance Lord Jagannātha was given in the whole of the Hindu world during Sāyaṇa's time (CE 1300-80).

S.C. De[25] mentions:

> Śrī Jagannātha is also referred to in the *Tantra Yāmala* and *Rudra Yāmala*. These references are assignable to about the eighth or ninth century CE. From the facts stated above there can be hardly any doubt that worship of Śrī Jagannātha was closely associated with Śaiva Tantrism in about the eighth and ninth centuries of the Christian era.

The learned scholar S.C. De should have been alert to know that the word Jagannātha used in *Tantra Yāmala* and *Rudra Yāmala* has been used for Śiva and not for the presiding deity of Puruṣottama-kṣetra (site), Purī.

R.N. Dash[26] has done similar mis-understanding when he states:

> Mahākavi Murari in his *Anargha-Rāghava Nāṭakam* has mentioned about the decoration of the breasts of Kamalā (Lakṣmī) by Puruṣottama (Jagannātha).

The above statement of Dash clearly shows that he is unable to differentiate between the use of the words Puruṣottama and Jagannātha.

Very rightly H.V. Stietencron[27] has expressed:

> An entirely different description of Puruṣottama is found in Murari's *Anargha-Rāghava Nāṭakam*, and in several texts belonging to the Gaṅga period, notably the *Gīta-Govinda* (twelfth century), the Utkala-Khaṇḍa of the *Skanda Purāṇa* (early fourteenth century), the *Kramadīpikā* (middle fourteenth century) and some Jagannātha passages of the *Rudra Yāmala Tantra* (probably fourteenth century). They describe Puruṣottama clearly in the form listed

25 S.C. De, "Erotic Figures in Temple Architecture", *OHRJ*, vol. XXXVIII, nos. 1-4, p. 102.

26 R.N. Dash, "The Depiction of Orissan Society and Culture in the Gitagovindam", *OHRJ*, vol. XXXVIII, nos. 1-4, p. 217.

27 H.V. Stietencron, "Early Temples of Jagannātha in Orissa: The Formative Phase", op. cit., New Delhi, 1978, p. 69.

above under 1.b: Puruṣottama seated on a lion throne, is joined with his consort Kamalā (Lakṣmī). The god is four-armed, wearing crown and all ornaments. He carries lotus (*padma*) in his upper right and the disk (*cakra*) in his upper left hand. With his lower left arm he embraces his consort Kamalā who is sitting on his left thigh, pressing her slightly against himself and touching her left breast with his hand, while his right lower hand is raised towards her breast in amorous play. The goddess who is also fully adorned with ornaments, has put her right arm around his neck, her hand resting gracefully on his right shoulder. With her left hand she too holds a lotus flower. And she is looking at his face which is lovingly turned towards her.

Stone images of this type, iconographically known as Lakṣmī-Nārāyaṇa or Kamalā–Puruṣottama, but locally also called Mādhava or Nīlamādhava, are found in Orissa, in the early Gaṅga period. They are clearly made in imitation of similar Hara–Pārvatī images of the late Somavaṁśī period which in turn derive from somewhat differently conceived Hara–Pārvatī images of the Bhauma period.

Puruṣottama as described in Murari Mishra's work is the description of Lakṣmī–Nārāyaṇa image which was worshipped as Puruṣottama and not Puruṣottama Jagannātha, as convincingly stated by learned scholar Dash. In this manner scholars are continuously repeating the error.

Purī is famous because the site happens to be the headquarters of its present presiding deity Lord Puruṣottama Jagannātha. The author had taken up a study named *Origin of Jagannātha Deity*. The author had established that an icon of Buddha was installed as Lord Jagannātha alias Viṣṇu-Kṛṣṇa by Ādi Śaṅkarācārya at the Govardhana Maṭha, founded by him at Purī and was made the male deity of Govardhana Maṭha. Latest study on first Jagadguru Śaṅkarācārya, places him in between the period 509–477 BCE.[28] S.D. Kulkarni informs:[29]

In determining the period of Ādi Śaṅkara, as 509 to 476 BCE, we have collected all possible evidence in favour of this date. The currently held view about Ādi Śaṅkara's period, at CE 788–820 is not backed by any record of any of the *pīṭhas* (*maṭhas*) founded by Ādi Śaṅkara.

---

[28] Swami Prakashanand Saraswati, *The True History and the Religion of India*, Delhi: Motilal Banarsidass, 2001, p. 502.

[29] S.D. Kulkarni (ed.), *Bhishma's Study of Indian History and Culture*, vol. IV, *Glorious Epoch*, 1993, Introduction and vol. XI; *Adi Sankaracarya: The Savior of Mankind*, Sri Bhagavan Vedavyasa Itihas Samshodhana Mandir, Bombay (Thane), 1987, *passim*.

Up-to-date study of the author[30] also emphasizes it:

> The earliest conception of Śakti and Śiva in union has also been discovered in the Mahānadī Valley in the form of stone sockets. These are in circular shape with a socket on the lower part and has components in the upper part which fit into the lower socket. The shape of this socket owes its origin to the rock shelter painting of Yogīmaṭh Ḍoṅger hill. Such a stone socket set was collected by the author from Mohangiri site and is preserved at the Manikyapur Museum of Bhawanipatna. It can be interpreted as the union of Śiva and Śakti, which represents the *yoga* of sexual transformation. Later it developed as *vajrolī* and *sahajolī* in the tāntric *haṭha-yoga* practice. Such a socket set was jointly collected by Baba Mishra and Pradeep Mohanty from the Kharligarh site of Bolaṅgīr district in Orissa state and exhibited at Manikyapur Museum of Bhawanipatna. Such an object has also been found from layer III (early historic phase), from Veerapuram in Andhra Pradesh, where it is interpreted as a votive *liṅga*.[31] The shape of such stone sockets had been utilized for the shape of Lord Buddha in the Amarāvatī cross-bar railing, which shows the presentation of Rāhula.[32]

Two sets of such stone sockets are found in the ruins of a stone eight-handed Mahiṣāsuramardinī temple at Baṛgāon village, situated on the left bank of Udanti River in Nuāpāḍā district. One half of such a socket is also found at Pātālagaṅgā site in Nuāpāḍā district. Later this shape evolved to be the image of Lord Jagannātha at Purī. Therefore Ādi Śaṅkarācārya should be given the claim and the credit for bringing in Lord Jagannātha as a Vaiṣṇava deity, and worshipped as male deity at Govardhana Maṭha.

In tenth century CE a great religious revolution took place and this Jagannātha deity of Govardhana Maṭha was made of wood and ceremoniously placed and set up as the presiding deity of Purī, the Puruṣottama-kṣetra and Jagannātha deity thereby came to be known as Puruṣottama Jagannātha, during the reigning period of Somavaṁśī king Mahāśivagupta Yayāti I, whose reigning period is assigned

---

30 J.P. Singh Deo, *Tāntric Hedonism of Mahanadi Valley (Uḍḍiyāna-Pīṭha)*, New Delhi: D.K. Printworld, 2004, pp. 31-32.

31 T.V.G. Sastri, K.N. Bai and J.V.P. Rao, *Veerapuram*, Hyderabad: Bhavani Printers, 1984, *passim*.

32 E.R. Stone, *The Buddhist Art of Nagarjunakonda*, Delhi: Motilal Banarsidass, 1994, Illustration no. 32.

between CE 925-955 by B.K. Rath,[33] and between CE 963-991, by B.K. Sharma.[34] So, it took about 1,600 years for Jagannātha deity worshipped in Govardhana Maṭha at Purī to evolve, develop and become Puruṣottama Jagannātha.

The Shape of Jagannātha Deity

The shape of Jagannātha deity owes its origin to the rock art of Yogīmaṭh Ḍoṅger (hill), belonging to the Neolithic period. Later it developed as stone sockets, representing the union of male and female principles of nature, which was also used to represent Lord Buddha in Amarāvatī *stūpa* railing and finally evolved as the shape of Jagannātha deity.

To know about the unique shape of Jagannātha deity, Buddhist tradition has to be given attention. According to K.C. Mishra:[35]

> In CE 1200 a Buddhist pilgrim named Lāmā Tāranātha[36] gave an account of a mysterious tradition regarding the construction of a Buddha image, which has some resemblance with the construction of the image of Lord Jagannātha. A certain brāhmaṇa named Kalyāṇa wanted to make an image of the Buddha. Accordingly, he built a temple and brought many carpenters including Viśvakarmā to make the image. The temple was to be closed for seven days so that the construction of the image could be completed. After five days, Kalyāṇa's mother apprehended the death of her son inside the temple. So, she opened it before the stipulated period was over and found there an image half made.

Such a tradition is also prevalent in Orissa regarding the construction of the image of Jagannātha.

> An archaeologist named L.A. Wadell, while giving an account of the Bauddha ruins of Monghyr has said that the people called the place, where the ruins of Bauddha temples were found, Indradyumna Gaḍa.[37] In the history of the construction of the temple of Jagannātha there is also the mention of the king named Indradyumna who is said to be the first builder

---

[33] B.K. Rath, *Cultural History of Orissa*, Delhi: Sundeep Prakashan, 1983, p. 62.

[34] B.K. Sarma, *The History of Somavaṁśī Rule in Orissa*, Calcutta: Punthi Pustak, 1983, p. 29.

[35] *TCOJ*, 1971, pp. 84-85.

[36] Ibid.; *Tales of Tāranātha* (quoted in *Prajatantra* Special Issue), Oriya daily newspaper, Cuttack, Sunday, 23 June 1963.

[37] Ibid.; *Prajatantra*, Sunday, 23 June 1963.

of the temple. So, it is evident that the tradition associated with Jagannātha was not localized in Orissa, but, popular throughout India with certain alternations.

M. Mansinha[38] gives references of two issues of English daily newspaper *The Statesman* thus:

> A parallel temple of Jagannātha rising from a Buddhist *stūpa*.
>
> Strongly supporting Percy Brown's theory that the present temple of Jagannātha, Purī, stands on an old Buddha-Mahāyānic structure, is the recent discovery in Maharashtra, of another temple of Jagannātha on a Buddhist *stūpa*, as described below.
>
> *Bombay, 30 June* — The recent discovery of the stupa complex at Pauni in Bhandara district of Maharashtra, has thrown light on the early history of Buddhist religion and architecture, reports UNI. The excavations have revealed that Pauni, situated on the ancient main route from central India to south India, was a great centre of Hīnayāna Buddhism, between fourth and second centuries BCE.
>
> The excavations this year have confirmed the varied and extensive nature of the ancient settlement. The mound which is now capped by the Jagannatha temple was a Mauryan *stūpa*, which seems to have been in worship for about four centuries.
>
> — *The Statesman*, 2 July 1969

The latest finding inside Puruṣottama Jagannātha temple complex of Purī, as stated by C.B. Patel[39] may be quoted:

> In this regard it is important to mention that recently the Archaeological Survey of India under the guidance of Dr. T. Satyamurty made some repair work in the base of the Garuḍa pillar inside the Naṭamandira area and found the remnant of an Aśokan pillar with typical Mauryan polish. The pillar goes deep into the platform. The author along with his colleague D.R. Pradhan visited the spot at the time of renovation and observed that

---

[38] M. Mansinha, *The Saga of the Land of Jagannātha*, Cuttack: J. Mohapatra & Co., Appendix III, p. 288.

[39] C.B. Patel, "Oldest Jagannātha Temple of Purī: The Buddhist and Somavaṁśī Connections", *Orissa Review*, July 2003, vol. LIX, no. 12, Public Relation Dept., Govt. of Orissa, Bhubaneswar, p. 65.

the entire Jagannātha temple complex platform area was man-made, resembling a platform of Buddhist establishment like a *stūpa*.

Swami Prahlad Giri[40] mentions:

"साँची में मिले हुए धर्मयन्त्रों की जगन्नाथ मूर्ति के साथ रूप से समानता है।"

Buddhist *stūpa*s and ruins of Sāñcī, Bharhut and Bodh-Gayā are dated to first century BCE by N.R. Ray.[41] In these Buddhist structures, the image of Buddha is depicted as modern Jagannātha deity. So, it can be said that from first century BCE the practice of making images of Buddha, like the modern Jagannātha deity had started.

There are many instances of antiquities of the images of Lord Buddha, resembling that of modern Puruṣottama Jagannātha deity at Purī.[42] As already stated, in two stone like sockets representing Lord Buddha in cross-bar railing of Amarāvatī *stūpa*, two hands were added and such a shape is found in the monolithic figure, near the south-east slope of Mahendragiri mountain, in Andhra Pradesh. The zone of Mahendragiri–Parlakhemandi has vast Buddhist remains.[43] One can also detect Buddhist remains in the vast archaeological wealth of the Gaṅga capital Kaliṅganagara.[44] The monolithic Buddha image of Mahendragiri–Parlakhemandi zone is misunderstood as Lord Jagannātha, by S.N. Rajaguru.[45] There are many images of Lord Buddha at the Buddhist monastery of Ladakh (Jammu-Kashmir) of north India, which resemble Lord Puruṣottama Jagannātha of Purī. These discoveries confirm that one of the images of Lord Buddha alias Puruṣottama Buddha Jagannātha evolved as Puruṣottama Jagannātha at Purī.[46]

---

40 Swami Prahad Giri, "अवतार और जगन्नाथ", *Unmana*, Cuttack: Souvenir of Akhil Bharat Jagannatha Consciousness Conference, 1984 (Hindi section), p. 16.

41 N.R. Ray, "Sculpture", *THACOTIP*, vol. II, *The Age of Imperial Unity*, 1968, p. 511.

42 J.P. Singh Deo, *Origin of Jagannātha Deity*, New Delhi: Gyan Publishing House, 2nd edn., 2003, pp. 79-96.

43 K.C. Dash, "Dantapura and Puspagiri", *The Journal of Orissan History*, vol. IX, June 1989, p. 9.

44 Ibid.; N.S. Ramaswami, *Monograph on Temples of Mukhalingam*, Govt. of Andhra Pradesh, Hyderabad, 1976, pp. 8-9.

45 S.N. Rajguru, *Śrī Purushottam-o-Śrī Mandira* (Oriyā), Bhubaneswar: Orissa Sahitya Academy, 1996, pp. 35-52.

46 J.P. Singh Deo, op. cit., 2nd edn., Appendix II, pp. 193-99; J.P. Singh Deo, *THOMV*, 2004, *passim*.

Trinity Conception

The earliest trinity antiquity of India is found with yogic conception in the prehistoric Rock Art of Yogīmaṭh Ḍoṅger (hill), discovered by the author on 21 December 1970, in Nuāpāḍā district of Orissa and assigned to the Neolithic period.[47] The line-drawn symbols painted in red-tint (orchel) colour show the creation and runs right to left. Paintings of bulls, rings and triple-strokes thrice are yogic conceptions which speak of prevalence of phallism and the trinity functioning of God as the creator, organizer and destroyer.[48] Three parallel lines are painted thrice, in this rock art of Yogīmaṭh Ḍoṅger, which is of great yogic and spiritual significance.

It is worth knowing the Vedic conception of Trinity of the Vedas. His Holiness Rashtraguru 1008 Swamiji Maharaj of Pītāmbarapīṭha, Datia deals with trinity:[49]

इदं विष्णुर्विंचक्रमे त्रेधा निदधे पदम्। समूल्हम्स्य पांसुरे॥

idaṁ viṣṇurviṁcakrame । *tredhā nidadhe padam* ।
samūlhamsya pāṁsure ॥

— *Ṛgveda*, I.22.17

This universe qualified and differentiated by name and form, is pervaded by Lord Viṣṇu; the entire universe is measured by the three steps of Lord Viṣṇu.

Explanation:

From the root "विष्नृ व्याप्तौ" (*viṣnṛ vyāptau*) is formed the word "विष्णु (Viṣṇu)" which means the all-pervading Supreme-Soul. His infinite power (*parā-śakti*) expresses itself in the threefold qualities. The *Brahma-tattva*, resulting from the plenitude of the *sattva*-quality, is called Viṣṇu. It is characterized by knowledge and bliss, Lord Viṣṇu is the symbol of full growth of knowledge and Supreme Bliss. The forms developed from *rajas* and *tamas* qualities are called Brahmā and Rudra. Śāntā (शान्ता) the unperturbed great-power expressed by will, knowledge and action, produces the divine triad (ब्रह्मा-विष्णु–रुद्र — Brahmā–Viṣṇu–Rudra) in the reverse order as Rudra, Viṣṇu and Brahmā. All these three gods are the subsidiary forms of Viṣṇu. The form resulting from the will, being full of purity, it is like the primal-Viṣṇu

[47] J.P. Singh Deo, *Cultural Profile of South Kosala*, Delhi: Gyan Publishing House, 1987, p. 20.

[48] J.P. Singh Deo, *THOMV*, 2004, p. 23.

[49] Maharaj Swamiji, *Vedic Upadesh* (*Vedic Teachings*), Sri Pitambara Sanskrit Parishad, Datia, Madhya Pradesh, 1st edn., July 1977, pp. 164-67.

who is also known by the appellation of Mahā-Rudra. In the Purāṇas, Viṣṇu has been designated as "Hari"; the Mahā-Rudra, as "Hara". The basic root "हृञ् (*hr̥ñ*)" in both these words being the same, the difference is owing to the termination added in inflection. The term "त्रेधा निदधे पदम् (*tredhā nidadhe padam*)" of the *mantra* denotes the trinity of Brahmā, Viṣṇu and Maheśa. Sage Yāska has traced the meaning of "विष्णु (Viṣṇu)" to the root "विश् (*viś*)" which means pervading the whole universe.

According to Ācārya Śākapūṇi (शाकपूणि) the term त्रेधा (*tredhā*) (threefold) includes the earth, the sky and the celestial region. Because of the gross character of the cosmic nature, Viṣṇu is beyond the comprehension of ordinary men. The wise alone can see his ultimate form. The highest place of primal Viṣṇu is that which is beyond the terrestrial, the mid and the celestial region; and it is also beyond Brahmā, Viṣṇu and Maheśa of the Triad. This secret has been explained in the "Viṣṇu-sūkta" of the Vedas, and has been described by the name "Nārāyaṇa" in the *Mahā-Nārāyaṇa Upaniṣad*. The *Viṣṇu Purāṇa* gives its detailed explanation. For the benefit of the devotees, the principles are enjoined in Nārada's philosophical treatise named *Pañca-Rātra* (पंचरात्र). *Śrīmad-Bhāgavata Purāṇa* explains the principle of love. The Bhāgavata cult has been preached by four varieties of reasonings (चतुर्व्यूह — *caturvyūha*), classified as Vāsudeva (वासुदेव), Pradyumna (प्रद्युम्न), Aniruddha (अनिरुद्ध) and Saṅkarṣaṇa (संकर्षण). Mādhavācārya has added a fifth variety called Nārāyaṇa (नारायण), making it a "पंचव्यूह (*pañcavyūha*)" in place of the "चतुर्व्यूह — *caturvyūha*" of the Bhāgavata cult. In the book *Tattva-Traya* (तत्त्वत्रय), the secret of Vaiṣṇava philosophy has been enunciated. In this way, Nārāyaṇa (नारायण), Vāsudeva (वासुदेव), Saṅkarṣaṇa (सङ्कर्षण), Pradyumna (प्रद्युम्न) and Aniruddha (अनिरुद्ध) are the names of the five different reasonings (पञ्चव्यूह — *pañcavyūha*). In the astronomical treatise named *Sūrya-Siddhānta* (सूर्यसिद्धांत), the sun has been considered as the fourth in this since the sun "चतुर्व्यूह — *caturvyūha*" is also one of the forms of Viṣṇu. In "विष्णुसहस्रनाम *Viṣṇusahasranāma*" (the thousand names of Viṣṇu) contained in the *Mahābhārata*, this theory of "चतुर्व्यूह — *caturvyūha*" has been accepted. Unlike the Pañca-Brahma *mantras* of the Śaivas, which take their origin from the Vedas, this theory of "चतुर्व्यूह — *caturvyūha*" of the Vaiṣṇavites is not found in the Vedic *mantras*. At the end of the second part of chapter II of *Vedānta Darśana*, Śaṅkarācārya has considered this theory as non-Vedic. According to Vallabhācārya, it is derived from the Purāṇas. The story of the incarnations of Viṣṇu is likewise, not found in the Vedas. The incarnation of R̥ṣabhadeva Buddha (ऋषभदेव बुद्ध) accepted in the Vaiṣṇava cult is also non-Vedic. Depending on exigencies of time, many such theories have been recognized in the Vaiṣṇava cult. The incarnations of Śrī Rāma and Śrī Kṛṣṇa are now worshipped as forms of Viṣṇu.

The twelve digits of the solar orb, and the sixteen, of the lunar orb, are related to these incarnations. They have been devised and made use of in the Tantra for devotional purposes. Both these incarnations represent the two elements of love and knowledge expressed by *sattva.* With Śrī Rāma is related mainly the solar digit in the form of knowledge, and hence the element of bliss plays a comparatively minor role in it. As a result of the slight influence exercised by the lunar orb, the epithet *candra* has been added to the name of Śrī Rāma, and he is accordingly called Śrī Rāmacandra. Nevertheless, the combination of the digits of the sun and those of the moon not being simultaneous, the development of the principle of bliss or love is negligible. However, springing from the Lunar dynasty, Śrī Kṛṣṇa, due to the influence of sixteen digits of the moon, has been considered as a perfect man (पुरुषोत्तम — *puruṣottama*). Hence the author of *Śrīmad-Bhāgavata* has said "कृष्णस्तु भगवान् स्वयम् (*kṛṣṇastu bhagavān svayam*)" (Kṛṣṇa is God incarnate). In the book named *Tattva-Traya* (तत्त्वत्रय), only these two incarnations have been given prominence. "सर्वविष्णुमय जगत् (*sarvaviṣṇumaya jagat*)" (the entire universe is pervaded by Viṣṇu). Acknowledging the theory that the whole universe is pervaded by Viṣṇu, the accepted principle of the Vaiṣṇavites is that of Advaita. Later on, the neo-Vaiṣṇavites explaining the Viṣṇava theory in the form of pure-Advaita qualified — Advaita, Dvaita-Advaita and Dvaita — have classified the Vaiṣṇava cult into four sub-sects; however, there is no difference of opinion so far as the recognition of all-pervading Lord Viṣṇu is concerned.

Saints like Sūradās and Tulsīdās have propagated the *bhakti* cult with the help of these two incarnations of Śrī Kṛṣṇa and Śrī Rāma respectively; and they have become a perennial source of worship of God and national life for Indians.

Attention goes to the following verse of the *Bhagavad-Gītā*:

यदादित्यगतं तेजो जगद्भासयतेऽखिलम् ।
यच्चन्द्रमसि यच्चाग्नौ तत्तेजो विद्धि मामकम् ॥ 15.12 ॥

yadādityagataṁ tejo jagadbhāsayate 'khilam ।
yaccandramasi yaccāgnau tattejo viddhi māmakam ॥ 15.12 ॥

The light of the sun that illumines the whole world, the light from the moon, and the light in fire — know this radiance to be mine.

Sri Sri Paramahamsa Yogananda[50] explains it:

> When this divine force vibrates more heavily or grossly, it becomes the electrons, protons and atoms of the universal structure.
>
> The sun and moon and fire are composed of the grosser light electrons, protons and atoms, which in turn are made of cosmic energy. And cosmic energy emanates from cosmic consciousness. Therefore it is the mind of spirit that manifests as the sun, moon, fire and all other objects and forces in the cosmos.
>
> In the microcosm of man, God's cosmic consciousness vibrates, through the individualized soul, as the astral light in the thousand-petalled lotus (the sun) that illumines with life the entire body (the world) through its reflection (the moon) in the subsidiary spinal *cakra*s and their radiating energies (fire).

The *Bhagavad-Gītā*[51] deals with three patterns of worship, three classes of food, three grades of spiritual practices, three kinds of giving and *auṁ-tat-sat*. These three varieties are sāttvic, rājasic and tāmasic.

It is worth quoting from the *Bhagavad-Gītā* which deals with *auṁ-tat-sat*, with its explanation, as given by Paramahamsa Yogananda:[52]

> ॐ तत्सदिति निर्देशो ब्रह्मणस्त्रिविधः स्मृतः ।
> ब्राह्मणास्तेन विदाश्च यज्ञाश्च विहिताः पुरा ॥ 17.23 ॥
>
> *oṁ tatsaditi nirdeśo brahmaṇastrividhaḥ smṛtaḥ* ।
> *brāhmaṇāstena vidāśca yajñāśca vihitāḥ purā* ॥
>
> *Auṁ-tat-sat* is considered to be the triple designation of *Brahman* (God). By this power were created, in the beginning, the brāhmaṇas (knowers of *brahman*), the Vedas, and the sacrificial rites.
>
> The unmanifested, the infinite, the changeless spirit is called *Para-Brahman*: the One Absolute. But during the cycles of manifestation, the nameless and formless is described as *auṁ-tat-sat* (or, often, *sat-tat-auṁ*) — so designated by the ancient sages.

In Bible, *sat-tat-auṁ* is spoken of as the Father, the Son and the Holy Ghost.

---

50 Sri Sri Paramahansa Yogananda, op. cit., vol. II, 2nd impression, 2002, pp. 941-42.

51 Ibid., pp. 987-1012.

52 Ibid., pp. 1006-09.

Auṁ (the "word" in Bible) is God the Holy Ghost, invisible vibratory power, the direct creator and activator of all creations.

Tat (That) is God the Son, the Christ or *kūṭastha* cosmic intelligence actively present in all creations.

Sat (Being, truth) is God the Father, beyond creation, existing in vibrationless unchangeability.

As the calm Ocean without waves and the ocean with waves in tumult are one and the same in essence, differing only in appearance, so also the unmanifested sea of spirit (*Para-Brahman*) and the manifested sea of spirit (*auṁ-tat-sat*) are the selfsame sole reality, differing only in form.

God as *sat* is the father of creation (*Īśvara*), though he exists beyond it. God as *tat* is the son or Christ (Kṛṣṇa or *kūṭastha*) intelligence that pervades the Universe, God as *auṁ* in the creative vibration that upholds the world through *prakṛti*, mother nature, his consort. It is the macrocosmic triple conception that has established itself in the microcosmic human relationship of father and mother, and their reflection in their offspring.

Man displays in himself the three divine manifestations. His body is the result of *auṁ* or vibratory forces. His Christ intelligence or *tat* exists in his omniscient spiritual eye between the eyebrows. This intelligence, individualized as his soul, is a reflection of cosmic consciousness or *sat* residing in the thousand-petalled lotus in the brain.

These three measures of spirit incarnate in man "from the beginning" are: the brāhmaṇas, *sat*, "knowers of God", the soul; the Vedas, *tat*, the soul's intuitive all-knowing intelligence; and the sacrificial rites, *auṁ*, the vibratory life that creates and preserves the body, empowering it to perform its divine and dutiful rituals of existence — including the ultimate sacrificial rites of *yoga* (one of which is meditation on *auṁ*) that reunite the soul with spirit. By this inherence, indigenous in the coming forth of mortal beings, the lord has endowed to man the way and the means and the irrevocable assurance — of salvation.

All *yogīs*, who perform the sacrificial rite of listening to the omnipresent holy vibration of *auṁ*, attain cosmic perception, Veda and by this expanding blessedness ascend to cosmic consciousness and become self-realized souls, the true brāhmaṇas or "knowers of *Brahman*".

Auṁ of the Vedas became the sacred word *huṁ* of the Tibetans, *āmīn* of the Muslims, and *āmen* of the Egyptians, Greeks, Romans, Jews and Christians. *Āmen* in Hebrew means "sure, faithful". *Auṁ* is the all-pervading soul emanating from the Holy Ghost as it performs its work of creating and maintaining the universal structure. *Auṁ* is the voice of creation, testifying to the divine presence in every atom.

> These things saith the *Āmen*, the faithful and true witness, the beginning of the creation of God. — Revelation 3:14
>
> In the beginning was the word, and the word was with God, and the word was God, all things were made by him (the word or *aum*); and without him was not anything made that was made. — John 1:1, 3
>
> Faith cometh by hearing, and hearing by the word of God. — Romans 10:17
>
> He who knows *auṁ* knows God. — Patañjali, great sage of ancient India, author of *Yoga-Sūtras*.
>
> *Auṁ* is the divinely empowered creator of all things, it manifests itself as cosmic light and cosmic sound. As the ocean roar is a conglomerated sound of all waves and is manifested in each wave, so the cosmic sound and the cosmic light are the aggregate of all animate and inanimate creation, and are manifested in each man as the light of life and may be heard by him as the astral sound of *auṁ*.
>
> Each seeker who wants liberation from the world of delusion must pass through the sphere of the Holy Ghost Libration and the sphere of Christ intelligence before he can reach God the Father beyond the phenomenal world. "No man cometh unto the Father (cosmic consciousness) but by me (Christ consciousness)." These words were spoken by Jesus from his oneness with the infinite Christ intelligence: "Believe me that I am in the Father, and the Father in me." — John 14: 6, 11
>
> Jesus promised to send to his disciples the Comforter, the Holy Ghost, to speed them on their way to self-realization. An advanced devotee can hear the sound of *auṁ* in his body and can see its light in his Spiritual eye, after he has become acquainted with these two limited manifestations, in the bodily sound and in his spiritual eye, then, by further spreading of his consciousness in omnipresence, he sees his small spherical eye of light expand into a cosmic sphere whose luminosity conflagrates the whole universe.
>
> Similarly, as the devotee listens to *praṇava*, the holy sound of *auṁ*, he forgets the restrictions of the human body and of space and can feel the *auṁ* of his

> body vibrating into a perception of his cosmic body. He feels his consciousness vibrating everywhere with the ever expanding *auṁ* sound. In ecstasy he suddenly sees his body as an atom or cell in the cosmic body. Perceiving the cosmic body as his own, he feels in it the cosmic *auṁ* sound and the Christ intelligence. By further advancement he becomes conscious of his presence not only in all creation but with God the Father beyond creation.

The distortion of the ancient Indian history has been done, because the English regime tried to destroy the culture and the religion of India by all means, and during that time, they deliberately produced such derogatory literatures in huge quantities that confused and misguided the whole world. The history of Bhāratavarṣa is since the creation of our *brahmāṇḍa*, 155.52 trillion years ago, with the unbroken continuity of Bhāratīya civilization.[53] The English people started demeaning the history and the religion of India, misguiding the whole world and destroying and fabricating the historic records. These people could do anything and everything to prove their point. Therefore the whole history and chronological dating of ancient history is perverted, mis-represented, twisted aside, put out of shape and turned aside from the true meaning and deformed.

Indian elite in general and the scholars in particular are so much under the influence of the writings of Western scholars that any fresh and independent conclusion about Indian history becomes jarring to them, if it goes beyond the ambit of Western writings. Very few Indian scholars have shown courage to deviate from the general guidelines of Indian history provided by their Western counterparts. The isolated efforts of these Indian scholars deal only with one or the other aspect of Indian history. But, in general, it has been proved beyond an iota of doubt that facts in our history have been twisted. Mischievous interpretations have been put on them and wrong conclusions have been drawn by most of the Western writers to suit their individual motive or whim.

H.K. Mahatab[54] is a victim to the post-British colonial efforts and, without taking care of the trinity conception of the great Vedic tradition, he states:

> With this background the mystery of Jagannātha, his name and his association of his brother and sister may be solved reasonably in the following manner.

[53] Swami Prakashanand Saraswati, *The True History and the Religion of India*, Delhi: Motilal Banarsidass, 2001, p. 476.

[54] H.K. Mahatab, "Culture of Orissa", *OHRJ*, vol. XXX, nos. 2-4, 1984, pp. 22-25.

> There were three images in very ancient times. During the Buddhist period, the chief of them was known as Jagannātha and the image between the two was considered as a female deity. It was further converted that she was the sister of the other two. When the worship of Kṛṣṇa-Vāsudeva was gaining ground in the eastern and southern India the image of Jagannātha which had been in existence for a very long time was taken to stand for Kṛṣṇa and the other male deity as a matter of course, was called Balarāma and the female deity who had been considered as the sister of the two was called Subhadrā. It is likely that at the time when Jagannātha was considered to stand for Kṛṣṇa, a *śakti* for each God had not been conceived. But by the time when a female deity was considered as the *śakti* for each God, the name of Jagannātha had been so firmly established that it was not possible to change it into any other. Thus the names of the deities remained as Jagannātha, Balabhadra and Subhadrā.

About the images of Jagannātha, Balabhadra and Subhadrā, Sir A. Cunningham makes the following observation in his book, *The Stūpa of Bharhut*.

> *Tri-Ratna Symbols*
>
> The principal Buddhist symbol of *tri-ratna* or "triple gem" which is found in all the countries wherever Buddhism prevailed. Mr. Beal calls this "the sacred symbol of the *maṇi*, or threefold gem, indicating the all Supreme Buddha", and in another place he described the symbol as "the triple object of their veneration, Buddha, the law and the Church". This triple symbol was a very favourite form of ornament for the point of military standard, of the centrepiece of a necklace. In the Bharhut sculptures the *tri-ratna* symbol is placed above the thrones of the Buddha, Viśvabāhū and Śākyamuni.
>
> Considerable interest attaches to the symbol of the *tri-ratna*, as there can be no reasonable doubt that the three rude figures of Jagannātha, his sister and brother, now worshipped with so much fervour in Orissa, have been directly derived from three of these symbols. I was first led to this opinion in 1851, by the discovery of three of these symbols set up together in one of the Sāñcī sculptures. Since then I have found these same three rude Jagannātha figures used in all the native almanacs of Mathurā and Benares as the representation of Buddha in the Buddha *avatāra* of Viṣṇu. This last fact seems to me to be conclusive but I may add that the Jagannātha figure in Orissa is universally believed to contain a bone of Kṛṣṇa. But as brāhmaṇas do not worship the relics of their God, I conclude that this bone must be a relic of Buddha, and that the rude figure of Jagannātha in which it is

contained is one of the old *tri-ratna*, or "triple-gem" symbol, of the Buddhist triad.

The able reviewer of Fergussons's *"Tree and Serpent Worship"* remarks, "One of General Cunningham's happiest hits in his derivation of the three fetish like figures of Jagannātha, his sister and brother, from three of the combined emblems of the Buddhistic Trinity, placed side by side as at Sāñcī. The resemblance he adds, is rude but unmistakable."

The same learned author has also dealt with the symbols of Buddha, *dharma* and *saṁgha* in his book, *The Bhilsa Topes,* Cunningham observes: 7. *Dharma,* or concrete nature, was, I believe neatly symbolized by a monogram which united the radical letters of the various elements of matter. According to the Pūjā-Khaṇḍa, all things with their *bīja mantras* (radicals), came from *svabhāva* (the self-existent), in this order.

From the *bīja* of the letter Y, air,
From that of the letter R, fire,
From that of the letter V, water,
From that of the letter L, earth,
From that of the letter S, Mount Sumeru.

Now it is curious that the old Pāli equivalents of these letters form, when combined together, a monogram of exactly the same shape as the symbol which I have attributed to *dharma*. In a place I have given this monogram, with the single letter which compose it placed in a line below. In all the monograms both of the bas-reliefs and on the coins, the symbol is crossed by a horizontal line in the middle, which I take to represent the lower stroke of the Pāli letter, n, the radical of "void space or vacuity". This, therefore, must be the fifth element, the *ākāśa* of the Hindus. The symbol is thus strictly composed of the five radical letters of the five elements, Y, air; R, fire; V, water; I, earth; and N, ether; which when combined contain the letter, S, for Mount Sumeru, as the letter O, M, or *manas* or mind. In a plate I have given all the different specimens of this symbol that I can collect from various sources.

From the foregoing considerations we may conclude that during the Buddhist period the Savaras of Orissa were converted to Buddhism. Either the original *stūpa* was converted or a new Buddhistic *stūpa* was constructed at Purī and the symbol of *tri-ratna* was put up there. By the first century BCE or the first century CE when Mahāyāna (the Great Path) Buddhism prevailed simple-minded Savaras began to worship the symbol of *tri-ratna*. The worship of symbol is still to be found in the worship of *svastika* which is really a combination of two Pāli letters, SU and TI, for *suti* is the Pāli form of *svastika*. The three symbols taken together were called Jagannātha. Jagannātha is another name for Buddha as known from Tibetan sources. So the name of Jagannātha is Buddhistic in origin. Later on Jagannātha was identified with Viṣṇu when Brāhmanism came to prevail.

Afterwards when worship of images came into vogue, the three symbols were represented on pieces of wood and Naturally, an attempt was made to give them the appearance of human beings as far as possible.

Of the three images Jagannātha was considered to stand for Buddha of Buddhism. *Dharma* in Buddhism is believed to be a female, so one of the images was supposed to be a female. In *saṁgha*, i.e. the monastic order of Buddhists the relationship between the monks and the nuns is that between brother and sister. The Savaras accordingly treated two of the images as brothers and the third as their sister. Of the three, Jagannātha was no doubt the most important.

From the antiquities discovered and discussed in earlier chapters, the conception of trinity is of the Neolithic period and, as discussed, it is of Vedic origin and therefore the view of Mahatab cannot be correct.

With this much of spiritual and metaphysical explanations of trinity conception, it is worth to know about the trinity worship, which developed in the Puruṣottama Jagannātha cult at Purī. According to Kedarnatha Mahapatra:[55]

> Great Śaṅkarācārya who in course of his spiritual conquest of the whole of India, stayed at Purī, which was well known by his time as a chief centre of religion and culture, and founded one of his four *pīṭha*s called *Bhogavardhana Pīṭha* here which has remained in existence till today. Śrī Padmapādācārya, one of his four disciples, who was also a Nambudiri Brāhmaṇa like his *guru* was placed as the first Jagadguru or spiritual head of this *pīṭha*. According to tradition Śaṅkara defeated the Buddhist *paṇḍit*s of this place by his vast learning and irrefutable arguments; converted most of them to his own faith and proclaimed Jagannātha Buddha as identical with the great Brāhmanical God Puruṣottama of the *Gītā*. This peaceful process of assimilation of a great Buddhist deity into the pantheon of Brāhmanism, strengthened its influence at Jagannātha Purī, which was a strong centre of Buddhism before his days. In commemoration of this great event, the images of Śrī Śaṅkara and Śrī Padmapāda were installed on the *ratna-siṁhāsana*

[55] K.N. Mahapatra, "Jagannāth Purī as a Centre of Culture through the Ages", *OHRJ*, vol. VI, no. 4, p. 297.

> of Jagannātha for which, it is known from *Mādalā-Pāñjī*, the chronicle of the Jagannātha temple written in Oriyā language, that their images were removed from that place during the reign of Divyasiṁha Deva II (CE 1793-98), Rājā of Purī.[56]

Even P.K. Pattanaik[57] also confirms by mentioning that the idols of Śaṅkarācārya and his disciple were removed to the southern gate and many other improvements were effected in the Purī temple, during the period of Divyasiṁha Deva II (CE 1793-98). Now, the idols of Śaṅkarācārya and his disciple Padmapādācārya are no more to be found in the boundary or campus of Puruṣottama Jagannātha temple at Purī.

With the visit of Rāmānuja[58] to Purī and his influence, Lakṣmī had become associated with Jagannātha in twelfth century CE. The Gaṅga period was therefore the formative phase of Jagannātha trinity and must have happened at a definite moment of the development of the cult. This has been proved by the discovery of inscriptions on Jagannātha temple, after the removal of lime plaster in recent years. Most of the inscriptions belong to the Gaṅga period.

Saint Rāmānuja alias third Jagadguru Rāmānujācārya (CE 1017–1137),[59] popularized the *Pāñcarātra* rites at Purī. The Pāñcarātra system emphasized Kṛṣṇa in his relations to his sister Ekānaṁśā and his brother Balarāma-Saṁkarṣaṇa. Ekānaṁśā was interpreted as a form of Durgā and Balarāma as a form of Śiva. Moreover the worship of *Sudarśana* was emphasized as well. Thus the Pāñcarātra system was befitting to take up the most important elements of the Jagannātha cult.[60] In Pāñcarātra philosophy Śiva came to be known as Balabhadra.[61] So, it can be said that Jagannātha cult in its final phase brought the synthesis of the main cults of Hinduism, Vaiṣṇavism, Śaivism and Śāktism. In the dilapidated brick temple of Turintiara village under Balipatna police station of Purī district, images of Balabhadra, Subhadrā and Kṛṣṇa are found carved in a chlorite stone. They are

[56] *The Mādalā-Pāñjī* Cuttack: Prachi-Samiti, p. 81.

[57] P.K. Pattanaik, *A Forgotten Chapter of Orissan History*, Calcutta: Punthi Pustak, 1979, p. 55.

[58] J.P. Singh Deo, *Origin of Jagannātha Deity*, New Delhi: Gyan Publishing House, 2nd edn., 2003, pp. 107-08.

[59] Swami Prakashanand Saraswati, *The True History and the Religion of India*, Delhi: Motilal Banarsidass, 2001, pp. 631-32.

[60] A. Echmann, H. Kulke and G.C. Tripathi, "The Formation of the Jagannātha Triad", *TCOJATRTOO*, 1978, p. 185.

[61] Ibid., pp. 187-89.

assigned to twelfth or thirteenth century CE and prove the popularity of triad worship in Orissa, during that period.

A. Echmann, H. Kulke and G.C. Tripathi[62] consider the year CE 1230 to have been the appropriate period for the establishment of the triad. It is their hypothesis and there is probability of finding new results if research is continued on this topic.

Definite period of the establishment of Jagannātha trinity is not yet known. It seems the trinity worship developed within twelfth-thirteenth centuries CE in the Gaṅga dynasty ruling period and the worship of Jagannātha trinity was well established when the Sūryavaṁśī Gajapati kings began to rule in fifteenth century CE.

About the new discoveries of antiquities of Lord Jagannātha, Sasanka Sekhar Panda[63] informs:

> Ultimately the apprehension of historians and scholars come true, when the ruins of an ancient Jagannātha temple site of the ninth century CE on the outskirts of Tentelkhunti village, situated on the right bank of river Tel, at a distance of around 40 km to the south-west of Bolaṅgīr town were discovered. The huge mound contains innumerable cut stone blocks, round *āmalaka* in four pieces, stone-made broken *nīlacakra* once adorning the temple top and many other sculptures of historical importance. All those antiquities have been brought out from underneath the earth by a local villager of the Kondh tribe named Trilochan Bhoi, during the last one year or so, single-handedly. Bhoi informed during my visit to this historical site on 29 June 2004 that three handless idols of the holy trinity Jagannātha, Balabhadra and Subhadrā have also been found underneath the earth during digging, which are at present installed and worshipped inside a hut constructed by the local villagers. The recent discovery authenticated the construction of the oldest temple of the holy trinity by the Somavaṁśī king Yayāti Keśarī some time in the ninth century CE as mentioned in the *Mādalā-Pāñjī*, the temple chronicle of Purī Jagannātha temple. . . . After discovery of these anthropoid forms of the holy trinity Jagannātha, Balabhadra and Subhadrā, made of stone, many intriguing questions arise regarding the origin of the Jagannātha cult and present wooden forms of the deities, enshrined in the Ratnavedī of the Jagannātha temple at Purī.

---

62 A. Echmann, H. Kulke and G.C. Tripathi, "The Formation of the Jagannātha Triad", *TCOJATRTOO*, 1978, p. 194.

63 S.S. Panda, "Antiquities of Lord Jagannatha an Amazing Finding", *The Youth World* (monthly), Arabinda Das (ed.), no. 27, January, 2005, p. 12. Bolangir.

As stated and dealt, the earliest semi-circular stone sockets as a set had been discovered from Kharligaṛh site, situated very close to Tentelkhunti village in Bolaṅgīr district. So, there is reason to believe that the semi-circular stone sockets finally evolved to the shape of Lord Jagannātha.

The new archaeological findings prove the present Sunabeda plateau and its vicinity of Nuāpāḍā district of Orissa state, to have been the site of nucleus of spiritual culture of the entire Mahānadī Valley. Further fieldworks, excavations, findings and studies are required to fill up the missing links. The holy triad probably evolved by absorbing the tribal, non-tribal and yogic conceptions, which emerged in the central Mahānadī Valley and finally Puruṣottama Jagannātha cult has evolved in establishing a harmonious cult and society in the greater Mahānadī Valley.

This work does not solve the mystery of the establishment of Jagannātha trinity. It is a study with latest findings and hypothesis only. Further findings, data and detailed studies of western Orissa region in future, will lead to the study of the development of the present-day Jagannātha trinity at Purī. The Puruṣottama Jagannātha cult has become purely Brāhmanical, during its development and is shrouded in legends, traditions, mythologies, superstitions and blind faiths, being in the clutch of *mukti maṇḍapa*. The images worshipped on the Ratnavedī are of Jagannātha, Balabhadra, Subhadrā, Sudarśana and miniature images of Lakṣmī, Sarasvatī and Mādhava, with the main deities. Originally Jagannātha culture has developed with a cosmopolitan outlook; therefore being propagated by His Divine Grace A.C. Bhaktivedanta Swami Prabhupada, it has practically entered most parts of the globe, through International Society for Kṛṣṇa Consciousness (ISKCON).[64]

The cult of Jagannātha, which developed in early medieval period of the Indian history, in the land of Kāmakalā, Uḍḍiyāna-Pīṭha and Erotic Art, has developed as a symbol of religious syncretism, where influences of all religions,[65] cults and *yoga*s are found, which makes a harmonious eclectic spiritual religion — all these are in keeping with the Vedic tradition.

---

64 J.P. Singh Deo, op. cit., 2003, pp. 110-11.

65 Niranjan Satapathy, *Religious Life in Orissa (A Study of the Inter-relation of Cults)*, Kolkata: R.N. Bhattacharya, 2000, pp. 145-60.

12

Jayadeva and the Gīta-Govinda

AFTER the age of *ācāryas* comes the age of *bhaktas* in Indian literature. The *bhakti* movement, which covers a span of over 1000 years, from CE 700 to 1800 can be studied in almost all the Indian languages.

Beginning with the exaltation of Śiva in the south, the *bhakti* movement veered towards Viṣṇu and the final achievement in this direction, in terms of Sanskrit poetry, remains Jayadeva's *Gīta-Govinda,* which has also been a part of the music and dance tradition of the eastern region since the twelfth century CE.

Arvind Mangrulker[1] has done a study — *Gīta-Govinda: Structure, Technique and Substance* — and states that Jayadeva, the poet and music-maker of the *Gīta-Govinda,* flourished in the twelfth century CE. Jayadeva has been claimed by Bengal, because the place of his birth was Kindubilva (modern Kenduli in Birbhum district), which is now in Bengal. Tradition, however, is very long and persistent that he belonged to Orissa. For various reasons this seems probable. We find a reference to Kindubilva in the *Gīta-Govinda* (3.10). Jayadeva also gives the names of his parents in the closing stanza of his poem as Śrī Bhojadeva and Ramādevī. Most probably, Padmāvatī, his wife, was a danseuse and Jayadeva used to sing songs from the *Gīta-Govinda* in accompaniment of her devotional temple dance as the leader of the troupe of musicians.

In all probability, this temple must have been the celebrated temple of Jagannātha at Purī, which was built some two centuries before the poet flourished. Puri was one of the great abiding centres of Vaiṣṇavite cult in India. That Jayadeva was the leader of the dancing-singing troupe is borne out by the almost opening verse of the *Gīta-Govinda.*

The entire *Gīta-Govinda* is full of word-play and charming ending rhyme. There

---

[1] Arvind Mangrulker, "Gīta-Govinda: Structure, Technique and Substance", *Annals of the Bhankarkar Oriental Research Institute,* 1983, vol. LXIV, pts. I-IV, Pune, pp. 149-63.

are some keywords such as a *rasa, madhu* and *vilāsa,* the meaning of which keeps on shifting furtively.

It is known from tradition that in the *sanctum sanctorum* of Vaiṣṇavite temples the *Daśāvatāra-Stuti* of the *Gīta-Govinda* was recited as a part of ritual at the time of worship, which is still continued at the Jagannātha temple of Purī and outside the precincts of the temple, in the open arena or in the *naṭa-maṇḍapa*. The *Gīta-Govinda* used to be dramatized and performed as a dance for the entertainment of lay devotees. The twofold — ritualistic and artistic — use flows easily from its composition.

The prelude to *Gīta-Govinda*, narrating the *daśāvatāra*, has been a favourite with young dancers whatever the technique under study, while the *aṣṭapadīs*, demanding greater interpretative powers have been presented by experienced exponents.

In fact, the *Gīta-Govinda*, in a compact form, can serve as an ideal dance-drama featuring three top exponents, for the characters are restricted to Kṛṣṇa, Rādhā and a confidante of Rādhā. That aside, what has brought Jayadeva's eloquent and impressive visualization of the estrangement and reunion of Rādhā and Kṛṣṇa to the dance stage is the inherent flavour of *rasa*, the *śṛṅgāra rasa*, the erotic sentiment — with both *vipralambha* (separation) and *sampanna saṁbhoga* (reunion), well balanced to exalt the mind to an awareness of the path of *bhakti* or loving faith.

It is not a night of romance that the poet is seeking, for that would only remain as ephemeral and transitory as a flash of revelation. Thus, Rādhā's anguish and anxiety are raised to the highest plane of longing — wanting to be possessed totally for eternal union and the ultimate bliss. Rādhā remains the individual soul, the *ātman*, seeking union with the *Paramātman*, the eternal soul. That is why the longing is placed close to eternal torment and total surrender.

Jayadeva, in his *Gīta-Govinda*, contemplates on the *śṛṅgāra rasa* to arouse the emotion of love to take us on the path of *bhakti*. And classical dance, that seeks the spiritual note on the sensuous scale, therefore often turns to Jayadeva to reveal the inner universal enlightened self. One does not, of course, expect either the dancer or the audience to be soaked in *bhakti*, but the classical dance techniques are well designed to recast the *rasa* of poetry and song in the resplendence of art. The influence of *Gīta-Govinda* on the Indian artistic traditions of India is very high.

Arvind Mangrulker claims Jayadeva to have been of Orissa and states:

> In the eastern part of India two types of folk dance have emerged culminating today by their sheer strength of tradition and beauty into classical dance forms: Oḍissī and Kucipuḍī. These dance forms have remained for hundreds of years locally bound and temple-locked. In fact, all our arts have been temple arts. If Jayadeva was an Oḍiyā person, as I think he was, some sort of seed form of Oḍissī dance tradition had something to do with the dance form supposed to be associated with the *Gīta-Govinda* in Jayadeva's days. One significant point to be noted in this connection is that no Oḍissī dance recital is complete even today without the *Daśāvatāra-Stuti*. There may be some more items from the *Gīta-Govinda*, but *Daśāvatāra-Stuti* is absolutely a "must". This is not so in other dance forms. This shows the most intimate connection between the *Gīta-Govinda* and Oḍissī dance.

Kindubilva village is situated in the Prācī Valley,[2] which is famous for the finding of *Daśāvatāra* images in different places. The finding of *Daśāvatāra* images had great influence in the mind of Jayadeva, who propagated the doctrine, giving topmost place to Śrī Kr̥ṣṇa as an *avatāra*. In the theory of Jayadeva, Kr̥ṣṇa has been given the place of an *avatāra* and around him the other incarnations have started. Thus it appears that the Prācī Valley was famous for the worship of *Daśāvatāra* images in various forms. There is every possibility that the celebrated Sanskrit poet Jayadeva was born at Kenduli in the Prācī Valley when the worship of such images was already prevalent there. Though he was a great devotee of Mādhava, his depiction of the theory of ten incarnations suggest that he gave topmost priority to Śrī Kr̥ṣṇa, who is taken as *avatārī* by him not as *avatāra*. There is every possibility that he was influenced by the Vāsudeva-Kr̥ṣṇa cult prevalent much earlier to that of other forms of Vaiṣṇavism in Orissa.

---

[2] P.K. Ray, *Archaeological Survey Report: Prachi Valley*, Bhubaneswar: Orissa State Archaeology, 1975, *passim*.

13

Erection of Sun Temple in a Folk Tale

FOR more than 700 years since its construction, Koṇārka has preserved the artistic heritage of a bygone age. Today, even in ruins, it attracts visitors and admirers of art from all parts of the world. The erection of a grand temple at this lonely place has been a subject of much speculation.[1]

K.S. Behera[2] comments on a little known temple near Koṇārka and mentions that to help the understanding of the temple in a wider context, we briefly discuss the important archaeological remains near Koṇārka, especially the temple of Triveṇīśvara, which is located at a distance of about 2 km to the north-west of the sun temple.

The traditional *kṣetra* of Koṇārka was not confined to the temple alone but embraced the surrounding areas. The *Koṇārka Kṣetra Māhātmya*[3] declares that this famous *kṣetra* was five *krośa* in extent. The *Brahma Purāṇa*[4] also asserts that the *kṣetra*, sacred to the thousand-rayed Sun God Koṇāditya, extends one *yojana*. No inscription or sculpture has yet been discovered at Koṇārka to throw light on the early history of the place. The Greek geographer Ptolemy (second century CE) mentions "Kannagara" which evidently stands for Koṇārka.[5] The *erbang* copper plate of Śambhuyaśa[6] seems to suggest that in the sixth century CE the Koṇārka area was included in his kingdom. The discovery of copper plates of Bhauma-Kara

---

[1] K.S. Behera, "Notes and Comments: (1) A Little Known Temple Near Koṇārka", *Journal of the Orissa Research Society*, no. 3. Oct. 1985, p. 45.

[2] Ibid., p. 45.

[3] *Koṇārka-Kṣetra-Māhātmya* (unpublished).

[4] *Brahma Purāṇa*, ch. 28.

[5] S.N. Majumdar, *Ancient India as Described by Ptolemy*, p. 70.

[6] *OHRJ*, vol. XII, no. 3, pp. 113-22.

kings from Terundia[7] and Caurāsī[8] suggest their supremacy over the locality. The surrounding area of Koṇārka came under the influence of Buddhism. In the village Baḍatārā (which literally means great Tārā) we find three images representing Tārā, Khasarpana Lokeśvara and Jambhala. The image of Tārā can be assigned to ninth-tenth centuries CE on the basis of the palaeography of the Buddhist formula — *ye dharma hetu prabhava* — inscribed on the backside of the slab. An image of crowned Buddha, seated in *bhūmisparśa-mudrā* has been discovered at Kuruma, at a distance of 8 km from Koṇārka. An image of Maricī has been fixed to a niche of the Rāmacaṇḍī temple. The discovery of these images indicates that the region of Koṇārka was an important centre of Buddhism during the eighth to tenth centuries CE.

The so-called Chāyādevī or Māyādevī temple[9] located in the south-western side of the enclosure of Koṇārka temple, seems to be a monument of the later Somavaṁśī period. Its architectural and sculptural style indicates that it was constructed before the main temple complex of Koṇārka. The existence of a sun temple at Koṇārka prior to the construction of a big temple by Narasiṁha I is known from the literary source.[10] That it was not the only monument of the place[11] is proved by the temple of Triveṇīśvara. According to the *Koṇārka Kṣetra Māhātmya*, Aṣṭa-Caṇḍī (eight Goddesses) and Aṣṭa-Śambhū (eight Śivas) were the guardian deities of the *kṣetra*, of these Triveṇīśvara is said to be one of the Aṣṭa-Śambhūs, whose shrine exists in the neighbourhood of Koṇārka. It is situated at a distance of about 2 km to the north-west of Koṇārka temple in the village Mādhipur. The original temple has been completely restored. A part of the *bāḍa* of the main deula still survives to indicate its former glory. The southern and western-central niches have the images of Gaṇeśa and Kārttikeya, respectively. The northern niche has the image of Pārvatī and a separate modern structure has been built over it. The original *bāḍa* is decorated with *nāga* and *nāgī* pilasters, female figures and elongated *khākharāmuṇḍī*s with *kalaśa* on the top. Of the *dikpālas*, *Īśāna*, seated on a bull, is seen on the north-east corner of the *vimāna*. The scheme of decoration has striking

---

[7] *EI*, vol. XXIII, pp. 211-16.

[8] *Journal of Bihar and Orissa Research Society*, vol. XIV, pp. 292-306.

[9] Debala Mitra, *Koṇārka*, New Delhi: Archaeological Survey of India, 1976, pp. 95-106.

[10] *JAS*, vol. III, 1961, pp. 60-61.

[11] According to Abul-Fazal, the famous chronicler of the time of Akbar, twenty-eight temples stood in its vicinity, six before the entrance and twenty-two without the enclosure and each had its separate legend. Vide, H.S. Jarrett and Jadunath Sarkar, *Ain-i-Akbari*, II, 140-41.

affinities with the Gaurī temple at Bhubaneswar and in point of date, these two may be regarded as close contemporaries. The female figures carved in alto-relivo and, particularly the elongated *khākharāmuṇḍīs* with *kalaśa* motif on the top, are similar to those on the Gaurī temple at Bhubaneswar.

One Buddha image with inscription is found at a temple named Kosaleśvara temple near Kañjiā village, close to Satyabādī (vide: *Samaj*, Oriyā daily newspaper, 7 January 1990). In Dharmakīrti village one Buddha image with inscription of Buddhist *mantra* is traced.

In the words of Debala Mitra:[12]

> There is no evidence to explain the selection of the site for building the temple. We have to assume that either the place enjoyed religious sanctity from before or, being on the sea-coast, it (rather *trikoṇa*) had commercial importance.

The purpose of erecting this stupendous temple is unknown. Sūrya is believed to be the healer of diseases and the bestower of wishes from very early times; and it is not unlikely that the temple is a worthy thanksgiving of the powerful ruler following either his recovery or the fulfilment of his prayer perhaps for a healthy son. That he had some genuine regard for this deity is shown by the name of his son Bhānudeva, the first solar name in that royal line. We should also remember in this connexion that the builder of this, Narasiṁha, was traditionally known as "Lāṅguliā" (one having a tail), the exact significance of which is not known. The explanation that he had a protuberance of the spinal cord seems to suggest that he had a physical deformity of some kind or other, of which he wanted to get cured by building a temple of Sūrya. Some scholars, however, surmise that the monument was erected as a memorial by the ambitious monarch after his successful campaign against the Muslims.

According to D.C. Ganguly,[13] the Gaṅga King Narasiṁha I succeeded his father Anaṅgabhīma III in CE 1238 and ruled till CE 1264. He has also earned undying fame by building the magnificent Sun temple at Koṇārka.

Raja G.C.H. Jagadeb[14] assigns the ruling period of Narasiṁha Deva I within CE

---

12 Debala Mitra, *Koṇārka*, New Delhi: Archaeological Survey of India, 1976, pp. 7-8.

13 D.C. Ganguly, "The Eastern Gaṅges", *THACOTIP*, vol. V, *The Struggle for Empire*, 1966, pp. 207-09.

14 Rājā Śrı Govind Candra Haricandan Jagadeb, *Utkal Empire Under Gaṅga Kings*, Berhampur, 1977, pp. 46-47.

1237-63 and states that in the lifetime of Rājā Rājeśvara Anaṅgabhīma Deb II, his son Narasiṁha Deva was administrating the country within the valley of Lāṅguliā River (river Nāgavalī) and was called as Lāṅguliā Narasiṁha Deva. The country around Lāṅguliā River Valley was once called Nandapur *sāmrājya;* in British regime, it was known as Jeypore *zamīndārī;* and at present it is known as Korapūṭ district. The history of Nandpur reveals the existence of kings named Lāṅguilā Bālādeb, etc. The names of kings or the people of a particular country are called by the name of the country for example Rājā of Haladiā is called Haladiā Rājā and the people are called Haladiā people, but neither the people nor the Rājā can be yellow in colour. So also Lāṅguliā Narasiṁha Deb cannot be presumed to have a tail or a dress with a tail as some writers presume. It was stated in *Mādalā-Pāñjī* that Lāṅguliā Narasiṁhā Deb laid the foundation of the Koṇārka temple in his 3rd Utkal *aṅka* of his reign and then left for southern expedition. His southern campaign lasted for twelve years.

So, this explains why the King Narasiṁha I was known Lāṅguliā Narasiṁha Deb. While writing on Koṇārka, M. Mansinha[15] addresses it as "The wonder that is Koṇārka" and concludes by mentioning:

> These great artists of Koṇārka have left absolutely no record of themselves. But to any seeing eye, the warm, living touch of those forgotten but glorious masters is still there in every inch of stone of the colossal structure they set up with such self-effacing devotion. The soul of 1200 poets who together wrote out this great epic, sought and realized deathlessness for their spirits, through pure worship of law and beauty, even as they worked like slaves under orders of an earthly king, because they knew the ineffable ecstacy of dedicating their daily task to the king of kings.

There are a number of folk tales, folklores, legends and stories regarding the Koṇārka temple. One folk tale on the completion of the Sun temple at Koṇārka is that the chief of the mason was Bisu Mahārāṇā. When he came to work at the construction site of Koṇārka temple, long twelve years ago, his wife was pregnant; who gave birth to a son named Dharmapada. In course of time Dharmapada went to school where the boys teased him as fatherless. Dharmapada insisted to see his father at Koṇārka. At last his mother sent some fruits of her garden and their favourite dog Balia and advised him to meet his father at Koṇārka. Dharmapada came to Koṇārka and completed the crowning elements of the

[15] M. Mansinha, *The Saga of the Land of Jagannātha*, Cuttack: J. Mohapatra & Co., p. 93.

temple. The masons were afraid of the king if he would know that a boy has completed the work. Therefore, Dharmapada, to save the 1,200 masons, jumped from the top of the temple to the sea.[16]

Among the Buddhist Pāli canon, one comes across a work named *Dhammapada*. The *Sutta Piṭaka*[17] incorporates the greatest literary works of Buddhism in prose and verse. It comprises the following five collections called Nikāyas: (1) *Dīgha*, (2) *Majjhima*, (3) *Saṁyutta*, (4) *Aṅguttara*, and (5) *Khuddaka*.

The *Khuddaka*[18] comprises the following texts: *Khuddakapāṭha, Dhammapada, Udāna, Itivuttaka, Sutta Nipāta, Vimānavatthu, Peṭavatthu, Theragāthā, Therigāthā, Jātakas, Niddesa, Paṭisambhidā-magga, Apādāna, Buddhavaṁsa* and *Cariyāpiṭaka*.

A.D. Pusalkar[19] mentions:

> The *Dhammapada*, the best known of the Buddhist canonical texts, is an anthology of 423 sayings of Buddha in verse divided into 26 *vagga*s or chapters, the stanzas being arranged by subjects. These stanzas are mostly taken from the other books of the Pāli canon, and embody the spirit of Buddha's teaching, if not the very words of the master. The *Dhammapada* is a fine exposition of the sublime ethical teachings of the Buddha and was a very popular text all over the Buddhist world.

Buddhism developed as a powerful factor not only of India but also of a large part of Asia. It is well known that during the period from third century BCE to second-third centuries CE, Andhra and particularly the entire eastern coastal belt[20] was studded with Buddhist monuments and Buddhism almost suppressed the growth of Brāhmanical vestiges.[21]

It is a sad plight to mention that scholars like K.C. Misra[22] observes, "historically Buddhism did not have great influence on Orissa".

---

16 A. Joshi, *Koṇārk*, Cuttack: Baneeshree, pp. 14-15.

17 A.D. Pusalkar, "The Pāli Canon", *THACOTIP*, vol. II, *The Age of Imperial Unity*, 1968, p. 398.

18 Ibid., p. 401.

19 Ibid.

20 S.R. Rao, "Kaverippumpattinam Excavations", *Transactions of the Archaeological South India (Madras)*, 1962-65, pp. 163-65; *Indian Archaeology: A Review, 1964-65*, p. 24.

21 I.K. Sarma, *The Development of Early Śaiva Art and Architecture*, Delhi: Sundeep Prakashan, 1982, p. 62.

22 K.C. Mishra, "Is Jagannātha Buddhistic?", in H.C. Das, C. Das and S.R. Pal (eds.) *Buddhism and Jainism*, Cuttack: Institute of Oriental and Orissan Studies, 1976, pp. 274-76.

Trapuśa and Bhallika, two merchants of Utkala, are stated to have been the first disciples of Buddha. It is known from *Aṅguttara-Nikāya* that Buddha gave them his hair, which was afterwards deposited in a *caitya* built by these two merchants in their native town Asitāñjana. The Nikāya *Mahāchatta-rasika-sutta* also states that Vassa and Bhanna of Utkala, on hearing the discourse of Buddha delivered at Jetavana, accepted his teaching.[23]

From *Avadānaśataka*,[24] it is known that Lord Buddha had visited South Kosala and had stayed for three months, at the then capital of South Kosala. South Kosala state was situated in the Upper Mahānadī Valley and to commemorate his visit, a tributary of Tel River, which starts from southern Khondmal district was named as Rāhula, after the name of Buddha's son. The rock-cut elephant of Dhauli may be regarded as the earliest Buddhist art in Orissa.

On the basis of the discovery of a few railing-posts, dated to first century BCE near the Bhāskareśvara temple in Bhubaneswar, K.C. Panigrahi[25] feels that there was a Buddhist *stūpa* at the site. The Bhāskareśvara temple contains a huge *Śiva-liṅga*, 9' high and 12' 5" in circumference. It seems, in reality, to have been the remnant of an Aśokan pillar whose Lion Capital and Bell Capital are now preserved at the Orissa State Museum.

It can be said that in early medieval period there was a Buddhist centre around Bhubaneswar and it is proved from the findings of images of Buddha, Lokeśvara and Tārā, which are now preserved at the Orissa State Museum.

The sites of Ratnagiri, Lalitagiri and Udayagiri in Cuttack district (now Jajpur district) have abundant Buddhist images, *stūpas* and antiquities. The antiquity of Ratnagiri may go back to the Gupta period and some of the images have Gupta art influence. So, it can be said that these sites were the centre of Buddhism from fourth century CE till the rise of the Somavaṁśī in tenth century CE. Archaeological Survey of India has published the *Report of Excavation of Ratnagiri* and it is a great contribution to the study of Buddhism in Orissa. Recent excavation carried out by the Archaeological Survey of India (ASI), Bhubaneswar Circle at Lalitagiri, has discovered an inscription of second century CE. Therefore it can be assumed that Lalitagiri was the ancient Buddhist site in that complex. ASI has also found a relic of Buddha.

---

23 N.K. Sahu, *Buddhism in Orissa*, Utkal University, 1958, p. 13.

24 Rajendralala Mitra, *The Sanskrit Buddhist Literature of Nepal*, Calcutta: Sanskrit Pustak Bhandar, 1971, p. 20.

25 K.C. Panigrahi, *Archaeological Remains at Bhubaneswar*, Calcutta: Orient Longmans, 1961, p. 171.

A Mahāyāna Buddhist establishment sprang up at Jayarampur in Bālāsore district. Metal Buddha images, stone images of Goddess and copper-plate of Gopacandra dated to sixth century CE have been found from there. The copper-plate records the grant of a village to the Mahāyānist *bhikṣu-saṁgha* for constructing a *vihāra* at Bodhipadraka, where the presiding deity was Avalokiteśvara.

Hiuen Tsang, the Chinese pilgrim, visited the territory of modern Orissa in CE 639 and from his record it is known that Buddhism was popular in the country of Wu (i.e. Oḍra). There were above 100 Buddhist monasteries and in his record, Puṣpagiri monastery, Po-lo-mo-lo-ki-li and city of Che-li-ta-lo are mentioned. The city of Che-li-ta-lo has been identified after excavation of the Buddhist monastery in Kuruma, near Koṇārka, near the sea, by the Orissa State Archaeology Department.

Kuruma, an ancient Buddhist site lies 8 km to the north-east of Koṇārka. Over a mound there Buddha in *bhūmisparśa-mudrā*, Avalokiteśvara in *lalitāsana* pose, Yamāri and Trivikrama-Viṣṇu are collectively worshipped inside a temporary shed by the local people as the *Yama-dharma* and accordingly the site is known as the Yamadharma-Pīṭha.[26] The Orissa State Archaeology Department had taken up excavation at Kuruma and informs that the Buddhist *vihāra*, which Hiuen Tsang saw, might be the original monastery flourishing during seventh-eighth centuries CE at Kuruma, which collapsed after a decade and followed by reconstruction during ninth-tenth centuries CE as revealed from the present excavated brick structures. We find from the accounts[27] of Hiuen Tsang that Che-li-ta-lo was situated to the south-east of the Wu-Tu country and was a remarkable seat of Mahāyāna Buddhism by the seventh century CE. On this basis, Kuruma and Citreśvarī located to the south-east of Koṇārka can take the place of Che-li-ta-lo of Hiuen Tsang account. These details prove that there was a Buddhist establishment and Buddhism was very popular around the present Koṇārka area.

A colossal image of Padmapāṇī 15' 8" in height is the largest Buddhist image, so far found in Orissa and it is found at Jajpur town. Close to Jajpur town is Solampur. Solampur seems to have been a flourishing establishment during Bhauma-Kara ruling period. Ratnagiri copper-plate of Somavaṁśī king Karṇa refers to Salonapura Mahāvihāra and the site may be identified as the modern Solampur situated near Jajpur.

The Birūpa-Citrotpala Valley was a prosperous Buddhist centre and its

[26] P.K. Ray, "Kuruka, An Ancient Buddhist Site", *OHRJ*, vol. XXIV-XXVI, p. 93.

[27] N.K. Sahu, op. cit., 1958, p. 84.

noteworthy centres were Ratnagiri, Lalitagiri, Udayagiri, Kulanagiri and Rāmeśvara. These spots seem to have been roaring in prosperity of Buddhism, during Bhauma-Kara period, because there are lots of ruins of *stūpa*s, monasteries and temples. ASI[28] had done excavation at Lalitagiri and had discovered tooth and hair relics of Lord Buddha, hermetically sealed in a stone box; which in turn was enclosed by another, twice over. Relics have been found at Ratnagiri and Udayagiri also.

The Orissa State Archaeology Department had surveyed the Citrotpala Valley. At Kolanapur site, situated on the eastern bank of Citrotpala River, Buddhist antiquities were discovered. P.K. Ray[29] states:

> On the basis of the engrate Buddhist sculptures; trial excavations were conducted by State Department of Archaeology. In order to get the chronological sequence of the site, the excavation has brought to light, structural remains made of ancient bricks of a collapsed Buddhist monastery. Such type of Buddhist *vihāra* has also been recovered in a place called Kuruma near Koṇārka. The recovery of loose Buddhist sculptures not only in this particular site but also in different areas of Citrotpala Valley give a clear picture that immediately after Ratnagiri complex, Buddhist monasteries were also built from *c.* ninth to eleventh centuries CE.

Surface findings of Buddhist images and existence of mounds at Talcher with Bhauma-Kara copper-plate discovery show Talcher area to have nourished Buddhist establishment during the regime of Bhauma-Kara rulers.

Images of Buddha and *bodhisattva*s are found on the surface of a mound at Khadipada-Mohanpārā in Bālāsore district. It seems to be a *vihāra* establishment. Only further excavation will give more details of this site.

There was an important Buddhist centre at Ayodhyā in Bālāsore district also. Images of Vajra-Tārā and Marīcī are found there. Ayodhyā, it seems, was a strong centre of Vajrayāna Buddhism. In most of the Buddhist sites of Orissa, Mahāyāna doctrine of Buddhism gradually transformed itself into Vajrayāna.

Modern Khichiṅg in Mayūrbhañj district was a large Buddhist settlement. The mound of Virāṭgaṛh has ruins of Buddhist creed. Other sites like Caṇḍiāsal, Itamuṇḍiā, Saṅkhurājāragaṛh and Kukudagaṛh contain Buddhist remains. From

---

28 *The Indian Express*, English daily newspaper, Vijayanagara, Sunday, 17 February 1991, pp. 1 and 3.

29 P.K. Ray, "Archaeological Remains of the Citrotpala Valley", *OHRJ*, vol. XXXII, nos. 1-2, p. 6.

these sites, many images of Buddha, Mañjuśrī, Lokeśvara, Vajrasattva, Jambhala, Vasundharā, Tārā and Marīcī have been found.

Achūtrājpur near Banpur was also a Buddhist centre and it is proved from Seone sculptures and a large number of Buddhist bronze images found there.

Buddhist vestiges are found at Ganiāpalī and Nāgarāj sites of Bargaṛh district. The Postgraduate Dept. of History, Sambalpur University, took up excavation and survey of Ganiāpali and Nāgarāj. N.K. Sahu[30] mentions that this monastery now excavated is the earliest of its kind in Orissa. Even in India, a structural monastery of this magnitude is rare during the fourth-fifth centuries CE. The Mucalinda Buddhist monastery of Ganiāpalī is a rare occurrence in the history of Buddhism in Orissa.

During the eighth and ninth centuries CE, Indrabhūti popularized Vajrayāna and his sister Lakṣmīkarā propounded Sahajayāna. Towards the end of tenth century CE Kālacakrayāna, an offsoot of Vajrayāna was introduced in Orissa.[31]

The whole Orissa is littered with images of the Mahāyāna and Vajrayāna pantheons of Buddhism. The noteworthy sites of Buddhist antiquities are Jayarāmpur, Khadipada-Mohanpārā, Solampur, Ayodhyā, Bhuinpārā and Kasbā, all in Bālāsore district; Khichiṅg, Rānībāgh and Udala in Mayūrbhañj district; Ratnagiri, Lalitagiri, Udayagiri, Kulanagiri, Rāmeśvara, Vajragiri, Kharia, Chauduar, Bhaneswarnasi and Kundeswar in Jajpur and Cuttack districts; Bhubaneswar, Kuruma and Achūtrājpur in Purī district; Talcher in Aṅgul district; and Bauḍh in Bauḍh district. Buddhist images have been found at Buddhakhol and Udayagiri or Gañjam district and one Mucalinda Buddha has been traced by the author at Ṭopīgāon village ruins, near Biśwanāthpur of Kālāhāṇḍī district on 15 December 1992. During the archaeological field survey of the district, one Buddha image in *bhūmisparśa-mudrā* was excavated at Rāṇīpur-Jharial in Bolaṅgīr district and is preserved at the Indralatha temple by the Orissa State Archaeology Department. One Buddha image in *bhūmisparśa-mudrā* was discovered by the author at the Māraguḍa Valley in 1968, it is now in much mutilated condition.

The study shows that from the tenth century CE onwards Buddhism in Orissa began to decline and the glamour of the Buddhist *vihāra*s remained for few centuries and faded out. Lord Buddha was made an *avatāra* of Viṣṇu, while revival of

---

30 N.K. Sahu, "Ganiapali", in K.C. Behera (ed.) *Interim Excavation Reports*, Sambalpur University: History Dept., 1982, p. 15.

31 N.K. Sahu, op. cit., 1958, *passim*.

Brahmanism took place. Lalmani Joshi[32] very rightly states that the acceptance of Buddha as an incarnation of Viṣṇu by Hinduism was a "well conceived and bold stroke of policy (which) cut the ground from under the feet of Buddhism".

According to tradition, Śaṅkara defeated the Buddhist *paṇḍits* of this place (i.e. Purī vicinity) by his vast learning and irrefutable arguments; converted most of them to his own faith and proclaimed Jagannātha Buddha as identical with the great Brāhmanical God Puruṣottama of the *Gītā*. This peaceful process of assimilation of a great Buddhist deity into the pantheon of Brāhmanism, strengthened its influence at Jagannātha Purī, which was a strong centre of Buddhism before his days.[33]

The author[34] has proved that Śaṅkara installed a Vaiṣṇava deity Jagannātha as the divinity, to be worshipped at the Govardhana Maṭha of Purī. It seems, thereby Śaṅkara made Jagannātha fully a Viṣṇu deity and the credit of first converting Jagannātha to a Viṣṇu-Kṛṣṇa deity should be given to Ādi Śaṅkarācārya. Finally, the instalment of Jagannātha as the presiding deity of Puruṣottama-Kṣetra, i.e. Purī, by Yayāti I, immortalized Jagannātha as Puruṣottama Jagannātha.

So, it can be claimed that the assimilation or conversion of one of the icons of Buddha as Puruṣottama Jagannātha was a great blow or suppression to the popularity of Buddhism in the coastal belt of Orissa and India in general. It seems, still then, some Buddhist monasteries were functioning at Kuruma, in the vicinity of Koṇārka and other places. Finally the construction of the Sun temple at Koṇārka by Gaṅga King Narasiṁha I in thirteenth century CE and the Sūrya-Viṣṇu religious culture there, gave a death blow to the functioning of the Buddhist *vihāra* at Kuruma. Because of this the folk tale or folklore of Dharmapada jumping from the top of the Sun temple of Koṇārka to the sea, developed. Further "Dharmapada" in Pāli connotation becomes "Dhammapada". *Dharma* is pronounced in Pāli language as *dhamma*. Even if the name "Dharmapāla" is considered, then it comes to notice that Dharmapāla was a Buddhist Yogācārya of Vijñānavāda school. N.K. Sahu[35] mentions Dharmapāla:

---

[32] L.M. Joshi, *Studies in the Buddhistic Culture of India*, Delhi: Motilal Banarsidass, 1987, p. 322.

[33] K.N. Mahapatra, "Jagannātha-Purī as a Centre of Culture Through the Ages", *OHRJ*, vol. VI, no. 4, p. 297; *The Mādalā-Pāñjī*, Cuttack: Prachi Samiti, p. 81.

[34] J.P. Singh Deo, *Origin of Jagannātha Deity*, New Delhi: Gyan Publishing House, 1991, pp. 68-69 and 71.

[35] N.K. Sahu, op. cit., 1958, p. 113.

> The scholastic tradition of Asaṅga and Vasubandhu, so ably maintained by Diṅnāga, Vasumitra and Sthiramati continued with great vigour by a fresh batch of scholars who flourished in the late fifth as well as in the sixth centuries CE. Dharmapāla, who came from Kāñcīdeśa, was a disciple of Diṅnāga and he appears to have spent some part of his life with his illustrious *ācārya* in Orissa where he popularized the Yogācāra school of thought. He was greatly respected by a large number of scholars because of his uncommon erudition and was invited to the University of Nālandā where he adorned the chair of Chancellorship for a long time. Like his great teacher, Dharmapāla was also an eminent logician and his commentary on the *Vijñaptimātratā-Siddhi* is a monumental work on the Vijñānavāda.[36]

The Pāla kings of Bengal ruled between eighth-ninth centuries. The second king of this dynasty was Dharmapāla,[37] whose reigning period is assigned to CE 770–810. The Pāla rulers were all Buddhists and among them the name of Dharmapāla is most significant as he was a great admirer, exponent of Buddhism and the founder of Vikramaśīlavihāra.[38]

So, it is definite that the names Dharmapāla, Dharmapada and Dhammapada (in Pāli) are connected in a manner with Buddhism. This folk tale of Koṇārka is a beautiful living example, in showing how sometimes, historical happenings develop into folk tale or folklore and preserve the occurrence of some account of event. Study of the historicity of this folk tale of the Sun temple at Koṇārka solves a problem of the cause of erection of this world famous temple.

---

[36] N.K. Sahu, op. cit., 1958; H. Ui, *The Vaiśeṣika Philosophy*, London: *OTF*, 1917, p. 2.

[37] R.C. Majumdar, "The Palas", *THACOTIP*, vol. IV, *The Age of Imperial Kanauj*, 1964, p. 45.

[38] Ibid., p. 271.

14

Erotic Art and the Land of Kāmakalā

THE whole Mahānadī Valley was the land of *Kāmakalā* and Uḍḍiyāna-Pīṭha (site). Kāma means desire and Kalā means art. As a whole *Kāmakalā* may be regarded as an erotic science. It is interesting to investigate the expressions of the art of Kāma, i.e. desire, expressed through the antiquities, sculptures and temple architectures of the Mahānadī Valley.

The circular stone sockets discovered from Nuāpāḍā and Kālāhāṇḍī districts are the symbols of union of male and female principles (i.e. union of Śiva–Śakti), and may be accepted as the earliest erotic art of the Mahānadī Valley, dated to early historical period. Eroticism pertains to sexual love, both amatory and amorous, leading to the expression of sensuousness in art.

The circular stone sockets owe their origin to the rock art of Yogīmaṭh Ḍoṅger of Neolithic period[1] and were used to represent Lord Buddha[2] on the cross-bar railing of Amarāvatī *stūpa* in Andhra Pradesh, where presentation of Rāhula is shown. Later this shape evolved to be the image of Lord Puruṣottama Jagannātha at Purī.[3]

The discovery of a rare stone with a right angle triangle, representing Śiva Kāmeśvara, Śakti Kāmeśvarī and Sāmarasya, in Patdaraha area of the southern Sunabeda plateau, signifies the *yantra* of creation. So, it can be taken as the second erotic art of the Mahānadī Valley.

Simple square temples were first built throughout the Mahānadī Valley. The

---

[1] J.P. Singh Deo, "The Pre-historic Cave Painting of Jogimath Donger", *OHRJ*, vol. XXII, no. 2, pp. 21-22.

[2] E.R. Stone, *The Buddhist Art of Nagarjunakonda*, Delhi: Motilal Banarsidass, 1994, illu. no. 32.

[3] J.P. Singh Deo, *Origin of Jagannātha Deity*, 2nd enlarged and rev. edn., New Delhi: Gyan Publishing House, 2003; Appendix II and plates.

J.P. Singh Deo, *Tāntric Hedonism of Mahānadī Valley, Uḍḍiyāna-Pīṭha*, New Delhi: D.K. Printworld, 2004, p. 32.

Māṭharas[4] ruled coastal southern Orissa during the fourth and fifth centuries CE and the Nalas[5] ruled the upper Mahānadī Valley during the third–fifth centuries CE. These two dynasties were credited with building square temples with *triratha* plan throughout the Mahānadī Valley.

A lot of experiments on the construction of stellate-planned temples took place in the upper Mahānadī Valley, comprising South Kosala state of ancient and medieval periods. Mention may be made of the Rāma temple at Sirpur (CE 595–605), the Indal Duel temple at Kharod (CE 650-60), the Siddheśvara temple at Palari (CE 675-85) and the Sabari temple at Kharod (CE 700-10).[6] One rare stellate planned ruined brick temple is found inside the Fort of Patnagaṛh.[7]

Another group of temples having the plans of two squares placed diagonally and intersecting each other at angles of 45° giving the shape of an eight-pointed star is of interest, because they are based on "Kāmakalā yantra". These are identified as "Kosalī Style of Rekha temples".[8] They are: (i) Pātāleśvara Śiva temple at Būḍhī Komnā (Nuāpāḍā district), (ii) Cheliā temple within Kansil village, adjacent to Rāṇīpur-Jharial complex (Bolaṅgīr district), (iii) Citawarī Devī temple at Dhobnī village near Damakeda village (Raipur district), and (iv) Temple ruins at Adhabhara village situated roughly 8 km south of Kharsiā (Bilāspur district, Chattisgaṛh). This style had influenced the construction of three tāntric temples at Bauḍ, situated on the right bank of central Mahānadī Valley which were constructed in the early part of Somavaṁśī rule, dating back to ninth century CE.[9]

About the three Śiva tāntric temples of Bauḍ, K.C. Panigrahi[10] mentions:

---

4 K.C. Panigrahi, *History of Orissa*, Cuttack: Kitab Mahal, 1981, p. 46.

5 C.B. Patel, *Dynastic History of Nalas*, Calcutta: Punthi Pustak, 1990, pp. 229-57.

6 Donald M. Standner, "Ancient Kosala and Stellate Plan", *Kaladarsana*, American Studies in the Art of India, G.W. Joanna (ed.), New Delhi: Oxford and I.B.H. Publishing Co., 1981, pp. 139, 141, 142 and 147.

7 J.P. Singh Deo, *Some Tāntric Esotericism of Orissa*, Kolkata: R.N. Bhattacharya, 2003, p. 142 and vide: Plan and photo of the ruined brick temple; J.P. Singh Deo, op. cit., 2004, pp. 199-200.

8 J.P. Singh Deo, op. cit., 2003, pp. 301-16; J.P. Singh Deo, op. cit., 2004, pp. 201-10; J.P. Singh Deo, *Cultural Profile of South Kosala*, New Delhi: Gyan Publishing House, 1987, p. 330.

9 D.C. Kuanr (state ed.), *Gazetteer of India, Orissa, Boudh-Khondamals*, N. Senapati (chief ed.), Cuttack, 1983, p. 33.

10 K.C. Panigrahi, *History of Orissa*, Cuttack: Kitab Mahal, 1981, pp. 392-93.

The Śiva temples at Bauḍ seems in all appearance to belong to the early period of the Somavaṁśī supremacy. The fine execution of the Muktesvara temple with its superb proportions and exquisite finish of the sculptures and other decorations indicate a resurgent movement linked up probably with the advent of the Somavaṁśī dynasty. Reference may be made in this connection to the three temples of Bauḍ situated in the Upper Mahānadī Valley which was included in the Kosala country, the original seat of power of the Somavaṁśīs. The three small temples of Bauḍ are of almost the same height and have identical architectural and sculptural peculiarities. The ground plan in each case is star like, which is most likely necessitated by the cult practised in these shrines. The Śaktis of the Śiva-liṅgas enshrined in them are also star like and these shapes indicate that both the temples and deities were made in the form of *maṇḍalas* or mystic figures, with the help of which the *tāntrikas* wanted to attain their *siddhis*. Barring these peculiarities in their planning, these three temples are otherwise linked up with the Mukteśvara in respect of other features. All these monuments and the Mukteśvara possess in common the same sub-divisions at the base, such as *pada, kumbha, paṭa, kani* and *vasanta* with leaf design in the *kumbha* linked up with a *caitya* arch above; the same form of rounded corners and the same kind of sunken panel marking the transition between the *vimāna* and *śikhara*.

We also find in them the same forms of the nine, not eight planets, in which Rāhu has been represented by a head, but not by a *mukha*, *caitya* arches, the dwarfs with uplifted hands as if supporting the *śikhara*, and the same form of pouncing lions with riders. What is however most significant is the fact that certain forms of decorations which are peculiar to the Mukteśvara alone and not to be found in other Bhubaneswar temples, except one or two that are its close contemporaries, are also to be found in these Bauḍ monuments. These decorations consist of a peculiar type of inter-lacing scrolls that occurs in its *śikhara* and the pitchers (*kumbhas*) carved in *alto relievo* in its *vimāna*. A large *caitya* arch flanked by the two Śaivite images holding a chain with a bell at the end dropped into a lotus medallion, which, in the Bhubaneswar temples, occurs for the first time on the Mukteśvara and then on the later temples with an imperfect knowledge of its character, is also to be found on the façades of the Bauḍ temples, though in a badly mutilated condition. The decoration in the *śikhara* of the Mukteśvara partly consist of a female figure opening a door with a parrot sitting at the top which has been repeated in several panels, and of the miniature images of Lakulīśa in various *mudrās*. These images, too, occur in

> the Bauḍ monuments in the same forms. The similarity in the major aspects of art and architecture of the Bauḍ temples and the Mukteśvara suggests that the former belong to the Somavaṁśī period, but they might have been erected by the Bhañja rulers, who were in the occupation of the territory.

Panigrahi supposes the three tāntric temples at Bauḍ to have been built either by Somavaṁśīs or the Bhañjas. But it seems to have been Somavaṁśī construction, because it was in Somavaṁśī alias Pāṇḍuvaṁśī ruling area that experimentation of construction of stellate planned temples took place and finally, temple plan of two squares placed diagonally and intersecting each other at angles of 45°, which gives the shape of eight-pointed star developed, as dealt and came to be known as "Kosalī Style of Rekha temples".[11]

About the three tāntric temples at Bauḍ, K.S. Behera[12] states:

> At Bauḍ town there are three small temples, within the compound of the Rāmeśvara temple, which have great significance from the architectural point of view. Of these temples, one faces west and the other two with the same architectural and sculptural features, face the east.

J.D. Beglar,[13] who visited the place in CE 1874-75, has left a concise account of the temples. Each of these temples stands by itself on a raised platform and each consists of a cell and its attached portico only. The plan will show the minute recesses and angularities in plan which produce so charming an effect in the variety of light and shade and confer an appearance of greater height from the continued cluster of vertical lines they really possess.[14] With these recesses and angularities the ground plan is in the shape of an eight-rayed star. The plan has been obtained on the principle of intersecting squares, but obviously this unique ground plan was due to tāntric necessity for not only the ground plan of the temple but also the Śakti of the Śiva-liṅga is star-shaped.

On the temples we find *navagraha* slabs, which are common in later temples. These are so profusely ornamented that Beglar remarked that "though small they are gems of art in their own humble way".[15] The clear-cut interlacing of *caitya-*

---

11 J.P. Singh Deo, op. cit., 2004, pp. 185-224.

12 K.S. Behera, *Temples of Orissa*, Bhubaneswar: Orissa Sahitya Akademi, 1993, pp. 35-36.

13 Cunningham's, *Archaeological Survey of India*, vol. XIII, pp. 118-19.

14 Ibid.

15 K.C. Panigrahi, *Archaeological Remains at Bhubaneswar*, Cuttack: Orient Longmans, 1961, pp. 158-59.

windows on the *śikhara* is arresting and similar designs are seen on the *anuratha-pāga* of the *deula* of the Mukteśvara temple at Bhubaneswar. These two temples, as Panigrahi[16] points out, possess many decorative elements in common and, therefore, may not have been far removed from each other in time. In shape and style of decorative treatment they differ considerably from the temples of the earlier period, but at the same time they do not possess the characteristics of the temples like the Brahmeśvara at Bhubaneswar, which was erected by the mother of the Somavaṁśī king Uddyotakeśarī. Therefore, we may assign them to the early period of the Somavaṁśī rule in Orissa.

It seems D.R. Das[17] was ignorant of the development of "Kosali Style of Rekha temple" in South Kosala region. Therefore, he was of the opinion:

> Temples in Orissa are mostly square, sometimes rectangular and rarely peripheral. A group of temples in this region, extremely limited in number and restricted to Western Orissa, are, however, built on a stellate plan. Every temple of this group is planned on the principle of two squares, placed diagonally and intersecting each other at 45° angles. So far stellate temples have been found at three sites in Orissa. These are Bauḍ in the Phūlbanī (now Koṇḍamal) district, Būḍhī Komnā in the Kālāhāṇḍī (now Nuāpāḍā) district and Kansil in the Bolaṅgīr district.

Das deals first with stellate-planned three temples of Bauḍ, then deals with stellate plan of Būḍhī Komnā temple and at last with the one at Kansil site. This erroneous dealing of Das was done, because, in general view, he had already written a book named, *Temples of Orissa: The Study of a Sub-Style.*[18] But the latest study of the author shows that the Kosali Style of Rekha temples was developed in South Kosala region which comprises the western part of modern Orissa and Chhattisgarh, with tāntric influence. It is sure that the Kosalī Style of Rekha temples architecture had influenced the development of *pañcaratha* plan temples of coastal Orissa, which was the matured form of Kaliṅga style. The matured *pañcaratha* planned temples, which had chronological development in their best forms in coastal Orissa, are the temples of Siṁhanātha, situated on an island in the Mahānadī River of Baramba area, the Mukteśvara temple of Bhubaneswar, the Liṅgarāja temple of Bhubaneswar, the Jagannātha temple of Purī and the Sun temple of Koṇārka. This shows the

16 K.C. Panigrahi, *Archaeological Remains at Bhubaneswar*, New Delhi: Orient Longmans, 1961, p. 159.

17 D.R. Das, "Stellate Temples of Orissa", *Art and Culture*, no. 1, July 1983, *passim.*

18 D.R. Das, *Temples of Orissa: The Study of a Sub-Style*, Delhi: Agam Kala Prakashan, 1982, *passim.*

influence of tāntric Kāmakalā Yantra on the temple architecture of the Mahānadī Valley. Hence the Mahānadī Valley which comprises Chhattisgarh and Orissa states is the land of Kāmakalā, i.e. erotic spiritual science of desire fulfilment. The highest desire of a human being is salvation or emancipation.[19]

In the land of Kāmakalā and Uḍḍiyāna-Pīṭha was born the great Yogī Matsyendranāth at Candravalī-Dhāmra, identified as the present Cāndbālī-Dhāmra region of Bhadrak district, as dealt in an earlier chapter. He was the founder of the Nātha cult and had systematized the *yoginī* cult and expounded it in his famous work *Kaulayānanirṇaya*, which has become the authoritative text of the cult.[20] According to *Haṭha-Yoga-Pradīpikā*,[21] a *yoginī* is one who practises *vajrolī*.

> If a woman practises *vajrolī* and saves her *rajas* and the man's *bindu* by thorough contraction, she is a *yoginī*.

Vajrolī-mudrā is a *haṭha-yoga* practice. It means "thunderbolt attitude" in which the muscles of the male sexual organ and lower urinary tract are contracted, redirecting sexual energy upwards — a practice of *haṭha-yoga* and Tantra. If *vajrolī-mudrā* is practised by a woman, it is called *sahajolī*.

The *Yoginī-Tantra*,[22] being a tāntric text of the eleventh century CE states that *ādi-pīṭha* (first site) of the *yoginī* cult is at a place where Someśvara-liṅga is worshipped.[23] Someśvara-liṅga is worshipped in the Someśvara Śiva temple,[24] which stands at the Rāṇīpur-Jharial site of Bolaṅgīr district of Orissa. Therefore, it can be stated that Rāṇīpur-Jharial is the *ādi-pīṭha* alias primal site of the sixty-four *yoginī* cult, where this cult evolved, at the right middle of the Mahānadī Valley and spread to different parts of the country.

With this background, it can be assumed that the Kosalī Style of Rekha Temple and sixty-four *yoginī* cult were developed in the central Mahānadī Valley

---

19 J.P. Singh Deo, op. cit., 2004, p. 231.

20 H.C. Das, *Tāntricism: A Study of the Yogini Cult*, New Delhi: Sterling, 1981, p. 3.

21 Swami Muktibodhananda Saraswati (comm.), *Haṭha-Yoga-Pradīpikā*, Munger: Bihar School of Yoga, 2nd edn., 1993, pp. 362, 558, 564.

22 K.L. Mishra (ed.), *Yoginī Tantra*, Lakshmi Venkatesvara Press, Saṁvat 2013 and Śakābda 1878, Uttara Khaṇḍa, Prathama Paṭala, pp. 241-42, verses 15-19.

23 R.P. Mishra, *Fragments of Indian Culture* (*Rāṇīpur-Jharial*), Calcutta: Punthi Pustak, 1995, p. 207.

24 D.R. Das, op. cit., 1982, pp. 26-29.

of south Kosala region, influencing the entire Mahānadī Valley, in its larger content and periphery. The author[25] had earlier stated:

> Kosalī Style of temple architecture developed in south Kosala during early Somavaṁśī rule or period and influenced the neighbouring territories. Thus, they influenced the Mukteśvara temple of Bhubaneswar, the temple within the Nurpur Fort and thousand-pillar temple of Warangal.[26] It seems, the Kosalī style of temple architecture had influenced the Lakṣmaṇa temple at Sirpur and Indralāṭh temple at Rāṇīpur-Jharial, to some extent, as these temples also consist of the sanctum proper and a *maṇḍapa* in front, with an ante-chamber (*antarāla*) connecting the two. The *kumbha*-shaped moulding of Kosalī style of temples, connecting the *maṇḍapa* and the *antarāla* of these two temples are practically same. The pillared *maṇḍapa* of Indralāṭh temple at Rāṇīpur-Jharial complex has fallen since long. The scattered stone pillars are now utilized as seats by the Orissa State Archaeology Department. Some influence is also noticeable between the Kosali style of temples and temples of *pañcaratha* plan, when the sharp edges of early Kosali style rounded up in later years. Nīlakaṇṭheśvara temple of Dadpur, in the district of Kālāhāṇḍī is a stone structure and seems to be a late medieval structure, with the influence of Kosalī style of temple architecture, in its plan. Here, it will be interesting to know the view of K.S. Behera, on the Brāhmanical temples of Orissa under the Somavaṁśīs. While giving the account, Behera[27] mentions that the Somavaṁśīs, who succeeded the Bhauma-Karas, came from south Kosala, but they did not introduce any unfamiliar line of development in art and architecture. The pillared *maṇḍapa* of the Kośaleśvara temple at Baidyanath (district Bolaṅgīr, now Sonepur district), with lateral transepts and large sculptures in the interior, seems to suggest that when the Somavaṁśīs were ruling the upper Mahānadī Valley, there was some central Indian influence of the temple architecture but as they proceeded towards the coastal region, they strengthened the traditional temple style. Hence, it is to be noted that there was influence of the plan of Kosalī style of temple architecture.

The number of intersecting squares developed particularly in the Cāḷukyan monuments of the eleventh-twelfth centuries CE in Gujarat. Even in the Hoysaḷa temples of Mysore the star-shaped plan became the usual fashion.[28]

---

[25] J.P. Ṣingh Deo "Kosali Style of Temple Architecture", *OHRJ*, vol. XXIV-XXVI, pp. 175-76.

[26] Ibid; *Caravan* (magazine), June (first), 1977, no. 60, p. 52.

[27] *Orissa Review: Monument Special*, Bhubaneswar, January 1976, p. 60.

[28] *THACOTIP*, vol. V, *The Struggle for Empire*, 2nd edn., 1966, p. 24.

> The maturity of structure, influenced each other and developed to such an extent that gradually the Cāḷukya–Hoysaḷa School of Architecture developed during eleventh–thirteenth centuries CE. This shows the plan of intersecting squares of Kosali style of early phase to have prevalence over these styles of architecture later.

The Kosali Style of Rekha temples which developed in the south Kosala region, influenced the construction of three tāntric temples at Bauḍ and developed *pañcaratha* temple plan in coastal Orissa during Somavaṁśī period.[29]

Orissa has a rich heritage of beautiful temples, which are full of sculptural motifs and excellent work, which shows the carving in their facial expression and sensuousness. James Fergusson was of the opinion, "There are more temples now in Orissa than in all the rest of Hindustan put together."[30]

The Orissan group of temples are regarded as of Nāgara style but the regional manifestation with the modifications and transformations in course of evolution has beautified the Orissa temples to such an extent that the temples of Orissa earned a name as the "Kaliṅga style", because of its distinguished peculiarities. An inscription on the capital of a pillar in the *mukhamaṇḍapa* of Amṛteśvara temple at Holal (Bellary district) mentions the "Kaliṅga style" type, along with the Nāgara, Draviḍa and Vesara styles.[31]

Panigrahi[32] had also stated that these three temples of Bauḍ have correlation with the Mukteśvara temple at Bhubaneswar. Mukteśvara temple has the *pañcaratha* plan with the *navagrahas* over its doorjamb. Therefore, it is sure that the Kosali Style of Rekha temple architecture with its tāntric cult had influenced the development of *pañcaratha* plan temples of coastal Orissa, which was the matured form of Kaliṅga style.

The study shows the development of a full-fledged temple architecture in the Mahānadī River Valley that took place with tāntric influence in the background.[33]

The Mukteśvara temple of Bhubaneswar is the most coquetting temple

---

[29] J.P. Singh Deo, *Tāntric Art of Orissa*, Delhi: Kalpaz Publications, 2001, p. 174.

[30] James Fergusson, *History of Indian and Eastern Architecture*, London, 1910, *passim.*

[31] Ibid., 2001, pp. 172-73.

[32] K.C. Panigrahi, *Archaeological Remains at Bhubaneswar*, New Delhi: Orient Longmans, 1961, pp. 87-93 and 159.

[33] J.P. Singh Deo, op. cit., 2004, p. 23.

structure, which attracts admiration, because of baroque. According to Charles Louis Fabri,[34] the baroque is ushered in by the eighth, to become flamboyant everywhere, from east to west, in the ninth to thirteenth centuries from Mysore to Koṇārka.

But stylistically, the Mukteśvara as well as the other masterpieces of the subsequent period, the Rājarānī, the most beautiful of all, or the Brahmeśvara, the Liṅgarāja and the Pārvatī — all in Bhubaneswar — belong to the world of the baroque; mannerism has been left behind, and in these magnificent works of art, among the best in India, the artist turns to that full, luscious romanticism that baroque means, rich, ornate, lush, a delight in excess, a love of profusion and multiplication, a passion for the beauty of the female form, a sensuous delight in the loveliness of the world.[35]

After the fulfilment of the baroque arts on temple architectures of Orissa, the words of Fabri[36] may again be quoted, when he stated:

> In many ways it is a matter for wonder that at so late a date, the middle of the thirteenth century, Orissan artists and artisans should have been capable of producing such a stunning masterpiece. For the thirteenth century marked in every way the decline of great art, and one may safely assert that nothing comparable to the Sun temple of Koṇārka has been produced anywhere in India at that time, let alone in Orissa. The exuberance of the Hoysaḷa rococo at Beḷūr and Halebiḍ, the monstrously over drawn sculpture pillars in south India, the almost sickly striving after stunning effect and the grossly over-decorated shrines of the twelfth century show everywhere the decline in taste, the end of great baroque art, with its superb sensitivity for ornamental values, for grace, beauty and charm. In its place comes the sheer, senseless desire for ornamentation, the ornament killing the design, weakening the strength of the composition, effeminating the human body which now becomes a mere carrier of jewels and scrolls and ornate work.
>
> On that basis alone Koṇārka is a kind of miracle, a last kick, as it were, of a great baroque art, after which nothing but death can follow. Indeed the hand of this death can already be felt at Koṇārka, and a careful observer can see the first signs of this moribund decline, notwithstanding the stupendous achievements of a few marvellous artists.

---

34 Charles Louis Fabri, *History of the Art of Orissa*, New Delhi: Orient Longmans, 1974, p. 126.

35 Ibid., pp. 140-41.

36 Ibid., pp. 166-68.

> The plan is grandiose, and the surviving parts of the temple are among the world's most impressive, most moving monuments. I pity anyone who can only spend a few hours at Koṇārka. The spell of the endless rhapsody of sculpture is so great that the visitor is unable to view the work with a critical eye.

The erotic sculptural arts show all the sexual acts for pleasure and the *yoga* for sexual transformation, i.e. both *mithuna* and *maithuna* are found in the entire Mahānadī Valley.

15

Erotic Art in Sculptures, Wood and Palm-leaf Manuscripts

MANY archaeological findings have proved that the Mahānadī Valley was the land of Kāmakalā and Uḍḍiyāna-Pīṭha (site). Kāma means desire and Kāmakalā is the science of love or erotic science. Eroticism is therefore pertaining to sexual love and amatory, which is amorous.

Kāmakalā-Vilāsa, written by Yogī Puṇyānanda, is a momentous literature of Tantra and Nāthism. The meaning of tantra and nātha requires definition. A tāntric text called the *Varāhī Tantra* gives an elaborate description of the main subjects of Tantra. They are summarized as:[1]

1. Consciousness.
2. The creation and destruction of the physical universe (*sṛṣṭi* and *pralaya*).
3. Worship of deities (Devī or Deva-pūjā).
4. Classification of beings.
5. The heavenly bodies — astronomy and astrology.
6. The different levels of awareness (*loka*s).
7. The psychic pathways and centres in the human framework (*nāḍī*s and *cakra*s).
8. Laws and duties in society.
9. Sacramental rites (*saṁskāra*s).
10. Consecration of forms of deities (*mūrti*s).
11. Incantation (*mantra*s).

---

[1] Swami Satyananda Saraswati, *A Systematic Course in the Ancient Tantric Techniques of Yoga and Kriya,* Munger: Bihar School of Yoga, 2nd edn., 1989, p. 322.

12. Magic circles (*maṇḍalas* and *yantras*).
13. Symbolic and invocative gestures (*mudrās*).
14. Spiritual practices (*sādhanā*).
15. Worship (*pūjā*) both internal and external.
16. Consecration of houses, wells, etc.
17. Description of holy shrines.
18. Magic (*yogamāyā sādhanā*).
19. Ceremonial rites and initiations (*dīkṣā*).
20. *Yoga* including *āsanas*, *prāṇāyāma* and meditative methods.
21. Medicine of many types, including Āyurveda which is a herbal science combined with yogic practices.
22. Science.

To this list we would add that Tantra also included alchemy, the art of living a fruitful and blissful life and the use of sexual energy as a means to unfold higher awareness.

It is known that knowledge is of different types — imitative, repetitive, derivative, educative and intuitive. Only intuitive knowledge reaches to the reality.[2] Intuitive knowledge is got through yogic path. They are *jñāna-yoga, rāja-yoga, bhakti-yoga, karma-yoga, haṭha-yoga, kuṇḍalinī-yoga, tantra-yoga, japa-yoga* and *laya-yoga*. As already observed, there is a *yoga* of sexual transformation also. According to Vedic and tāntric paths, sex has three purposes — pleasure, procreation and *samādhi*. *Samādhi* means to be observed in a particular type of consciousness, which takes place with the rise of *kuṇḍalinī*. *Kuṇḍalinī* is a gift of Tantra.[3]

It is worth to know the definition of *savikalpa samādhi* and *nirvikalpa samādhi*, by S.R. Sengupta.[4]

---

[2] J.P. Singh Deo, *Origin of Jagannātha Deity*, New Delhi: Gyan Publishing House, 2nd enlarged and rev. edn., 2003, Preface.

[3] Swami Satyananda Saraswati, *Kundalini Tantra*, Munger: Bihar School of Yoga, 2nd edn., 1992, *passim*.

[4] S.R. Sengupta, *Mother Cult*, Kolkata: Firma K.L.M., 1977, pp. 106-07.

Savikalpa Samādhi

Savikalpa Samādhi is of four types. Each of them is described below:

1. ***Savitarka samādhi***: Self-absorption in the duality of structure in consciousness with latent sense of controversy in the consciousness is called *savitarka samādhi.*
2. ***Savicāra samādhi***: Self-absorption in the duality of structure in consciousness with a latent sense of discretion in the consciousness is called *savicāra samādhi.*
3. ***Sānanda samādhi***: Self-absorption in the duality of structure in consciousness with an all-absorbing bliss is called *sānanda samādhi.*
4. ***Sāsmita samādhi***: Self-absorption in the duality of structure in consciousness with a latest sense of self-existence is called *sāsmita samādhi.*

Nirvikalpa Samādhi

There are two practice under Nirvikalpa Samādhi:

1. ***Bhāva-pratyaya-videha samādhi***: Consists in self-absorption without the least trace of duality in consciousness with complete self-indentification with the nature of God, without the light of consciousness. It has three sub-divisions — *prakṛti-pratyaya, aham-pratyaya* and *mahat-pratyaya,* i.e. self-consciousness lost in nature, egotism and *bodhisattva.*
2. ***Pūrṇa-pratyaya samādhi***: Self-absorption in the secondless unique conscious absolute self of the Supreme Self without the least trace of duality is called *pūrṇa-pratyaya-nirvikalpa samādhi.* It is possible when the five waves of mind cease to function and the *sādhaka* transcends the basic evolution. *Pūrṇa samādhi* attained as a result of the realization of the identity of self with the absolute self of God without the least trace of duality in the self-revealed consciousness liberates an individual soul from the ills of the world and world knows no other existence except the Supreme Being. The sages say that of these eight varieties of *samādhi, pūrṇa-pratyaya-videha samādhi* alone can liberate the soul.

Now, let us know about the purposes of sex, which are pleasure, procreation and *samādhi.*

The subject of *kāma* (desire)[5] was taken up precisely with the same care, seriousness and objectivity as that of *dharma* and *artha*, or as any other technical topic, by the Vedic *ṛṣis*. *Bṛhadāraṇyaka Upaniṣad* of *Śukla Yajurveda* symbolizes women as a medium of sacrifice, her lap as sacrificial altar, her hairs as sacrificial grass, her skin as soma grass and copulation as the act of sacrifice. It proclaims a series of rules and advises its followers to observe them unmistakably for choiceable progeny. Auddālakī Śvetaketu, apparently a Vedic sage, first gave an exposition in 500 chapters, which Pāñcāla Bābhravya condensed in 150 chapters, under seven definite sections (*adhikaraṇas*): (i) general principles (*sādhāraṇa*), (ii) sexual union (*sāṁprayogika*), (iii) courtship and marriage (*kanyāsaṁprayuktaka*), (iv) the wife (*bhāryādhikārika*), (v) wives of other people (*pāradārika*), (vi) the prostitute (*vaiśika*), and (vii) secret love of extraneous stimulation (*anpaniṣadika*). Of these topics, Duttaka, at the request of the courtesans of Pāṭaliputra, chose the sixth (*vaiśika*) as his special subject and his example was followed by Cārāyaṇa, Suvarṇanābha, Ghoṭakamukha, Goṇardiya, Goṇikāputra and Kucumāra, each of whom wrote a monograph on one of the remaining subjects in the order given above. In view of the fractional and specialized nature of separate treatises and difficulty of mastering, Bābhravya's extensive work as a whole, the Śāstra was getting lost and Vātsyāyana's professed object was the writing of a comprehensive compendium within a reasonable dimension.

Vātsyāyana's *Kāma-Sūtra* is the oldest literature surviving in India for sexual pleasure. In contrast to the ideas of chastity and asceticism, sex is not opposed to the attainment of the higher goal of spiritual development.

All the works after Vātsyāyana are just repetitions with little variations, changes and additions. On sexual morality, the physiology and the psychology of sexual intercourse remain the same at present, as it was from time immemorial.

Dāmodaragupta, author of *Kuṭṭanīmata*, adorned the court of Jayāpīḍa Vinayāditya, the king of Karkoṭaka dynasty, who ruled Kashmir during CE 779–810.

The other works on erotic literature may be mentioned serially. The *Rati-Rahasya* of Kukkoka was composed sometime before twelfth century CE. This work was generally known as *Kukkaka* alias *Koka Śāstra*.

The *Nāgara-Sarvasva* of Padmaśrī was written between the tenth and fourteenth centuries CE. The *Pañcasāyaka* of the Maithilī Jyotirīśvara Kaviśekhara was composed

[5] J.P. Singh Deo, *Tāntric Art of Orissa*, Delhi: Kalpaz Publications, 2001, pp. 31-33.

in the first half of fourteenth century CE. Mahārāja Prandhadevarāya of Vijayanagara (fifteenth century CE) composed *Ratiratna-Pradīpikā* in seven chapters which is an elaborate treatise on sexual pleasure. The *Kāmasamūha*, of Ananta, discussing almost all aspects of love, was written in CE 1457. *Kandarpacūḍāmaṇi* of King Vīrabhadra of the Vaghela dynasty was composed in CE 1577. *Anaṅgaraṅga*, of Kalyaṇamalla was composed in the sixteenth century CE. The *Rati-mañjarī*, in sixty verses only, of some unknown Jayadeva (different from the author of the *Gīta-Govinda*), is almost entirely on the subject of sexual union (*sāṁprayogika*).[6]

There are erotic literatures in Oriyā language also. Kavi Samrāṭ Upendra Bhañja was born between CE 1675 and 1680. He was the grandson of Dhanañjaya Bhañja (and the son of Nīlakaṇṭha Bhañja), who ruled over Ghumsar, with capital at Kulāda in Gañjam district of Orissa.[7] It was Upendra Bhañja, who wrote *Pañcasāyaka*, an Oriyā poetry. The work begins:[8]

> Salutation to Gaṇeśa.
> An individual ignorant of erotic art is equal to a beast.

The speciality of Upendra Bhañja is that he deals with *Candra-Cālana*, the erogenous zones of female during different moon days, medicine and has described sixty-four sexual poses (*bandhas*).

Gopāla Bhañja, who belonged to the Bhañja family of Mayūrbhañj in Orissa, had also composed *Cauṅsaṭhī Rati Bandha*, in Oriyā language, whose 19 palm-leaf manuscripts are preserved at the Orissa State Museum, Bhubaneswar.[9] A palm-leaf manuscript of *Pañcasāyaka*, composed by Upendra Bhañja is also found in the Orissa State Museum.[10] Orissa has contributed significantly to the erotic science for pleasure and *samādhi*, because the whole details of foreplay and *yoga* of sexual transformation are found in its sculptural art and literature.

So, the whole land of the Mahānadī Valley is the land of *Kāmakalā-Vilāsa*. Kāma

6 Sushil Kumar De, *Ancient Indian Erotics and Erotic Literature*, Kolkata: Firma K.L.M., 2nd edn., 1969, *passim*; Narendra Nath Bhatacharyya, *History of the Indian Erotic Literature*, New Delhi: Munshiram Manoharlal, 1975, *passim*.

7 Somanath Rath, "Upendra Bhanja", *Sidelights on History and Culture of Orissa*, M.N. Das (ed.), Cuttack: Vidyapuri, 1977, pp. 692-701.

8 J.P. Singh Deo, *Tāntric Hedonism of Mahānadī Valley* (*Uḍḍiyāna-Pīṭha*), New Delhi: D.K. Printworld 2004, pp. 255-70.

9 Subas Pani, *Illustrated Palmleaf Manuscripts of Orissa* (*A Selection from Orissa State Museum*), Cuttack, 1984, pp. 81-82.

10 Ibid., p. 85.

means desire, Kalā means art and Vilāsa means sport, play or enjoyment of pleasure.[11] Therefore, the author calls it, "the art of desire in beatitude". Who is in beatitude with the art of desire? It is the creator Himself.

The author deems it fit to quote the *Bhagavad-Gītā* (ch. 13) where it deals with *puruṣa* and *prakṛti* (spirit and nature):[12]

> Verse 19 — Know that both *puruṣa* and *prakṛti* are beginningless, and know also that all modifications and qualities (*guṇas*) are born of *prakṛti*.
>
> Verse 20 — In the creation of the effect (the body) and the instrument (the senses), *prakṛti* is spoken of as the cause; in the experience of joy and sorrow, *puruṣa* is said to be the cause.
>
> Verse 21 — *Puruṣa* involved with *prakṛti* experiences the *guṇas* born of nature. Attachment to the three qualities of *prakṛti* causes the soul to take embodiment in good and evil wombs.
>
> Verse 22 — The Supreme Spirit, transcendent and existing in the body, is the detached beholder, the consenter, the sustainer, the experiencer, the Great Lord, and also the highest self.
>
> Verse 23 — Whatever his mode of life, he who thus realizes *puruṣa* and the three-fold nature of *prakṛti* will not again suffer rebirth.

Now, it is important to study about the Nātha cult. Śrī Ādināth is one of the names given to Lord Śiva, who is the Supreme Cosmic Consciousness. In Tantra there is the concept of Śiva and Śakti. Śiva is the eternal consciousness of the cosmos and Śakti is his creative power. The Cosmic Consciousness or Universal Spirit is known by many names. In Sāṁkhya philosophy, it is *puruṣa*, in Vedānta it is *Brahman*.[13] From *Haṭha-Yoga-Pradīpikā*, it is known that Yogī Matsyendranāth had the knowledge of *haṭha-yoga*. He gave it to Gorakhnāth and others.[14] P.K. Bandyopadhyay[15] states:

[11] Gopal Chandra Praharaj, *Pūrnnachandra Ordia Bhāshā Kosha*, vol. V (Consonants, pha-ma), Cuttack, 1936, p. 5731.

[12] Sri Sri Paramahansa Yogananda, *God Talks with Arjuna: the Bhagavad-Gītā*, vol. II, Kolkata: Yogoda Satsanga Society of India, 2nd impression, 2002, pp. 889-94.

[13] Swami Muktibodhananda Saraswati (Comm.), *Haṭha-Yoga-Pradīpikā*, Munger: Bihar School of Yoga, 2nd edn., 1993, p. 21.

[14] Ibid., p. 27.

[15] P.K. Bandyopadhyay, *Nātha Cult and Mahānadī (A Study in Syncretism)*, Delhi: B.R. Publishing Corporation, 1992, pp. 5 and 63-64.

> The Nātha cult which has derived much of its character from estoric Tantrism and the Śaivite tradition is a perfect example of amlgam. . . . A Nātha *yogī* must be acquainted with *piṇḍa-vicāra*, a deeper understanding of the constitution of the body.

According to Swami Satyananda Saraswati:[16]

> Tantra aims to transform every action in life into a ritual, so that the individual performs every action and thought with a feeling of worship and awareness. The action of bathing, dressing, sitting for worship offering various symbolic sacrifices, sexual relations, stages of development from inception in the womb, birth to marriage, etc. are transformed into worship. The aim of Tantra is to unleash the cosmic energy in man, so that he rises to higher levels of awareness.

These observations show that Swami Harshananda[17] is very correct when he mentions:

> Again the temple represents this world in all its aspects, the actual and the ideal. The imposing *gopurams* at the entrance reflect the awesome grandeur of the external world. The friezes and sculptures on the external walls of the temple proper depict the animal world and the mundane life of ordinary human beings including the ridiculous side and the aberrations. Criticism is often voiced against the *mithuna* figures (figures of amorous couples) that adorn most of the temples on their exterior walls. These figures, obviously connected with fertility rites, are considered to be auspicious. More often, they are iconographical representations of creation and of the bipolar nature of this created world, which is described in philosophical treatises as arising out of the union of *prakṛti* and *puruṣa* (nature and spirit). Uninhibited eroticism as found in the temples at Koṇārka (Orissa) and Khajurāho (Madhya Pradesh) is perhaps the outcome of Tantricism.

Erotic Art

Erotic arts are mostly found on the temple architectures of India. Stella Kramrisch[18] rightly remarks that the plan of the temple is akin to a *yantra* or linear diagram used by the worshipper for a localization of each of the aspects and powers of God in their hierarchy with regard to the centre, the immovable principle.

[16] Swami Satyananda Saraswati, op. cit., 1989, p. 335.

[17] Swami Harshananda, *All About Hindu Temple*, Mysore: Sri Ramakrishna Ashrama, 2nd edn., 1981, pp. 12-13.

[18] Stella Kramrisch, *The Hindu Temple*, Calcutta: University of Calcutta, 1946, p. 338.

The use of mystic diagrams (*yantras*) is primarily found in tāntric cult, which as a special religious philosophical concept came into use by fifth or sixth century CE. Tantra is an erotic cult, because of its mysterious sex-oriented rituals. The object of the sex act in Tantra is not the ecstatic pleasure of intercourse only, but the "oneness" that the man and woman experience when they are in such a sexual "high".[19]

The ancient temple plan of India was a simple square — a ritual diagram first mentioned in *Śulba-Sūtras*.[20] The square grid of the *vāstu-maṇḍala* reflected Vedic cosmology, which saw the world as square and again prescribed for temples was *vāstupuruṣa-maṇḍala* in the sixth-century *Bṛhat-Saṁhitā*.[21] With this developed the experimentation of stellate plans in the upper Mahānadī Valley and "Kosalī Style of Rekha temples",[22] which developed as the matured form of *pañcaratha, saptaratha* and *navaratha* temple architectural plans in the coastal belt of Orissa. Plastic arts of sensuousness with erotic depiction developed as mentioned in Śilpaśāstras of Orissa:[23] — 1. *Bhuvana-Pradīpa*, 2. *Śilpa-Prakāśa*, 3. *Saudhikāgama*, 4. *Baya Cakada* (a book of accounts and building chronicle of the Sun temple of Koṇārka), 5. *Śilpa-Sāriṇī*, 6. *Vāstusūtra Upaniṣad*, and 7. *Śilpa Ratnakośa*.

Such amount of Śilpaśāstras has not yet been found in any other state of India. This shows that specialization of Śilpaśāstras and temple construction received special privilege in the cultural heritage of Orissa. The medieval temple was not just a religious institution or place of worship. It was a ritualistic, yogic and socio-cultural institution with royal-aristocratic patronage and influence. The whole *Kāma-Sūtra* or the Hindu art of love making, meant for pleasure, procreation and *samādhi*, and all human aspects of life were depicted on the temple architecture.

---

19 Arvind and Shantakale, *Tantra: The Secret Power of Sex*, Bombay: Jaico Publishing House, 1976, p. 5.

20 Michnel W. Meister, "Muṇḍeśvarī: Ambiguity and Certainty in the Analysis of a Temple Plan", *Kalādarśana* (*American Studies in the Art of India*), J.C. Williams (ed.), New Delhi: Oxford and I.B.H. Publishing Co., 1981, p. 83; C.P.S. Dhatta, *Early Astronomy and Cosmology*, London, 1932, Apte, "Constructive Geometry", p. 14; see quotation from *Śulba-Sūtras* in note 10.

21 *Kalādarśana*, op. cit., 1981, p. 79.

22 J.P. Singh Deo, *Some Tāntric Esotericism of Orissa*, Kolkata: R.N. Bhattacharya, 2003, pp. 301-16; J.P. Singh Deo, *Tāntric Hedonism of Mahānadī Valley (Uḍḍiyāna-Pīṭha)*, New Delhi: D.K. Printworld, 2004, pp. 185-210.

23 R.P. Das, "The Study of Silpa Shastra", *Reference Orissa*, A.N. Tiwari (ed.), Bhubaneswar: Enterprising Publisher, 1999, pp. 174-81.

Nude women exposing *pudendum, fellatio, cunnilingus, zoophilia, mithuna, maithuna* and all types of sensuousness are found in the sculptural arts.

Words *mithuna* and *maithuna,* need clarification. *Mithuna* means common sex practice for pleasure but *maithuna* with its yogic interpretation has been explained by Swami Muktananda Saraswati:[24]

> ***Maithuna:*** According to Tantra, the interaction between man and woman may have one of the three purposes — procreation, pleasure and *samādhi.* Householder *sādhakas* experience this relationship without any inhibitions, conflicts or guilt, as apart of *sādhanā* for *samādhi.* In general, the climax of this experience is lost before one is able to deepen it, but for spiritual purposes, the climax must be prolonged so that the dormant, "silent", centres of consciousness are awakened and start to function continuously in daily life.
>
> *Maithuna* then is not merely physical union, but union with a view to *samādhi,* the purpose is clear — awakening of *suṣumnā,* raising the *kuṇḍalinī* from *mūlādhāra cakra* and exploding the unconscious areas of the brain.
>
> The practice of *maithuna* requires strict preparation by both partners and certain *haṭha-yoga* practices must be perfected. Initially a woman develops control of the lower centres through *paścimottānāsana, śalabhāsana, vajrāsana, suptavajrāsana* and *siddha yoni āsana. Śīrṣāsana* is also important in regulating the reproductive hormones and harmonizing influxes to the brain. *Mūla bandha, uḍḍiyāna bandha, śāmbhavī-mudrā, sahajolī-mudrā* and *kumbhaka* (breath retention) must also become so spontaneous that there is no difficulty in using these techniques at the height of *maithuna.*
>
> On the emotional level, both husband and wife must be purified of dependency and possessiveness. They must also have transcended the usual stereotyped masculine and feminine behaviour, to the point where both are able to achieve fulfilment by wholehearted acceptance of the role of woman as *guru.*
>
> It is at the initiative of the woman, and under her guidance, that *maithuna* takes place. She performs all the necessary preliminaries and marks her husband's forehead, telling him where to meditate. In ordinary relationships, the man takes the aggressive role and the woman submits. But in *maithuna,* the woman takes the lead and the man becomes her medium.

---

[24] Swami Muktananda Saraswati, *Nawa Yogini Tantra,* Munger: Bihar School of Yoga, 2nd edn., 1983, pp. 64-65.

> A wife must be able to arouse her husband, yet to help him maintain his *bindu*. If her husband loses control, it is because the woman has not conducted the ritual correctly.
>
> In Tantra it is said that Śiva is merely a *śava*, a corpse, without Śakti. Śakti is the priestess. At the birth of the cosmos Śakti is the creator and Śiva is the witness, so in Tantra the woman has the status of the *guru* and the man of disciple. The tāntric tradition is actually passed on from the woman to the man, it is the woman who initiates.
>
> That woman who is able to keep her *rajas* above means of retention of the orgasm is the real *yoginī*. The practice of *vajrolī* gives *siddhi* to the body — it becomes handsome, smooth, bright and attractive. This is the divine practice of *yoga* that gives liberation through enjoyment (*Haṭha-Yoga-Pradīpikā*).

Devangana Desai[25] states that our study of sexual representation in the Indian culture convinces us that there is no philosophical or rational motivation behind it. Its presence in religious art is a pointer to the continuity and persistence of primitive and popular cultural elements in a civilized society. Far from being an anomaly in Hindu culture, erotic motifs were in harmony with the religious environment to which they belonged and with the majestic, courtly and artistic temples they decorated. They were *alaṁkāra*s.

Here, the author does not agree with Desai, when she claims that there is no philosophical or rational motivation behind the sexual representation in the Indian culture. Some of the erotic sculptures are based on the poses described in the *Kāma-Sūtra* and are not the works of the imagination of the artists, though some poses are sexo-yogic poses. For an instance, an example can be given of a sculpture of Koṇārka (see cover page of this book), which is yawning position as described in Vātsyāyana's *Kāma-Sūtra*.[26] The description goes — "When she raises her thighs and keeps them wide apart and engages in congress, it is called the 'yawning position'." Such a sculpture dated to eleventh century CE[27] is also found at Khajurāho temple. This shows the erotic sculptures to have features and were not chiselled by the artists, in their own imagination. The artists were guided by Śilpaśāstras and *sthāpaka* masters, who were usually and popularly brāhmaṇas. For example,

25 Devangana Desai, *Erotic Sculptures of India: A Socio-Cultural Study*, New Delhi: Tata McGraw Hill Publishing Company, 1975, p. 203.

26 Sir Richard Barton and F.F. Arbuthnot (trs.), *Vātsyāyana's Kāmasūtra*, Delhi: Orient Paperbacks, 1982, pp. 77-78.

27 Ibid., pp. 77-78 (vide the sketch on p. 78).

Śilparatnakośa (a glossary of Orissan temple architecture), was composed by Sthapaka Nirañjana Mahāpātra.[28]

So, it can be said that the erotic art of temple architecture gave easy access to the common individuals of both sexes, who could learn the arts of *Kāma-Sūtra*, without reading them in literatures. Except the extra-martial bestiality, the erotic art, chiselled on temple sculptures are all human, worthy to be practised in sex life, as the grandest knowledge taught by the ancients to promote maximum contentment and happiness among couples and to concrete their relationship.[29]

Erotic Sculptures of Orissa

The purpose of the erotic sculptures of Orissa is to let one know the art of love-play, with the art of wooing, so that one can ensure the peak of sexual satisfaction of the woman partner, before he ejaculates. There are a few *maithuna* sculptures also, which depict the *yoga* of sexual transformation, from sex to superconsciousness, or from sex to salvation.

The *Śilpa-Prakāśa*, the tāntric Śilpaśāstra from Orissa belonging to the period between ninth and twelfth centuries CE, mentions that the *Kāmakalā yantra* or the symbolic representation of sex should be camouflaged by the portrayal of erotic figures on it. Generally speaking, the true tāntric art is functionally related to *upāsanā* and *sādhanā* to attain the non-dual *sahaja* state.[30]

Because of Tantra influence, the whole life, erotic art and few sexo-yogic poses are found among the sculptures of Orissa. Some sensuous sculptures are depicted on combs, toilet trays, furniture and articles of daily use also. These show the sensuous tastes of the cultured elite.

A sexual scene is depicted on a sculpture of Ratnagiri, where a male while enjoying sexual intercourse with a female is having hair-cut by a male barber. It is said to be a tāntric hair-cutting ritual.

A sculptural scene, showing a youth having bestiality (i.e. the sexual relation of a human with a beast) with a cow or a buffallo, is seen at the Liṅgarāja temple of Bhubaneswar. This shows the forbidden sexual behaviour and morality, prevalent during the construction of the temple.

---

[28] Bettina Baumer and Rajendra Prasad Das (eds.), *Śilparatnakośa*, Delhi: Motilal Banarsidass, 1994, *passim*.

[29] Kenneth Anderson, *Secrets of Sex*, Mumbai: Jaico Publishing House, 1973, *passim*.

[30] Devangana Desai, op. cit., pp. 199-200.

Among the sculptural art of Koṇārka, Debala Mitra[31] mentions that the meaning of one particular scene is not clear. Here a robeless woman (rarely a man) is seen standing with flames of fire between the legs. It might mean that the woman is performing an abortion or having some Āyurvedic treatment.

Ramendra Nath Nandi[32] draws attention to an important sculptural scene of Orissa. He remarks that the eight erotic composite reliefs shown in the top sections of the vertical outer flat ribs of the Vārāhī temple at Kakatpur illustrate tāntric associations of the Mother Goddesses. The sculptures refer to the process of eight-phased copulation practised by left hand tāntrics.[33] The process known as *aṣṭa-kāmakalā-prayoga* is also referred to in an unedited tāntric text in Sanskrit language and Oriyā script.[34] The phases sculptured in the Vārāhī shrine are *vaśīkaraṇa* (bringing the maiden under control), *sammohana* (enchanting her), *ākarṣaṇa* and *uccāṭana* (attracting and preparing her for the sex act), *yonyābhiṣeka* (consecration of the female organ), *puraścaraṇa* (preliminary stage of the act), *rajopāna* (drinking of the *raja*), *prastāva* (proposal) and *nivṛtti* (return to the normal state).[35] These sculptures represent most of the characteristics of the tāntric form of worship. The male figures appear nude with their genital organ standing erect, which indicates the sexual orgies characteristic of the left-hand tāntric worshippers. The corpse-seat in the sculptures is also a feature of extremist tāntric rites.

The erotic sculptures of Orissa can be divided into two broad divisions, i.e. the coastal belt and the hinterland.

The sculptural art of the Upper Mahānadī or hinterland of Orissa and Chhattisgarh appears heavy and cumbersome, while that of coastal belt has grace and elegance, which have been a distinguished quality of Orissa sculptures, but it was left to the artists of the Rājarānī, Liṅgarāja and Koṇārka temples to exploit them to the fullest limit.[36] Stella Kramrisch[37] had said, "Architecture in Orissa is but sculpture on a gigantic scale."

---

[31] Debala Mitra, *Konārak*, New Delhi: Archaeological Survey of India, 1976, p. 47.

[32] R.N. Nandi, *Religious Institutions and Cults in the Deccan* (*c.* AD *600–1000)*, Delhi: Motilal Banarsidass, 1973, p. 131.

[33] Ibid.; N.N. Vasu (ed.), *V.V. Mirashi Felicitation Volume*, p. 350.

[34] Ibid.

[35] Ibid.

[36] N.R. Ray, "Sculpture in Orissa", *THACOTIP*, vol. V, *The Struggle for Empire*, 1966, p. 654.

[37] K.S. Behera, *Temples of Orissa*, Bhubaneswar: Orissa Sahitya Akademi, 1993, p. 7.

The human body, sensuous love and joy are well depicted in the Orissan plastic art in bold relief. The chiselled expressions are massive representation of the totality of life and the erotic scenes are the silent speech, suggesting the beauty of healthy physical relation between woman and man, with no shame, because it is a part of human life. They express the secrets of the art of sex-acts. They seem to express, "Come on, do it and derive practical happiness of life. The one skilful in the art of love-play can give greater pleasure to the partner, than an average individual." This seems to be the expressive language of the simple and beautiful sculptures, which have sensitive modelling.

It is a matter of practice and experience, through which one gains long duration in the sex-act, which promotes contentment and happiness. Therefore, contribution of Orissa, especially in erotic sculptural art can be freely acknowledged as masterpieces.

The carving of female and male figures with curves, in eternal youth, sensuousness, displaying different skills, by the Orissan artists is based on the eternal principles of sex life.

T.N. Mishra[38] states:

> Moreover, the male figures are often shown with protruding stomachs or disproportionate bodies which indicate that they were not adept in *yoga* or *haṭha-yoga*. The eternal bliss of the non-dual state is rarely reflected in the sculptural depictions. Only a handful sculptures of Orissa and Khajurāho present lovers in a state of bliss.

It is true that such male figures with disproportionate bodies are found in sculptural arts of temples. They can be explained as expression of debauchee. An example of the name of a village named Kusaṅga, in Bolaṅgīr district of Orissa can be referred. The author[39] had mentioned that Kusaṅga is an important tāntric site in Bolaṅgīr district. The name Kusaṅga means, bad company. The *yoga* of sexual transformation most probably had turned at least to debauchee there, during the late medieval period and, therefore, the name Kusaṅga developed.

The sculptural arts are the free expressions of every aspect of human life, because as already expressed and hinted, Tantra aims to transform every action in life into a ritual, so that the individual performs every action and thought with a feeling of

38 T.N. Mishra, *Yoga-Tantra and Sensuousness in Art*, New Delhi: D.K. Printworld, 2003, p. 99.

39 J.P. Singh Deo, *Some Tāntric Esotericism of Orissa*, Kolkata: R.N. Bhattacharya, 2003, p. 280.

worship and awareness. From one's own feelings, actions and mental interests, an individual can know that in what state, condition, mode of existence and perturbed condition, he/she is suffering. The sculptural arts are the free expressions of all human actions and behaviours, with a tāntric influence.

Erotic Art in Wood, Palm-leaf Manuscripts and Paintings of Orissa

Orissan craftsmen had excelled in wood carving art too. Among the surviving timber works, mention may be made of a *maṇḍapa* or open pavillion in the small hamlet of Puruṣottampura in the district of Gañjam, about 25 miles from Chatrapur, which stands in front of the Kapileśvara temple, and the timber temple of Birañji-Nārāyaṇa or Birañci-Nārāyaṇa (probably Viriñci-Nārāyaṇa) at Buguḍa, near Aska and Bhañjanagar.[40] For wooden craftmanship, Gañjam district is famous in Orissa.

Wood is a perishable material, therefore ancient wooden workmanship are not found in plenty.[41] Almost all the Indian art history speaks of timber works. So, it shows that there was constant practice of wooden work, throughout India.

Few teak wooden erotic arts, made by the carpenters of Gañjam district, are surviving within a Jagannātha temple of a small village, Brahmanpara, within the Sinapali Block area of Nuāpāḍā district.

Wooden erotic arts are found on the door of the *siṁha-dvāra* alias main gate of the Varāha temple at Aul, in Kendrapāḍā district of Orissa. The construction of Varāha temple was started by the seventh Rājā of Aul, Rājā Nilakhaṇṭha Deb II in CE 1702.

Orissa made significant contributions to erotic literature also. The *Pañcasāyaka*, composed by Kavi Samrāṭ Upendra Bhañja, unsurpasses all others, because it deals with sixty-four sexual poses (*bandhas*). Gopāla Bhañja, who belonged to the Bhañja dynasty of Mayūrbhañj, had also composed *Cauṅsaṭhī Rati Bandha*, literature in Oriyā language, which is not yet published. A number of works survive as palm-leaf manuscripts, but unfortunately such palm-leaf manuscripts earlier than the seventeenth century CE have not yet been acquired by the Orissa State Museum, so far.

---

40 C.L. Fabri, *History of the Art of Orissa*, Calcutta: Orient Longman, 1974, pp. 181-83.

41 Wooden palisades have been unearthead near modern Patna in Bihar, which are the ruins of ancient Pāṭaliputra. Many wooden shrines, especially the Padmanābhapuram Palace of Kerala, some erotic wooden arts of Kerala and few wooden constructions in Kashmir and in the foothills of the Himalayas are noteworthy traces of wooden art work.

Painting on palm leaves is usually done by means of a stylus made of iron. The delineation of the figures of human beings or animals is only possible by means of drawing on this medium through very simple outlines. After the outlines are formed various indigenous mineral colours obtained from *hiṅgula, harītāla, harītakī, goracanā, kumkum, kajjala, gerū,* etc. are applied wherever necessary. In plain ones, after etching, a vegetable colour is uniformly applied over the illustrated portions.

Referring to the merits of the palm-leaf paintings of Orissa, O.C. Ganguly[42] observes:

> If the Orissan etchings in their severe simplicity and poverty of means in the vivid actions of their figures and their power of depicting gestures and movements in spite of the severe simplicity and austerity of their lines telling their story within the utmost economy of means — a virtue no doubt imposed by the poverty of executive appliances.

The author is concerned with the erotic art, on the palm-leaf mansucripts, as shown on the plates. With these positions (*bandha*s) recommended by the ancients, one can keep the sex-life, sex-acts and love-making always fresh and not stale, as it is wise to keep the love-making always by love-play in different ways, using different techniques at different places.

Painting has a long history in Orissa, which has been summarized by K.S. Behera,[43] when he writes that Orissa has a fine tradition in painting. The great temples and wonderful achievements in sculpture have so far overshadowed this aspect of Orissan art. Orissan painting covers a wider range — pre-historic painting, historical paintings, illustrated palm-leaf manuscripts, painted manuscripts on paper, *paṭa* paintings, etc. The prehistoric paintings are found in the forests of western Orissa in Sambalpur, Sundargaṛh and Kālāhāṇḍī districts in such places as Ulapgaṛh, Maṇikmada, Ūṣa Koṭi, Yogīmaṭh and Guḍahāṇḍī. Their systematic study remains yet a desideratum. In the historical periods, the paintings which adorned the crude walls of Khaṇḍagiri-Udayagiri caves have all vanished, but paintings on Rāvaṇa Chāyā at Sītabhiñjī (Keoñjhar district) still struggles to survive. The scene depicts a royal procession and treatment of it is "at par with the quality of the Ajantā, Bāgh cave frescos of the Gupta period".

---

42 H.C. Das, *A Guide to Orissa State Museum*, Bhubaneswar, 1981, pp. 59-60.

43 K.S. Behera, "An Introduction to the Cultural Heritage of Orissa", *Sree Neelachala Seva Sangha Shree Jagannatha Smarika*, 1984, New Delhi: Basanta Panchami, 1984, p. 14.

The paintings represented by illustrated palm-leaf and paper manuscripts are in the indigenous styles. The themes are generally drawn from works like the *Gīta-Govinda*, the *Amarū-Śataka* and *Bhāgavata Purāṇa*. The *paṭa* paintings of Purī have a tradition which goes back to an earlier period. These paintings are so called because they are executed on cloth, but being brightly painted with Jagannātha and other icons, religious and even historical themes they possess a peculiar charm and originality of their own.

Durga Prasad Patnaik[44] divides the Orissan paintings into three main schools. The first is the Gañjam or Dakṣiṇī, second is Purī and the third is Campāmāḷ. The Dakṣiṇī prevails in Gañjam district, the centre of old Orissan culture. Ghumsar, Khalikoṭ, Dharakoṭ, Khemuṇḍī, Parala, Ichāpur, Tikali, Mañjūsā, etc. are the areas where this style prevails.

The Purī style is found in Purī and its adjacent areas like Pratāpapur, Bālāpur, Raghurājpur and others. Sonepur and Sambalpur are the areas where Campāmāḷ style prevails. Each school differs from the other. The physiognomy of Purī and Gañjam schools is closer to each other whereas the Campīmāḷ school is quite different. It bears the character of Indonesian paintings.

The remark of late Charles Louis Fabri[45] on the painting in Orissa, may be quoted here. "*En passant*, that a very large number of illustrated manuscripts that I have examined in public and private collections in Orissa, have erotic illustrations, is of interest." Further he says that women appear without blouses, as far I can see, as late as the early ninth century,[46] paintings. Cloth painting, locally known as *paṭa-citra* and mural paintings on the wall of houses are styles still surviving among the coastal area.

> This schematic treatment of parts of the body, etc. is a matter of considerable interest. I have watched present-day artisans at work, and was astonished to see how these readymade formulae are employed with an almost unbelievable rapidity, the stylus running with utmost ease to form every eye always the same; every nose always the same; every chin all the same; and every limb in what ever position, always identically drawn, with the same, few, economic and sweeping lines.[47]

---

[44] D.P. Patnaik, "Orissan Art", *Sidelights on History and Culture*, M.N. Das (ed.), Vidyapuri, Cuttack, 1977, pp. 479-80.

[45] C.L. Fabri, *History of the Art of Orissa*, New Delhi: Orient Longman, 1974, pp. 189-90.

[46] Ibid., p. 191.

[47] C.L. Fabri, *History of the Art of Orissa*, New Delhi: Orient Longman, 1974, p. 189.

I believe the few illustrations of the sculptures and palm-leaf etching given in plates will stimulate the couples to indulge in erotic sports, arts and skilfulness, which, in turn, will promote maximum contentment and happiness with aesthetic pleasure, and will concrete their relationship.

Sensual Art of Orissa

Orissa is celebrated for its sculptural fare, where the erotic and sensual cameos express the beauty, youth and charm of women. The inspired orgy of magnificence arts, including the beautiful *alasa-kanyā*s (indolent damsels) are sure to make one's sensual excitement. Thus, a strong sensual element is almost ubiquitous. Rare sensitivenesses, carved with inspiration in sculptures, are superb in execution.

Female figures are shown in many graceful poses with *surā-sundarī*s in Orissa. N.L. Mathur remarks,[48] "The Orissan artist has shown consummate ability and creative imagination in depicting scenes from life with remarkable vividness and realism. . . ." There are also sculptures of numerous couples engaged in a great variety of amorous antics. These figures are representations of *mithuna*s. Percy Brown[49] feels, "But nowhere are its observances more blatantly exploited than on the walls of the temple of the Sun at Koṇārka."

This Koṇārka Sun temple, noted for its arthitectural and sculptural beauty as well as for the depiction of the erotic sentiment in various poses, is also a museum of female-figures engaged in various other activities.[50] They are:

1. With a baby in the left arm, the mother gives a gentle push to other child to move forward.
2. Dexterity in drumming and dancing.
3. A couple.
4. Acrobatics — the human pyramid (by about a dozen women).
5. Vegetable hawker, on her way to the market, troubled by monkeys.
6. Holding the *caurī* in the right hand to render service to some deity in a temple.

---

48 N.L. Mathur, *Sculptures in India: Its History and Art*, New Delhi: Caxton Press, 1976, p. 44.

49 Ibid.; Percy Brown, *Indian Architecture (Hindu & Buddhist)*, Bombay: D.B.Taraporewala, 1959, *passim*.

50 *Little Known Aspects of Women in Konarka*, Dept. of Tourism and Cultural Affairs, Govt. of Orissa, Bhubaneswar, 1975, *passim*.

7. The mother with her baby held on the right thigh for breast feeding.
8. Immediately after bath.
9. The beloved wife on the shoulders of the henpecked husband.
10. Relaxing.
11. Renouncing family life.
12. A friend in need is a friend indeed.
13. In the sanctum of the temple in devotional fervour.
14. A famished woman (with the bones of the body clearly seen).
15. Awaiting lover's arrival.
16. In the service of the Lord.
17. Holding the child.
18. In a musical trance.
19. With a pet-parrot on the right shoulder.
20. Putting the mark of vermilion on the forehead.

Sahajayāna developed in Uḍḍiyāna-Pīṭha, which is the Mahānadī River Valley. Grandiose conception of the idea of *sahaja*, the Sahajayāna remains as a way of propitiating the primitive instincts and desires, i.e. sex, hunger and the like, and in advocating the principle, it challenges all established religions with their rigour of discipline, orthodoxy and formalities. Thus *sahajayāna* appears as an open protest for all sorts of religious formalism and yogic rigourism and it lays emphasis on developing the human nature for the realization of *śūnyatā*, the ultimate truth. So the *sahajīya*s profess the principle of satisfying all the needs of the physical body which is the abode of all the *tattva*s, *pīṭha*s and deities, and without which no *siddhi* can be attainted.[51] The whole yogic process of the Sahaja school is found to be based on a highly sublime aspect of the sex, where the *sādhaka* is to embrace and sport with the female *śakti*, variously called as the *cāṇḍālī, domْbī, śavarī, yoginī, nairātma sahaja sundarī,* etc. The bliss that comes out of this sexo-yogic practices is generally divided into four stages — *ānanda, paramānanda, viramānanda* and *sahajānanda.* The final stage — Sahajānanada — is known as the state of *mahāsukha*, at the attainment of which "the senses are absorbed within, all

[51] N.K. Sahu, *Buddhism in Orissa*, Utkal University, Cuttack, 1958, p. 139.

thought processes are annihilated, all the seeds of existence are destroyed; it is full of lustre of the bliss, it is like the vacant sky and yet cool and sweet".[52]

Iṅdrabhūti was the king of Sambhala in Uḍḍiyāna and his sister Lakṣmīkarā was married to King Jalendra of Laṅkāpurī in eighth-century CE. Lakṣmīkarā was the propounder of Sahajayāna knowledge. N.K. Sahu[53] locates Sambhala and Laṅkāpurī of tāntric Buddhist period in Orissa and claims Sahajayāna philosophy to have developed in the upper Mahānadī Valley.

So, in the land, where Sahajayāna was propagated, the sensual art seems to have been in superb expression and condition. Late Mayadhar Mansinha[54] gives full justice to the Orissan dreams in stone, when he remarks the following, on the love-play and the woman in Orissan art:

> ***THE LOVE-PLAY***: And in the vast, bewildering confusion of biological unfoldment that is life, is not the union of two sexes, the central factor? If the Upaniṣads sang ecstatically that all beings are born in joy, what exactly could that be but that of union, the complete mingling of two hearts, two souls, and two bodies, that is love? Could that be obscene, indeed? By what logic the master-artists, who took the temple walls as their canvas for the whole life, could have left out the central factor of creation, that is love?
>
> We have no right to judge art with the yardstick of prudery and unintelligent and arbitrary social conventions. Viewed with the angle of vision of those devoted artists and builders, who wore out their precious lives for giving a local habitation to their faiths by turning a temple into an epitome of the visible world and a home of the world soul, the so-called obscene sculptures should surely appear as innocent and common place as sex in children or flowers.
>
> They might hurt our sophisticated eyes and offend our sense of hypocritical elegance only so long as we miss the broad viewpoint of conception of these temples.
>
> ***THE WOMAN IN ORISSAN ART***: But the supposed offending figures are indeed few compared to the vast, bewildering panorama of life that stretches

---

[52] N.K. Sahu, *Buddhism in Orissa*, Utkal University, Cuttack, 1958, pp. 140.

[53] Ibid., pp. 147-52.

[54] M. Mansinha, *The Saga of the Land of Jagannatha*, Cuttack: J. Mohapatra & Co., pp. 72-75.

> before our eyes on these walls. The royal processions, the march of armies in full panoply, the religious discourses, the charming defile of deer, elephants and ducks, the frolics of monkeys, the penances of *yogīs*, the obsequitous attitudes in royal courts, the animals of the jungle and the water, and all imaginable happenings in social life are depicted in stone, representing life, in fittingly apparent confusion. But woman emerges out of this confusing tangle as the loveliest strand running through the whole and as the central factor in the whole creation that she really is. The great anonymous artists of Orissa seem to have devoted the best of their skill, imagination and devotional labour to recreating the women of their dreams in stone, shaping them with as perfect charm and loveliness as would be possible to impart to such a hard substance by any sculptor of any country in the world. Women waiting expectantly for their lovers with doors ajar, as on the temples of Brahmeśvara and Mukteśvara; women waiting under *aśoka* trees, as on the Rājarānī; women writing letters to their lovers or getting ready to welcome them, as on the Liṅgarāja; women dancing and playing on all varieties of musical instruments, with enchanting abandon and naivete, as on the walls of Koṇārka; and above all, women completely surrendering to their lovers, the warm ecstasy of consummation blazing on their glowing cheeks — these cannot fail to draw anything but elegant, nostalgic and serenely mistful emotion in any except the grossest of human minds. A few crude vulgarities on the temple walls of Jagannātha should not be allowed to sway the judgement of connoisseurs regarding the so-called obscenities in Orissan sculpture. To one vulgar representation, there are scores that express soul-stirring human romance with uncommon elegance and grace. Indeed, no poet depicted women in finer lyrics than did these medieval stone-artists of Orissa. These dreamers in stone have created some of the most superb female figures in the whole world of art, representing the eternal feminine, the eternal charmer.

And again it is only to those with jaundiced eye, that Orissa's story of art might appear to be nothing but morbid obsession with woman or love-play. The Orissan masters have expressed all human emotions and situations with remarkable skill, covering extremely interesting examples of the heroic, the sublime, the fantastic, not excluding even the most repulsive, as part of life's spectacle on earth.

Famous connoisseurs of Orissa's art-heritage have testified the capacities of Orissan artists for varied sculptural expressions and their performance as consummate builders, with a veiled message for even the ultra-modern artist.

Speciality of Erotic Art in Orissa

Too much of unhappiness prevail in humanity. The ancients of India very minutely had observed sexual incompatibility to have been the seed of all strife and disagreement. Hence sex science developed and literature on sex had been produced in abundance. Erotic sculptures were displayed on temples, as already stated, according to the rules of Śilpaśāstras and the erotica was for publicity purposes also, because like today the ancients had no newspapers, magazines, radios and televisions. The Erotic Art is therefore not pornography. Erotic Art is available in sculptural arts, wood arts, palm-leaf manuscripts and paintings. The speciality of erotic art in Orissa is that the whole erotic art shows all aspects of sex life, beginning from the approach, embrace, kiss, fellatio, exciting the female and male genitalia, caressing, erotic stroking, coital articulation, *aṣṭa-kāmakalā-prayoga* and different poses alias *bandha*s.

According to P.S. Rawson:[55]

> The entire sculptural scheme is dominated by erotic groups, superbly cut, once painted and now world famous. . . . In Orissa today a tradition of illumination on narrow strips of palm-leaf still survives. The oldest known examples are probably fifteenth century, but there can be no doubt that this particular tradition preserves perhaps the most faithful record of what was in earlier times a widespread genre of Hindu art. Classical Hindu texts are impressed with the stylus on to the leaf-strip and colour is rubbed into the impressions; drawings to illustrate them are executed in the same way, and are painted in bright, clear colours. The figure types and conventions of design in the recent illustrations parallel very closely those which appear in the eleventh-century sculpture.
>
> The creative climax of the Erotic Art was reached in Orissa and if through this book, the individuals learn and practise the sex art, by which they derive happiness and reach sexual bliss, then the author will regard the effort in producing this book a success and at least that will be the speciality of the Erotic Art of Orissa.

For those who are interested in the *yoga* of sexual transformation, for them also there are erotic arts of Śyāmakālī, Dakṣiṇakālī and *maithuna* in *viparīta-rati* (inverted sexual intercourse also called *puruṣāyita*) with Mahākāla (Śiva). The *Niruttara-*

---

[55] P.S. Rawson, "Early Art and Architecture", *A Cultural History of India*, A.L. Basham (ed.), Delhi: Oxford University Press, 2nd impression, 1984, p. 207.

Tantra, Paṭala II, gives a slightly different version of this *dhyāna* or practice. With this background, it can be claimed that the erotic arts of Orissa mainly deal with pleasure of sex and *yoga* of sex.

16

Kāmākhyā and the Yoga of Sexual Transformation

PRIMEVAL Yoni alias Yonigātra and Sixty-four Yoginī temples have been traced at the middle right of Mahānadī River Valley, i.e. in Nuāpāḍā and Bolaṅgīr districts of Orissa. Therefore the author[1] is of the opinion that the nucleus of spiritual culture of the Mahānadī Valley was developed at Nuāpāḍā district. Among the Śākta literatures of Assam, *Yoni-Tantra, Bṛhadyoni-Tantra* and *Yoginī-Tantra* texts are found in plenty. Mention may be made of the *Kālikā Purāṇa* and the *Devī Bhāgavata* also.

J.A. Schoterman,[2] the critical editor of *Yoni-Tantra,* states that six of its manuscripts are written in Bengali script which he has edited and two manuscripts written in Oriyā are also found in Orissa. He holds that the most important in determining the origin of the text is Paṭala IV:

> *kocākhyāne ca deśe ca yonigalrasamīpataḥ* ॥ 2 ॥
>
> *gaṅgāyāḥ paścime bhāge mādhavī nāma viśruta* ।
> *gatvā tatra maheśāni yonidarśanamānasaḥ* ॥ 3 ॥
>
> *ahaṁ cātra niśam devī yonipūjanatatparaḥ* ।
> *bhikṣācāraprasaṅgena gacchāmi cadivāniśam* ॥ 4 ॥
>
> *mādhaviyonisadṛśi nāsti yonir mahītale* ।
> *tatkucau kaṭhinau durgeyonis tastyāḥsupinatā* ॥ 5 ॥

We are thus informed that in a country called Koca, near Yoni Gātra, on the western side of the river Ganges, a certain Mādhavī is known to exist whose *yoni* is equalled on earth; it is an object of constant veneration for Mahādeva, who is the narrator in this fourth Paṭala of the *Yoni-Tantra*. The

[1] J.P. Singh Deo, *Tāntric Hedonism of Mahānadī Valley (Uḍḍiyāna-Pīṭha),* New Delhi: D.K. Printworld, 2004, p. 71, fig. 5.

[2] J.A. Schoterman, *The Yoni Tantra,* New Delhi: Manohar, 1980, pp. 3-4, 9 and 38-39.

> country called Koca is unmistakably modern Cooch Behar, north of Bangladesh. . .. Thus summarizing this section on the origin of the *Yoni-Tantra,* he concludes that its origin is in the region of Cooch Behar near Kāmarūpa centring around the cult of Mādhavī.

The country of Koca, on the *paścima* (west) of Gaṅgā River, as mentioned in *Yoni-Tantra,* should have been Kosala country, i.e. South Kosala, because the primeval *yoni,* as discussed in earlier chapter is the *yoni* of Pātālgaṅgā site, Nuāpāḍā district, under a bamboo thicket, formed naturally. It seems to be a spelling mistake or vague negligence of the unqualified writer alias copy-writer of *Yoni-Tantra,* which was composed under the Vaiṣṇava influence in the late medieval period. According to Schoterman,[3] the establishment of Vaiṣṇava tāntric literature can be attributed to the late medieval period (thirteenth century CE onwards), especially the post-Caitanya centuries. So, it can be surmised that the central right Mahānadī River Valley had contributed much to the origin of esoteric yogic *sādhanās* (spiritual practice), which spread to other parts and its glorious spiritual achievements are now forgotten, lost and bereft of recognition.[4]

According to N.R. Mishra:[5]

> Assam has a rich stock of Śākta literature in both Sanskrit and Assamese. Some of the well-known Sanskrit works are the *Kālikā Purāṇa,* the *Yoginī-Tantra,* and the *Mahābhāgavata Purāṇa,* which is popularly known as *Devī Bhāgavata.*
>
> The extant *Kālikā Purāṇa* is one of the most important Śākta sacred texts. It is said that this scripture was written in or around Assam before eleventh century CE to celebrate the worship of Śakti.
>
> The *Yoginī-Tantra* is a major tāntric text which is widely believed to be written in sixteenth century CE. The book has two sections with several chapters in each one of them. While the first section mainly deals with different esoteric practices and the supremacy of the Śakti, the second section focuses on different sacred places of Kāmarūpa and the socio-cultural life of this period. In this second section it is very clearly said that the Devī who is rare elsewhere resides in every house of Kāmarūpa.

---

3 J.A. Schoterman, *The Yoni Tantra,* New Delhi: Manohar, 1980, p. 17.

4 J.P. Singh Deo, op. cit., 2004, p. 121.

5 N.R. Mishra, *Kāmākhyā: A Socio-Cultural Study,* New Delhi: D.K. Printworld, 2004, pp. 20-21.

kāmarūpam devīkṣetraṁ kutrāpi samaṁ na ca ।
anyatra viralā devi kāmarūpe gr̥he gr̥he ॥
— 2.6.152

The *Yoginī-Tantra* also very openly states that the *dharma* of Yonipīṭha is the *dharma* of the Kirāta people.

sarveṣo yoginī pīṭhe dharmaṁ kairātajaṁ mataṁ ॥
kāmarūpe na saṁyāsaṁtathā dīrghatamaṁ priye ।
na tājet sāmisaṁ devibrahmacaryamataṁ na ca ॥
— 2.9.13.14

Here in Kāmarūpa the practice of continence, giving up non-vegetarian diet, undergoing long penance, etc. are not obligatory. Like the *Kālikā Purāṇa* this scripture also has many stories which have implicit sociological meanings. Scholars like Shastri[6] have studied the destruction of the Kāmākhyā temple on the basis of the *Yoginī-Tantra*.

N.R. Mishra further states:

The *Devī-Bhāgavata* is also another Śākta Upapurāṇa. It is said to have been written in tenth or eleventh century CE in Assam or its contiguous areas of North Bengal.

While dealing on the Upapurāṇa, R.C. Hazra[7] deals about *Kālikā Purāṇa* and *Devī Bhāgavata*:

The present *Kālikā Purāṇa* which was written somewhere in, or very near about, Kāmarūpa in Assam, is regarded as one of the most authoritative works by the comparatively late Nibandha writers especially as regards Śakti worship. It deals with the exploits and worship of Kālī or Kālikā, who is primarily the *yoga-nidrā* and *māyā* of Viṣṇu, but who later became the wife of Śiva as Satī, daughter of Dakṣa, and Kālī or Kālikā, daughter of Himavat, for the good of the world; and in connection with these topics it narrates many interesting stories (including that of the birth of Sītā and Naraka from the sacrificial ground of King Janaka of Videha) and introduces chapters on the mountains, rivers and holy places of Kāmarūpa, duties and conducts of kings,

---

[6] B. Shastri, "Destruction of the Kāmākhyā Temple as Referred to in the Yogini Tantra", in P.C. Choudhury (ed.), *Journal of the Assam Research Society*, vol. XXXVI, Guwahati, 1979-80, pp. 1-8.

[7] R.C. Hazra, "The Upapuraṇas", *The Cultural Heritage of India*, vol. II (*Itihāsas, Purāṇas, Dharma and other Śāstras*), Calcutta: The Ramakrishna Mission Institute of Culture, 1969, pp. 280-81.

construction of forts, manners and customs, and so on. This Upapurāṇa was written not later than CE 1100 and most probably in the tenth or eleventh century, and it contains valuable materials for the study of the social, religious and even political history of Kāmarūpa. . . .

The *Devī Bhāgavata*, though a work of the eleventh or twelfth century CE claims to be the real *Bhāgavata Purāṇa* and includes the Vaiṣṇava Bhāgavata among the Upapurāṇas. But it really is an Upapurāṇa adapted carefully by its author to the description of the *Bhāgavata Purāṇa* contained in the *Matsya, Agni, Skanda* and other Purāṇas. An examination of this work shows that its author was a Smārtta Śākta brāhmaṇa of Bengal, lived for a long time in Banaras, and then wrote this work for infusing Śākta ideas into the members of different sects by adapting it, as far as practicable, to the views of these sectaries. It conceives of a central Goddess named Devī Śrībhuvaneśvarī, who is a maiden having four hands and three eyes and living in a region called Maṇi-Dvīpa. She holds a noose (*pāśa*) and a goad (*aṅkuśa*) in two of her hands, and assures granting boon and safety with the other two. In her supreme state she is identical with *Para-Brahman* and *Paramātman*, but in creation she takes to the *guṇas*, and divides herself into *puruṣa* and *prakṛti*, and it is she who appears as Durgā, Gaṅgā, and others for accomplishing different objects.

The *Devī Bhāgavata* lays special stress on *bhakti* (devotion) as a means of realizing Devī, and takes *jñāna* (knowledge) to be the same as *bhakti* in its highest state. It holds the Vedas in high esteem and decries the Tantras whenever they go against the Vedas.

There is no *yoginī* temple in Kāmākhyā or north-east India. It is a wonder that manuscripts of *Yoni-Tantra, Bṛhadyonitantra* and *Yoginī-Tantra* are mostly available in north-east India. *Yoni-Tantra* and *Yoginī-Tantra* mainly deal with *yoga* of sexual transformation. Schoterman[8] is of the opinion:

The *sādhaka* should, however, never ridicule a *yoni*, nor should he show disgust nor shame (*Yoni-Tantra*, VI.27ab). His behaviour towards women should not be offensive (VII.14.ed.). *Maithuna* should only be performed by the *sādhaka* for ritual purposes, never for worldly enjoyment in which case the *sādhaka* is condemned to hell (V.3).

There is difference between the words *mithuna* and *maithuna*. *Mithuna* means sex for pleasure, but *maithuna* means sex for *yoga* of sexual transformation, i.e. from sex

[8] J.A. Schoterman, op. cit., p. 21.

to *samādhi*, salvation, God realization and rise of *kuṇḍalinī*. Swami Muktananda Saraswati[9] explains *maithuna*, as discussed in ch. 15.

Haṭha-Yoga-Pradīpikā,[10] an authoritative work on *haṭha-yoga* of Nāthism, gives the following narration, while identifying a *yoginī*.

> पुंसो विदुं समाकुध्या सम्यगभ्यासपाटवात् ।
> यदि नारी रजो रक्षद्धज्रोत्या सापि योगिनी ॥ 99 ॥
>
> *puṁso viduṁ samākudhyā samyagabhyāsapāṭavāt* ।
> *yadi nārī rajo rakṣaddhajrotyā sāpi yoginī* ॥ 99 ॥
>
> — Chapter 3

> If a woman practises *vajrolī* and saves her *rajas* and the man's *bindu* by thorough contraction, she is a *yoginī*.

These prove that *yoni* cult and *yoga* of sexual transformation migrated to Kāmākhyā region of north-east India in some uncertain early medieval period, because as H.D. Bhattacharyya[11] mentions that from about the tenth century a composite Tantra, drawing materials from Brāhmanic, Buddhistic and Nāthist circles, grew up, and some deities, adepts, cults and practices became common to all of them, though the traditions did not always tally among the different communities and localities. Denominationally and geographically considered, Vedācāra is patronized in Maharashtra; Vaiṣṇavācāra among the Rāmānuja and Gauḍa schools; Dakṣiṇācāra among the Śaṅkarites of the south; Śaivācāra and Vīrācāra among the Liṅgāyats and Vīraśaivas; and Vāmācāra, Siddhāntācāra and Kaulācāra among the Śāktas of Kerala, Gauḍa, Nepal and Kāmarūpa. The first three disfavour both Vīrācāra and Bauddhācāra, while the others extol them.

> Let us turn now to certain other specific beliefs and speculations of the Tantras, and try to trace their antecedents. The Śaiva Āgamas, the Vaiṣṇava Saṁhitās and the Śākta Tantras agree on one point, namely, that a female principle representing the Śakti or energy must be associated with the ultimate reality or the source or locus of power considered as male. This power is not only the cause of manifestation, but is also responsible for differentiation, and

---

[9] Swami Muktananda Saraswati, *Nava Yogini Tantra*, Munger: Bihar School of Yoga, 2nd rev. edn., 1983, pp. 64-65.

[10] Swami Muktananda Saraswati, *Haṭha-Yoga-Pradīpikā* (*Light on Haṭha Yoga*), Munger: Bihar School of Yoga, 2nd edn., 1993, p. 362.

[11] H.D. Bhattacharya, "Tāntric Religion", *THACOTIP*, vol. IV, *The Age of Imperial Kanauj*, 1964, pp. 323-24.

hence a diversified world in time and space, including finite individuals, comes into being because of the association of the male and the female, as in the generation of the world of living things. An elaborate philosophy developed in all the schools — Śaiva, Śākta and Vaiṣṇava, professing to explain the different types and stages of evolution, the first two approximating each other in their main outlines and the last perhaps slightly antedating them both. This origin of the cosmos is to be distinguished, however, from the birth of children to the divine pair as in Purāṇic accounts of the birth of Gaṇeśa and Kārttikeya, for instance, when Śiva and Śakti are considered anthropomorphically. The universe, so originated, has a systaltic process, inasmuch as the created world returns to its source in course of time, when Śakti comes to repose in the Lord, either temporarily in *pralaya* at the end of a cosmic cycle (the philosophers of *karma* and the Paurāṇikas mostly favouring this partial dissolution), or finally by the efforts of finite souls who, by religious practice, yogic concentration, contemplation and meditation realize their oneness with God and annul their finitude. The general tendency of the Tantras is to accept the world in both its physical and mental aspects as real; only that matter or *prakṛti*, as such, was not accorded independent existence as in the Sāṁkhya system, but was supposed to be under the control of the spirit and, in fact, the body was regarded as the seat of the divine in every part thereof.

Tradition of Seven Tāntric Maidens and "Śaśi Sena Kāvya"

With the background of *Yoni-Tantra*, the *yoginī* cult developed in the central Mahānadī Valley, and the first Sixty-four Yoginī temple came up at Rāṇīpur-Jharial site of Bolaṅgīr district. As already dealt, this tāntric cult evolved as the *yoga* of sexual transformation, for which some haṭha-yogic practices are required.

From Gazetteer,[12] it is known that:

> Patnagaṛh was the capital of the kingdom of Patna under the Cauhān rule from its foundation in the middle of the fourteenth century CE till 1872, when Bolaṅgīr became the seat of the Durbar government. Even before the advent of the Cauhāns, Patnagarh was the seat of administration where a sort of oligarchical form of government consisting of eight chieftains was functioning. In the twelfth century CE when the Telugu Coḍas were ruling

[12] N.K. Sahu (state ed.), *Gazetteer of India: Orissa, Bolaṅgīr*, N. Senapati (chief ed.), Cuttack, 1968, pp. 488-89.

> over the tract Patna (Paṭnāgaṛh) was the headquarters of an administrative division called Patna Daṇḍapāṭa. Thus the place had considerable political importance and its history was closely connected with that of Western Orissa for several centuries. It was admirably suitable to be the headquarters of a powerful kingdom being surrounded on three sides by the river Svarṇarekhā and its tributary Māyābatī. Under the Cauhāns, Patnagarh was a highly fortified township and was impregnable from all sides. . . .
>
> Patnagarh is long since known as Kaunri Patna or Kumārī Patna after the seven tāntric maidens who lived in this township for some time and practised esoteric rites. These maidens were popularly known by their assumed names Gangi Gauduni, Sua Teluni, Jnanadei Maluni, Netai Dhobaṇī, Luhukuti Luhuruni, Sukuti Camaruni and Patrapindhi Saharuni. There are popular tales and tradition in western Orissa, depicting the occult practices and tāntric activities of these maidens. They seem to be the followers of Lakṣmīkarā who propounded Sahajayāna Buddhism in western Orissa in the ninth century CE. As late as the sixteenth century CE the Patna kingdom was known as Kaunri Patna after the name of the headquarters town of that name, as known from the *Nirguṇa Māhātmya* of the poet Caitanya Dās.

This narration shows that N.K. Sahu considers the famous seven tāntric maidens of Paṭnāgaṛh area to be the followers of Lakṣmīkarā, who propounded Sahajayāna Buddhism. But this is not so, as it seems that the seven tāntric maidens of Paṭnāgaṛh area continued the secret esoteric tāntric rituals of *yoga* of sexual transformation and of the *yoginī*s, which had originated earlier in the central right Mahānadī Valley. It seems N.K. Sahu was ignorant of the development of the *yoga* of sexual transformation or *yoga* which leads from sex to super-consciousness in this locality and its inclusion in Hinduism or Vedic culture, as expounded in the *Bṛhadāraṇyaka Upaniṣad* (vi.4.2-3 lines) of the *Śukla Yajurveda*.[13] *Bṛhadāraṇyaka Upaniṣad* symbolizes woman as a medium of sacrifice, her lap as the sacrificial altar, her hair as sacrificial grass, her skin as *soma* grass and copulation as an act of sacrifice. It proclaims a series of rules and advises its followers to observe them unmistakably for a choice progeny. The *Chāndogya Upaniṣad* portrays woman as a sacrificial fire and the generative organs as fuels.[14]

---

[13] J.P. Singh Deo, op. cit., p. 135.

[14] R.P. Mishra, *Sahajayana: A Study of Tāntric Buddhism*, Calcutta: Punthi Pustak, 1991, p. 4.

While dealing on the *Mādalā-Pāñjī*, Anirudha Das[15] remarks:

> Now, the *karaṇa*s are writing the *pāñjī*s in their own houses. When the recording was being made with some ceremonies some 40 years back, offerings of the *prāsāda* of the Jagannātha temple used to be made to two images installed in the Chuḍaṅga (Choḍagaṅga) Sāi in Purī town. This offering was known as *kartā-kheyi*s, or dish of offering to the master, and *kheyi* means share. The offering to Balabhadra used to be again offered to Vimalā, the oldest deity of divine energy inside the temple premises. A portion of it used to be removed and offered to a stone image in Chuḍaṅga Sāi by Baḍu Mahāpātra, an important servant of the temple, and some to the image of Hanumān and some to the image of a female deity called Gāreḍi Suṇi, installed in a small temple. Now, this rite has been discontinued and Mahāpātra sells away his share of the offering of *prasāda* in the temple.
>
> Two images of stone, installed in a small miniature temple in Chuḍaṅga Sāi, of a male and another of a female, are of much significance. The beautiful male figure is seated on a throne and armed with bow and arrow. On both his sides are the figures of two attendants, one holding the royal umbrella and another a *cāmara*. On the pedestal, there is the image of a man with an elephant and another one with a horse. To this royal image, offerings stated above are made as the master's share and people till now believe that this is the image of Anantavarma Choḍagaṅga Deva, the builder of the great Jagannātha temple. During the past few months, the writer has visited some old temples and to his surprise he has seen some images which can be appropriately identified as the image of the kings who have built the temples.
>
> The image of this female figure by the side of this male is quite helpful to identify the male figure with reference to the accounts recorded in the *Mādalā-Pāñjī*. Seated on something like a stool, the figure appears to be busy with work on something which is called a *udkhala* or a wooden device commonly used for husking paddy. This also represents a tāntric or black-magic operation. This image is popularly known as *gāreḍi suṇi* in the locality which means the lady practising witchcraft. With reference to the episode of Choḍagaṅga Deva as narrated in the *Mādalā-Pāñjī* and the offerings which used to be made on the tenth day of the bright fortnight of Āśvina, can it not be identified as the *guru-mā* of Choḍagaṅga Deva? There appears to be legendary connection between the two images. It is known from the *Mādalā-*

[15] A. Das, "The Mādalā Pāñji", *OHRJ*, vol. XIV, nos. 3 and 4, pp. 5-7.

Pāñjī that due to the treachery of Vāsudeva brāhmaṇa, Choḍagaṅga Deva conquered Orissa. It has already been stated that Choḍagaṅga Deva learnt witchcraft from Netai Dhobaṇī to whom he was devoted as a disciple and a God-son. These two images are very old. People say that on the pedestal of this female figure, there was the figure of a male in the pose of learning something from the female figure; but due to the thick coating of vermillion (*chuā*) and sandal paste which was about half an inch thick, on both the images, it has been destroyed. With great difficulty the coating was removed by mild chiselling to enable us to make a drawing of both the images.

It will not be out of place here to give a little introduction of Netai Dhobaṇī. The name Netai Dhobaṇī is well known in the folk tales, stories of witchcraft, etc. in many parts of Orissa. People still believe that many people and specially children are influenced by evil spirit as a result of which they are diseased and sometimes they die also. So, one adept in witchcraft is called and one recites, *nahebāra boli kāhāra ājñā, kitai mā, patra sauruni, netai dhobaṇī, sidha sauruñi, Jnanadei maluni ra koṭi ājñā*. So, in the names of all these ladies, such as Kitāi Mā, Patra Sauruni, Netai Dhobaṇī, Sidha Sauruñi and Jnanadei Maluni, the person well versed with the *mantra* to cure possession by evil spirit cures the patient. In many parts of western Orissa, Netai Dhobaṇī is worshipped by certain classes of people. She has been described in the *Mādalā-Pāñji*, as the Nagara-Devī or deity of the capital. Considered from all angles, it is difficult to disbelieve that the image in question is not of Netai Dhobaṇī.

The above narration of witchcraft by Anirudha Das requires explanation. Witch[16] means a woman regarded as having supernatural or magical power or a minor evil spirit. Witch-craft therefore means a craft or practice of witches — the black art, sorcery and supernatural power.

Swami Satyananda Saraswati[17] now Paramahansa, explains the magic of supernatural power:

Magic occurs in the realm of the material universe (*māyā*). Everything that happens around us in the world, whether the birth of a child, the growth of a tree, a flying bird or the digestive process, it is really magic. What can be more magical than the incredible phenomena occurring around us every

[16] William Geddie (ed.), *Chamber's Twentieth Century Dictionary*, New Delhi: Allied Publishers, first Indian edn., 1964, p. 1278.

[17] Swami Satyananda Saraswati, *A Systematic Course in the Ancient Tantric Techniques of Yoga and Kriya*, Munger: Bihar School of Yoga, 2nd edn., 1989, pp. 337-38.

> second of the day? All that magic rites involve is the manipulation of the universal magic around and within us. Modern science, in a sense, does this through various energy manipulations: electrical, mechanical, biological and so forth. The tāntric *yogī* or magician invokes cosmic forces, psychic forces, etc. by means of *mantras*, *maṇḍalas*, rites and other tāntric practices. If you don't think this is possible, then we don't intend to persuade you otherwise. In fact, we again point out that there is no reason why you should believe anything without personal experience. Only keep open mind to possibilities, and remember that magic rites have been practised all through the history of mankind.

The basic premise of magic is that the macrocosm is reflected in the microcosm, though in fact the relationship is far deeper than this. Therefore change in the outer world, in the phenomenal universe and in the individual himself can be invoked by magical means. The microcosm is the gateway to the macrocosm. Undertaking of the inner leads to understanding of the outer. Understanding of *māyā* leads to its mastery.

In Tantra, magic is to be used to bring about positive changes in one's being and surroundings. Unfortunately, magic is easily open to abuse in all forms of black magic. This leads to a person's downfall, for negative actions lead to negative repercussions on the magician. There is a tendency for the misapplied use of magic to rebound. Tantra, of course, discourages misuse of magic. It advocates that magic should be used to bring about harmony, it should be in accordance with one's nature (*dharma*). This is often called white magic. But magic is magic; it is only misappropriate or appropriate use that transforms it into black or white magic. The power is there in each individual; it is the way that it is used that is important. If it is used properly then it can lead to extraordinary experiences, higher awareness and knowledge. If used wrongly, for personal gain or for purpose of revenge, then the practitioner will suffer.

Most people are either very sceptical about magic, or they regard it as supernatural. But actually it is no more than an extension of one's natural faculties beyond the range that most people comprehend and experience. Magical power is real as real . . . as anything else that exists. But it is beyond the normal experience. The power of magic stems from the dictum of the *Viśvasāra Tantra* which says:

> What is here is elsewhere;
> What is not here is nowhere.

It stems from the dictum of Hermes Trismegistus of ancient Egypt, who said:

> "What is below is an image of that which is above; and that which is above is an image of that which is below for the purposes of magic or miracle."
>
> All tāntric and yogic practices are a form of magic invocation, for they are trying to tune you in with something else, whether it is inner peace, knowledge or whatever. And the greatest form of magic is *nirvāṇa, samādhi, kaivalya* or whatever you want to call the state of enlightenment.
>
> Christ was a magician, for he performed miracles. Buddha was a magician, Mohammed was a magician, Moses was a magician, together with an innumerable number of *yogī*s and saints throughout the ages. A *guru* is a magician, let there be no doubt about this. And so on. Magic merely covers the aspects of existence which are beyond normal low states of awareness. It is magic brought about by spiritual practices that will take you to indescribable states of consciousness, knowledge and bliss.
>
> Magic is the process of spiritual alchemy, for it fuses the individual consciousness with the supreme consciousness. It transmutes the mortal into the immortal. Man finds his real nature. It is by looking inside that one discovers the secrets of the universe and the supreme secret. This is magic.

There are many esoteric tales and stories in western Orissa, the middle Mahānadī River Valley. P.M. Nayak[18] also states Sonepur too was the ancient seat of Tantra, the abode of the seven tāntric sisters. The Satbandh (seven tanks) of the town is traditionally associated with them. *Mantra*s in which their names are invoked are chanted: "Go, disease go; for this is the command of Kaunri Kāmacaṇḍī; Madana Maluni, Netai Dhobaṇī, Sukuti Camaruni, Luhukuti Luhuruni, Gangi Gauduni, Patrapindhi Saharuni, Sua Teluni, go, for Īśvara and Pārvatī order you a crore of times to go". Madana or Jnanadei Maluni and Netai Dhobaṇī are believed to be the inhabitants of Sonepur. Jagabandhu Singh[19] in *Prācīna Utkala* tells the story of Chodagaṅga Deva, who saw Netai Dhobaṇī at Sonepur on his way to coastal Orissa cook with one feet in the burning hearth and her child in the boiling cauldron. Even today in Sonepur the washermen worship Netai, the *mālī*s worship Madana and the *lohāra*s worship Sukuti as their tutelary deities. Pt. Gopinath Panigrahi quotes Ramchandra Panigrahi, an old brāhmaṇa of Sonepur, who used to locate

---

[18] P.M. Nayak, "A Fresh Look at Sasisena Kavya", *Confluence*, vol. I, P.M. Nayak (ed.), Registrar, Sambalpur University, Burla, 1992, p. 72.

[19] Jagabandhu Singh, *Prācīna Utkala* (Oriyā), Purī, 1929, p. 101.

the house of Madana and her flower garden close to the west of the present palace.

While narrating about the places of interest, about Sonepur, N.K. Sahu[20] says that, in fact, Sonepur territory was a stronghold of tāntric Buddhism and in the tāntric Buddhist literature it is referred to as Laṅkā. Lakṣmīkarā, daughter of Rājā Indrabhūti of Sambal (Sambalpur) in the ninth century CE, is known to have married the son of Rājā Jalendra of Laṅkā (Sonepur). (It is a printing mistake. Lakṣmīkarā was a sister of King Indrabhūti. She married Prince Sevola, the son of King Jalendra of Laṅkāpur. Jalendra is also known as Jālandhara.) Lakṣmīkarā is regarded as one of the traditional eighty-four *siddhas* of India and she is famous for propounding Sahajayāna system of Buddhism. Jayadratha who translated *Sambara Tantra* (*Tantra* of Sambal), into Tibetan also belonged to Laṅka (Sonepur).

> A work called *Śaśi Senā*, written by Pratap Ray, describes Jnanadei Maluni, one of the seven tāntric maidens, as resident of Sonepur. Śaśisenā was the daughter of some feudatory chief of western Orissa. She was in love with Ahimāṇikya, the son of the Dīwān, when both of them were reading in the school. After their marriage, which was secretly performed by the help of the teacher, who officiated as priest, they came and lived at Sonepur which was also then known by its second name Kamitapura. Jnanadei Maluni, also known as Madana Maluni, the tāntric maiden, who was then living in Sonepur, was charmed by the beauty of Ahimāṇikya and when he once went out alone to the bazaar, she induced him to come to her place where Ahimāṇikya was transformed to a lamb by dint of her esoteric art. This tāntric maiden used to reconvert him into human form in the night, while at day time the unfortunate man remained as a lamb. In the meantime, Śaśisenā having lost her husband remained in guise of a man, so that she could not be molested by malevolent persons and could search her husband everywhere in the town. She subsequently got an appointment under the Rājā of Sonepur and became a soldier in the army. Very soon she earned reputation for her courage and heroism, particularly when she once killed a man-eater tiger at the risk of her life. The Rājā being pleased with Śaśisenā desired to give his daughter in marriage to her. As Śaśisenā could not reveal her identity she was forced by circumstances to marry the daughter of the Rājā. She, however, described her misfortune to the newly-married girl and the latter being full of sympathy for her did not reveal anything about her identity. Both of them searched for Ahimāṇikya by all possible means. They excavated a tank at a place in the west of Sonepur town and

[20] N.K. Sahu (state ed.), op. cit., pp. 494-95.

> constructed four temples on four sides of the tank. A grand festival took place on the day of consecration of the tank. Jnanadei Maluni came to see the festival at night with Ahimāṇikya who was then in human form. Ahimāṇikya could recognize Śaśisenā and not being able to contact her, he wrote a few lines on the wall of one of the temples by a piece of chalk informing her that he had been taken captive and transformed as a lamb by the tāntric maiden Jnanadei Maluni. Śaśisenā could know everything about her husband from the writing. She told the Rājā that she would sacrifice some lambs before the Goddess Bhagavatī and that the lamb possessed by Jnanadei Maluni be brought for that purpose. The Rājā at her request brought Ahimāṇikya who was then in the form of lamb, from Jnanadei Maluni. It was then known that the lamb was no other than Ahimāṇikya and by the order of the Rājā, Jnanadei Maluni brought him back to human form. Śaśisenā and Ahimāṇikya met together and at the desire of the Rājā, both his daughter and Śaśisenā became the wives of Ahimāṇikya.

The stories of seven tāntric maidens and Śaśisenā are popular in the folk tales of Assam. P.M. Nayak[21] asserts that the story of Śaśisenā is widely prevalent in the eastern states of India. These facts and the discussions show that the *Yoni-Tantra* and *yoga* of sexual transformation of *yoginī* cult had shifted from the central Mahānadī River Valley to the eastern states of India and especially to Kāmākhyā and Assam tracts.

R.K. Mishra[22] states that the land of Netai Dhobaṇī and Patrapindhi Saharuni Sauruni (names of two legendary women Tantra practitioners of Orissa) is now bereft of that mystical aura that was once lit up by Nāgārajuna, the Buddhist tāntric alchemist in the Caves of Keoñjhar and by the silhouetted magic masters who haunted the Virajā-Kṣetra, Prācī Valley, Ekāmra-Kṣetra, Hirapur and Cilkā belt in the east and the hinterlands of Kālāhāṇḍī including (Māraguḍa) and Bolaṅgīr (including Rāṇīpur-Jharial, Yogī Surda) and Sonepur.

R.K. Mishra makes the same mistake like N.K. Sahu in regarding the tāntric maidens to be of Buddhist tāntric following. The whole narration shows the gradual development of Tāntricism and the tāntric maidens were the followers of *yoni* and *yoginī* Tantras. These yogic Tantras of sexual transformation became popular

---

21 P.M. Nayak, op. cit., pp. 69-76.

22 R.K. Mishra, "Śakti Cult in Orissa: An Iconographic Overview", *Studies in Śāktism*, K.C. Mishra (ed.), Institute of Orissan Culture, Bhubaneswar, 1995, p. 154.

throughout India, during early medieval period. Therefore, for survival, probably Buddhism developed tāntric Buddhism.[23]

While camping at Khariar in 2003, anthropologist Gitanjali Nayak of Purī informed the author that in between Ānandapur and Ghaṭagāon Tāriṇī villages of Keoñjhar district, a high school named Patra Sauruni exists. This proves that the occult teaching of Patrapindhi Saharuni was popular in Keoñjhar district in bygone days, among some followers. The name of Patra Sauruni High School in Keoñjhar district seems to be the last remnant of the tradition of the seven tāntric maidens of the central right Mahānadī Valley before it went to the Assam region.

The Name Nīlācala

Another tradition of the Mahānadī Valley is the name Nīlācala. In *Puruṣottama Kṣetra Māhātmyam* of *Skanda Purāṇa*,[24] hill Nīlācala is mentioned for the first time. According to Rajendra Chandra Hazra,[25] the *Skanda Purāṇa* is a voluminous work consisting of a very large number of parts, most of which have not yet been printed. Though, like the other Purāṇas, the *Skanda* also was subjected to additions and alterations more than once, there are chapters in it which were written earlier than CE 1000, but it seems to contain little which can be dated earlier than CE 700.

Gopinath Mahapatra,[26] while dealing with Śavari-Nārāyaṇa, states that according to a fifteenth-century work, *Sāralā Mahābhārata*, written by Sāralādās, the concept of Śavari-Nārāyaṇa originates from the following story. Gālamādhava was a king of Kāñcan Nagara. He was a worshipper of Lord Viṣṇu. Once he, upon a vow to fast, remained without food. One day he went out in quest of the image of Viṣṇu and in the course of his search, he noticed that Śavari-Nārāyaṇa was being worshipped by the Śavaras on a hill called Dhauli, near Bhubaneswar, Orissa. Gālamādhava brought the idol to Nīlādri as described by the deity and worshipped him. The Śavaras called this idol as Śavari-Nārāyaṇa.

> This story has another version also. Śavari-Nārāyaṇa, originally worshipped at Dhauli, was brought to Nīlācala by Indradyumna. But the people, who worshipped the idol, were delivered from the bondage of life (died). Lord Hara then ordered Yama to remove the idol to Purī. Here also the

[23] J.P. Singh Deo, *Tāntric Art of Orissa*, Delhi: Kalpaz Publications, 2001, pp. 201-02.

[24] Gopinath Mohapatra, *The Land of Viṣṇu (A Study of Jagannātha Cult)*, Delhi: B.R. Publishing Corporation, 1979, p. 228.

[25] R.C. Hazra, "The Purāṇas", op. cit., 1969, p. 263.

[26] Gopinath Mohapatra, op. cit., pp. 7-8.

worshippers (of the idol) met with the same fate. Yama then removed it to Śavara village. But the idol did not like to stay in Śavara Palli and wanted to remain at Nīlācala. Gālamādhava thus took the idol back to Nīlācala.

According to K.C. Mishra:[27]

> A reference can justifiably be made here to a commonly prevalent notion that the temple of Jagannātha is on a mountain and therefore it is called Nilādri, Nilācala or Nīlagiri. But neither is the temple situated on a mountain, nor is there any mountain in the vicinity of Purī. The temple is really situated on a sand-hill and is called Nīlagiri (blue mountain) only on grounds of analogy. The Liṅgarāja temple at Bhubaneswar is called Svarṇādri or Svarṇagiri though this temple too is not on a mountain. Most probably, it is called so because Kailāsa, the abode of Śiva, has several names as Hemakūṭa, Svarṇakūṭa or Svarṇagiri, etc. and one of the names has been chosen for the Liṅgarāja temple. So, it may be presumed that the name Nīlagiri was adopted for the Jagannātha temple because the name Svarṇādri was used for the Liṅgarāja temple. It is also probable that because of the lofty structure of the temple of Jagannātha, it came to be metaphorically compared with a hill or *giri*, from which it assumed the name Nīlagiri. And, as the local tradition goes a sandhill did actually exist.

The latest archaeological finding of this Nīlācala site of Purī, over which the Puruṣottama Jagannātha temple stands, may be stated as reported by C.B. Patel:[28]

> In this regard it is important to mention that recently the Archaeological Survey of India under the guidance of T. Satyamurty made some repair work in the base of the Garuḍa pillar inside the Naṭamandira area and found the remnant of an Aśokan pillar with typical Mauryan polish. The pillar goes deep into the platform. The author along with his colleague D.R. Pradhan visited the spot at the time of renovation and observed that the entire Jagannātha temple complex platform area was man-made, resembling a platform of Buddhist establishment like a *stūpa*. Many scholars believe the Buddhist origin of Jagannātha and opine that Purī was an ancient seat of Buddhist cult. The reference to Buddha's tooth relics of Orissa, theory of Buddha's birth in Orissa, conversion of Aśoka to Buddhism

---

[27] K.C. Mishra, *The Cult of Jagannātha*, Calcutta: Firma K.L. Mukhopadhyay, 1971, p. 21.

[28] C.B. Patel, "Oldest Jagannātha Temple of Purī: The Buddhist and Somavaṁśī Connections", *Orissa Review*, vol. LIX, no. 12, July, 2003, Information and Public Relation Departments, Bhubaneswar, Orissa, p. 65.

> in Purī district lend support to this contention. Fergusson is of the opinion that "there can be little doubt that the temple (of Jagannātha at Purī) now occupies that site where formerly stood the *pagoḍā* containing the celebrated tooth relics." Alexander Cunningham has reported that in a Sāñcī *stūpa*-sculpture, he has noticed Buddha, *dharma* and *saṁgha* representation which can be identified as the Jagannātha of Purī. He further says that the second *dharma* aspect of Buddhist trinity is taken as a female form and can be identified with Subhadrā.

C.B. Patel[29] further mentions that one group of scholars opines that the site was originally a natural hillock over which a Buddhist establishment has developed since early time. Another group of scholars believe that the present elevated platform of 8 m height was constructed by the Buddhist for erection of a Buddhist *stūpa*. During 2003-04 tha Garuḍa pillar at the Naṭa Maṇḍapa was repaired by Archaeological Survey of India. During the course of repair work, the author along with Dr. Satyamurty, superintendent, Archaeological Survey of India, was present. It was observed that the pillar in question is a fossilized wood, while the lower portion below is a Chunar sandstone (!) of which Aśokan pillars were built. Hence, there is great possibility that originally the Śrī Jagannātha temple complex at Purī was a Buddhist establishment. Scientific excavation will confirm this in future.

The name Nīlācala is also traced at Kāmākhyā site of north-east India.

According to N.R. Mishra:[30]

> The Kāmākhyā temple which is situated atop the Nīlācala hill to the west of Guwahati (91°42'E – 26°10'N approximately) is at present an important part of a sacred complex. This complex not only houses many other temples but also a whole set of people connected with them. The main temple (Kāmākhyā temple) has the *pīṭha* of Goddess Kāmākhyā and two shrines of Lakṣmī and Sarasvatī nearby. Other major Devī temples in the complex belong to Goddesses like Kālī, Tārā, Bhuvaneśvarī, Chinnamastā, Bagalā, Bhairavī and Dhūmāvatī. There are some minor temples of various goddesses in this complex too. They are the Śītalā temple, the Lalitā-Kāntā temple, the Jaya-Durgā temple, the Vana-Durgā temple, the Rājarājeśvarī temple, the Śmaśāna-Kālī temple, the Kālī temple of Abhayānanda Dharmaśālā and the Śaṅkheśvarī temple. These temples are considered minor only from the

[29] C.B. Patel, "Conservation Issues of Shree Jagannātha Temple of Purī", *OHRJ*, vol. XLVIII, no. 1, p. 147.

[30] N.R. Mishra, *Kāmākhyā: A Socio-Cultural Study*, New Delhi: D.K. Printworld, 2004, pp. 23-24.

> point of view of comparatively less number of devotees going there. There are five temples of Lord Śiva in this complex. They belong to different manifestations of Lord Śiva like Kāmeśvara (*umānanda*), Siddheśvara, Amṛtakeśvara (*heruka*), Aghora and Koṭiliṅga (*tatpuruṣa*). Here a temple of Lord Viṣṇu as Kedāra (Kamaleśvara) is also situated near the northern side of the main temple. Another temple of Lord Viṣṇu known as Gadādhara is found in north-western direction of the Kāmākhyā temple. A temple of Lord Viṣṇu as Pāṇḍunātha is situated in the eastern foothills of Nīlācala which is known as Pāṇḍu. Lord Gaṇeśa, in his four different forms as Nandī, Bhṛṅgī, Mahākāla and Gaṇapati guards the four gates of this sacred complex. The complex is also dotted with a few sacred ponds (*kuṇḍas*) which are associated with various *pūjās* and rituals. These ponds are Saubhāgya Kuṇḍa, Durgā Kuṇḍa, Bhairavī Kuṇḍa, Amṛtadhārā Kuṇḍa, Ṛṇamocana Kuṇḍa and Gayā Kuṇḍa. The complex has a number of *āśramas* and *dharmaśālās* which are meant for saints and holy men. These are like Daśamaṇi Akhāṛā, Abhayānanda Dharmaśālā, Kalipur Āśrama, Nigamānanda Āśrama, Satsaṅga Āśrama, Tapoban Āśrama and Bijay Kṛṣṇa Āśrama.
>
> Various *pūjās* and festivals are performed in different temples round the year by both brāhmaṇa and non-brāhmaṇa personnel. These personnel have settled in this complex for generations. Their society is not only functionally integrated by itself but is also marked by its own peculiarities.
>
> This sacred complex, which is referred to as Kāmākhyā-dhām or more simply Kāmākhyā attracts large number of devotees. They come not only from this region but also from different parts of this country. In fact, this temple of the north-east remains an integrating force not only among the people of this region but also serves as a major link with the peninsular mainland.

In peninsular India, the Mahānadī Valley was and is the land of Kāmakalā, Uḍḍiyāna-Pīṭha and erotic art, where *yoga* of sexual transformation and the *yoginī* cult had developed in early and medieval periods, but these esoteric yogic practices gradually migrated to north-east India as *Yoni-Tantra*, and *Yoginī-Tantra* texts are mostly found in Bengal and north-east India.

Kālikā Purāṇa (eleventh century CE) clearly speaks of Jagannātha as Bhairava and Kātyāyanī as Bhairavī in Orissa (Uḍḍiyāna).[31] While dealing about the tāntric palm-leaf manuscripts of Orissa, N. Mishra[32] states:

---

[31] H.C. Das, "Religions of Orissa", *OHRJ*, vol. XXX, nos. 2-4, p. 132.

[32] N. Mishra, "Palm-leaf Manuscripts of Orissa", *OHRJ*, vol. XXX, nos. 2-4, pp. 81-82.

Orissa was famed as an important centre of tāntric cult from sixth century CE. The first Uḍḍiyāna-Pīṭha was in Orissa which can be testified from the scriptures. The presiding deities of Tantra system, Bhairava and Bhairavī are identified as Vimala and Virājā. Besides, the Goddesses Maṅgalā, Bhagavatī, Bhadrakālī, Carcikā, Bhaṭṭārikā, Samalai have immense popularity in Orissa. All these might have paved the way for composition of Tantra, *Oḍḍiyāna Tantra, Udubhāsvara Tantra, Oḍḍamareśvara Tantra,* though they do not bear any names of the scribes. They are believed to have been written in Orissa which can be testified from the naming and subject matter of the manuscripts. Apart from this, many novel additions have been found in *Sāṅkhyāyana Tantra, Yoginī-Tantra, Kumārī Tantra, Kumāra Tantra* and *Yoni Tantra,* which have relevance to their being scribed in Orissa. *Bhuvaneśvarī Pallava* dedicated to Gajapati Puruṣottama Deva, *Śāradā-Śāradārcana Paddhati, Yantracintāmaṇi* of Godāvara Miṣrā, *Śakti Pratimā Pratiṣṭhā* of Vidyākaraṇa Vājapeyī, *Durgotsava Candrikā* of Vardhana Mohapatra, *Tāriṇīkula Sudia Taraṅgiṇī* of Rāmacandra Udgātā, *Durgā Yajña Dīpikā* of Jagannātha Ācārya, *Bhubanesvarī Prakāśa* of Bāsudev Ratha, *Vana-Durgā-Pūjā* of Raghunātha Dāsa, *Śivārcanā Paddhati* and *Jhānavallī Tantra* of Lakṣeśvara Rath are famous as tāntric texts in Orissa.

Besides these, 123 Tantra manuscripts and 73 tāntric supplements are preserved in the manuscript section of the Orissa State Museum, Bhubaneswar.[33] The manuscripts *Yoni Tantra* and *Yoginī Tantra,* mainly deal or are concerned with the *yoga* of sexual transformation. Therefore, it is certain that *yoga* of sexual transformation had migrated to Kāmākhyā region of north-east India, from the central right Mahānadī Valley.

[33] M.P. Dash (comp.), *A Descriptive Catalogue of Sanskrit Manuscripts of Orissa,* vol. V (*Tantra Manuscripts*), Bhubaneswar: Orissa State Museum, 1965, *passim.*

17

Sensuousness in Art

AT the request of the All India Radio, Trichinopoly, Sri Aurobindo Ghosh[1] had given a message, that was broadcast on 14 August 1947. In this message, Sri Aurobindo had said:

> The spiritual gift of India to the world has already begun. India's spirituality is entering Europe and America in an ever increasing measure. That movement will grow amid the disasters of the time, more and more eyes are turning towards her with hope and there is even an increasing resort not only to her teachings, but to her psychic and spiritual practice . . . the initiative can come from India and although the scope must be universal, the central movement may be hers.

In the words of Satyavrata R. Patel:[2]

> Indian art is more abstract or philosophical, Greek more human and naturalistic. A knowledge of the myths and symbolism in which the art is rooted is needed. Otherwise in the case of Indian art the response of the onlooker would be to draw a blank. Indian art is closer to nature; there are flowers, birds or the like. And there is not merely physical nature, the supernatural and the lower worlds too are delineated. The whole cosmos is sought to be depicted in all its multiplicity and wideness. Hence Indian art is many sided, deeper and may not attract at first sight. Greek art makes fewer demands on the capacities of the observer. But Indian art portrays all human activities, sacred and profane, secular and religious, from sex to salvation. It embraces all life, even the cosmos in its vast existence. . . .[3]

---

1 "A Message from Śrī Aurbindo: The 15th of August 1947", Appendix II, Adwaitya P. Ganguly, *Vedanta Philosophy for the Unity of Mankind*, New Delhi: Vikas Publishing House, 1995, p. 102.

2 Satyavrata R. Patel, *East and West: A Cultural Dialogue*, Bombay: Bharatiya Vidya Bhavan, 1992, pp. 74, 79 and 131.

3 Ibid.; Śrī Aurbindo, *The Foundation of Indian Culture*, chapter of arts.

> In particular, Indian Art is cosmic, perennial and universal. India evolved art-forms that brought with them intimate relations with the whole cosmos, all orders of being, sub-human and super-human and the transcendental whole from which all is derived. India ceaselessly and systematically created abstract or generic symbols and images. Super-human and animalistic forms, cosmic motifs and significances inform it. It created devices for revealing the face of the ultimate reality of the imponderable values and meanings of the eternal varities of existence. . . .
>
> India mastered many fields, from sex to salvation, from the conscious to the superconscious, and was equally at home with reason and mysticism, intellect and intuition, vision and action. From the dawn of history, India had an integral approach throughout, till the barbarian onslaught disturbed life's balance and her life force withdrew itself into a cell, the spark of creativity having departed from life. The barbarian onslaught broke her very existence at a physical level and her soul languished. All along, both in theory and in practice India stressed both the fullness of outer and inner life, and the material splendour of her civilization right up to the British conquest unmistakably reveals that despite all the disorders of her life. There is again, as we noted, a deeper interrelation between spirit and matter, since material growth leads to and sustains culture and even spiritual growth. Unless there is a feeding of life's energies no further growth or development is possible. The spiritual is one such possibility. And without the energy of matter the spirit cannot flower. Very often spiritual poverty and cultural poverty go together. The departure of the leavening influence of spirit, results in outer darkness. Often, contrarily, material expansion foreshadows spiritual growth.

Search of the cradle of civilization[4] has begun and it has been found that nothing could be farther from the truth. Just as the Vedic seers and sages have given rise in subsequent centuries to an unparalleled profusion of metaphysical ideas and lofty spiritual ideas in the wisdom schools, they also have provided the impetus for ingenious and diversified scientific and other secular knowledge. This knowledge can be found embedded in the rich secondary literature on astronomy, mathematics, medicine, architecture, grammar, phonetics, etymology, art, music, dance, sexology, statecraft, weaponry and ethics in general. While dealing on "The Birth of Science in Ritual", scholars[5] of "The Cradle of Civilization" have also stated:

---

[4] George Feuerstein, Subhash Kak and David Frawley, *In Search of the Cradle of Civilization*, Delhi: Motilal Banarsidass, 1999, pp. 41-42.

[5] Ibid., p. 199.

> Incidentally, the sky and earth altars were correlated with the male and female gender respectively. Sexual-symbolism is pervasive in the Vedic religion. Thus the Adhvaryu priest was deemed male while the Neṣṭṛ priest, who was typically associated with the Goddesses, represented the female gender. The Vedic texts speak of the "copulation" between the chants and the formulas, the former being considered feminine and the latter masculine. There are numerous "couplings" (*mithunī-karaṇa*) of this type in the Vedas and the subsequent ritual literature. It is in this Vedic custom that we must look for the seeds of the metaphysics of medieval Tantrism, which views the cosmos as the product of Śiva's and Śakti's divine embrace (*maithuna*).[6]

Looking forward of the intelligentsia has already begun. It finds expression in the words of K. de B. Codrington:[7]

> War does not only disrupt the publication of books, but also the writing of books. On the eve of India's independence, an enquirer, at three leading bookshops in London, found an array of books on Indian politics, but not one book on Indian history or Indian art. The reproach is common to the West and the East. Problems do not spring up overnight. They grow, and if they are to be understood rightly, their growth must be studied. In any case, there are other things to talk about in India than politics. India is not merely a problem. There is more to her than religious schism, party politics or hypothetical constitution building. Her history, her literature, her art, her manifold ways of life, exist as accomplishments. Whatever happens in the future, her accomplishment in the past cannot be neglected, nor indeed her accomplishment in the present. The royal society has been fit to acknowledge the work of living Indian scientists with its highest honours. Like Indian Science, Indian Art and letters are living things. Apart from the obvious political conflict, and the flood of verbiage which it engenders, the genius of the country, with its general human values and individual charms, is still open to the student, who will take up the book and read. Ancient Greece is no more, and Rome is hardly what it once was. The Oriental empires of the Nile and the Tigris are dead. Only in China and India has tradition survived from the beginning. No man who boasts himself

6 George Feuerstein, Subhash Kak and David Frawley, *In Search of the Cradle of Civilization*, Delhi: Motilal Banarsidass, 1999, For a detailed study of the sexual symbolism of the Vedas, see S.A. Dange, *Sexual Symbolism from the Vedic Ritual*, Delhi: Ajanta Publications, 1979, *passim*.

7 K. de B. Codrington, *The Study of Indian Art*, Varanasi: Chowkhamba Sanskrit Series Office, 1988, pp. 158-59.

> a humanist can afford to neglect them. Surely, on our part, we can, now, admit that the honours schools of our universities are not everything? And would it not be wise for all who love India to seek to make her ancient contribution to humanism, as widely known as possible? In spite of war, in spite of disputes, in spite of the fault of loquacity, it is still possible to appreciate the things that last. But the traditions of appreciation have to be preserved. Culture is, to a very large extent, remembering. The dark ages were worth forgetting. It can happen again.

According to *Mahānirvāṇa Tantram*:[8]

> The river Ganges, the Mahānadī — the residence of the spiritual guide, and the celebrated shrines, these are the *tīrtha*s or the holy places of pilgrimage in the *Kali-yuga*.

Spiritual guide alias master (*guru*) is found to the seeker, but the temples and sculptural arts with their sensuousness of expression have much to speak to the mundane world. Therefore, the author[9] had earlier expressed that the iconographical masterpieces representing the haṭha-yogic features with sensual expressions are found in this area. Stones do not speak, only yogic masters show and interpret their expressions to the common man.

A series of temples were constructed in Orissa from sixth to thirteenth century CE, the most important of them being Paraśurāmeśvara (CE 750), Mukteśvara (CE 950), Liṅgarāja (CE 1000) and Rājārānī (CE 1150) at Bhubaneswar, the Jagannātha temple of Purī (twelfth century CE) and the gigantic Sun temple at Koṇārka (thirteenth century CE). About the evolution of temple architecture in Orissa, K.S. Behera[10] is of the opinion that Orissan temple-style was in full vigour in the wake of the vast religious and cultural resurgence that took place when the Śailodbhava kings ruled from the middle of the sixth century till the first quarter of the eighth century. The temple building activities gained momentum under the Bhauma-Karas (CE 736–959), the Somavaṁśīs (CE 950–1112) and reached the climax during the Gaṅga period (CE 1112–1435). The activity continued even under the Sūryavaṁśi-Gajapatis (CE 1435–1542), though on a very small scale.

[8] Manmatha Nath Dutt (ed.), *Mahānirvāṇa Tantram* (A prose; English translation), Varanasi: Chowkhamba Sanskrit Series Office, 2nd edn., 1979, p. 135.

[9] J.P. Singh Deo, *Tāntric Hedonism of Mahānadī Valley (Uḍḍiyāna-Pīṭha)*, New Delhi: D.K. Printworld, 2004, p. 74.

[10] K.S. Behera, "Brahmanical Temples of Orissa", *Orissa Review (Monument Special)*, Public Relation Dept., Govt. of Orissa, Bhubaneswar, January 1976, p. 58.

In tradition of sculptures in Orissa, mention may be made of decorative female figures, secular scenes with figures, animal figures, decorative motifs like *kīrttimukha*, *caitya* window and scroll works. Even bestiality is depicted. Cult images are found in plenty. Purāṇic representations in temple art are found, as deciphered by Kedarnath Mohapatra.[11] The most remarkable are the erotic figures. Among the erotic sculptures, all scenes of sex for pleasure, i.e. *mithuna* and *yoga* of sexual transformation, i.e. *maithuna* are found.

Mayadhar Mansinha[12] describes Orissa dreams in stone and about the love-play scenes:

> And in the vast, bewildering confusion of biological unfoldment that is life, is not the union of two sexes, the central factor? If the Upaniṣads sang ecstatically that all beings are born in joy, what exactly could that be but that of union, the complete mingling of two hearts, two souls, and two bodies, that is love? Could that be obscene, indeed? By what logic the master-artists, who took the temple walls as their canvas for the whole life, could have left out the central factor of creation, that is love?
>
> We have no right to judge art with the yardstick of little pruderies and unintelligent and arbitrary social conventions. Viewed with the angle of vision of those devoted artists and builders, who wore out their precious lives for giving a local habitation to their faiths by turning a temple into an epitome of the visible world and a home of the world-soul, the so-called obscence sculptures should surely appear as innocent and common-place as sex in children or flowers. They might hurt our sophisticated eyes and offend our sense of hypocritical elegance only so long as we miss the broad viewpoint of the builders in the total cosmic conception of these temples.

In the words of N.L. Mathur:[13]

> The supreme achievement of Orissa's architectural genius is the Sun temple at Koṇārka about 20 miles north-east of Purī, built during the reign of Narsiṁha Deva (CE 1238-64). The temple is conceived of as a *ratha* or chariot

[11] Kedarnath Mohapatra, *Purāṇic Representations in Temple Art of Orissa*, Bhubaneswar: Kedarnatha Gaveshana Pratisthana, 2002, *passim.*

[12] Mayadhar Mansinha, *The Saga of the Land of Jagannātha*, Cuttack: J. Mohapatra & Co., pp. 72-73.

[13] N.L. Mathur, *Sculpture in India, Its History and Art*, 2nd rev. and enlarged edn., New Delhi: National Museum, 1976, pp. 44-45.

of the Sun God drawn by seven caparisoned horses. The wheels of the gigantic solar car are carved with remarkable skill and are the most perfect. The outer surfaces of the temple are embellished with exquisite sculptures, portraying any subject or motif known, fantastic human and animal forms. Its huge proportion and elaborately decorative carvings and designs are unmatched in other temples in India. The sculptures executed in hard stone, are large, vigorous and full of warmth of life. Percy Brown remarks, "Few buildings can boast of such an unrestrained abundance of plastic decoration as this vast structure, every portion of the exterior being moulded and chiselled either in form of abstract geometrical ornament, conventional foliage, mythical animals, fabulous beings half-human with half-serpent coils, figures satanical and figures divine, of every conceivable motif and subject known to the Indian mind, and in a technique which ranges from patterns cut with the minute precision of a cameo to powerfully modelled groups of colossal size."

The Orissan artist has shown consummate ability and creative imagination in depicting scenes from life with remarkable vividness and realism. A representation of a farewell of a soldier armed with sword and shield about to take leave of his wife and child for the field of battle has been very realistically executed. The beautiful female figures of drum, flute and cymbal players exquisitely chiselled are redolent with exuberant vitality and their plastic flesh of stone vibrates with an innate lust for life. There is a headless figure of a drummer playing on her *mṛdaṅga,* posed between her thighs. In the intensely graceful posture of the jewelled feet, the artist skilfully suggests the rhythmic movements of the dance. Another drummer is playing on the drum with both of her hands. The rapt expression of the face is indicated in the delicate contours of the cheeks. A cymbal player gracefully handles large discs held in her sensitive figures. Another captivating figure of cymbal player is in a characteristic pose of supreme grace and dignity. The flute player stands in a stately pose, holding a long piping instrument. As a portrayal of a celestial musician, it is a veritable masterpiece of great distinction and power. These superbly proportioned heavy bosomed musicians of enchanting beauty seem to sing a wild and rapturous hymn of worldly existence in various forms — the joys and pleasures of a full life. There are also sculptures of numerous couples engaged in a great variety of amorous antics. These figures are representations of *mithunas*. Percy Brown feels, "But nowhere are its observances more blatantly exploited than on the walls of the temple of the Sun at Koṇārka." The colossal animal sculptures in the round are also of high artistic merit. A pair of rampant lions hovering on prostrate elephants is of monumental grandeur. A row of moving elephants is occupied in the sport of uprooting trees in a playful mood. The spirited horses and the warriors vainly trying to hold them down, depict the spirit of life. Havell describes it as one of the grandest examples of Indian sculpture extant. He further says, "Here Indian sculptors have shown that they can express with as much fire and passion as the greatest European art the pride of victory and the glory of triumphant warfare; for not even the homeric grandeur of the elgin marbles surpasses the magnificent movement and modelling of this Indian Achilles, and the superbly monumental horse in its massive strength and vigour is not unworthy of comparison with Verrocchio's famous masterpieces at Venice."

In addition to these sculptures, there is a standing image of the Sun God which has been very artistically carved. A monumental sculpture of Bṛhaspati (Jupiter), son of Ṛṣi Aṅgīrasa is one of the finest portraits of a planet.

Rekha Jhanji[14] argues against the view that the classical Indian art is akin to spiritual activity and concludes by mentioning that it is only with respect to the temporary nature of the psychic state of desirelessness that the aesthetic experience can be distinguished from mystical ecstasy. But there is another very important feature of the aesthetic experience which gives it a *sui generis* character. And that stems from the peculiar role and surface qualities of the art work play in aesthetic enjoyment. While a meditator (*sādhaka*) may concentrate on the image of Buddha or Naṭarāja in order to envision and inculcate the moral and spiritual qualities associated with these two deities, a *rasika* enjoys the structure of these two sculpted forms. The former transcends the form, while the latter keeps coming back to the visual and kinetic form; and it is in this return to the sensuous qualities that he derives his primary aesthetic pleasure. Since he is free of any desire associated with these sensory experiences, which is the normal accompaniment of any sensory experience in everyday life, he is filled with a feeling of untainted joy. This joy is associated with all *rasa*s, be it the aesthetic rendering of the terrible (*bhayānaka*) or of pathos (*karuṇa*) or even of the odious (*bībhatsa*); for it is the transfiguration involved in artistic rendering with/which generates this joy. Even if the spectacle arouses pathos, fear or anger, the very configuration of elements generates a certain joy. This explains our enjoyment of tragedies, of crime thrillers or of horror films.

To this view of Rekha Jhanji, a befitting reply is found in the words of Swami

---

[14] Rekha Jhanji, *The Sensuous in Art*, Simla: Indian Institute of Advanced Study, Delhi: Motilal Banarsidass, 1989, pp. 58 and 69.

Satyananda Saraswati,[15] when he explains the ritualistic worship in Tantra, by mentioning that Tantra aims to transform every action in life into a ritual, so that the individual performs every action and thought with a feeling of worship and awareness. The action of bathing, dressing, sitting for worship, offering various symbolic sacrifices, sexual relations, stages of development from inception in the womb, birth to marriage, etc. are transformed into worship. The aim of Tantra is to unleash the cosmic energy in man, so that he rises to higher levels of awareness.

The author gives emphasis on the pleasure and *samādhi* aspects of the sensuousness in art. The available art on palm-leaf, painting of sixty-four sexual poses and sculptural arts on temple architecture of Orissa testify for them. It is only in Orissa and its Oriyā language that description of sixty-four sexual *bandha*s alias poses are found.[16] The traditional painters of Orissa still go on painting the sixty-four poses in their inheritance style.

In the words of Mayadhar Mansinha:[17]

> But ethics apart, haven't the artists of Koṇārka so abundantly demonstrated their capacity to delineate also the delicacy of sublime human love and the deepest mysteries of faith? Only master-artists could create the sculptures now named "the Kiss", or "the Lovers" the joyous, ecstatic abandon of dancers and musicians and the divine light, grace and peace on the face of the various Sun images of Koṇārka. The wheels of Koṇārka, now famous all over the world, are not only grand and resplendent enough to be the wheels of the heavenly chariot of the God of gods, but amazingly full of the delineation of life, symbolizing the wheel of life, that is this *saṁsāra*. One indeed needs the vision of poets to understand what, to prudes, may appear as merely immoral, to inhale the pervasive beauty, colour and aroma in the totality of Koṇārka, and to say, like the great artist Abanindranath Tagore, "The ever old and the ever new dance-sport of the whole universe is going on day and night under the sportive *kadamba* tree of love, sacred to the gods, to the accompaniment of burning lamps of divergent colours placed round the bejewelled throne of the bodyless god of love." Here (in Koṇārka) nothing is silent. Stones are ringing with the deep resonance of the *mṛdaṅga* (drum), stones are running like frisky, spirited horses, pulling the car at

[15] Swami Satyananda Saraswati, *A Systematic Course in the Ancient Tāntric Techniques of Yoga and Kriya*, Munger: Bihar School of Yoga, 2nd edn., 1989, p. 335.

[16] J.P. Singh Deo, op. cit., 2004, Appendix, pp. 255-70.

[17] Mayadhar Mansinha, op. cit., pp. 86-87.

> top speed. Stones have blossomed out here like ever-blooming flowers in the bowers, embracing all quarters in their thousand arms of shining green.

The Hindu sages have turned every aspect of human culture — including art, drama, music, medicine, astronomy and language — into a tool of spiritual awakening and realization.[18] The erotic art also depicts the same in unspoken language.

It is worth quoting George Feuerstein, Subhash Kak and David Frawley,[19] "The Vedas are the earliest available expression of perennial philosophy or universal spirituality." Their revelatory knowledge contains depths that, in the words of R. Panikkar, "Still resound in the heart of modern man."[20] Panikkar, a Roman Catholic priest and professor of Religious Studies, is one of the most appreciative interpreters of the Vedas. In his book *The Vedic Experience*, we find the following passage that fittingly describes our present endeavour as well: "The Vedic experience introduces nothing alien to modern man, but helps him to realize his own life and emphasizes an often neglected aspect of his own being. In this sense the Vedas occupy a privileged position in the crystallized culture of man. They are neither primitive nor modern. Not being primitive, they present a depth, a critical awareness, and a sophistication not shown by many other ancient cultures. Not being modern they exhale a fragrance and present an appeal that the merely modern does not possess."[21]

T.N. Mishra[22] mentions:

> The erotic figures on temples represent tāntric *sādhaka* in the non-dual state of divine bliss: we know that this *sādhanā* was not meant for pleasure but was undertaken as a ritual act and, in this light, only a few sculptures were found relieved according to haṭha-yogic discipline. Moreover, the male figures are often shown with protruding stomachs or disproportionate bodies which indicate that they were not adept in *yoga* or *haṭha-yoga*. The

---

[18] George Feuerstein, Subhash Kak and David Frawley, *In Search of the Cradle of Civilization*, Delhi: Motilal Banarsidass, 1999, p. 276.

[19] Ibid., p. 275.

[20] Ibid.; R. Panikkar, *The Vedic Experience: Mantramanjari*, London: Darton, Longman and Todd, 1979, p. 9.

[21] George Feuerstein, Subhash Kak and David Frawley, *In Search of the Cradle of Civilization*, Delhi: Motilal Banarsidass, 1999, p. 275.

[22] T.N. Mishra, *Yoga-Tantra and Sensuousness in Art*, New Delhi: D.K. Printworld, 2003, pp. 98-99.

> eternal bliss of the non-dual state is rarely reflected in the sculptural depictions. Only a handful sculptures of Orissa and Khajurāho present lovers in a state of bliss. The esoteric rites (*vidhis*) of Pāśupata (who influenced many Aghorī tāntric sects) are considered relevant in explaining certain erotic depictions on temples by the famous iconographists. But it is wondered whether the tāntric esoteric doctrines were ever exposed to the general public. The initiated persons were not to expose their practices in front of the common people. Only specially initiated persons (and that too, *vīra* type not *paśus*) had the privilege of practising the ritual of sex. Tāntric literature advocates strict secrecy of the rituals. The true tāntric art is functionally related to the *upāsanā* and *sādhanā* to attain the non-dual *sahaja* state. The theory of the *maṇḍala* or mystic circle, Tantras or Mystic diagram aided the *sādhanā* to reach his spiritual goal. Such art is non-decorative, it is cultic. The tāntric shrines of India are, therefore, not associated merely with erotic display.

It is true that male figures are often shown with protruding stomachs or disproportionate bodies, which indicate that they were not adept in *yoga* or *haṭha-yoga* and *yogīs* in sculptural arts of temple architecture. Examples can be given of a few sculptures of this type in the Sun temple at Koṇārka.[23] It is nothing but debauchee. Example the name of a village named Kusaṅga,[24] in Bolaṅgīr district of Orissa. The name Kusaṅga means bad company. The *yoga* of sexual transformation most probably had turned at least to debauchery there, during late medieval period and therefore Kusaṅga, name developed. This is the hypotheses of the author, from tāntric-yogic point of view. The Jagannātha temple, the Śiva temple and the Kusaṅgi temple are found there.[25]

Therefore, A.L. Basham[26] is very correct when he states:

> Meanwhile Buddhism steadily lost ground, though it was still very much alive in Bengal and Bihar when the Muslims occupied these regions. Both Buddhism and Hinduism had become affected by what is generally known

---

23 Ristam J. Mehta, *Koṇārka: The Sun Temple of Love*, Bombay: D.B. Taraporevala Sons and Co., 1969, Pls. 8, 19, 55 and 68.

24 J.P. Singh Deo, *Some Tāntric Esotericism of Orissa*, Kolkata: R.N. Bhattacharya, 2003, pp. 280-81.

25 Ibid.; *The Forgotten Monuments of Orissa*, vol. I, New Delhi: Publication Division, Govt. of India, 1995, pp. 51-52.

26 A.L. Basham, "Medieval Hindu India", *A Cultural History of India*, A.L. Basham (ed.), Delhi: Oxford University Press, 2nd impression, 1984, pp. 58-59.

> as Tāntricism or Tantrism, emphasizing the worship of goddesses, especially the Mother Goddess, the spouse of Śiva, known by many names. With this came sexual mysticism, and the sacramentalization of the sexual act, which was performed ritually by circles of initiates. Other socio-religious practices, looked on as reprehensible by most modern Hindus, became more common in this period. Among these were the burning of widows on their husband's funeral pyres, wrongly called *satī* (*suttee*), child marriage, animal sacrifice, female infanticide, and the religious prostitution of the *devadāsī*. One feels that there was a definite lowering in the value of human life in comparison with the days of the Guptas, when, according to Chinese accounts, even the death penalty was not inflicted.
>
> When the Turkish horsemen swept through the Gaṅgā plain, Hindu culture was tending to look inwards and backwards — inwards to the private life of the spirit and backwards to the hallowed norms of the distant past. In many respects the legacy of this period to later times was a negative one. Yet, in the spiring temples built during this period all over India, the age endowed posterity with monuments of enduring splendour and beauty. The parallel with the medieval period in Western Christendom is a close one. Here too there was in some respects a cultural decline, in comparison with the days of the great empire destroyed by the barbarians. But in this time new forms of religious literature and art appeared, as well as glorious monuments to faith such as the older empire could never have built.

What is true to the mundane, is false to the spiritually advanced *yogī*.[27] Therefore Swami Satyananda Saraswati is of the opinion that sexual union is also a powerful *maṇḍala*. That is why it can be a means to meditation. When a man and a woman make love, then they are creating a magic circle, a *maṇḍala*.

One should not forget that every aspect of human life is depicted on the sculptural arts of temple architecture. Gaja-Siṁha motif is most important, from *haṭha-yoga* point of view with its unspoken language of expression.

Gaja-Siṁha Motif

Gaja-Siṁha motifs generally adorn the entrance gate (*siṁha-dvāra*) of main temples of Orissa and India in general, which is considered to be one of the most sacred, attractive and embellished decorative motifs of Orissa sculpture, in general. These innovative presentations are also reflecting the ancient artistic excellence of Orissa

[27] *ASCITATTOYAK*, 2nd edn., 1989, p. 336.

in the hands of contemporary artists, craftmen and further giving a new lease of life to the ancient near-extinct magnificent art idioms of Orissa.

Earlier O.C. Ganguly[28] had done a study on "Lion on Elephant's Motif in Orissa Art". He[29] had quoted Manmohan Gangoly and had narrated:

> Manmohan Gangoly (*Orissa and Her Remains*, 1912, pp. 203-04) deals with *śārdūla* combined with the elephant motif. The passage is quoted below:
>
> The victory of the Keśarīs must have been an epoch-making event, or else its representation would not have influenced the architecture of Orissa in such a remarkable degree, for almost all the temples of medieval times in the Purī district are invariably found to contain in the narrow recesses between the pilasters representations of a lion standing over a crouched elephant. These lions are, as a matter of fact, fantastic monsters having leafy horns, pointed ears, elaborate manes and a beaded tassel dangling from the mouth. . . . This is the sculptor's *śārdūla* which is not obtained in nature. From this conventional representation of *śārdūla* we should not come to the conclusion that the Oriyas had no knowledge of the physiognomy of a lion, in support of the above remark; the lion of the Jagamohana of the Mukteśvara temple may be cited by way of illustration.
>
> The lion has been represented in various situations. It is seen on both sides of the main entrance as a guard or a *dvārapāla* and towering over a crouched elephant. It is seen in a similar posture projecting from the Rekha of the sanctum at a definite height. It is also placed on the roof of the *jagamohana*, and is invariably found in one of the three following postures: (1) Udā-Sinhā, or flying lion, as in the temple of Yukti Kedāreśvara, (2) Jhāppāsinhā or rampant lion, as in the temple of Kedāreśvara, and (3) Kṣepāsinhā or mad lion as in the temple of Mukteśvara. The lion is also noticed in the intervening space below the *āmalaka śilā* referred to already. The representation of the lion is called Dupiccā-Siṁhā or two lions placed back to back.
>
> The problem is, when does the lion and elephant device first appear in Orissa, and who is responsible for the design? M.M. Gangoly, relying on current craftmen's tradition asserts that it appeared after the advent of the Keśarī dynasty which subjugated and supplanted an earlier ruling dynasty (could it be the Gajapati dynasty) which was symbolized by the elephant.

---

[28] O.C. Gangoly, "Lion on Elephant's Motif in Orissan Art", *OHRJ*, vol. IV, nos. 1 and 2, pp. 1-5.

[29] Ibid., pp. 2-5.

But the present writer claims to have proved that the motif is earlier than the earliest medieval temples in Orissa and appears to have been formulated in some part of Magadha, during the Gupta period.

This is proved by a fragment of a large bronze piece dug up at Nālandā (Bihar) during an excavation undertaken by the Archaeological Survey, Eastern Circle, during the year 1916-17 (see *Annual Report, Eastern Circle, 1916-17*, p. 2), where the piece is described as "a large metal column with elaborate capital showing a lion above an elephant". On the basis of other finds dug up from the site, this piece has been ascribed to the Gupta period, so that it cannot be claimed that the device is an original invention of Orissan craftsmen. The writer drew the attention of scholars to the pattern and its significance in an article published in the *Modern Review* in 1918. This bronze piece is about 3' in height and the question is, what was the use of this metal column? We can only make plausible guesses. If it had any structural function, it might have been one of the legs of a throne for placing an image or one of its uprights. Alternately, it might have been used as the base or pedestal of a lamp-stand.

Whatever may have been its function, it offers a clinching evidence that the design was first formulated during the Gupta period in Bihar or some related culture-areas. But then we have still to explain the significance of this design, why is the lion placed on the back of an elephant? If it was used for a seat for any image, that seat (*āsana*) was meant to be a *siṁhāsana* (a lion seat) so that for such a seat the effigy of a lion should be an appropriate motif. We have several images of the Buddha placed on a lion-seat. But if the effigy of a lion is a relevancy design for a lion-seat, why does the elephant come in?

The answer is provided by an old traditional verse found in the older anthologies, which describes the character of a lion, and which is very familiar to scholars:

> *vibharti vegaṁ pavanātirekam* ।
> *bhinatti nityaṁ karirāja-kumbham* ॥
>
> *karoti vāsam giri-rāja-śṛṅge* ।
> *tathāpi siṁhā paśurevanānyaḥ* ॥

Translation — "It may possess a swiftness more than the air. It may be habitually breaking the skull of the king of elephants. It may reside on the pinnacle of the king of hills. The lion is yet no other than a beast."

The above verse suggests a clue to the significance of the motif, namely —

> that it is the traditional habit and character of a lion — to smash the head of an elephant to kill it.
>
> Tradition also asserts that the skull of the king of elephants conceals a valuable treasure, a precious pearl, known as Gajamaṇi. It does not occur in the heads of all elephants but only in the skull of an animal of the super-type (*mukti-kamna gaja gaje*). This tradition of the search for the precious pearl inside the head of a *Gajarāja* may be assumed to be the motive of the lion hunting for it by smashing its head. . . .
>
> So in the absence of appropriate textual authority to support this fine and impressive human conception, one is unable to suggest the actual significance of the motif and as this type does not appear to have been frequently repeated anywhere else, we can only justify the motif as a fanciful and personal interpretation of the Narasiṁha type devised by an artist endowed by wild and creative imagination.
>
> The lion and the elephant motif attains a superbly monumental expression in the gigantic pair at the entrance to the *jagamohana* at Koṇārka. Majestically stylized the lions are pure, rampant, energetic, awesome in their prowess and majesty. Such is the interesting history of an ancient artistic motif treated in Orissan art with a singular distinction and originality.

This narration shows that there is confusion on knowing the purpose of Gaja-Siṁha motifs. This is because of the bereft of yogic intuitive knowledge. The knowledge which is acquired from teachers and from books are imitative, repetitive, derivative and educative. Another knowledge which is above these types of knowledge is intuitive. Only intuitive knowledge reaches to the reality. Intuition means the power of the mind which immediately perceives the truth of things without reasoning or analysis: a truth so perceived, immediate knowledge in contrast with mediate.[30]

Only through yogic path one can attain intuitive knowledge or experiences of different *samādhis*. To be observed in a particular type of consciousness is called *samādhi*. There are ten kinds of *yoga* — *jñāna-yoga, rāja-yoga, bhakti-yoga, karma-yoga, haṭha-yoga, kuṇḍalinī-yoga, tantra-yoga, japa-yoga, laya-yoga* and *yoga* of sexual transformation.[31]

---

30 J.P. Singh Deo, *Tāntric Art of Orissa*, Delhi: Kalpaz Publications, 2001, p. 213.

31 Ibid., pp. 29 and 31-37.

Orissa is the only state of India, which has produced the maximum number of literature in art and architecture.[32] They are: (1) *Bhuvana-Pradīpa,* (2) *Śilpa-Prakāśa,* (3) *Saudhikāgama,* (4) *Baya-Cakada* (a book of accounts and building chronicle of the Sun temple of Koṇārka), (5) *Śilpa-Sāriṇī,* (6) *Vāstusūtra Upaniṣad* and (7) *Śilpa Ratnakośa.*

From *Śilpa Ratnakośa,*[33] it is known that the main *vimāna* (temple) is in the form of the *puruṣa* (man). In religious Hindu *yoga* and art, importance is given to the human body alias individual self.

Gaja-Siṁha motif is a symbolism of *haṭha-yoga. Haṭha-yoga* practices were designed by the *ṛṣis, yogīs* and sages of old, for the evolution of mankind. This important yogic science was gradually ignored by the serious-minded people and was wrongly taught by others. Therefore, it became necessary to re-introduce the proper system of meditation. This is how the system of *haṭha-yoga* was founded. It was at this time that Matsyendranāth founded the Nātha cult, which believed that, before taking to the practices of meditation, one must purify the body and its elements.[34] In recent years R.P. Mishra[35] has established that Luipa or Matsyendranāth was Nātha *siddha* and was born in Candradvīpa, Cāndavāli-Dhāmra region of Bālāsore (present Bhadrak district) in Orissa.

In *Śiva-Saṁhitā,*[36] the following verse regarding *khecarī-mudrā* is found:

सिद्धोनां जननी ह्येषा मम प्रणाधिकप्रिया ।
निरन्तरकृताभ्यासात्पीयुषं प्रस्यहं पिबेत् ।
तेन विग्रहसिद्धिः स्याम्मृस्युमतङ्गकेसरी ॥ 32 ॥

siddhonāṁ jananī hyeṣā mama praṇādhikapriyā ।
nirantarakṛtābhyāsātpīyuṣaṁ prasyahaṁ pibet ।
tena vigrahasiddhiḥ syāmmṛsyumataṅgakesarī ॥ 32 ॥

---

32 R.P. Das, "The Study of Silpa Sastras", *Reference Orissa,* A.N. Tiwari (ed.), Bhubaneswar: Enterprising Publishers, 1999, pp. 174-81.

33 Bettina Baümer and Rajendra Prasad Das (eds.), *Śilparatnakośa* (*A Glossary of Orissan Temple Architecture*), Kapila Vatsyayan (general ed.), New Delhi: Indira Gandhi National Centre for the Arts and Motilal Banarsidass, 1994, fig. 1, pp. 32-33.

34 Swami Satyananda Saraswati, "Swamiji Speaks on *Haṭha-Yoga*", *Haṭha-Yoga-Pradīpikā* (*Light on Haṭha Yoga*), commentary by Swami Muktibodhananda Saraswati, Munger: Bihar School of Yoga, 2nd edn., 1993, pp. 2-3.

35 R.P. Mishra, *Sahajayāna: A Study of Tāntric Buddhism,* Calcutta: Punthi Pustak, 1991, p. 165.

36 Rai Bahadur Srisa Chandra Vasu, *The Śiva Saṁhitā,* New Delhi: Munshiram Manoharlal, 4th edn., 1990, p. 47.

> O, my beloved! know this to be the source of all success, always practising it let him drink the ambrosia daily. By this he obtains *vigraha siddhi* (power over the microcosm), even as a lion over the elephant of death.

Again in *Śiva-Saṁhitā*, while dealing on *uḍḍiyāna bandha*, the following verse is found:

> नाभेरुर्ध्वमघश्चापि तानं प्रश्चिममाचरेत् ।
> उड्डुयानबंध एष स्यात्सर्वदः खौघनाशनः ॥
> उदरे पश्चिमं तानं नामेरूर्ध्वं तु कारयेत् ।
> उडगनाख्याडत्र बन्धोयं मृत्युमातङ्गकेसरी ॥ 48 ॥
>
> *nābherūrdhvamaghaścāpi tānaṁ praścimamācaret* ।
> *uḍuyānabandha eṣa syātsarvadaḥ khaughanāśanaḥ* ॥
>
> *udare paścimaṁ tānaṁ nāmerūrdhva tu kārayet* ।
> *uḍaganākhyāḍatra bandhoyaṁ mṛtyumātaṅgakesarī* ॥ 48 ॥
>
> When the intestines above and below the navel are brought to the left side, it is called *uḍḍiyāna-bandha*, the destroyer of all sins and sorrows. The left side viscera of the abdominal cavity should be brought above the navel. This is *uḍḍiyāna-bandha*, the lion over the elephant of death.

In Indian spiritual and yogic traditions lion is given the highest or first position in animal kingdom, because it is the most self-controlled and majestic animal. Even *Haṭha-Yoga-Pradīpikā*,[37] deals of *siṁhāsana* (lion's pose) and verse 15 of ch. 2 of the same text mentions:[38]

> Just as lions, elephants and tigers are gradually controlled, the *prāṇa* is controlled through practice. Otherwise the practitioner is destroyed.

These references in Haṭha-yogic literature prove that lion symbolism is given importance in Indian yogic *sādhanā* and lion is known as the king of the animal kingdom.

In the ancient and medieval periods of Indian history, the spiritual yogic masters (*gurus*) used to speak of "elephant like mind", which in modern times has changed into "monkey like mind". Therefore, in *Śiva Saṁhitā*, *vigraha-siddhi* (power over the microcosm) ever, as a lion over the elephant of death is mentioned. In spiritual yogic path one should kill the elephant-like mind, i.e. conquer the fickle elephant

[37] Swami Muktibodhananda Saraswati (Comm.), *Haṭha-Yoga-Pradīpikā*, Munger: Bihar School of Yoga, 2nd edn., 1993, pp. 113-15.

[38] Ibid., p. 159.

mind, and become like a lion. Lion is the most courageous, self-restrained or sense-controlled animal and therefore conspicuous.

In the words of K.S. Behera:[39]

> The *Gaja-Siṁha* or the "lion standing on elephant" motif is another interesting device, which is notable alike for its symbolic significance and imaginative handling. The gigantic pair in front of the Naṭamandira of Koṇārka shows this motif at its best. The lion, with open mouth, lolling tongue, flamboyant manes, protruding eyes, stands over the recumbent elephant. The majesty and vigour of the lion in contrast to the attitude of helplessness of the elephant are well expressed by the sculptor.

The *Gaja-Siṁha* motif, which has its unspoken language, but only expression, teaches an individual to become lion like and reach *vigraha siddhi* (power over the microcosm) in yogic sense.

In higher intuitive wisdom and knowledge, there is no difference of religion, caste, creed or nationality. It is the realization, achievement and observation in consciousness that counts. Therefore *Ṛgveda* (5.60.5) declares, "Here, there is none greater, none smaller. All have gathered together here for advancing common welfare of all." The studies of Vedas show that the Vedas constitute the root of all religious, social, cultural, political and economic thoughts of mankind. The existential blissful consciousness is the source of all creation. The Energy of the Lord or by whatever name one recognizes it, it is truth, beauty and goodness. The Vedas are his breath, man is his expression. The tenets of Vedic Sanātana Dharma with its scientific yogic rationalism can help human beings in the flowering of their genius to its fullest potential. The fundamental truths of life, as revealed to us by the Vedas, can make our lives healthy, wealthy and wise.

Very recently D.G. White[40] has studied the *siddha* traditions in medieval India from alchemical sources and demonstrates for the first time that the medieval disciplines of Hindu alchemy and *haṭha-yoga* were practised by one and the same people and they can only be understood when viewed together. This is the way to a new and more comprehensive understanding of medieval Indian mysticism, within the border context of South Asian Hinduism, Buddhism, Jainism and Islam.

---

[39] K.S. Behera, "Traditions in Sculpture", *Art Tradition of Orissa*, Bhubaneswar: Orissa Sahitya Akademi, 1983, p. 39.

[40] D.G. White, *The Alchemical Body* (*Siddha Traditions in Medieval India*), New Delhi: Munshiram Manoharlal, 2004, *passim*.

The *Gaja-Siṁha* motif is one of the most important yogic symbolisms, which is not easily understood. Therefore, the author[41] is of the opinion that study of yogic development which evolved Uḍḍiyāna-Pīṭha (site) shows the natural unfoldment of symbolism and erotic mysticism, which is a silent expression of the antiquities of the Mahānadī Valley, so eagerly awaiting to be exposed and expounded for guidance to the modern *Kali-yuga* (age) people. Great discoveries have been done, but human beings have forgotten to delve into the self. The self-indulgence of the author in discovering the secrets of the Mahānadī Valley has spotlighted the evolution of yogic erotic mysticism.

As *Gaja-Siṁha* motifs are mostly found in Orissa, it proves that *haṭha-yoga* was much developed in this area and it requires a yogic mind to understand yogic symbolism and expression.

Gaja-Siṁha motif is therefore an important symbolism of Vedānta philosophy and *yoga*, which looks for cosmic laws, known as *ṛta*s (the cosmic order) in the *Ṛgveda*, to which the entire mankind is conditioned.[42] It seems, Orissa has much to teach the modern world.

---

41 J.P. Singh Deo, *Tāntric Hedonism of Mahānadī Valley (Uḍḍiyāna-Pīṭha)*, New Delhi: D.K. Printworld, 2004, p. 57.

42 Adwaitya P. Gangoly, *Vedanta Philosophy for the Unity of Mankind*, New Delhi: Vikas Publishing House, 1995, p. 69; Madhu Khanna (ed.), *Ṛta: The Cosmic Order*, New Delhi: D.K. Printworld, 2004, *passim*.

Plates

Pl. 1 *Yoni* of quartzite stone and ferruginous colour

Pl. 2 Broken stone *yoni* of ferruginous colour

Pl. 3 Red stone *yoni*

Pl. 4 *Yoni* in *Bhairavī-Yantra* shape, with a spot (*bindu*) at the centre

Pl. 5 Stone Śākti

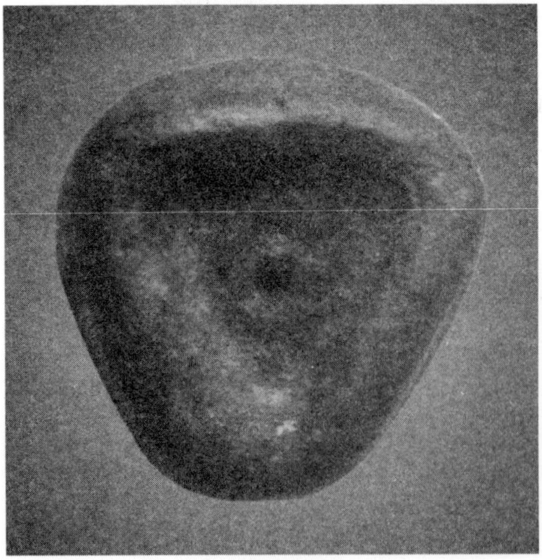

Pl. 6 *Yoni* as *Bhairavī-Yantra*, with a spot (*bindu*) at the centre

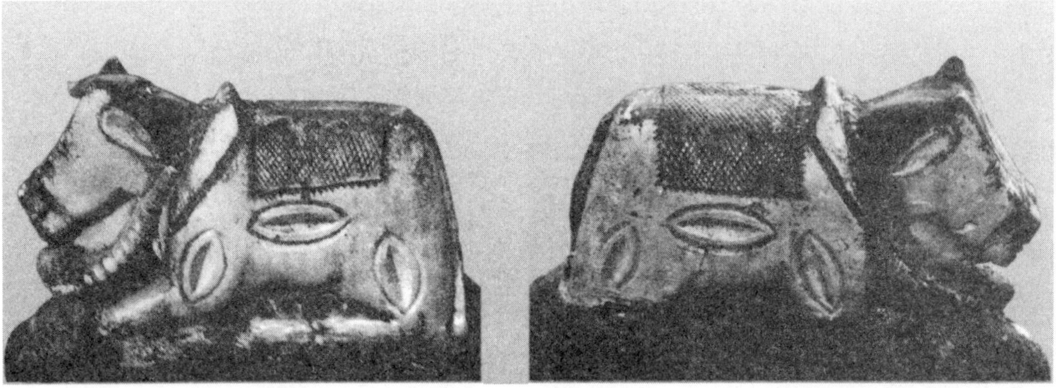

Pls. 7-8 Stone Nandī bull with three *yonis* chiselled on its both side of the body

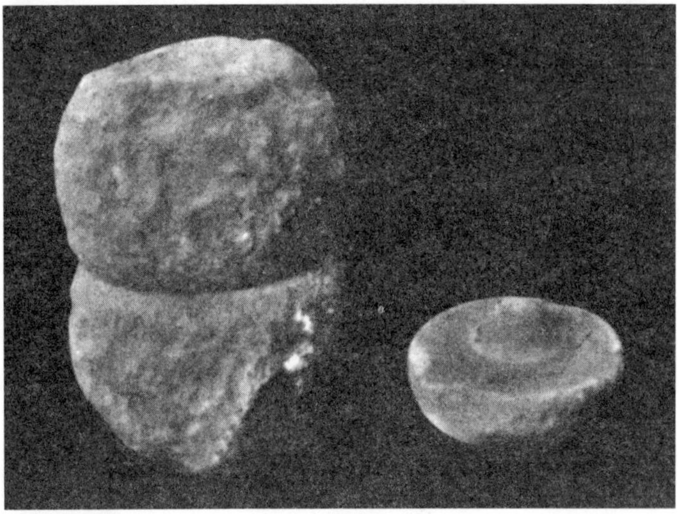

Pl. 9 Two circular stone sockets, 26 cm in diameter. They have components which fit into each other, thereby showing the union of male and female principles. The inner parts are polished

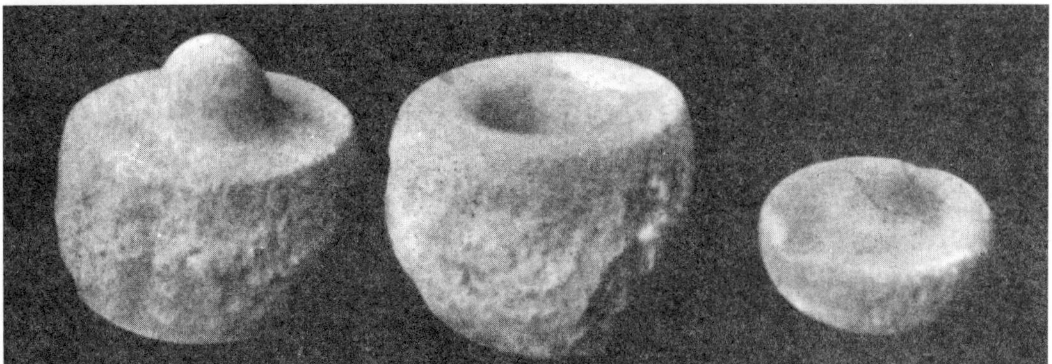

Pl. 10 Exposed stone sockets

Pl. 11 Buddha represented at the centre, like the stone sockets findings

Pl. 12 Stone with right angle triangle *yantra*, with three spots (dots), at the three corners

Pl. 13 Dakṣiṇa Kālī as found in a northern niche of the Kedāreśvara Mahādeva temple

Pl. 14 *Paṭṭa-citra* painting of Dakṣiṇa Kālī

Pl. 15 Six-headed and twelve-handed Kārttikeya

Pl. 16 Six-headed and two-handed Kārttikeya as *pārśva-devatā* in a niche

Pl. 17 Six-headed and two-handed Kārttikeya as *pārśva-devatā* in a niche

Pl. 18 Six-headed and twelve-handed Kārttikeya as *pārśva-devatā*

Pl. 20 Lower portion of eight-handed, nude dancing Gaṇeśa

Pl. 19 Eight-handed, nude dancing Gaṇeśa

Pl. 22 Eight-handed *nṛtya* (dancing) Gaṇeśa, *pārśva-devatā* of the Trilochanpur temple

Pl. 21 Six-handed Gaṇeśa of yellow colour

Pl. 23 Pātāleśvara Śiva temple of brick construction, at Būḍhī Komnā village

Pl. 24 Three tāntric Śiva temples at Bauḍ, Bauḍ district, Orissa

Pl. 25 The Kapileśvara temple of Bauḍ

Pl. 26 Śivā-Śakti as found as the presiding deities, inside the Bhubaneswar temple

Pl. 27 Erotic sculptures of the Mukteśvara temple

Pl. 28 Erotic sculptures of the Mukteśvara temple

Pls. 29-32 Erotic sculptures of the Sun temple

Pls. 33-36 Erotic sculptures of the Sun temple

Pl. 37 Umā–Maheśvara with *ūrdhva-liṅga* (*penis erectus)* at the Khiching Museum

Pl. 38 Gaja-Siṁha at the Sun temple

Pls. 39-41 Wooden art on the gate of the Siṁhadvāra (lion gate) of Varāha temple at Aul

Pls. 42-45 Wooden art on the gate of the Siṁhadvāra (lion gate) of Varāha temple at Aul

Pl. 46 Wooden art on the gate of
the Siṁhadvāra (lion gate) of Varāha temple at Aul

Pls. 47-48 Palm-leaf etching of sexual poses, found on the palm-leaf manuscript of "Cauṅsaṭhī Rati Bandha"

Pls. 49-50 Palm-leaf etching of sexual poses, found on the palm-leaf manuscript of "Cauṅsaṭhī Rati Bandha"

Pls. 51-52 Palm-leaf etching of sexual poses, found on the palm-leaf manuscript of "Cauṅsaṭhī Rati Bandha"

Pls. 53-54 Palm-leaf etching of sexual poses, found on the palm-leaf manuscript of "Cauṅsaṭhī Rati Bandha"

Pls. 55-56 Palm-leaf etching of sexual poses, found on the palm-leaf manuscript of "Cauṅsaṭhī Rati Bandha"

Pls. 57-58 Palm-leaf etching of sexual poses, found on the palm-leaf manuscript of "Cauṅsaṭhī Rati Bandha"

Pls. 59-60 Palm-leaf etching of sexual poses, found on the palm-leaf manuscript of "Cauṅsaṭhī Rati Bandha"

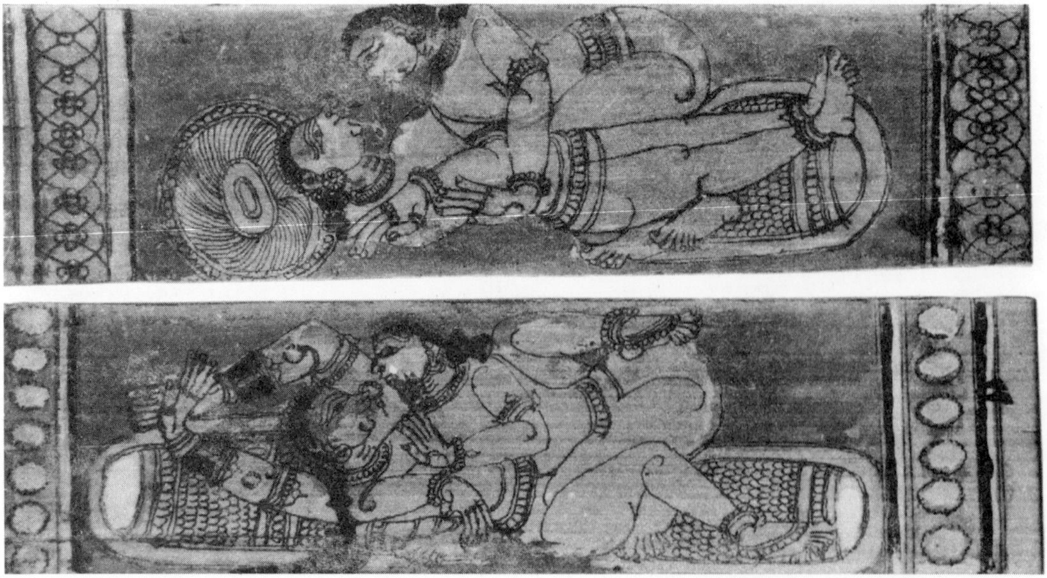

Pls. 61-63 Palm-leaf etching of sexual poses,
found on the palm-leaf manuscript of "Cauṅsaṭhī Rati Bandha"

Pls. 64-66 Palm-leaf etching of sexual poses,
found on the palm-leaf manuscript of "Cauṅsaṭhī Rati Bandha"

Glossary

ādi	:	Primate, primal.
Aditi	:	Mother of the gods.
Āgama	:	Testimony, revelation, the philosophy and scriptures in which Śiva teaches Śakti. Last books of the Vedas, appropriate to the *Kali-yuga* and Tantra Śāstra.
ahaṁkāra	:	Faculty of ego, awareness of the existence of "I", centre of individual, mental, emotional, psychic and physical functioning.
artha	:	Literally means object. Also refers to wealth, one of the *puruṣārtha*s.
bhūpura	:	Terrestrial plane of existence.
bīja	:	Seed.
bindu	:	Point, point of potential energy and consciousness, nucleus. In Tantra and *haṭha-yoga* it also represents a drop of semen.
Brahmā	:	One of the holy trinity, Cosmic Creator, potentiality of *mūlādhāra cakra*.
Brahman	:	Etymologically it means "ever expanding", limitless consciousness; name of Supreme Consciousness according to Vedānta philosophy. Monistic concept of absolute reality.
cakra	:	Circle, wheel or vortex; prāṇic/psychic centre in the subtle body responsible for specific physiological and psychic functions; conjugating point of *nāḍī*s.
cit alias *chit*	:	Supreme Consciousness.
darśana	:	The vision to greet.
gātra	:	Hole.
haṭha-yoga	:	Science of *yoga* which purifies the physical body by means of *ṣaṭ karma — āsana, prāṇāyāma, mudrā, bandha,* concentration, as a prelude to *rāja-yoga* and *samādhi*.
icchā	:	Will.
Īśvara	:	Cosmic causal body of sound, also known as *para-bindu, para-śabda,* Supreme Being, God.

jñānā	:	Knowledge, cognition, wisdom.
kāma	:	Desire.
kriyā	:	Activity, dynamic yogic practice.
kṣetra	:	Site.
kuṇḍalinī	:	Human being's spiritual energy, capacity and consciousness.
madhyamā	:	Middle.
mantra	:	Subtle sound vibration, process of Tantra for liberating energy and expanding consciousness from the limitations of mundane awareness.
māyā	:	Cosmic illusion.
nāda	:	Subtle sound vibration, the vibration created by the union of Śiva and Śakti *tattvas*.
nāḍī	:	Flow; subtle channel in the prāṇic body conducting the flow of Śakti, comparable to the meridians of acupuncture.
Paśupati	:	Lord of the animal kingdom.
paśyantī	:	Cosmic subtle body.
piṇḍa-vicāra	:	Deeper understanding of the constitution of the body.
prakāśa	:	Light, illumination, internal or subtle illumination.
prakṛti	:	Nature, manifested Śakti, universe, vehicle of *puruṣa* (consciousness) according to Sāṁkhya philosophy.
prāṇa	:	Vital energy force sustaining life and creation, permeating the whole of creation and existing in both the macrocosmos and microcosmos.
pūjā	:	Worship.
puruṣa	:	Pure consciousness according to Saṁkhya philosophy. Can also refer to a man or human being.
puruṣārtha	:	Purpose of the consciousness, the four basic needs of desires — *dharma, artha, kāma* and *mokṣa*.
Rudra	:	Name of Lord Śiva in the Vedas; also indicates the first aspect of nature, *tamas*. Generally signifies transformation through destruction. Rudra is said to have sprung from Brahmā's forehead and is one of the Holy Trinity.
śabda	:	Sound.
sādhaka	:	Spiritual practitioner; a person who is striving on the spiritual path for self-realization, true reality and cosmic consciousness.

Śakti	:	Vital energy, force, creative, potential force, vehicle of consciousness.
samādhi	:	Culmination of meditation, state of oneness of mind with the object of concentration, supramental consciousness, the eighth stage of *aṣṭāṅga yoga*.
saṁhāra	:	Dissolution.
saṁsāra	:	Unending cycle of birth and death.
Śāstra	:	Written composition on a subject, formally or systematically.
siddhānta	:	Established doctrines.
siddhi	:	Perfection, enhanced prāṇic and psychic capacity, paranormal or supernormal accomplishment; control of mind and *prāṇa*.
śilpa	:	Art, architecture, sculpture.
Śiva	:	The third God of the Hindu triad, destroyer and reproducer.
śloka	:	Verse.
sṛṣṭi	:	Creation.
sthapaka	:	Architect, sculptor.
sthiti	:	Steadiness, steady state of created universe, upholding of creation.
tattva	:	Element, true or real state.
trikoṇa	:	Triangle.
vaikharī	:	Gross.
Vāk	:	*Nāda*, *śadba*, word, manifest sound.
vāmā	:	Left, contrary, opposite.
Viṣṇu	:	One of the Holy Trinity, the Cosmic Preserver; also refers to the vital capacity of *maṇipūra cakra*, which stores and distributes *prāṇa*, so that health and stamina are maintained in the body.
yajña	:	Fire ceremony in which oblations are offered into a sacred fire, accompanied by chanting of *mantras*.
yantra	:	Precisely calculated geometrical symbol representing specific conformations of forces of Śakti and consciousness, viz. *Śrī-yantra*, *Kālī-yantra*, etc. A process of concentration upon specific forms employed in Tantra to liberate potential energy and consciousness within an individual.
yoni	:	Female vulva.

Bibliography

Antiquary, Gazetteers, Journals, Magazines, Memoirs, Papers, Proceedings, Quarterlies and Reports

Annual Administrative Report of Archaeological Dept., Gwalior State, 1924-25.

Archaeological Survey of India, *Annual Reports 1905-06 and 1913-14.*

Behera, S.C. (ed.), *Interim Excavation Reports*, History Dept., Sambalpur University, Burla, 1982.

Behuria, Nrusinha Charan (chief ed.), *Orissa State Gazetteer, Orissa State*, vol. II, Cuttack, 1991.

Caravan, June (first), 1977, English magazine, no. 60.

Descriptive List of Exhibits at the Nagpur Museum.

Gazetteer of India, Orissa, Sambalpur; Cuttack, 1971.

Indian Antiquary, vol. XII.

Indian Archaeology — A Review, 1964.

Indian Express, English daily newspaper, Vijayanagaram, Sunday, 17 February 1991.

Indian Historical Quarterly, vols. X and XXVI, no. 1.

Jhankar, Oriya monthly magazine, Cuttack, July, 1991.

Journal of Bengal Art, vol. 4, 1999.

Journal of the Assam Research Society, vol. XXXVI, Guwahati.

Journal of the Bihar and Orissa Research Society, vols. II and XIV.

Journal of Orissa Research Society, no. 3, October, Bhubaneswar, 1985.

Kala Jharan — Kalahandi Utsav 2002, Souvenir, District of Culture, Bhawanipatna, 2002.

Kesharwani, S.N., "The Sītā Mātā Temple at Deorbija", *Prachya Pratibha*, vol. V, no. 2, July 1977, Delhi: Agam Kala Prakashan.

Kuanr, D.C. (state ed.), *Orissa District Gazetteers, Kalahandi*, N. Senapati (chief ed.), Cuttack, 1980.

———, *Gazetteer of India, Orissa, Boudh-Khondmals*, N. Senapati (chief ed.), Cuttack, 1983.

Mangrulker, Arvind, "Gita-Govinda: Structure, Technique and Substance", *Annals of the Bhandarkar Oriental Research Institute*, vol. LXIV, pts. I-IV, Pune, 1983.

Memoirs of the Archaeological Survey of India, nos. 23 and 44.

Mishra, R.P., "Primal Yoginī Piṭha, Rāṇīpur-Jharial and Its influence on the Culture of Western Orissa", *Souvenir — Bolangīr Loka Utsabha*, 2001, Bolangir, 2001.

———, "Indralat Brick Temple of Rāṇīpur-Jharial and Its Cultural Heritage", *Souvenir — Bolangir Loka Utsabha*, 2003, Bolangir, 2003.

Nayak, P.M. (ed.), *Confluence*, vol. I, Sambalpur University, Burla, 1992.

New Aspects of History of Orissa, vol. II, Dept. of History, Sambalpur University, Burla, 1978.

Orissa Review, vol. XXXVI, no. 12, July 1970, Information and Public Relation Depts., Govt. of Orissa, Bhubaneswar, 1970.

Orissa Review — Monument Special, A.N. Tiwari (editor-in-chief), Information and Public Relations Depts., Govt. of Orissa, Bhubaneswar, January, 1976.

Pradhan, Sadasiba, "Rock Art Heritage in Orissa", *Souvenir* (*Orissa History Congress — Silver Jubilee Session*), 2-3 November 2003, History Dept., Sambalpur University, Burla, 2003.

Prajatantra (Special Issue), Oriya daily newspaper, Cuttack, Sunday, 23 June 1963.

Proceedings and Transactions of the 7th All India Oriental Conference, Baroda, 1938.

Proceedings of the Indian History Congress, X Session.

Rūpam, no. 1, 1926.

Ray, P.K., *Archaeological Survey Report — Prachi Valley*, Orissa State Archaeology, Bhubaneswar, 1975.

Sahu, N.K. (state ed.), *Gazetteers of India, Orissa, Bolangir*, N. Senapati (chief ed.), Cuttack, 1968.

The Journal of Kalinga Historical Research Society, vol. II.

The Journal of Orissan History, vol. IX, June 1989.

The Orissa Historical Research Journal, vols. II, no. 2; III, nos. 1 and 2; IV, nos. 1 and 2.; VI, no. 4; XII, no. 3; XIII, no. 2; XIV, nos. 3 and 4; XXII, no. 2; XXX, nos. 2-4; XXIV-XXVI, XXX, nos. 1-2; XXXV, XXXVIII, nos. 1-4; XXXX, nos. 1-4; XLI, nos. 1-4; XLII, nos; XLVI, no. 3; XLVII, no. 3 and XLVIII, no. 1.

The Youth World, English monthly, no. 27, January 2005, Bolangir, Orissa.

Unmana, Souvenir of Akhil Bharat Jagannath Consciousness Conference, Cuttack, 1984.

Vasu, N.N. (ed.), *The Archaeological Survey of Mayurbhanj*, vol. I.

Yoga — Ganga Darshan Issue, vol. XXI, no. 12, December 1983, Bihar School of Yoga, Munger, Bihar.

Inscription

Epigraphia Indica, vols. I, III, XXI, XXIII, XXIV, XXVI, XXVII and XXXI.

Inscriptions of Orissa, vols. II and IV, Bhubaneswar.

Sanskrit Text

Avalon, Arthur (ed.), *Śāradā-Tilaka Tantram*, Delhi: Motilal Banarsidass, Delhi, repr. 2001.

Brahma Purāṇa.

Bhāgavata Purāṇa.

Bṛhadāraṇyaka Upaniṣad.

Gaṇeśa Purāṇa.

Kalyāṇa (Hindi), year 48, *aṅka* 1, Gorakhpur: Kalyan Press.

Kaulāvali Tantra, Calcutta.

Koṇārka Kṣetra Māhātmya, unpublished.

Matsya Purāṇa, Rama Pratap Tripathi (tr.), Hindi Sahitya Sammelan, Prayag, Saṁvat in 2003 and also Jamna Das (ed.), Delhi: Akhtar, 1972.

Mishra, K.L. (ed.), *Yoginī-Tantra*, Bombay: Lakshmi Venkatesvara Press, Saṁvat 2013 and Śakābda 1878.

Mudgala Purāṇa, unpublished.

Pañcaviṁśa Brāhmaṇa, W. Caland (ed.), Calcutta, 1931.

Ray, Ram Kumar (tr.), *Kulārṇava Tantra*, Varanasi: Prachya Prakashan, 1983.

Śākta Pramoda, Bombay: Sri Venkatesvara Press, 1951.

Śatapatha Brāhmaṇa with Sāyaṇa's commentary, A. Weber (ed.), 2nd edn., Varanasi, 1963.

Taittirīya Brāhmaṇa, Anandarshrama Sanskrit Series, 3 vols., Poona, 1898.

Viṣṇudharmottara Purāṇa, Bombay: Venkatesvara Press, 1912.

Woodroffe, Sir J. and M.P. Pandit, *Kulārṇava Tantra*, Delhi: Motilal Banarsidass, repr. 1984.

Secondary Sources

Abbott, E. and N.R. Godbole (eds.), *Stories of Indian Saints*, Delhi: Motilal Banarsidass, 1999.

Agrawala, Vasudeva S., *Śiva Mahādeva the Great God* (*An Exposition of the Symbolism of Śiva*), Varanasi: Prithivi Prakashan, 2nd edn., 1984.

Anderson, Kenneth, *Secrets of Sex*, Mumbai: Jaico Publishing House, 1973.

Art Tradition of Orissa, Bhubaneswar: Orissa Sahitya Akademi, 1983.

Arvind and Shantakale, *Tantra: The Secret Power of Sex*, Mumbai: Jaico Publishing House, 1976.

Bandyopadhyay, P.K., *Nāth Cult and Mahānadī* (*A Study of Syncretism*), Delhi: B.R. Publishing Corporation, 1992.

Bandyopadhyay, Pranab, *The Goddess of Tantra*, Calcutta: Punthi Pustak, 1987.

Banerjea, J.N., *Purāṇic and Tāntric Religion*, Calcutta, 1966.

Banerjee, R.D., *History of Orissa*, vol. II, Calcutta, 1932.

———, *The Haihayas of Tripuri and Their Monuments, Memoirs of Archaeological Survey of India*, no. 23, Calcutta, 1931.

Barton, Sir Richard and F.F. Arbuthnot (trs.), *Vātsyāyana's Kāmasūtra*, Delhi: Orient Paperbacks, 1982.

Basham, A.L., *The Wonder that Was India*, London: Sidgwick and Jackson, 1969.

———, (ed.), *A Cultural History of India*, Delhi: Oxford University Press, 2nd impression, 1984.

Bäumer, Bettina and Rajendra Prasad Das, *Śilparatnakośa* (*A Glossary of Orissan Temple Architecture by Sthapaka Niranjana Mahaptra*), Delhi: Motilal Banarsidass, 1994.

Behera, K.S., *Temples of Orissa*, Bhubaneswar: Orissa Sahitya Akademi, 1993.

Behera, S.C., *Rise and Fall of the Sailodbhavas*, Calcutta: Punthi Pustak, 1982.

Bhandarkar, Sir R.G., *Vaiṣṇavism, Śaivism and Minor Religious Systems*, Varanasi: Indological Book House, 1965.

Bhattacharya, B., *The World of Tantra*, New Delhi: Mushiram Manoharlal, 1992.

Bhattacharya, D.C., *Iconology of Composite Images*, New Delhi: Munshiram Manoharlal, 1980.

Bhattacharyya, N.N., *History of the Śākta Religion*, New Delhi: Munshiram Manoharlal, 1974.

———, *History of Indian Erotic Literature*, New Delhi: Munshiram Manoharlal, 1975.

———, *History of Tāntric Religion*, New Delhi: Manohar, 2nd repr., 1987.

Bobby, G., *Looking for Dilmum*, New York: New American Library, 1974.

Bose, D.N. and H. Haldar, *Tantras: Their Philosophy and Occult Secrets*, Delhi: Eastern Book Linkers, 1992.

Bose, N.K., *Canons of Orissan Architecture*, New Delhi, Cosmo Publications, 1982.

———, *Indian Temple Designs*, Calcutta: R.N. Bose, 1981.

———, *Orissa Architecture*, Calcutta, 1931.

Briggs, George Weston, *Gorakhnāth and the Kānphaṭa Yogīs*, Delhi: Motilal Banarsidass, 1989.

Brown, Percy, *Indian Architecture (Hindu & Buddhist)*, Bombay: Taraporevala Sons & Co., 1959.

Chakravarty, Minoti, *Religious Life in the Kaḷachuri Empire*, Calcutta: Punthi Pustak, 1999.

Chatterjee, Asim Kumar, *Cult of Skanda Kārttikeya in Ancient India*, Calcutta: Punthi Pustak, 1970.

Chawdhri, L.R., *Practicals of Yantras*, New Delhi: Sagar Publications, 1984.

Chela, Buddhananda, *Moola Bandha the Master Key*, Munger: Bihar School of Yoga,

Bihar, 2nd edn., 1984.

Codrington, K. de B., *The Study of Indian Art*, Varanasi: Chowkhamba Sanskrit Series Office, 1988.

Cunningham, A., *Archaeological Survey of India*, vol. XIII.

Dange, S.A., *Sexual Symbolism from the Vedic Ritual*, Delhi: Ajanta Publications, 1979.

Das, B.S. (ed.), *Glimpses of Orissa*, Kolkata: Punthi Pustak, 1986.

Das Chittaranjan, *A Glimpse into Oriya Literature*, Bhubaneswar: Orissa Sahitya Akademi, 1982.

Das, D.R., "Stellate Temples of Orissa", *Art and Culture*, no. 1, July 1983.

———, *Temples of Rāṇīpur-Jharial*, Calcutta: Calcutta University, 1990.

Das, Dipakranjan, *Temples of Orissa (The Study of a Sub-style)*, New Delhi: Agam Kala Prakashan, 1982.

Das, H.C., *A Guide to Orissa State Museum*, Bhubaneswar, 1981.

———, *Tāntricism: A Study of Yoginī Cult*, New Delhi: Sterling Publishers, 1981.

Das, H.C., C. Das and S.R. Pal (eds.), *Buddhism and Jainism*, Cuttack: Institute of Oriental and Orissan Studies, 1976.

Das, M.N. (ed.), *Side Lights on History and Culture of Orissa*, Vidyapuri, Cuttack, 1977.

Das, Mamata, *Origin and Development of Gaṇeśa in the Purāṇas*, Berhampur: Upagupta Publications, Orissa, 1996.

Dasgupta, S.B., *Obscure Religious Cults*, Calcutta: Firma K.L.M., 1976 and 1995.

Dasgupta, S.N., *A History of Indian Philosophy*, vol. V.

Dash, M.P. (comp.), *A Descriptive Catalogue of Sanskrit Manuscripts of Orissa*, vol. V (Tantra Manuscript), Bhubaneswar: Orissa State Museum, 1965.

De, Sushil Kumar, *Ancient Indian Erotics and Erotic Literature*, Calcutta: Firma K.L.M., 2nd edn., 1969.

Dehejia, Vidya, *Early Stone Temples of Orissa*, New Delhi: Vikas Publishing House, 1979.

———, *Yoginī Cult and Temples: A Tāntric Tradition*, New Delhi: National Museum Publication, 1986.

Deo, P.K., *Memoirs of a Bygone Era*, New Delhi: Minerva Press, 2000.

Desai, Devangana, *Erotic Sculptures of India: A Socio-Cultural Study*, New Delhi: Tata McGraw Hill 1975.

Donaldson, Thomas E., *Hindu Temple Art of Orissa*, vol. I, The Netherlands: E.J. Brill, Leiden, 1985.

Douglas, Nik, *Tantra Yoga*, New Delhi: Munshiram Manoharlal, 1971.

Dutt, M.N. (ed.), *Mahānirvāṇa Tantram (A Prose, English Translation)*, Varanasi: Chowkhamba Sanskrit Series Office, 2nd edn., 1979.

Eschmann, A., H. Kulke and G.C. Tripathi (eds.), *The Cult of Jagannāth and the Regional Tradition of Orissa*, New Delhi: *Manohar*, 1978.

Fabri, Charles Louis, *History of the Art of Orissa*, Calcutta: Orient Longman, 1974.

Frawley, David, *Hinduism: The Eternal Tradition* (*Sanatana Dharma*), New Delhi: Voice of India, 1995.

———, *Tāntric Yoga and the Wisdom Goddesses*, Delhi: Motilal Banarsidass, 1996.

———, *The Rigveda and the History of India*, New Delhi: Aditya Prakashan, 2001.

Ganguli, M.M., *Orissa and Her Remains*: *Ancient and Medieval* (*District Puri*), London: W. Thacker & Co., 1912.

Ganguly, Adwaita P., *Vedanta Philosophy for the Unity of Mankind*, New Delhi: Vikas Publishing House, 1995.

Geddie, William (ed.), *Chamber's Twentieth Century Dictionary*, New Delhi: Allied Publisher, 1st Indian edn., 1964.

Georg, Feuerstein, Subhash Kak and David Frawley, *In Search of the Cradle of Civilization*, Delhi: Motilal Banarsidass, 1999.

Getty, Alice, *Gaṇeśa: A Monograph on the Elephant-faced God*, New Delhi: Munshiram Manoharlal, 1992.

Ghosh, Devabrata (ed.), *Ānandalaharī*, Calcutta: Sanskrit Book Dept., 1986.

Gopinatha Rao, T.A., *Elements of Hindu Iconography*, vol. II, Madras, 1916.

Gupte, R.S., *Iconography of the Hindus, Buddhists and Jains*, Bombay: Taraporevala, 1972 and 1974.

Handbuch Der Orientalistik II, ABT., IV. Band 2. ABSCHN, Hindu Tantrism, Leiden/ Koln: E.J. Brill, 1979.

Harshnanda, Swami, *All About Hindu Temple*, Mysore: Sri Ramakrishna Ashrama, 2nd edn., 1981.

Jagadeb, Raja, "Śrī Govind Chandra Harichandan", *Utkal Empire Under Gaṅga Kings*, Berhampur, 1977.

Jhanji, Rekha, *The Sensuous in Art*, Simla: Indian Institute of Advanced Study, Delhi: Motilal Banarsidass, 1989.

Jons, Veronica, *Indian Mythology*, London, 1968.

Joshi, Arjun, *Koṇārka*, Cuttack: Baneeshree.

———, *New Light on the Cultural Heritage of Orissa*, Cuttack: Baneeshree, 1979-80.

Joshi, L.M., *Studies in the Buddhistic Culture of India*, Delhi: Motilal Banarsidass, 1987.

Khanna, Madhu (ed.), *Ṛta: The Cosmic Order*, New Delhi: D.K. Printworld, 2004.

Khare, G.H., *Mūrtti Vijñāna* (Marāṭhī), Poona, 1939.

Kramrisch, Stella, *The Hindu Temple*, Calcutta: University of Calcutta, 1946.

———, *Treatise on Indian Painting and Image Making*, 2nd edn., Calcutta: Calcutta University Press, 1928.

Kulkarni, S.D. (ed.), *Bhishma's Study of Indian History and Culture*, vol. IV, 1993 and vol. XI, 1987, Bombay: Sri Bhagvan Vedavyasa Itihas Samshodhana Mandir.

Kumar, Pushpendra, *Śakti Cult in Ancient India*, Varanasi: Bhartiya Publishing House, 1974.

Little Known Aspects of Women in Koṇārk, Bhubaneswar: Dept. of Tourism and Cultural Affairs, Govt. of Orissa, 1975.

Mahadevan, T.M.P., *The Hymns of Śaṅkara*, Delhi: Motilal Banarsidass, 1986.

Mahapatra, Kedarnath, *Purāṇic Representations: In Temple Art of Orissa*, Bhubaneswar: Kedaranatha Gaveshana Pratisthana, 2002.

Mahatab, H.K., *History of Orissa*, vol. I, Cuttack: Prajatantra Press, Prajatantra Prachar Samiti, 1959.

Majumdar, R.C. (gen. ed.), *THACOTIP*, vol. I, 1965; vol. II, 1968; vol. IV, 1964 and vol. V, 1966.

Majumdar, S.N. (ed.), *Ancient India as Described by Ptolemy*, Calcutta, 1927.

Mansinha, M., *The Saga of the Land of Jagannāth*, Cuttack: J. Mohaptra and Co.

Mathur, N.L., *Sculpture in India: Its History and Art*, New Delhi: Caxton Press New Delhi, 1976.

Mehta, Rustam J., *Konarka: The Sun Temple of Love*, Bombay: D.B. Taraporevala Sons and Co., 1969.

Mirashi, V.V., *Corpus Inscriptionum Indicarum*, vol. IV, pt. I, Ootacumund: Archaeological Survey of India, 1955.

Mishra, Baba, *Medieval Orissa and Cult of Jagannath*, New Delhi: Navrang, 1995.

Mishra, K.C., *The Cult of Jagannath*, Kolkata: Firma K.L.M., 1971.

——— (ed.), *Studies in Śāktism*, Bhubaneswar: Institute of Orissan Culture, 1995.

Mishra, K.L. (ed.), *Yogini Tantra*, Lakshmi Venkatesvara Press, Saṁvat 2013 and Śakābda 1878.

Mishra, N.R., *Kāmākhya: A Socio-Cultural Study*, New Delhi: D.K. Printworld, 2004.

Mishra, R.P. (ed.), *Culture and Collections*, Kolkata: Punthi Pustak, 1996.

———, *Fragments of Indian Culture*, Kolkata: Punthi Pustak, 1995.

———, *Sahajayāna (A Study of Tāntric Buddhism)*, Kolkata: Punthi Pustak, 1991.

Mishra, T.N., *Yoga-Tantra and Sensuousness in Art*, New Delhi: D.K. Printworld, 2003.

Mitra, Debala, *Koṇārk*, New Delhi: Archaeological Survey of India, 1976.

Mitra, Rajendralala, *The Sanskrit Buddhist Literature of Nepal*, Calcutta: Sanskrit Pustak Bhandar, 1971.

Mohapatra, G., *The Land of Viṣṇu (A Study of Jagannāth Cult)*, Delhi: B.R. Publishing Corporation, 1979.

———, *Śrī Jagannāth Tattva* (Oriyā), Cuttack: Nalanda, 1989.

Nandi, R.N., *Religious Institutions and Cults in the Deccan (circa,* AD *600–1000)*, Delhi:

Motilal Banarsidass, 1973.

Nema, S.R., *Political History of the Somavaṁśī Kings of South Kosala and Orissa*, New Delhi: Oriental Publishers, 1978.

Nigam, L.S. (ed.), *Iconography* (*Zetetic on Rare Icon from Tala*), Delhi: Sharada Publishing House, 2000.

Notovitch, N., *The Unknown Life of Jesus Christ*, Calcutta: Nababharat Publishers, 1981.

Śaṅkara: The Missionary, Bombay: Central Chinmaya Mission Trust, 1978.

Sri Aurobindo, *The Foundation of Indian Culture*, Pondicherry, 1975.

Panda, L.K., *Śaivism in Orissa*, Delhi: Sundeep Prakashan, 1985.

Pani, Subas (ed.), *Illustrated Palmleaf Manuscripts of Orissa* (*A Selection from Orissa State Museum*), Bhubaneswar, 1984.

Panigrahi, K.C., *Archaeological Remains at Bhubaneswar*, New Delhi: Orient Longman, 1961.

———, *History of Orissa*, Cuttack: Kitab Mahal, 1981.

Panikkar, R., *The Vedic Experience: Mantramanjari*, London: Darton, Longman and Todd, 1979.

Patel, C.B., *Dynastic History of Nalas*, Calcutta: Punthi Pustak, 1990.

Patel, Satyavrata R., *East and West: A Cultural Dialogue*, Bombay: Bharatiya Vidya Bhavan, 1992.

Pattanaik, P.K., *A Forgotten Chapter of Orissan History*, Calcutta: Punthi Pustak, 1979.

Pradhan, B.C. "Śāktism", *Cultural Heritage of Orissa*, vol. II, pt. I, B.C. Ray (ed.), Bhubaneswar: Centre for Advanced Studies in History and Culture, 1996.

Pradhan, S., *Rock Art in Orissa*, New Delhi: Aryan Books International, 2001.

Praharaj, Gopal Chandra, *Purnnachandra Orida Bhāshā Kosha*, vol. IV, 1934 and vol. V, 1936, Cuttack.

Purnanāthji, *Gorakṣa Siddhānta Saṁgraha* (Hindi).

Rajguru, S.N., *Oḍisha-ra-Itihāsa*, pt. I (Oriyā), Cuttack: Grantha Mandir, 1985.

———, *Sri Purushottam-o-Sri Mandira* (Oriyā), Bhubaneswar: Orissa Sahitya Academy, 1996.

Ramachandra Rao, S.K., *Yantras*, Delhi: Sri Satguru Publications, 1988.

Ramaswami, N.S., *Monograph on Temples of Mukhaliṅgam*, Govt. of Andhra Pradesh, Hyderabad, 1976.

Rath, B.K., *Cultural History of Orissa*, Delhi: Sundeep Prakashan, 1983.

Sahu, N.K., *Buddhism in Orissa*, Cuttack: Utkal University, 1958.

———, *Odiā Jatira Itihasa* (Oriya), pt. I, Bhubaneswar: Orissa State Bureau of Text Book Preparation and Production, 1974.

Saraswati, His Divinity Dharm Chakravati Swami Prakashanand, *The True History and the Religion of India*, Delhi: Motilal Banarsidass, 2001.

Saraswati, Swami Muktananda, *Nava Yogini Tantra*, Munger: Bihar School of Yoga, 2nd edn., 1983.

Saraswati, Swami Muktibodhananda (comm.), *Haṭha-Yoga-Pradīpikā*, Munger: Bihar School of Yoga, 2nd edn., 1993.

Saraswati, Swami Satyananda, *A Systematic Course in the Ancient Tāntric Techniques of Yoga and Kriya*, Munger: Bihar School of Yoga, 2nd edn., 1989.

———, *Kuṇḍalinī Tantra*, Munger: Bihar School of Yoga, 2nd edn., 1992.

Sarma, Bina Kumari, *The History of Somavaṁśī Rule in Orissa*, Calcutta: Punthi Pustak, 1983.

Sarma, I.K., *The Development of Early Śaiva Art and Architecture*, Delhi: Sundeep Prakashan, 1982.

Sastri, T.V.G., K.N. Vai and J.V.P. Rao, *Veerapuram*, Hyderabad: Bhavani Printers, 1984.

Satapathy, N., *Religious Life in Orissa: A Study of the Interrelation of Cults*, Kolkata: R.N. Bhattacharya, 2000.

Satpathy, Sarbeswar, *Śākti Iconography in Tāntric Mahāvidyās*, Calcutta: Punthi Pustak, 1991.

Schoterman, J.A. (ed.), *The Yoni Tantra*, New Delhi: Manohar, 1980.

Sengupta, Sudhir Ranjan, *Mother Cult*, Kolkata: Firma K.L.M., 1977.

Sharma, R.K., *The Kaḷachuris and Their Times*, New Delhi: Sundeep Prakashan, 1980.

Sharma, V.S., *The Sarvadarśana Saṁgraha of Mādhavācārya* (Hindi), Varanasi: Chowkhamba Vidya Bhavan, 1964.

Shukla, D.N., *Hindu Canons of Iconography and Paintings*, Gorakhpur, 1958.

Singh Deo, J.P., *Cultural Profile of South Kosala*, New Delhi: Gyan Publishing House, 1987.

———, *Tāntric Art of Orissa*, Delhi: Kalpaz Publications, 2001.

———, *Origin of Jagannāth Deity*, New Delhi: Gyan Publishing House, 1st edn., 1991, 2nd enlarged edn., 2003.

———, *Some Tāntric Esotericism of Orissa*, Kolkata: R.N. Bhattacharya, 2003.

———, *Tāntric Hedonism of Mahānadī Valley (Uḍḍiyāna-Pīṭha)*, New Delhi: D.K. Printworld, 2004.

Singh, Bhagwan, *The Vedic Harappans*, New Delhi: Aditya Prakashan, 1995.

Singh, Jagabandhu, *Prācīna Utkala* (Oriyā), Puri, 1929.

Sinha, Kanchan, *Kārttikeya in Indian Art and Literature*, Delhi: Sundeep Prakashan, 1979.

Sircar, D.C., *The Śākta Pīṭhas*, Delhi: Motilal Banarsidass, 1973.

Sivaramamurti, C., *Nataraja in Art: Thought and Literature*, Publication Division, Govt. of India, National Museum, New Delhi, 2nd edn., 1994.

Sree Neelachala Seva Sangha Shree Jagannath Smarika, New Delhi, Basanta Panchami, 1984.

Stone, E.R., *The Buddhist Art of Nagarjunakonda*, Delhi: Motilal Banarsidass, 1994.

Subramanian, V.K., *Saundaryalaharī of Śaṅkarācārya*, Delhi: Motilal Banarsidass, repr. 1986.

Svoboda, Robert E., *Aghora*, New Delhi: Rupa and Co., 1993.

Swamiji Maharaj, *Vedic Upadesh* (*Vedic Teachings*), Datia: Shri Pitambara Sanskrit Parishad, 1st edn., July 1977.

Swarup, Ram, "Introduction to the Reprint", *Mohammed and the Rise of Islam*, D.S. Margoliouth, New Delhi: Voice of India, 1985.

The Cultural Heritage of India, vol. II, Calcutta: The Ramakrishna Mission Institute of Culture, 1969.

The Forgotten Monuments of Orissa, vol. I, New Delhi: Publication Division, Govt. of India, 1995.

The Mādalā-Pāñjī, Cuttack: Prachi Samiti, repr., Bhubaneswar: Utkal University, 1928.

Tiwari, A.N. (ed.), *Reference Orissa*, Bhubaneswar: Enterprising Publisher, 1999.

Transactions of the Archaeological Society of South India, Madras, 1962-65.

Vanamali, *Śrī Śiva Līlā*, New Delhi: Aryan Books International, 2002.

Vasu, N.N. (ed.), *V.V. Mirashi Felicitation Volume.*

Vasu, Rai Bahadur Srisa Chandra, *The Śiva-Saṁhitā*, New Delhi: Munshiram Manoharlal, 4th edn., 1990.

Viśva Koṣa (Bengali), vol. 13,, Kolkata.

Wall, O.A., *Sex and Sex Worship in the World*, Delhi: Inter-India Publication, 1979.

White, David Gordon, *The Alchemical Body*, New Delhi: Munshiram Manoharlal, 2004.

Williams, J. (ed.), *Kalādarśana* (*American Studies in the Art of India*), New Delhi: Oxford and I.B.H. Publishing Co., 1981.

Woodroffe, Sir John, *The Garland of Letters* (*Studies in the Mantra-Sastra*), Madras: Ganesh and Co., 6th edn., 1974.

———, *Śakti and Śākta*, Madras: Ganesh & Company, 8th edition, 1975.

———, (tr.), *Tantraraja Tantra and Kāmakalā-Vilāsa*, Madras: Ganesh and Co., 8th edn., 1971.

Yogananda, Sri Sri Paramahansa, *God Talks with Arjuna: the Bhagavad-Gītā*, vols. I and II, Kolkata: Yogoda Satsanga Society of India, 2nd impression, 2002.

Index